DMU 0508514 01 0

AF744567

VN
ERSITY

The Economic Analysis of Environmental Policy and Law

The Economic Analysis of Environmental Policy and Law

An Introduction

Michael Faure

Professor of Comparative and International Environmental Law, Maastricht University, The Netherlands

Göran Skogh

Professor of Economics, Linköping University, Sweden

Edward Elgar

Cheltenham, UK • Northampton, MA, USA

© Michael Faure, Göran Skogh 2003

All rights reserved. No part of this publication may be reproduced, stored in a retrieval system or transmitted in any form or by any means, electronic, mechanical or photocopying, recording, or otherwise without the prior permission of the publisher.

Published by
Edward Elgar Publishing Limited
Glensanda House
Montpellier Parade
Cheltenham
Glos GL50 1UA
UK

Edward Elgar Publishing, Inc.
136 West Street
Suite 202
Northampton
Massachusetts 01060
USA

DE MONTFORT UNIVERSITY
LIBRARY:
B/code
Fund: 119 Date: 29/3/04
Sequence:
Class: 341.4
Suffix: FAU

A catalogue record for this book
is available from the British Library

Library of Congress Cataloguing in Publication Data
Faure, Michael (Michael G.)
The economic analysis of environmental policy and law : an introduction / Michael Faure, Göran Skogh.
p. cm.
Includes bibliographical references and index.
1. Environmental law—Economic aspects. 2. Environmental policy—Economic aspects. I. Skogh, Göran, 1943– II. Title.

K3585 .F378 2003
363.7—dc21

2002041378

ISBN 1 84376 234 X (cased)

Typeset by Manton Typesetters, Louth, Lincolnshire, UK.
Printed and bound in Great Britain by MPG Books Ltd, Bodmin, Cornwall.

Contents

Figures

Tables

Boxes

Abbreviations

BAT	best available technique
BATNEEC	best available technique (or technology) not entailing excessive costs
BPM	best practical means
CBA	cost–benefit analysis
COM	(European) Commission
ECHR	European Convention on Human Rights
ECJ	European Court of Justice
ECR	European Court Reports
EU	European Union
EV	expected value
FCCC	Framework Convention on Climate Change
GATT	General Agreement on Tariffs and Trade
GDP	gross domestic product
IAEA	International Atomic Energy Agency
IPPC	integrated pollution prevention and control
MPC	marginal profit for the collective
MR	marginal revenue
NEA	Nuclear Energy Agency
NGO	non-governmental organization
NNP	net national product
NPV	net present value
OPEC	Organization of Petroleum-Exporting Countries
PP	private profit
PPP	polluter pays principle
TC	total cost
TPC	total profit for the collective
TR	total revenue
TRC	total revenue for the collective
VPP	victim pays principle
WTA	willingness to accept
WTO	World Trade Organization
WTP	willingness to pay

Acknowledgements

This book originates from a lawyer's and an economist's common interest in the economic analysis of law. In 1986 when we first met, our research was focused on accident law and insurance. Gradually we also applied the economic analysis to pollution regulation and accidental damage to the environment. Our joint interest and effort soon developed into a longstanding friendship.

We found that the economic tools could contribute to a clarified environmental policy, and to a better use of legal rules. We were struck by the many persons in the environmental policy debate who claimed that environmental pollution should be abated without taking the costs into account. The fact that traditional environmental economics focuses on instruments such as emission trading and taxes, although these were of minor practical use, was also striking. Environmental law is primarily about various forms of regulations, liability rules and enforcement. Nevertheless, instruments such as licensing, zoning, expropriation and penal sanctions are not addressed in traditional environmental economics. Hence, we found a gap between environmental economics, environmental law and policy that we wanted to bridge.

In putting together this book we have benefited from the generous cooperation of many people. The main forum for intellectual interchange has been the European Association of Law and Economics, EALE. We learned a great deal at its conferences and we owe a debt of gratitude to many colleagues and friends throughout Europe and the USA. First of all, we want to thank the former president of the EALE, Professor Roger van den Bergh.

Since 1986, the EALE has been organizing conferences jointly with the International Association for the Study of Insurance Economics (Geneva Association). This cooperation was due to the longstanding support given by Professor Orio Giarini, former Secretary General of the Geneva Association. We are grateful to him and the Association for valuable exchange of thoughts, especially on liability and risk that is the topic of part IV of the book.

In the mid-1990s we jointly taught environmental law and economics at the International Institute of Industrial Environmental Economics at Lund University. The idea of the book took shape during this period. Demanding and extremely stimulating students in the Master of Science programme in Environmental Management and Policy made it clear to us that there was a need for a book on environmental policy and law in which basic insights from environmental law and economics are applied. We are very grateful to them, and to all the colleagues of the Institute, most particulary the former Director, Professor Karl Lidgren, Dr Thomas Lindquist and Dr Lars Hansson.

We also thank all those who provided the practical assistance necessary to make this book possible. We are grateful for research assistance given by Jesper Katz, Caroline Swarén and Johan Eklund at Linköping University, and for secretarial help from Elaine Padbury at the International Institute of Industrial Environmental Economics, Marina Jodogne and Yleen Simonis at Metro, Maastricht University and Christina Svensson at Linköping University. The kind support of our publisher Edward Elgar, and most particularly of Senior Commissioning Editor Dymphna Evans, has been a great help in the final stages of this project.

Finally, financial support from the foundation Forum for Law and Economics and the Torsten and Ragnar Söderberg Foundations is gratefully acknowledged.

Michael Faure
Göran Skogh
Maastricht/Linköping
March 2003

1. Introduction and summary

1. ECONOMICS AND THE ENVIRONMENT

Global pollution, population growth, extinction of species and the threat to complete ecosystems are serious environmental problems of our time. The protection of human civilization and the environment requires, therefore, changes in the use of resources, production methods and consumption patterns. There are in the environmental debate many suggestions on appropriate measures, but there are no simple solutions to the problems. The responsibility is also unclear. It may be argued that the ultimate responsibility lies with the politicians. Yet the formation of attitudes and the implementation of political changes is undertaken by the public, including many households, firms and public institutions.

'*Environmental Law*' constitutes a major part of the framework within which all institutions and individuals act. An understanding of the interrelation and effects of legal policy instruments is, therefore, of vital importance for the future.

Much attention in the debate is paid to general environmental principles such as sustainable development, the polluter pays principle, the precautionary principle, and so on. Increasingly such policy declarations can be found in documents with legal binding force, such as constitutions or treaties. In addition, environmental governance is based on a large number of different laws, for example land laws, city planning, production and emission standards, licences, safety regulations, civil liability, administrative and criminal sanctions, taxes, deposits and compulsory insurance.

The economic effects ensuing from the application of environmental legal rules are, to some extent, the object of study in *environmental economics*. The starting-point in this literature is usually a closer examination of charges or subsidies to ameliorate the environmental harm. Parallel to this line of investigation one may also follow an approach based on the seminal work of Hotelling (1931), which examines the exploitation over time of non-renewable natural resources. Of prime importance also is the concept of social cost–benefit analysis (CBA), which began to be applied to environmental problems in the 1960s. Together with population growth, economic development and the environmental concerns of the Third World, these areas briefly constitute the standard textbook of environmental economics.

The economic analysis of law, also referred to as '*law and economics*', has been growing rapidly in the USA since the beginning of the 1970s, and is now widely recognized in the rest of the world. Contemporary economic analysis of law is sometimes referred to as 'new' law and economics. The 'old' law and economics analysis was linked to taxation and the regulation of markets or competition law. Lawyers sometimes required the assistance of economists to help them answer economic questions related to such laws. In the 'new' law and economics it is the economists who formulate the relevant questions: the law is the subject of study. Today the economic analysis of law covers most fields of law, including the origin of legal systems.

The economic studies pertaining to environmental law are plentiful and powerful. A huge amount of research on the economics of legal regulations has emerged since the beginning of the 1970s and has added substantial knowledge to the economics of environmental laws pertaining to licensing, safety regulations, insurance and environmental crime. Today, the externality problem is analysed in terms of the cost for the involved parties to undertake and control mutually beneficial agreements. When externalities cannot be eliminated by agreement, some form of intervention may be warranted. Pigouvian taxes are treated as one of many measures, comparable, for instance, to zoning, safety regulations and liability, as well as insurance and funds for the financing of environmental damage.

In addition to economic analysis, other social science theories may be used to explain the content of legal rules. This is especially the case for political theories related to *public choice* that attempt to explain legislation as a product of demand by interest groups and supply as a product of the power play among wealth-maximizing politicians. Also, in the environmental area it is highly useful to combine economics with political interest group theory.

2. THE AIM OF THE BOOK

So far the results of this law and economics research have been poorly integrated into traditional environmental economics texts. For instance, the setting of legal standards, private and public insurance, liability, safety regulation and criminal sanctions are occasionally mentioned, but the interrelation of the many legal and economic instruments has not been properly analysed.

Although there are many excellent books on environmental economics, their scope is narrow. Their main focus traditionally is corrective taxes, whereas many other instruments that are more important in the legal environment are often neglected. Similarly, there are many good books on environmental law, but, traditionally, most of these books have been oriented towards environmental law within specific national systems. Today, however, increasing attention is being paid to comparative and international environmental law. In comparative environmental legal studies, the legal systems of two or more countries are compared. International environmental legal research attempts to identify the general principles of environmental law common to all legal systems, and focuses on remedies for transboundary environmental pollution. Nevertheless, most of this research still mainly deals with the legal aspects of pollution; that is, up until now the economic and environmental effects of the various laws have not been taken into consideration.

The aim of this book, then, is to attempt to fill the gap between environmental economics and environmental law with a study on '*environmental law and economics*'. Hence the area of traditional environmental economics is extended with an economic analysis of the law in order to reach a broader understanding of the general aspects of environmental law and policy. In addition, an attempt is made to integrate comparative and international environmental law by presenting legislation and the case law of Europe, together with other international examples.

The economic analysis will thus be combined with comparative environmental legal analysis. This integration is of great benefit since solutions in various national legal systems differ. The economic analysis has the advantage that the rules in the diverse legal systems can be investigated according to principles, without having to discuss in detail the laws of particular countries. We will examine legal solutions, in particular legal systems, and will give the economic explanation for some of the observed differences; that is, we shall apply a comparative law and economics methodology.

Finally, it should be noted that we do not attempt to use economics as the only input of value in legal rule-making. Indeed, we will also demonstrate limits to economics, and the need for ethical norms. Where possible, we shall also point to the distribution consequences of various legal solutions.

3. READERSHIP

Our interest in writing this book is partly due to our own research in environmental law and economics, and partly due to our educational experience. We have both been teaching the subject of economics of environmental law for some time and have been struck by the fact that no textbook on the topic is available. We have seen that there has been a great interest among students from various natural and social sciences in the environmental policy issues presented in some of our classes. Thus a primary reason for our book is to provide teaching material for this subject.

Yet the book has also been written for academic scholars. It will be of interest to students of various social and natural sciences interested in environmental policy and law. Economic analysis leads not only to conclusions with respect to the efficiency of certain existing legal rules; it may also be used to test the effectiveness of legislative action. On the other hand, it is also important to clarify the limits and shortcomings of economics.

As the book has been written for readers of varying backgrounds, this inevitably has consequences for the depth of both the legal and the economic analysis. Presentations of the law will focus on the essence of the legal solutions and leave out details of less importance to the analysis. The economic analysis will be presented in a manner easily understandable to non-economists. Mathematical proof of certain statements will not be provided. The number of references and notes in the text has been minimized for simplicity. The 'Further reading' sections at the end of the chapters are aimed to provide a starting point for interested students. At the end of the book there is an index and an extensive list of references.

The book provides the necessary foundations for the economic analysis of law. It is addressed to readers unfamiliar with economics. An economic scholar may, therefore, find some sections of limited interest. Yet most of the book should also appeal to scholars of economics, especially those unfamiliar with law and economics. It demonstrates, once again, the wide applicability of economic concepts to various social problems. Indeed, it should be of great benefit for environmental economists to read about, among other things, liability and insurance in controlling environmental risks, and about the similarities and differences between safety regulations, charges and criminal sanctions for the protection of the environment.

We hope that the book will function as a stimulating introduction to law and economics in general. The book contains the most important parts of an 'Introduction to Law and Economics' course: economic principles, property rights, transaction costs, regulation, tort, insurance and crime. The teacher of such a course will easily be able to add articles in areas such as 'contracts', 'corporations' and 'procedures' not covered in the book.

Finally, it should be noted that the book is written by a Belgian lawyer and a Swedish economist. The difference in national and professional background can be observed in the text and in the choice of examples. We hope that the mixture of experience, knowledge and style will contribute to the richness of the book. It is up to readers to use their own examples and experiences to supplement the material provided here.

OUTLINE AND SUMMARY

Part I Rights and the Environment

The book is divided in four parts following this introduction.

Chapter 2 constitutes the beginning of Part I. Here we examine various types of rights to the environment. Some of these rights originate from principles of environmental policy. Of special interest are:

(i) the sustainable development principle;
(ii) the prevention principle;
(iii) the precautionary principle;
(iv) the polluter pays principle; and
(v) the proximity principle.

These principles are briefly presented in Chapter 2. In connection with the presentation we give an introductory overview to economic problems and controversies related to these principles.

Environmental principles were first political declarations without legal force. Later, some of them became included in documents with legal status. For instance, many modern constitutions in Western European countries explicitly provide for a right to a clean environment. Hence environmental policy principles also constitute environmental law. The *right* to a clean environment implies a *duty* of the state to protect the citizens. Indeed, the sustainable development principle also includes a duty to protect future generations. These rights, below named '*social rights*', were introduced by political and legislative decisions in the past with the aim of influencing politics in the future. It is obviously a different issue whether these principles or social rights can also be considered as '*subjective rights*', meaning that they can be enforced by citizens in a court. That may be doubtful in respect of the notion of sustainable development. Moreover, the right to a clean environment can also be seen as a human or natural right based on ethical or religious grounds, existing independently of politically decided treaties or constitutions.

Besides the moral and legal rights to a clean environment there are '*private property rights*', which are fundamental for the environment. Here it is important, however, to separate and clarify the environmental issue in relation to the political controversy over property rights. Property rights have been a political issue throughout history; many wars have been fought for the right to land, and since the Industrial Revolution numerous political struggles have centred on the right to the means of production. Liberal and conservative parties defend private ownership, while socialists argue in favour of collectivization. In the environmental debate it is often held that profit-seeking owners destroy the environment, for example, by cutting down forests, using pesticides in agriculture, and polluting water and air. Economists claim, to the contrary, that private property rights are fundamental to the protection of the environment. Furthermore, private ownership is also basic to the market economic system. Indeed, economists claim that efficient property rights in a well-functioning market economy should be: universal, exclusive, transferable and enforced (Tietenberg, 2000, p. 62). Lawyers, on the other hand, working with the task of clarifying and protecting rights, know that these requirements can never be met. 'Property rights' is, in other words, a vague concept.

Our analysis of property rights and the environment is divided into two chapters. Chapter 3 presents the economic analysis of exclusion for the protection of scarce resources. A point here is that lack of control may cause the extinction of exhaustible resources such as forests, fish, birds and mammals. The 'tragedy of the commons', that is, overexploitation of open access to scarce resources is presented and illustrated. Certain economic conditions can, in combination with some biological conditions, lead to extinction. The most serious environmental problems are related to the global commons such as the air, the ozone layer, and the high seas that cannot be fenced and controlled.

In Chapter 4 we relate the economic analysis of exclusivity and control of scarce resources to legal property rights. The exclusive use and control of a resource is often said in the economic literature to be synonymous with private property rights. But exclusivity does not necessarily mean that it is protected by law, and thus constitutes a legal right. Occupation may be the origin of exclusivity, but it is, of course, better if the right to exclusion is assigned by the state. The avoidance of conflicts and wars is an urgent issue to both man and the environment. The chapter studies common versus private ownership and the fundamental role of property rights for the economic market system. That does not mean that a liberal market economy based on private property rights is the best political solution to most problems. In fact, the free market economy includes many forms of common and collective ownership that apparently have certain advantages. It is noted that property rights is a bundle of rights specified in various laws that may be changed by, for example, legislation. Property rights is thus a relative concept. Human rights and rights of the environment are, on the other hand, sometimes said to be natural rights, and as such existing independently of the current political or economic system. A strength of property rights is that it can be motivated on pure economic grounds.

Part II Resources, Prices and Sustainable Growth

In Part II we present principles of economics. The presentation is limited to the standard price theory model. The model is based on a given set of institutions, including legal order, markets, firms and households. This theory is sufficient for a fruitful discussion on the use of non-renewable resources like metals and oil, whose the virgin ores diminish, and resources such as water that will remain, but of poor quality. We also use this traditional economic theory for a discussion of economic progress and sustainable growth.

Chapter 5 outlines the basic theory of prices in competitive markets. First we examine the benefits of bilateral exchange. Thereafter, the chapter deals with demand and supply. The following environmental applications concern non-renewable resources such as minerals and fossil fuels.

Existing virgin ores are diminishing, which frightens many in the environmental debate. This has also resulted in environmental policy and legislation supporting, for example, wind power and recycling, with the aim of maintaining the global resource base. Nevertheless, economists are normally not unduly worried about reductions in available resources, because increased scarcity will be reflected in prices that will modify behaviour. If supply goes down, prices will go up. Higher prices increase the search for new resources and for substitutes. In fact, the price of many metals and other raw materials has not gone up since the beginning of the nineteenth century, and many resources, including energy, have become cheaper. In the long run, there will be less oil in the ground, but there will always be reserves left that are too costly to detect and exploit. When scarcity increases there will be a search for alternatives, for example recycling, solar energy, wind and nuclear power. Indeed, the current investments in 'green' alternatives can be seen as an early adaptation to a belief in future rising prices of oil and other resources. We also present the concepts of consumer and producer surplus, and the 'paradox of value', that is, the common confusion between total and marginal values. The paradox has its environmental application in relation to the subsidy to 'necessities', such as water, and the implied misuse of the natural resource.

Market failures are treated in Chapter 6. First, economic value, and the useful information derived from prices in a well-functioning market, are explained. Thereafter, we introduce the concepts of external effects and corrective Pigouvian charges. The impact of monopoly is briefly presented by an example of the oil cartel OPEC (Organization of Petroleum-Exporting Countries). Public goods and taxes are also introduced. A basic understanding of private versus public goods, as well as the excess burden of public spending, is needed in the later analysis. Yet the concepts are used here in a brief comment on the debate on 'green taxes'. An environmental policy application is on the 'circular flow' concept. The idea is that 'circular thinking' and production is an improvement in relation to 'linear thinking'. Our argument is that prices are useful for the orientation of producers and consumers in the economy, which is also true for the production and treatment of waste. We question the belief that pre-industrial societies managed better to match the use of resources compared with our industrial society. Another doubted view is that minimization of waste is preferable. Certain methods, such as reuse and recycling, are said to be superior to landfilling. Minimization of waste, however, may be costly and perhaps even result in a loss of resources. Therefore, a critical analysis is needed.

The credit market and the economic valuation of risks and risky projects are treated in Chapter 7. Basics on the financial market are included as well. The reason for introducing these concepts is, of course, that they are needed for an understanding of the following examination of environmental matters that depend fundamentally on savings for the future as well as on concepts such as risk and uncertainty.

In addition to the general introduction to the analysis of credit and risk, three important environmental applications are presented. First, the concepts of risk neutrality and risk aversion are related to results in psychological research on human risk perception. Bounded rationality appears to cause systematic failures in the perception of catastrophic losses with very low probabilities. Individuals also appear to underestimate 'controllable' risks of, for example, eating, driving and skiing. These phenomena, and their exploitation in the mass media, may also explain irrational attitudes and misleading behaviour in relation to environmental matters.

Second, the net present value of a resource is used as a measure of the economic value of the property rights to an asset. The net present value formula indicates that risk reduces the value of property. If the risks include a political risk, that is, risk of confiscation or arbitrary political changes, this reduces the value of property due both to the reduced expected value and the risk aversion of property owners. Arbitrary, short-sighted *ad hoc* politics thus reduces value. On the other hand, long-term politics based on legal rules for changes in law and taxes creates a value. Hence net present value gives a measure of the economic value of legal certainty and the economic value of legal protection of property rights. It also illustrates the controversial issue of expropriations and takings for the protection of the environment.

Third, the discounting of future benefits and costs in a net present value formula shows that effects more than 50 years ahead are practically neglected in the economic calculus. Hence there is no economic consideration of future generations derived from price theory. This may obviously have important consequences for the concept of sustainable development.

Chapter 8 examines the principle of sustainable development and relates it to economic growth. The interpretation of the sustainability principle that we use is that it aims at economic growth, under the constraint of sustainable resources for the future. The constraint of sustainability is motivated by the presumption that the amount of natural resources is given. The idea is that the exploitation of virgin resources results in increased scarcity that may in the future cause starvation. The classical economists Thomas Malthus and David Ricardo held this pessimistic view, which is also basic to environmental politics and to current legislation.

However, there are more optimistic forecasts. While the pessimistic view is based on the idea that natural resources limit long-term growth, the optimists present another explanation of growth and conditions for sustainability. The availability of natural resources is neither a necessary nor a sufficient condition for sustainability. Indeed, countries with huge resources, like the former Soviet Union as well as countries in Africa and Latin America, remain poor, while East Asia and Europe have many prosperous nations although their natural resources are rather limited.

Traditional economic explanations for growth are physical capital and technological improvements. Investments and natural resources have been transferred to machinery, infrastructure and knowledge. These production factors may well compensate for the reduced stock of virgin sources.

It is widely accepted by economists that a driving force behind economic growth is 'economies of scale'. That is, specialization and large-scale production increase the output without an equally large increase of inputs. Large-scale production, however, presumes transportation, which causes negative externalities. Similarly, huge production and consumption pollute and threaten biodiversity. Hence physical capital and technical knowledge are not enough for sustainable growth either. Moreover, skilled technicians are not a guarantee of increased wealth or quality of life. These facts have increased the interest in institutional explanations of the kind we stress in this book.

In sum, the view that 'resources will come to an end and mankind will thus be starving in the future' is too simplistic and misleading. New resources, that is, of physical and human capital, are continuously created by investments that will have a value in the future, although it is discounted. The misuse of resources depends to some extent on negative externalities, that is, insufficient legal institutions protecting property rights, controlling corruption, and promoting social norms, reducing free-riding and establishing incentives for socially productive work.

The legal sustainability principle targets future generations. But benefits and costs far ahead are discounted to zero in the economic calculus. Economists have tried in various ways to include considerations for future generations by, for example, special discount rates for environmental investments, option values of species and social contracts among various generations. Our view is that the economic model based on preferences of the current generation is not suited to answer the question of how future generations should be treated. Of course, the present generation may have preferences regarding future generations and their environment, but such social norms cannot be explained by economics – norms and morals are matters of ethics.

Part III Transaction Costs and the Law

In Part II, we analysed public and legal regulations within the framework of a given economic system where the markets, firms and the legal system are assumed to be given. This is the traditional economic approach to environmental matters, familiar in most textbooks on economics. The approach is usefully applied to resource economics, economics of growth and so on, as was demonstrated in Part II. Nevertheless, the approach is insufficient for an analysis of institutions such as property rights and specific environmental laws. In Part I we started by introducing some basic institutional economics of rights. Here, in Part III, which starts with Chapter 9, we continue and apply institutional economics to specific legal rules. The approach explains institutional arrangements by the use of the transaction costs concept. The analysis is normative, thus assuming that the goal of law is to reduce transaction costs in trade. And in case there is no trade, we assume that the law should minimize the total costs of harm caused in the absence of private agreements. The norm is individualistic, and in accordance with the Pareto criterion. In other words, what parties freely accept in trade is good for society. In situations where there is no exchange, the law-maker should legislate or regulate, as the parties would have done in a world without transaction costs. This approach structures the analysis of law. The result of a contract in a world without transaction costs is used as the norm for efficient rules of law. The approach fits well with most environmental laws that regulate negative externalities and free-riding due to some type of transaction costs.

The chapter concludes with two applications. One is to the environmental policy of extended producer's responsibility for durable goods. Does it matter who in the production chain is responsible for the recycling of goods? Transaction costs analysis offers an approach and an answer. The other application is to international relations where there is a *de facto* injurer's right to compensation contrary to the polluter pays principle. The result states that it may be efficient that the polluted industry (the Western world) pays the polluter (the Third World) to reduce its pollution.

A law-maker searching for efficient rules has to weigh the marginal benefits and costs of all involved. Practical methods for this weighing are presented in Chapter 10. First we describe social cost–benefit analysis (CBA). In CBA the costs and benefits of various parties are added together. If the benefits exceed the costs, the project or legal rule is preferable. This summation is based on utilitarian assumptions: (i) that the government aims at maximum social welfare; (ii) that money, at the margin, has the same utility for everyone; and (iii) that prices reflects the opportunity cost of resources. These are, of course, strong assumptions. Nevertheless, CBA is widely used. It is one-dimensional and thus a simple instrument for judgements – all is counted in money, and profitable projects should be chosen.

Of course, there are many problems with the idealized CBA. One is measuring benefits and costs. For instance, in environmental legislation costs may be identifiable while the benefits in terms of a cleaner environment may be impossible to measure. This is why many studies are in practice limited to cost-effectiveness analysis.

We survey standard measurement methods used in CBA. Thereafter we review aspects of public choice theory that question the assumption in CBA, that is, that the goal of government (or the law-maker) is to maximize social welfare. Of course, the government may be motivated by special interests rather than the public interest. Calculation of maximal social wealth is, therefore, of limited relevance for the policy-maker. Nevertheless, an estimation of costs and benefits, or groups of winners and losers, is in the general interest.

A fundamental critique of CBA, and of economic analysis in general, states that economic weighing should not be applied in areas such as human welfare and the environment. Ethical values should govern politics and law rather than an economic calculus. We defend the view that weighing of costs against benefits is necessary in a world with scarce resources. When weighing is denied, scarcity is neglected with inefficiency as a result, that is, a waste of resources.

Ethical norms are, contrary to economics, often expressed in absolute terms – investment should be safe, the water should be clean, life should always be protected, and so on. Nevertheless, safety and cleanliness are relative and gradual matters. We speculate why many environmental issues are presented in absolute terms rather than in more realistic relative terms. One reason may be that policy norms are often a result of a political compromise. It is presumably easy to agree on a positive statement that disregards costs. Another reason may be that we teach in imperatives such as: 'You shall not commit crime' or 'Pollution is bad'. It may be an effective teaching method, although crime and pollution appear in all societies.

A basic principle in normative economics is that free trade is beneficial to the traders and to society as a whole. Yet environmental ethics claims that trade may be immoral. Trade with waste is assumed to be bad, especially international trade. According to the proximity principle, and the Basel Convention, waste should be handled and recycled locally. We discuss and question these general ideas, although there are obvious situations where free trade may be limited.

The chapter is completed with a section on the valuation of life in economic calculations. Morally it may be argued that life should not be valued in monetary terms. However, failure to put a value on human lives in the calculations of projects implies a zero value. We present methods to give an economic value to a saved or lost life.

In Chapter 11 we examine the regulation of industry. Environmental policy on industrial emissions is usually based on guidelines. Industry should use best available techniques (BAT), or some similar standard. Such vague and general standards delegate power to an environmental agency that has to implement the law. Other standards, such as emission standards or quotas, are more demanding on industry. A problem is that the agency normally lacks information on the industry it is supposed to control. It therefore has to negotiate with industry. As a result, the agency may be more or less captured by industry.

There is a trend in environmental policy favouring 'integrated pollution prevention and control' (IPPC). One aspect of IPPC is that sometimes uniform rules are suggested for industry in different nations, for example within the EU. This can be explained to some extent by the desire 'to harmonize marketing conditions' for industry within Europe. However, the impact and valuation of pollution varies among countries. Uniform rules in terms of harmonization may thus end up with solutions ill suited to local preferences and conditions.

In Chapter 12 we discuss land law. The use of land is much more regulated than private non-fixed property. Geographical plans regulate which areas are used for residence, farming, industry, roads and so on (so-called zoning). It is up to the owner to locate within this framework. Daily decisions relating to crops, planting of trees, domestic paint and the like are often up to the owner, but are sometimes regulated by the authorities as well. We give various explanations for this phenomenon of an increased regulatory intervention in the case of land. One is that the value of real estate depends on location and, thus, is due to investments and other activities in the surrounding area. Property owners, therefore, try to influence the use of an estate belonging to others by political activities. A second explanation is that neighbours are in a small-number bargaining relation. Thus there is no simple market solution to their conflicts – disputes may continue without settlement for generations. Legal rules and/or an independent judge may be necessary for solving conflict. A third explanation is that land has multiple uses. It may be used for farming, trespass and tourism at the same time. Agreements among those involved may not be feasible. Transaction costs may be large, especially if the parties are unknown to each other.

Environmental issues that we discuss in this respect are zoning and nuisance law. An important issue here is timing of settlements. Should first-comers be legally protected in a conflict with newcomers? Under which conditions should a newcomer have the right to settle and disturb a first-comer? Zoning is the most common method of regulating disputes on spatial resources. Owners are, therefore, limited to their right to use their property and settle in areas where their business is permitted. Transaction costs and costs in investments forgone in a relocation are important in the economic analysis of land law.

Environmentalists sometimes argue that all polluted land should be cleaned up, also at very large costs. Yet the need for cleanliness varies a great deal in different areas. Having the same requirements for purity everywhere is a waste of resources. Indeed, zoning is a way of utilizing economies of scale. That is, by dividing land into zones for residence, industry, national parks and so on, we can have both wilderness and a polluting industry. If all were industry, or national parks, we would be worse off.

In Chapter 13 we examine environmental taxes, charges and tradable permits. Such measures to regulate negative external effects are traditionally favoured by economists and extensively treated in traditional environmental economics texts. Relative to their practical importance, the charges seem over-investigated. Also from a legal point of view fees and charges are of rather limited interest, compared with, for instance, physical planning and zoning, which are legal instruments of large practical importance.

We apply the Coasean property rights approach in a section on tradable permits. Tradable permits are practical in situations where a number of actors can trade on a market for permits. Efficiency is established by the fact that the highest bidders of the permits will pay for them. Charges, that is, Pigouvian environmental taxes, are similar to tradable rights. The main difference is distributive. That is, in the case of taxes (tradable permits) the users have to pay to the state (the initial owner) for the right to pollute. Tradable permits and charges are applicable when the target is to reduce some pollution and there are a number of actors in the market. For instance, traffic volume, use of oil or pesticides may be efficiently reduced by charges.

Part IV Risk and Liability

Many serious environmental problems are related to uncertainty. New substances, techniques and production systems create new risks that need to be covered by someone. That is, we want to avoid random victimization. We also want to prevent accidents.

Part IV deals with risk and liability. In Chapter 14 we present the economic theory of tort liability and accident prevention. A simple model examines the difference between negligence and strict liability. Given certain assumptions, one reaches the conclusion that both a negligence and a strict liability rule will lead to a minimization of the social costs of accidents. However, in a more complicated setting there remain differences between the rules. Under a negligence rule in principle no cases of liability could be found since an injurer would always follow the due care standard required in the legal system and would thus never have to compensate his victim. Under a strict liability rule on the other hand victims would always receive compensation. If the assumption of risk neutrality is relaxed and if only one of the two parties were risk-averse, for instance the victim, the choice between negligence and strict liability could result in a preference for one of these rules depending upon which party is risk-averse. Also the administrative and information costs of the rules differ. The strict liability rule seems to have the disadvantage that a legal case will follow with every accident since the injurer is always bound to compensate. Court costs can, therefore, be expected to be high. On the other hand, the negligence rule seems to have high information costs for the judge, who will have to determine in a particular case what the marginal costs and marginal benefits of care-taking were.

In Chapter 15 we will investigate the applicability of liability rules when the simplifying assumptions are relaxed. A major problem in environmental liability is that 'nature' does not claim for compensation. Another problem is that the liable party may be unable to pay. We study risk aversion and bankruptcy, which cause a demand for insurance and/or guarantees. A main issue here is the role of insurance. Thereafter, we examine liability and risk taking when the probabilities of accidents are unpredictable or unknown. Many environmental hazards are new and thus inexperienced. Accidents are caused by new systems, substances and products in a complex and largely unknown way. The insurance industry is usually not willing to accept such hazards. Risk-sharing agreements are an alternative to insurance, which is studied next. Further alternatives are funds for the coverage of environmental damage, and increased solvency margins for hazardous industries. Thereafter, we study the efficiency of strict liability at unpredictable losses, and the coverage by first-party insurance and by public compensation schemes.

Chapter 16 studies the economics of environmental crime. Regulations for the protection of the environment are often suggested without consideration of the problem of enforcement. In reality, enforcement of environmental regulations may be weak, or even absent. Regulations are, therefore, sometimes held to be dull environmental instruments. Nonetheless, regulations combined with administrative or criminal sanctions are frequent.

The most important difference between the economic model of tort liability and the model of criminal liability is that all criminal polluters are not detected. A low detection rate reduces the incentive to protect the environment. Rare detection increases the required sanction, which, in turn, causes bankruptcy problems.

There is a trade-off between optimal deterrence and enforcement costs, since an increase in the detection rate requires an increase in policing costs. Fines are financial transfers that move the amount from the offender to society, while imprisonment means a cost in terms of freedom and production lost, and resources used in the criminal justice system. Fines are thus preferable. However, the probability of detection of environmental pollution is often very low while the environmental damage may be large. In that case the optimal sanction to deter pollution becomes high. The optimal monetary sanction required for deterrence often exceeds the offender's assets. Consequently non-monetary sanctions, such as imprisonment, may be used.

The major advantage of the fine therefore only applies when the damage of crime is small and the insolvency risk can be controlled. That may be the case with violations of regulations that (i) are simple to detect, and (ii) are considered a danger *ex ante*.

Chapter 17 overviews the combination of various measures such as property rights legislation, licences, industry regulation, charges, deposits, land use regulations, tort liability, insurance and criminal sanctions. In addition, levels of government are discussed. We ask what the criteria for central decision-making are, that is, we investigate principles for environmental regulation on an international (EU) level and on a local level. Chapter 17 concludes the book.

FURTHER READING

Introductory Texts and Overviews

Ackerman, B.A. (ed.) (1975), *Economic Foundations of Property Law*, Boston: Little Brown and Company.

Bouckaert, B. and De Geest, G. (eds) (2000), *Encyclopedia of Law and Economics* (5 vols), Cheltenham, UK and Northampton, USA: Edward Elgar.

Cooter, R. and Ulen, T. (2000), *Law and Economics*, 3rd edn, Reading: Addison-Wesley.

Cropper, M.L. and Oates, W.E. (1992), 'Environmental Economics: A Survey', *Journal of Economic Literature*, **30**, 675–740.

Kiss, A. and Shelton, D. (1997), *Manual of European Environmental Law*, 2nd edn, Cambridge: Grotius Publications.

Mueller, D.C. (1979), *Public Choice*, Cambridge: Cambridge University Press.

Newman, P. (ed.) (1998), *The New Palgrave Dictionary of Economics and the Law* (3 vols), London: Macmillan.

Pearce, D.W. and Turner, R.K. (1998), *Economics of Natural Resources and the Environment*, New York and London: Harvester Wheatsheaf.

Posner, R.A. (1998), *Economic Analysis of Law*, 5th edn, New York: Aspen.

Sands, P. (1995), *Principles of International Environmental Law I. Frameworks, standards and implementation*, Manchester: Manchester University Press.

Seerden, R., Heldeweg, M. and Deketelaere, K. (2002), *Public Environmental Law in the European Union and the United States: A Comparative Analysis*, The Hague: Kluwer.

Tietenberg, T. (2000), *Environmental and Natural Resource Economics*, 5th edn, New York: HarperCollins.

PART I

Rights and the Environment

2. Principles of environmental policy

Prevention is better than cure.

1. INTRODUCTION

In this chapter we present general principles of environmental policy. We also give a brief introduction to economic issues related to these principles. The purpose is to provide an introductory framework for the remainder of the book. A more detailed analysis of specific laws regulating the use of specific environmental resources, such as property law, administrative law, tort law and criminal law, will follow later.

In Section 2 we present the principle of sustainable development. This principle promotes economic growth, given that future generations must meet their needs. The principles of prevention and precaution are outlined in Section 3. The general idea here is that 'prevention and precaution are better than cure'. At a general level this saying appears to be a good economic guideline. Nonetheless, economic efficiency requires that costs and benefits are balanced. Indeed, there are circumstances in which the costs of prevention and/or precaution exceed the benefits both to the society and to the environment.

The polluter pays principle is discussed in Section 4. The notion that the polluter should pay for the damage caused is a widely accepted economic principle. Nevertheless, it has been questioned by, for example, Ronald Coase (1960) in the famous Coase theorem that is briefly introduced. This theorem is one of the underpinnings of the rest of the book.

In Section 5 we present the proximity principle, which states that environmental damage ought to be rectified at the source. This view may have general appeal as a guideline in life – each and every person should keep his own backyard clean. The idea is that waste handling and recycling are preferably undertaken by the party that creates the waste. In Section 6 we examine environmental rights in constitutional law. Many modern constitutions in, for example, Western European countries explicitly provide for a right to a clean environment. Hence environmental policy principles have also become environmental law. Section 7 discusses the economic nature of environmental principles. Finally, Section 8 concludes.

2. SUSTAINABLE DEVELOPMENT

The concept of '*sustainable development*' is mentioned in the 1972 Stockholm declaration and the 1992 Rio declaration, which in Principle 4 states that the 'right to development must be fulfilled so as to equitably meet the developmental and environmental needs of present and future generations'. Important also is the commitment to integrate environmental considerations into economic and other developments. The term 'sustainable development' was also introduced in 1987 in a report of the World Commission on Environment and Development called *Our common future*, usually referred to as the Brundtland Report. The report defines sustainable development as a 'development that meets the needs of the present without compromising the ability of future generations to meet their own needs'.

Further, the EC Treaty, as amended by the Treaty on the European Union (better known as the Treaty of Maastricht), states in Article 2 that:

> The Community shall have as its task, by establishing a common market and an economic and monetary union and by implementing common policies or activities referred to in Articles 3 and 4, to promote throughout the Community a harmonious, balanced and sustainable development of economic activities, a high level of employment and of social protection, equality between men and women, sustainable and non-inflationary growth, a high degree of competitiveness and convergence of economic performance, a high level of protection and improvement of the quality of the environment, the raising of the standard of living and quality of life, and economic and social cohesion and solidarity among Member States.

This text is referred to in the legal literature as the principle of sustainable development. It requires the European Union to promote a harmonious, balanced and sustainable development of economic activities. It may be impossible to define the concept with precision.[1] Yet it seems obvious that it is basically economic – the principle aims at economic growth, within the constraints of sustainable resources (widely defined) for the future. In other words, economic growth is the target, and it should be realized (at least in the European Union) in a free common market with a high level of employment, and a high level of protection and improvement of the quality of the environment.

Economic growth is usually measured by the increase in *gross domestic product* (GDP), which summarizes the total economic value of products and services produced in one nation during a year. The GDP measure is much questioned, not least in the environmental debate: how should the depletion of natural resources be accounted for? How shall we guarantee that a civilised and wealthy society will remain for future generations?

We will not be able to answer all these questions, but in Part II we will try to clarify the economic analysis and valuation of environmental policy principles. Principles of economics, such as beneficial exchange, the formation and function of prices, investments, risk-taking, and the rule of law in the market economy, are fundamental to the understanding of economic growth and its impact on the environment. It is also important to understand implicit and explicit norms of economics, and the limits of economic analysis. The most demanding environmental questions are, to a large degree, ethical or moral, that is, beyond economics. Our intention below is limited to a study of the wide-ranging abilities, but also the limits, of economics.

3. THE PREVENTION AND PRECAUTIONARY PRINCIPLES

The *principle of prevention* states that actions should be taken before pollution, damage or environmental impairment has occurred (Article 174 (2) of the EC Treaty). The same principle can also be found in international environmental law, for instance, in the 1972 Stockholm declaration, and in Principle 11 of the 1992 Rio declaration. The principle requires that an activity that may cause damage to the environment be prevented or controlled at an early stage. This principle is, like the other principles, not legally binding in itself, but functions as a general policy guideline.

A loss can often be prevented at much lower cost than that of the loss itself. The idea that prevention is better than cure is, therefore, a good economic rule of thumb. The costs of taking preventive action, for example by careful treatment of toxic substances or by investments in abatement technology, are often lower than curing the environmental pollution or damage. Nonetheless, prevention is not always preferable. Extensive preventive measures may very well be more costly than the damage prevented. Indeed, if all possible preventive measures are made in a certain area the costs in terms of physical, human and environmental resources may far exceed the benefits. A basic principle in economics, which we will repeat many times in this book, is that benefits and costs should be compared and balanced at the margin. A firm that maximizes profit will undertake prevention as long as the marginal costs are smaller than the marginal benefits, and authorities performing investments based on a cost–benefit calculus may perform a similar balancing on a community or on a social level. Social cost–benefit calculus will be dealt with in Chapter 10. The balancing of costs of prevention is crucial, for instance in the analysis of accidents and torts (see Chapter 14), and in the economic analysis of criminal law (see Chapter 16).

Article 174 (2) of the EC Treaty also states that community policy on the environment should be based on the *precautionary principle*. The principle can also be found in national environmental legal systems and in international environmental law. The legal basis for the principle may be found – *inter alia* – in Principle 15 of the Rio declaration, which provides that 'where there are threats of serious or irreversible damage, lack of full scientific certainty shall not be used as a reason for postponing cost-effective measures to prevent environmental degradation'. This precautionary principle has now been adapted in several international environmental treaties. One example is the 1992 Baltic Sea Convention, which states that preventive measures are to be taken when there is reason to assume that harm might be caused even when there is no conclusive evidence of a causal relationship between inputs and their alleged effects. Another example constitutes Article 3 (3) of the well-known Framework Convention on Climate Change (FCCC) of 9 May 1992, which states:

> The parties should take precautionary measures to anticipate, prevent or minimise the causes of climate change and mitigate its adverse effects. Where there are threats of serious or irreversible damage, lack of full scientific certainty shall not be used as a reason for postponing such measures, taking into account that policies and measures to deal with climate change should be cost-effective so as to ensure global benefits at the lowest possible cost.

Here it can be noted that the economic notion of cost–benefit analysis is linked to the (legal) precautionary principle.

Most legal scholars link the precautionary principle with the preventive principle, although some make a distinction between the two. The precautionary principle, which has its roots in the German 'Vorsorge Prinzip', dictates that if there is a strong suspicion that a certain activity may have environmentally harmful consequences, it is better to act before it is too late. In that sense the precautionary principle goes a step further than the preventive principle, since the former dictates that action must be taken as a precaution, meaning that one should not wait until scientific evidence incontrovertibly shows a causal connection between a certain activity and possible environmental damage. This principle is, therefore, important in cases where there is a presumption, but as yet no clear and convincing scientific evidence of certain undesirable environmental effects. Even in the absence of absolute proof the precautionary principle dictates that tentative and indicative scientific data are sufficient grounds on which to take measures to protect the environment. Within the context of international environmental law this means that legal action must be taken to address highly threatening environmental issues such as ozone depletion and climate change, even if full scientific certainty is not established. However, as the definition of the precautionary principle in the Climate Change Convention showed, the actions taken still have to be cost-effective.

If, on the other hand, the general opinion is that a polluting industry should be allowed to continue its practices if uncertainty prevails, we might talk about

BOX 2.1 THE DUDDRIDGE CASE

Citizens are not always successful when they try to ask for policy measures to reduce environmental harm, using the precautionary principle. A well-known case in the United Kingdom dealt with citizens who were arguing that non-ionizing radiation in electromagnetic fields will or might expose children to risks of developing childhood leukaemia. Therefore, they required the UK Secretary of State to take measures to limit non-ionizing radiation. Their argument was that the Secretary of State was obliged to take precautionary action if there was the slightest possibility of risk of serious harm to environmental health. Experts argued that there might be a possibility of a connection between electromagnetic fields and childhood leukaemia, but they saw the need for further research. The case was tried by the High Court, which examined whether Article 130R of the EC Treaty[1] created an obligation on the Secretary of State to apply the precautionary principle to his consideration under the British Electricity Act. The High Court held that it was the clear intention that the policy envisaged in Article 130R was to be brought into effect by the introduction of EC measures. It was for the EC Council of Ministers to adopt measures necessary to implement the policy. Therefore the Court ruled that the principles in Article 130R did not create an obligation on the Secretary of State to take national action in accordance with it. It held that the Secretary of State could lawfully apply the precautionary principle to exercise his powers under the 1989 Electricity Act, but that the precautionary principle did not oblige to do so. In sum, the High Court held that the precautionary principle did not force the UK Secretary of State to take measures.

Note:
1. As a result of the Maastricht Treaty this became Article 174.

Source: Based on High Court, 3 October 1994. *Regina* v. *Secretary of State for Trade and Industry, ENDS report*, 237, October 1994, pp. 41–21.

'*industrial optimism*'. In such a regime, the burden of proof is on the party that wishes to ban an activity. If, instead, the general opinion is that the activity should not be allowed if uncertainty prevails, we have the precautionary principle. Here, the party that wishes to allow an activity must prove that it is socially profitable. Industrial optimism has been the dominating attitude in many countries during the twentieth century. The belief that benefits normally exceed the potential harm of industry has been strong. The fact that some in society will be harmed has been accepted because of the belief in over-riding benefits. Economic growth, and the accumulation of capital and knowledge, as well as the development of the social security systems of the welfare state, were supposed to compensate for the potential damage (see Chapter 8). Although the meaning of the precautionary principle is not quite clear yet, it may be seen as a shift in approach to decision-making under uncertainty. Industrial optimism has lost its dominant position, but is still important. Indeed, industrial operations continuously take place with the belief that, on the whole, the benefits exceed the costs. On the other hand, bans and restrictions on toxic substances, obsolete production techniques and so on are also frequent. Indeed, the precautionary principle is often used in national environmental law in the standard-setting process (see Chapter 11). This usually leads to imposing stricter emission standards to prevent certain environmental risks, even if the effects are not certain.

BOX 2.2 NUCLEAR POWER AND INDUSTRIAL OPTIMISM

The precautionary principle may be the over-riding theme today; however, industrial optimism has guided industries, policy-makers and legislators since the Second World War. This can be illustrated by the legislation concerning nuclear power in the early 1960s. Most of the conventions which came into being within the framework of either the Nuclear Energy Agency (NEA) or the International Atomic Energy Agency (IAEA) started from a belief that the enormous benefits of the industry should not be hindered by obstacles like potential accidents. The preparatory proceedings for the Paris Convention for example, made clear that the (international) legislator wished to limit the liability of the licensee of a nuclear power plant. As a result financial caps were introduced, which limited the exposure to liability of the nuclear industry. This fitted with the general optimism concerning the benefits of nuclear power. The corresponding role of the legislator was, therefore, to facilitate industrial development instead of hindering it. However, as we shall demonstrate below, the financial caps which were introduced as a result of this industrial optimism can largely be considered as having had potential adverse effects on safety (see Chapter 15).

A precautionary principle forcing the administration and industry to invest in measures when there is scientific uncertainty about the need to take these measures worries many industrialists and economists. The principle may lead to over-regulation in that costly precautions are taken without evidence that this will lead to a reduction in environmental harm, and may bring about a waste of scarce resources. A general problem here is the asymmetry of information over time; that is, the costs of prevention and precaution are

BOX 2.3 COMMUNICATION ON THE PRECAUTIONARY PRINCIPLE

On 2 February 2000 the European Commission launched a communication on the precautionary principle. The goal of this communication is to establish guidelines for applying it and to avoid unwarranted recourse to the precautionary principle as a disguised form of protectionism. The Commission holds that recourse to the precautionary principle supposes that scientific evaluation does not allow the risk to be determined with sufficient certainty. The implementation of an approach based on the precautionary principle should hence start with a scientific evaluation, identifying the degree of scientific uncertainty. This is referred to as risk assessment. The precautionary principle plays a role in the second stage, being that of risk management. Given the scientific information on the uncertainty, decision-makers have to take the political responsibility to determine the 'acceptable' level of risk for society. When measures are indeed necessary based on the precautionary principle, the Commission holds that these measures should among others also be based on an examination of the potential benefits and costs of action, or lack of action. However, the Commission stresses that this is not simply an economic cost–benefit analysis. The scope of this consideration is much broader and includes non-economic considerations, such as the efficacy of possible options and their acceptability to the public. Measures taken on the basis of the precautionary principle should also be periodically reviewed in the light of scientific progress and amended as necessary.

Source: Based on EU Commission on the precautionary principle, COM (2000), 1.

available today and are calculable, while the benefits and costs to the environment in the future may be diffuse and hard to estimate.

If risks are systematically avoided this can sometimes cause high costs, whereas the benefits are sometimes doubtful. For instance, Anthony Ogus (1995) gives the example of the display screen equipment directive 1990,[2] which governs the use of display screens throughout industry and commerce. It requires employers to meet standards relating to, for example, the design of the screen, desk and chair, and environmental factors. While health problems which may arise from the use of display screens have been the subject of concern in the debate, there is no hard evidence indicating serious effects.

4. THE POLLUTER PAYS PRINCIPLE

Principle 16 of the Rio declaration provides that:

> National authorities should endeavour to promote the internalisation of environmental costs and the use of economic instruments, taking into account the approach that the polluter should, in principle, bear the costs of pollution, with due regard to the public interest and without distorting international trade and investment.

Similarly, Article 174(2) of the EC Treaty states that community policy on the environment shall be based on the principle 'that the polluter should pay'. This *polluter pays principle* (PPP) has an obvious intuitive appeal – it is the wrongdoer who is responsible and should pay. In economics the polluter pays principle is well established, but also questioned. The economics of the polluter pays principle goes back to the work of Pigou (1920). It is common knowledge in economics that prices inform buyers and sellers about opportunity costs, that is, the resources required to produce goods and services on the market. The parties in the markets are thereby guided, and their decisions are coordinated via prices. However, the informative correctness of prices depends on the assumption that all affected are included in the trade and accept the terms. If the prices do not include compensation to all involved, there is an imperfection, or lack of *internalization* of costs or benefits, that is, an *external effect* in the economy.

Thus negative external effects prevail when someone causes harm without considering the consequences to others. Indeed, many environmental problems are due to technical, chemical and biological changes that may be harmful to individuals and the environment. A large portion of environmental economics is concerned with the question of how such negative external effects can be internalized in the economic system. The traditional reply has been to recommend charges for environmentally hazardous activities, that is, the advice to apply the polluter pays principle via charges on, for example, cars, alcoholic beverages and energy.

This seemingly straightforward and still well-established principle was questioned, however, in the 1960s by Ronald Coase. In his famous *Coase's theorem* he states that the distribution of rights – here the right to pollute without a duty to compensate victims, or the victim's right to be compensated for pollution (PPP) – has no importance from an economic efficiency point of view. In other words, it could be equally efficient if the victim paid the wrongdoer not to pollute. This norm we name the *victim pays principle* (VPP). Note that the theorem refers to a situation where two or more parties are able to trade without any *transaction costs*, that is, costs to search, to bargain, to contract and to enforce agreements. Coase's point is that in this situation the parties have a common interest in maximizing the joint value of the trade, that is, in efficiency. Once the joint benefit is maximized they have an individual interest in getting as large a proportion as possible.

To illustrate the theorem we use a simple example in Box 2.4 below.

Economists following the Pigou (1951) tradition advocate that externalities such as environmental pollution should be internalized by imposing a corrective tax or charge on the polluting activity. A charge equal to the costs caused by the smoke from the factory in Box 2.4, that is, $600, would create an incentive to reduce pollution by installation of a filter. Note that the charge distributes the income to the state, not to the victim.

The charge is thus only one option. Ronald Coase (1960) opposed the general approach focusing on charges and claimed that either a PPP or a VPP rule would result in efficiency (a filter in Box 2.4). Coase stressed the reciprocal nature of harm. In this case it refers to the fact that the pollution is not just caused by the factory emitting pollutants; one could equally regard it as a case where the presence of neighbours limits the rights of the factory. It is, therefore, more useful to view this as a case of conflicting uses of property rights.

As various legal rules may result in efficiency, the PPP cannot be motivated solely on efficiency grounds. In fact, the PPP may rather be understood via distributive considerations. In other words, if the polluter is rich (industry) and the victim is poor (the general public), it may motivate a '*deep pocket*' or '*ability to pay*' principle, that is, the PPP.

When someone is disturbed or harmed, it may seem natural that the victim should have the right to compensation. But a polluter may claim, on reasonable grounds, that the right to pollute is part of the owner's rights. Assume, for instance, that a factory was first located in a sparsely populated area and is afterwards confronted by neighbours who move into the vicinity of the nuisance, and thereafter claim compensation or demand relocation of the factory. If the neighbours move in, aware of the nuisance, it is not obvious

BOX 2.4 THE COASE THEOREM: A FILTER EXAMPLE

Assume that a factory is emitting smoke and that three people who live near it are claiming $200 each because of the alleged damage to their health. Assume, furthermore, that the emissions are affecting only the three victims. In this example, we can disregard the fact that the emissions may be damaging the environment. There is no feasible way in which the victims can prevent this damage to their health. The factory on the other hand can eliminate all the emissions by installing a filter costing $300.

The first question that must be answered is what the socially optimal result entails: installation of the filter or not. To be able to answer this question, we must specify the social economic goal. Here, we assume that the social goal is the maximization of the joint benefits, minus costs of the pollutant to the victims. Since a cost of $600 (3 victims each claiming damages of $200) can be avoided by investing just $300, the optimal solution is obviously to install the filter.

Another possible solution would be a relocation of the factory or the victims, but we assume that relocation costs would be substantially higher than the $300 a filter would cost.

Coase's theorem holds that if the transaction costs are zero, an optimal allocation of resources will always take place, irrespective of the contents of the governing legal rule. The optimal allocation of resources in this example is the installation of the filter. Indeed, the filter will be installed no matter what the contents of the legal rule are. If the law holds the factory owner liable to pay compensation to the victims, the installation of the filter is obviously in the interest of the factory. By installing the filter costing just $300, the factory can avoid having to pay compensation to the victims (of $600). Under this legal regime, which one may for now call a PPP regime, the optimal result will follow.

The same, however, is true if the factory is not liable and victims bear their own damage according to a 'right-to-pollute' regime or a victim pays principle (VPP). Given the zero transaction costs assumption, they will get together and negotiate with the factory to persuade it to install the filter. By paying the factory the price of the filter, the victims are still better off since the total costs of the damages are considerably higher than the costs of the filter. Hence, in either case, that is the PPP or the VPP rule, the efficient outcome will follow.

This result merits several comments. First, it should be stressed that it is not clear at first sight what price the victims will pay the factory in the VPP regime. Depending upon its bargaining power, the factory may well claim more than just the price of $300 for the installation of the filter. In the end, the victims may have to pay up to (almost) $600 for the filter if the factory is a tough bargainer. Then the benefit of the installation is to the factory.

Second, a mixture of the PPP rule and the VPP rule prevails if the right to compensation is given to only one of the three victims. The outcome will also be efficient in this case. Assume that only victim A has a right to compensation. At first glance it may seem better for the polluter to pay $200 instead of installing the filter. However, victims B and C are willing to pay the polluter $200 each to make the polluter install the filter. Their payment to the polluter, plus the eliminated compensation to A, make it economically profitable for the polluter to install the filter.

A general conclusion that can be drawn from the example is that when several parties are involved, the right to pollute or right(s) to compensation can be placed on *any* of the parties with the same outcome, given that the transaction costs are negligible.

Note that the efficient outcome may not follow if the parties behave *strategically*. In order to improve their own position, the parties may misinform and threaten each other, which may result in no agreement at all. By the assumption of zero transaction costs, we have excluded strategic behaviour and other bargaining and contracting costs.

The theorem only deals with efficiency, not with distributional aspects. Although the efficient outcome will hold in the different distributions of rights, there is a distributional difference: on PPP the factory in our example pays for the filter; on VPP the victims do. Hence the contents of the legal rule matter from the perspective of the wealth distribution of the parties. The liable party must, of course, have resources available to pay. There is no risk of bankruptcy in the example. Hence the Coase theorem fits best when the parties involved are solvent, profit-maximizing firms.

that the first-comer should compensate the newcomer (this issue is discussed in Chapter 12).

Similarly, the PPP is an internationally accepted rule. Nonetheless, international aid is an area where the VPP is often the rule rather than the exception. One example of this is the investments made by Western European countries today in reducing environmental harm caused by Eastern European industry. For example, the investments in nuclear safety in Bulgaria may well be efficient, but show that in fact it is not the polluter, but rather the victim who pays. Furthermore, in tort law strict liability corresponds to the PPP while the negligence rule corresponds to the VPP. There are arguments in favour of strict liability when dangerous industries pollute and cause accidents. However, there are arguments in favour of negligence as well (see Chapters 14 and 15).

All in all, the PPP is undoubtedly a workable starting-point, corresponding to the economic notion that an externality can be internalized by exposing that polluter to the full costs of his activity. However, in reality the applicability is limited – a point we will return to in later chapters.

5. THE PROXIMITY PRINCIPLE

A general aim in environmental policy is to reduce the enormous amounts of waste produced, especially in the technically highly developed countries. A basic idea in this respect is that the waste should be treated, and if possible eliminated, at the source. If the waste cannot be eliminated, the material may be recycled, and if that is not is possible it may be burnt. Landfills and disposals are seen as the worst alternative. This *proximity principle* may seem sound housekeeping, but has considerable economic limitations. An efficient treatment of waste, as all other goods, requires that the party with comparative advantage perform the production or service. An efficient alternative to waste treatment at the source is often, therefore, to trade the waste to other parties that can deal with it.

The notion that waste should as a priority be eliminated at source is, therefore, in conflict with freedom of trade. This conflict is obvious in, for instance, the European Community context where it has been unclear whether the basic freedoms of the common market, such as the free movement of goods, also apply to waste and to polluting and dangerous goods. In other words, should individual Member States of the Union be allowed to restrict the free movement of goods for reasons of environmental protection? According to the provisions of Article 28 (and following) of the Treaty a Member State cannot restrict or prohibit the import of a certain (polluting) product. Article 28 of the Treaty provides that quantitative restrictions on imports and

BOX 2.5 THE DASSONVILLE CASE

The European Court of Justice decided in this case that 'all trading rules enacted by Member States which are capable of hindering, directly or indirectly, actually or potentially, intra-community trade, are to be considered as measures having an effect equivalent to quantitative restrictions'. Hence every potential import hindrance, with or without distinction, to domestic or imported products, falls in principle under this prohibition. In this respect one can think of a national ban on a certain polluting compound (such as asbestos) or concentration of a certain toxic compound in products to fall under the prohibition of Article 28. Hence a strict interpretation of the Dassonville case would mean that the goal of the realization of the common internal market is considered so important that products that are harmful to the environment can also cross the national borders of the Member States without any limitation.

Source: Based on ECJ 11 July 1974, *Procureur du Roi* v. *Dassonville*, Case 8/74, ECR [1974], p. 837.

all measures having equivalent effect shall be prohibited between Member States.

However, an elaborate case-law has been developed with respect to the trade-off between the free movement of goods versus environmental protection. An important exception can be found in Article 30 of the Treaty. This exception allows Member States to restrict intra-community trade if the measures taken are justified 'on grounds of … the protection of health and life of humans, animals or plants'. These measures 'shall not, however, constitute a means of arbitrary discrimination or a disguised restriction on trade between Member States'. The grounds on which Member States can restrict intra-community trade have been interpreted in a series of decisions of the European Court of Justice (ECJ). The conclusion is that measures taken have to be 'necessary and proportionate to the goal to be reached'.[3] The example of a prohibition of asbestos, as being a substance dangerous to the health and life of humans, animals and plants, could well be justified by the exceptions mentioned. On the other hand, the Court also decided that a general import prohibition on not-dangerous wastes cannot be justified under the article.[4]

Since the Danish bottles case (Box 2.6) it is accepted that environmental protection can be one of the 'mandatory requirements' that can restrict the

BOX 2.6 THE CASSIS DE DIJON CASE AND THE DANISH BOTTLES CASE

An important exception to Article 28 is created by the European Court of Justice in the Cassis de Dijon case.[1] The Court held that a national trade-restricting measure can be justified if, first, it applies in a non-discriminatory way to both national and imported products; second, if the goal of this measure is a mandatory requirement – such as public health – and, third, if the impact of the measure is proportionate to the interest that needs to be protected by it. This idea was extended to the field of the environment in the Danish bottles case,[2] where the European Court decided that the environment can be classified as a mandatory requirement. The Court held that environmental protection is an interest that can justify a national environmental policy with trade-restricting effects, such as *in casu* a mandatory system of returnable containers for beer and soft drinks.

Notes:

1. ECJ 20 February 1979, *Rewe-Zentral AG* v. *Bundesmonopolverwaltung für Branntwein* (Cassis de Dijon), Case 120/78, ECR [1979], p. 649.
2. ECJ 20 September 1988, *Commission* v. *Denmark* (Danish bottles), Case 302/86, ECR [1988], p. 4607.

applicability of the free trade principle of Article 28. This exception is broader than the one offered by Article 30. For the applicability of Article 30 it is necessary that human, animal or vegetal life or health is at stake, whereas this is not required under the rule of the bottles case.

A condition for the applicability of the environmental protection exception is that the national measures taken apply to national and imported products in a non-discriminatory way. But even this non-discrimination principle has been relaxed. The Court held in the Walloon case (see note 4) that the principle of preventive action at source can justify an import restriction that only applies to foreign waste. The Court held that there was no violation of the non-discrimination principle although the prohibition in the Walloon regulation only applied to foreign waste. This principle of preventive action at source is apparently considered to have priority over the freedom of trade and non-discrimination principles.

How is the trade-off between free trade and environmental protection addressed from an economic point of view? First it should be noted that, as just shown, free trade is a cornerstone in, for example, the Treaty of Rome.

A fundamental argument in favour of free trade is that integration of states by trade contributes to a peaceful development and to an end to armed conflicts. The idea of peace-creating trade has a long history. For instance, eighteenth-century philosophers like Montesquieu and Condorcet argued that trade refines the human being – the trader travels without a sword, is peaceful and takes nothing without agreement of the trading partner. Concepts like honour, trust and loyalty are important for the businessman (Hirschman, 1982). This belief in the honourable and trustworthy trader is controversial, of course. Nonetheless, the idea of an extended network and of long-term relations based on a mutually beneficial ground is of great importance both in European politics and in mainstream economic thinking.

Another reason for the priority and protection of free trade is its fundamental importance in the market economy system. Waste can usually – as other goods and services – be traded in a mutually beneficial way due to comparative advantages and the utilization of economies of scale. It may, for instance, be possible that the French can incinerate waste at lower costs than the Dutch or Belgians. A trade of waste from Belgium or the Netherlands to France would in that case be beneficial. Some countries may be able to use certain waste products for secondary goals. Such a trade is

BOX 2.7 TRADE IN WASTE: MORALISTS VERSUS RATIONALISTS

Frey (1997) recently showed that economists (considered as 'rationalists') regard trade in waste totally differently from 'moralists', who look at the environment as an ethical issue. Moralists would be strongly against trade in waste, arguing that dealing with waste remains a fundamental responsibility of the state which cannot be delegated (the very notion of the proximity principle). Economists on the other hand would see no reason why the fundamental law of comparative advantage governing international trade should not apply to waste. All participants could gain if countries were allowed to ship the waste to the country best equipped to deal with it. The waste-exporting country would pay a lower price than if the waste had to be treated internally and the waste-importing country could make a profit by providing a service at comparatively low cost. This battle, so Frey argues, has apparently been won by the moralists, since many treaties, such as the Basel Convention, explicitly prohibit the export of waste, contrary to economic logic.

allowed under the 1992 Basel Convention, which regulates transboundary trade of waste, and the ban on trade does not apply if the waste is reused or recycled. Nevertheless, there is a danger when waste is moving across borders. The lack of monitoring by administrative agencies may increase the probability that the waste escapes any control, and is therefore discharged illegally.

Another general problem in the international exchange of goods and services is that an industry or a nation may gain by unilateral restrictions on trade. That is, customs and other forms of protection may benefit a domestic industry, but at the same time harm foreign industries. If many nations individually protect their industries, all will be harmed by reduced trade. In other words, the ability to free-ride on other nations' liberal trade makes it complicated to uphold a system of free trade. Hence continuous efforts must be made to maintain and develop international free trade of goods and services. Representatives of 120 nations met, for instance, in 1994 to sign the Uruguay Round of the General Agreement on Tariffs and Trade (GATT). It became a revised version of the 1948 GATT Convention, which attempted to lower tariff barriers to world trade. The World Trade Organization (WTO) has the status and power to oversee and enforce the agreement.

A problem with the enforcement of the agreements of free trade is the presence of various more or less hidden technical hindrances that can be used to protect own industry and, thereby, free-ride on the liberal trade rules. It may also be hard to separate negative attitudes to trade that are ethically grounded and mere protectionism 'in a green dress'. That is, environmental protection can be used as an argument for protection, which, in turn, explains the resistance and suspicion in relation to environmental requirements and limitations.

It may well be efficient, for instance, from an economic point of view, to ship waste to the Sahara desert and store it there at relatively low costs where potential environmental harm is very low. Here we assume, of course, that the waste is not dangerous, toxic or traded illegally. Nonetheless, these kinds of trades are prohibited by international conventions partly for ethical reasons. The proximity principle apparently has a strong ethical appeal, being the basic idea that a community should treat its waste problem itself and not export it to its neighbours or to less developed countries. Note, however, that the ethical and 'green' argument can also be used to favour specific economic interests, notably a domestic waste-handling industry in an industrially developed country as described in Box 2.8.

BOX 2.8 THE DUSSELDORP CASE

The possible protection of a domestic industry has been shown recently in a case brought before the European Court of Justice where the relationship between competition law and the proximity principle had to be decided. National regulations may force the local industry for example to bring all industrial waste to one (monopolized) waste treatment plant or incinerator and prohibit all export of waste on the basis of the proximity principle. In those cases the question obviously arises whether the national Member States have the right to force their national industry to use an expensive waste treatment on the basis of the proximity principle, or whether the export ban should be considered illegal. The European Court of Justice decided against an 'abuse' of the proximity principle to justify an export ban on waste. Such a general export ban (by *in casu* the Netherlands) was held to violate European Law.

Source: Based on ECJ, 25 June 1998, Case C 203/96, Chemische afvalstoffen Dusseldorp B.V.

6. THE RIGHT TO A CLEAN ENVIRONMENT

The environmental policy principles are, as mentioned in the introduction, included in many national constitutions. The right to a clean or good environment is formulated here, in some form or another, as a human right. For instance, in 1994 Article 20a was added to the German constitution (the Grundgesetz), which made environmental protection a state principle. Article 20a of the German constitution emphasizes a principle of precaution and an environmental duty at all state levels towards the goal of environmental protection. It does not, however, grant an actionable right to the citizen. Thus it is, according to German legal doctrine, not to be considered a 'fundamental environmental right'. Other constitutions also guarantee the protection of the environment, for instance, the Greek constitution of 1986 in Article 24, where protection of the environment is formulated as a duty of the state. Finally we could point to the Dutch example, where Article 21 of the constitution provides for a legal basis for environmental protection. This was introduced in the revision of the constitution in 1983 and states that the duty of the government is aimed at the inhabitation of the land and the protection and improvement of the environment. Again, legal doctrine holds that the article lays an obligation on the government without actually serving as a legal basis for claims by civilians against the state.

These developments in modern constitutions are in line with pleas in environmental legal doctrine to introduce environmental human rights into the law. The 'environmental protection rights' in constitutions or conventions usually refer to a duty of the authorities to protect citizens against environmental degradation. It is, however, usually argued as well that these social rights do not confer individually actionable subjective rights on citizens (see Chapter 4, Sections 9 and 10).

There are, nevertheless, a number of interesting cases where citizens have used the traditional human rights, notably the right as laid down in the European Convention on Human Rights of 1950, to argue that some cases of environmental pollution might constitute a violation of these traditional human rights. Several articles of the Convention have been used in that respect.

BOX 2.9 THE FREDIN CASE

The background to the Fredin case is Article 1 of the first protocol to the European Convention of Human Rights, which protects private property. The Court recognized in the case of *Fredin* v. *Sweden* that 'in today's society the protection of the environment is an increasingly important consideration', and tested whether the interference with a private property right to achieve environmental objectives was proportionate or disproportionate in the context of Article 1 of the first protocol. It held that this interference was not inappropriate, meaning that environmental protection measures can in fact override private property rights.

Source: Based on ECHR, Judgement of 18 February 1991, Series A, no. 192, p. 14, para. 48.

The question has also risen whether severe cases of environmental pollution might be considered as a breach of Article 8 of the European Convention on Human Rights (ECHR), which provides that, *inter alia*, 'everyone has the right to respect for his private … life and his home … and there shall be no interference by a public authority with the exercise of the right except such as is in accordance with the law and is necessary in a democratic society in the interests of the economic well-being of the country … '. Citizens living in the neighbourhood of London's Heathrow Airport alleged that excessive noise forced them to endure unreasonable disturbance caused by air traffic, flying in accordance with governmental regulation, which would constitute a breach of Article 8. The Court rejected the allegation, arguing that it had to strike a fair balance between the competing interests of the individual and the community as a whole. The Court apparently judged that this fair balance had not been upset, given, *inter alia* the significant measures to abate noise pollution that had been taken by the government, following international standards.

BOX 2.10 THE LOPEZ OSTRA CASE

In the December 1994 case of *Lopez Ostra* v. *Spain*, the European Court of Human Rights held that there was a violation of Article 8 of the European Convention because of the pollution caused by a waste treatment plant. Experts showed an unacceptable emission of toxic fumes and damage to the health of the people living in the immediate vicinity of a waste treatment plant. Physicians had testified that the health of Mrs Lopez Ostra's daughter had been seriously damaged and recommended that she should move. The Court held that there was a violation of Article 8. The town had allowed the plant to be built on its land and the state of Spain had subsidized the plant's construction. The Court considered in this case that the state did not succeed in striking a fair balance between the interests of the town's economic well-being – that of having a waste treatment plant – and the applicant's effective enjoyment of her right to respect for her home and her private and family life. Accordingly the Court held that there had been a violation of Article 8. Legal doctrine holds that this case may have important implications, especially for countries in Europe with less developed legislation and rules, in respect of all kinds of environmental problems and huge pollution problems caused by outdated and ill-equipped factories. It shows that serious environmental issues can lead to a question under Article 8. This case also shows that there is apparently less of a distinction between the traditional human rights, where it was accepted that they were actionable, and social rights, where it was generally held that they were not. This case apparently leads to a fusion between human rights and social rights.

Source: Based on A.W. Heringa, 'Private life and the protection of the environment', *European Court of Human Rights*, 9 December 1994; *Lopez-Ostra* v. *Spain*, *Maastricht Journal of European and Comparative Law*, 1995, 196–204.

Moreover, some nearby residents had been compensated for disturbances resulting from aircraft noise (see Chapter 12, Section 5).

7. CONCLUSIONS

In this chapter we have given an introductory presentation of the main environmental principles that will be studied in detail later in the book. The principles concern sustainable development, precautionary measures, prevention, polluter's responsibility, waste treatment at source, and the right to a clean environment.

These principles have different functions. General declarations serve as political instruments putting the environment on the political agenda. They also formulate a vision to guide the general public. Later, the principles become included in legal documents and will thus be interpreted and applied in specific legal situations. The application becomes complicated due to the different functions of policy declarations and legal rules. One function of law is to solve conflicts where the parties have different interests. The legal rules and their interpretations have various effects on citizens, effects that may be poorly understood. Vagueness is here a problem.

The principles are not only statements of political intent, or legal rules to be implemented and followed. The principles have important economic dimensions too. That is, costs and benefits for different parties have to be compared and weighed. Limited resources, together with unsatisfied needs, now and in the future, make economic analysis of the environmental principles of great importance. *Economics* is the science of rational use of scarce resources. A rational analysis of the use of scarce resources is of fundamental importance today and in the future. As such it can help to improve welfare as well as the environment.

Nonetheless, in the environmental debate economics is often seen to be in conflict with environmental goals. The reason may be that 'economic' here is synonymous with 'short-sighted interest in monetary values'. It may be true that many economists are narrowly interested in profit. However, economic science studies the rational use of resources, given preferences for goods and services over time. That is, the goal, taste or time preference (short- or long-sightedness) of the analyst, or of the studied economic agent (which may be individuals, firms or states), is beyond economic analysis. We will return to the basics of economics in Chapter 5.

In other words, environmental policy principles have economic effects that are best analysed by economic methods. Sustainable development requires a balanced development of economic activities. Similarly, the principle of prevention requires that action should be taken before damage has occurred. A loss can often be prevented at lower cost than that of the loss itself. Yet there are situations where prevention is not preferable because of its costs. Similarly, the polluter pays principle make economic sense, but Coase's theorem tells us that there are situations where a victim pays rule may be preferred. In order to reach the most efficient solution it is important to compare and balance the benefits and costs at the margin. A basic economic principle is that the party with comparative advantage in producing a good or service should perform it. That is true, for example, in the case of waste treatment. The best waste handler is obviously not always the producer at the 'source' – it may be any party in the chain of production and consumption, or some external party specialized in the field. Moreover, the transfer of production to the party with a comparative advantage requires trade, and environmental policy is ambivalent about trade. Free trade is, on the other hand, held to be fundamental to economic growth. Obviously, there may be a conflict between environmental policy, efficient waste treatment and trade.

To avoid an inefficient use of the scarce resources of our planet, which, indeed, is the same as protecting the environment, the policy documents and their legal implementation need a careful economic basis and analysis. This conviction motivates the rest of this book.

NOTES

1. This definition in Article 2 of the EC Treaty has been amended on various occasions.
2. Directive 90/270, *Official Journal*, 1990, l 156/14.
3. ECJ 20 May 1976, *De Peijper*, Case 104/75, ECR [1976], p. 613.
4. ECJ 9 July 1992, *Commission* v. *Belgium*, Walloon waste, Case C-2/90, ECR [1992], p. I-4431.

FURTHER READING

Frey, B.S. (1997), *Not just for the money. An economic theory of personal motivation*, Cheltenham, UK and Lyme, USA: Edward Elgar.

Ogus, A.I. (1995), 'Quality control for European regulation', *Maastricht Journal of European and Comparative Law*, **2**, 325–38.

Porges, A. (1995), 'The New Dispute Settlement: From the GATT to the WTO', *Leiden Journal of International Law*, 115–33.

van Calster, G. (1996), 'The WTO Committee on Trade and Environment: Exploring the Challenges of Free Trade', *European Environmental Law Review*, 44–51.

Vig, N.J. and Kraft, M.E. (eds) (1997), *Environmental Policy in the 1990s, Reform or Reaction?*, 3rd edn, Washington, DC: CQ Press.

3. Exploitation and protection of endangered species

> The tragedy of the commons is averted by private property …, but the air and waters … cannot readily be fenced, so the tragedy … must be prevented by different means.
>
> Hardin (1968)

1. INTRODUCTION

Serious environmental problems are related to overexploitation of the global commons such as the air and the high seas, and to the irreversible extinction of rare species. Economists – and scientists like Hardin in the quotation above – claim that the absence of enforced 'property rights' can explain these fundamental problems. In other words, property rights are fundamental for the protection of the environment. By 'property rights' is meant the property holder's exclusive control of a scarce resource. The legality and the public protection of the exclusion rights is not their immediate concern, but it is usually taken for granted. In this chapter we limit ourselves to this economic approach to exclusive 'property rights'. The legality of rights will be discussed in the next chapter. We begin in Section 2 with examples describing the importance of the exclusive control of resources in order to avoid depletion. In Section 3 we examine the general free-rider problem. How 'the tragedy of the commons', under certain economic and political conditions, in combination with some biological facts, can lead to extinction is analysed in Sections 4 and 5. Conclusions are presented in Section 6.

2. EXCLUSION OR EXTINCTION

To give an intuitive understanding of the importance of exclusive control of resources, it may be useful to present several examples. The first is taken from a seminal article by Harold Demsetz (1967), where he comments on an anthropological investigation of the economy of hunting practised by the North American Indians during an earlier age. At that time the presence of the white man changed the situation for the Indians. The demand for meat and skins increased at the same time that hunting methods became more refined. As a consequence, the buffalo that had roamed freely for centuries nearly became extinct. On the other hand, beaver colonies in Canada survived in spite of great demand and extensive hunting. No detailed explanation of why this occurred had been given in the existing anthropological studies so far. Demsetz's contribution was to furnish an explanation for this phenomenon: the beaver colonies survived because the Indian tribes in Canada divided the hunting territory among themselves. In this way, their interest was in not exploiting the resource. The 'right' to beaver could be upheld because the domain of the beavers was relatively stationary. The Indians also lived sta-

BOX 3.1 THE EFFECT OF PROPERTY RIGHTS ON THE DEVELOPMENT OF THE SAMI VILLAGE STRUCTURE

Another interesting study examines Scandinavian Sami village structures from the Middle Ages up to the eighteenth century (Lundgren, 1987). During the Middle Ages the Sami lived stationary lives, clustered in circular villages where they fished and hunted within the areas of closest proximity. The wild reindeer were of great significance, but the Sami did not follow the reindeer during their wanderings. In the seventeenth century, however, conditions changed in several ways. Among other things, North American fur-hunting increased, which lowered the price of skins. The Sami sold skins on international markets to Danes via the North Sea, to Swedes in the south, and to Russians in the east. Moreover, the climate worsened, and the Swedish bailiffs began to collect higher and higher taxes. The increasing scarcity brought with it an intensified quest for reindeer. In order to keep a check on regeneration, the reindeer were marked and followed during their wanderings. As a consequence, the villages of the Sami changed form gradually and took on the appearance of today, that is, a stretch of habitation from mountain slopes to forest tracts according to the pathways of the reindeer. The reason the reindeer flocks did not die out is, perhaps, in accordance with Demsetz's theory; that is, the Sami were successful in claiming the reindeer within their own territory where they could be controlled so that overexploitation did not occur. The Indians never had the possibility of following 'their' buffalo over prairie lands.

tionary lives and provided for themselves within well-defined boundaries, which is how they could ensure that 'outsiders' did not trap their animals. It was a different situation, however, with the buffalo. They roamed over large areas and were hunted by different tribes and settlers. Because none of these groups could exclude others from hunting and thereby gain the fruits of regeneration, it was in everyone's interest to hunt the buffalo within reach. Since the buffalo was such an easy prey, its fate was sealed.

Another explanation related to the buffaloes is that the white man intentionally killed them to worsen the position of the Indians. If that is true, it strengthens the argument that the lack of control creates an incentive to overexploitation.

3. FREE-RIDERS

From the examples above, it should be clear that open access to a common resource may cause extinction of species and the depletion of natural resources. Due to the seriousness of the problem, this state of affairs has been named the '*tragedy of the commons*'. Yet the examples above also indicate that it may be possible under some circumstances to escape the tragedy through exclusion and control.

Upon closer examination it is easy to see that the tragedy of the commons is due to a more general problem, usually named the '*free-rider problem*'. That is, if individuals in a group glean advantages at the cost of the collective, they become the so-called 'free-riders'. The problem with free-riders is sometimes also called a *1/N-problem*. Why this is so can be seen in the following example. A collective containing *N* individuals is in possession of a scarce resource that may generate benefits due to efforts by the members. If benefits are divided within the collective, that is, if everyone receives 1/*N* of the results, inefficient utilization will occur, the reason being that the efforts expended by the members are not proportional to the benefits being divided. If the individual member, for example, exerts an effort corresponding to 100 and this generates an income to the collective of 900, it is in the collective's interest that the individual's work be undertaken. However, if the collective is made up of 50 individuals, only 900/50 = 18 falls to the one doing the work. Therefore, it is not in the interest of the individual to make such an effort. Individual sacrifices result in an income to the collective, but only a fraction of this income falls to the individual. The same applies to everyone else in the collective. A poor outcome can be expected, provided there is not a steering mechanism to stimulate everyone to work for the collective's best interests.[1]

In the example above, the benefits were divided within the group, while the costs were carried by the individual. It may, however, also be the case that the free-rider is the individual, and the collective is harmed. Traffic congestion is one such example that we have chosen to illustrate numerically. Assume that identical individuals have a revenue of 100 per day in salaries, and no choice of transportation to work other than a car. Furthermore, assume that travel time is valuable to the individual because, for example, revenue from the job is diminished by the time spent driving to the work site. Driving takes 20 minutes – as long as there is no congestion. The time cost is assumed to be 1 per minute, which means that the time cost at no congestion is 20. Hence, the net private profit, *PP*, equals 100 – 20 = 80. However, if more than 200 cars are on the road at the same time, congestion occurs and travel time increases. Indeed, if there are 700 cars on the road, the travel time is 180 minutes, which causes a loss of 80 for each of the individual drivers.

The three left columns of Table 3.1 show how private profit is assumed to vary. The number of cars, *N*, is in Column 1 and the average time cost, *ATC*, in column 2. In column 3 we see the net private profit of driving, *PP*. For simplicity, we assume that all individuals in this society are car drivers, and that no disturbances other than congestion exist. The total profit for the collective, *TPC*, is, then, equal to the sum of the private profits of all the individuals. In the fourth column we present how *TPC* varies with the number of cars on the road. *TPC* is derived simply by multiplying the number of cars (column 1) by the private profit of each driver (column 3). The marginal profit to the collective, that is, the added profit of the last one hundred cars, is presented in the fifth column. This marginal profit to the collective, MPC_{100}, is calculated as the difference between the new and the old *TPC* when one hundred cars are added.[2] Finally, in order to be able to compare the net private profit of a single driver with the marginal profit to

Table 3.1 Costs of congestion

Number of cars (1) N	Average time cost (2) ATC	Net private profit (3) PP $100 - ATC$	Total profit for the collective (4) TPC $N \times PP$	Marginal profit of the collective of 100 new cars (5) MPC_{100} $TPC_N - TPC_{N-100}$	Marginal profit to the collective of one more car (6) MPC_1 $MPC_{100}/100$
100	20	80	8 000	8 000	80
200	20	80	16 000	8 000	80
300	25	75	22 500	6 500	65
400	35	65	26 000	3 500	35
500	60	40	20 000	–6 000	–60
600	90	10	6 000	–14 000	–140
700	180	–80	–56 000	–62 000	–620

the collective, we divide MPC_{100} by 100. This will give MPC_1, which is the marginal profit to the collective by one more driver.[3] MPC_1 is presented in column 6.

As long as there is no congestion (up to 200 cars), the private profit, *PP*, and the MPC_1 coincide (80). Hence there is no conflict between the individual and the collective interest. However, at 300 or more cars, the private profit of driving is greater than MPC_1. The reason for this is the congestion that an additional car causes to everyone else on the road in the form of reduced speed for all cars. When 500 cars are on the road, each individual still has a private profit from driving of 40. The last 100 car drivers have a joint private profit of 4 000 that must be added to the *TPC*. However, the value lost due to the increased time everyone else must spend on the road must also be factored into the *TPC*. The time loss is 25 minutes for each of the 400 original drivers, equalling a total cost of 10 000. It follows from this that the net loss to society is 6 000. It is, thus, a social cost to allow the last 100 individuals to drive.

Assuming that the goal is maximization of social profit, *TPC*, Table 3.1 shows that it is in the interest of the collective to limit the number of cars to 400.[4] This is where the *TPC* is at its maximum (26 000). Nevertheless, the end result is 600 cars as this is the level reached when people start driving as long as the private profit, *PP*, is positive. When there are 600 cars on the road, Table 3.1 shows that the private gain is 10 per driver, giving a *TPC* of 6 000. Thus the loss to society of having 600 instead of 400 cars is 20 000.

Now, let us analyse a curve using increments of one, as in Figure 3.1, instead of Table 3.1. The number of cars in hundreds is on the horizontal axis, while the vertical axis indicates total profit to society, *TPC*, in thousands. Graphically, *TPC* is the distance between the curve and the horizontal axis.

As above, the optimum for society is 400 cars. Nevertheless, individuals will drive to work as long as they expect a private gain, however small. This

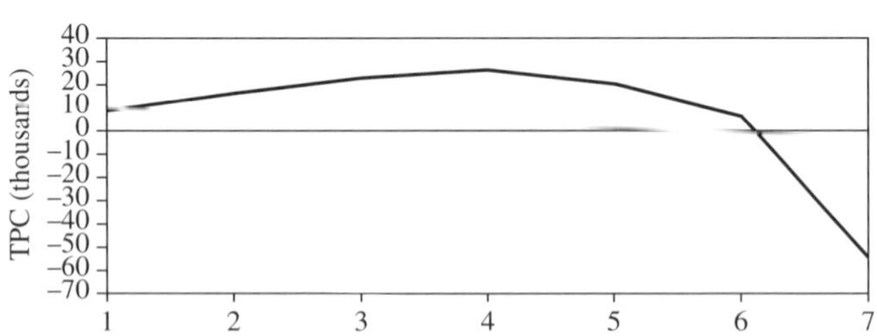

Figure 3.1 Cars and social profit, TPC

BOX 3.2 COSTS OF CONGESTION

According to *The Economist*, 6 December 1997, the European Commission calculated the external cost of road transport, including accidents, infrastructure, environmental pollution, and congestion at US$308 billion a year, that is, the equivalent of 4 per cent of the GDP of the EU. Half of this cost is due to congested roads.

Obviously, some control of traffic congestion is required. One option is to build more or broader roads, another is to tax cars, to introduce tolls at peak hours or subsidize public transport. Quotas for traffic are also possible. Nonetheless, there are many big cities that remain extremely congested and polluted, harming, first of all, their own populations.

will continue until the number of journeys is somewhat larger then 600, where there is no private gain at all. Since all drivers are in the same situation, no one in the collective gains from driving. This is the worst outcome of the free-rider problem.

4. OVERFISHING

Exploitation of fishing grounds has frequently been used as an example of the tragedy of the commons. Here, we will explain the ‘overfishing problem’ and how it may lead to the extinction, or not, of a species of fish.

A renewable resource such as fish can be harvested in a steady flow for ever. Yet if too much is caught at one time, the stock may become depleted and there may be no more fish to catch. The size of the stock determines the growth of the stock, which is the flow that may be caught without diminishing the stock. The growth depends mainly on two biological factors: (i) the food supply, and (ii) the density of fish. The food supply is negatively correlated, and the density is positively correlated, with growth. If the stock is small, the food supply will be plentiful; however, the low density makes it more difficult for the fish to find a mate. If, on the other hand, the stock is large, there is less food, but it is easier to find a mate.

Given these biological facts of a specific species we can, as in Figure 3.2, draw an economic graph showing the sustainable total collective revenue, *TR*, of fishing, equivalent to the *TPC* curve in Figure 3.1. The *TR* curve is based on biological facts described above and two further assumptions:

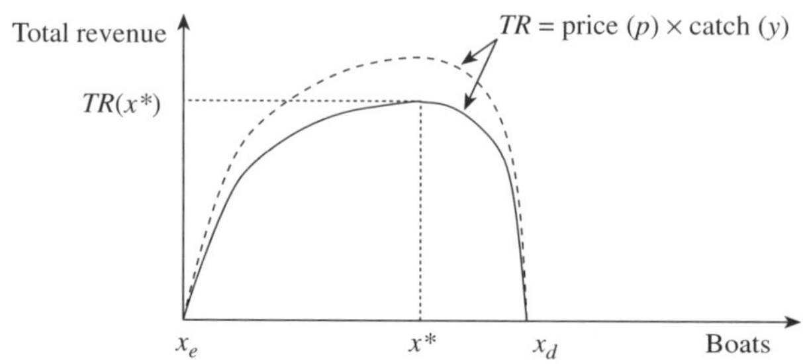

Figure 3.2 The total revenue from fishing

(i) the price of fish (p) is assumed to be constant, thus independent of the catch (y). *TR* equals the price of the fish times the catch of fish. An increase in price will shift the *TR* curve upwards as shown by the dotted line in Figure 3.2;

(ii) the catch (y) is assumed to be equal to the growth at various levels of fishing. Hence the same stock and catch can remain over time.

The horizontal axis in Figure 3.2 represents the number of boats, x. $x_e = 0$ at the origin corresponds to the natural equilibrium with no fishing and no growth of the stock. The maximum revenue of fishing is reached at x^* number of boats. However, the individual fishing boat will continue to fish as long as there is a private gain, that is, at x_d. At x_d the catch is zero because no stock is available, that is, depletion prevails.

In order to obtain a more realistic picture, we now include fishing costs (Figure 3.3). On the vertical axis we have the total cost and total revenue. The cost of a boat with equipment is assumed to be constant and equal to c. Hence the total cost of fishing, *TC*, equals $c \times x$, which is illustrated by the straight line in Figure 3.3. The total revenue, *TR*, is assumed to vary with the number

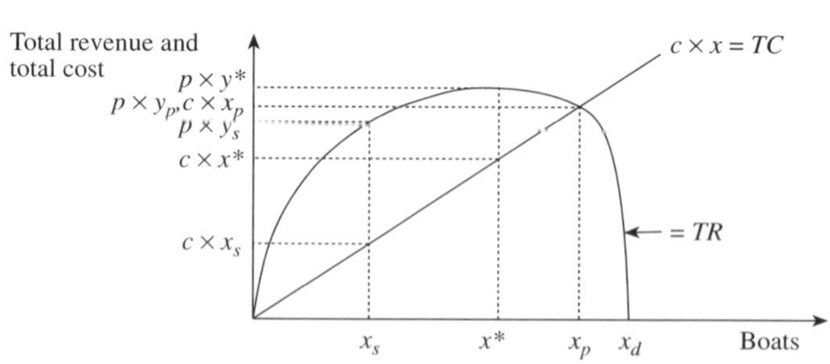

Figure 3.3 The overfishing problem

of boats, as in Figure 3.2. Inserting costs in the figure changes the results of Figure 3.2. First of all, we find that the optimal number of boats seen from a collective, or social, point of view is where the total profit, *TR* – *TC,* reaches its maximum. Thus the new optimum catch is x_s, which is less than the optimum without fishing costs, x^*. Second, in this new situation the best a single boat can do is to go out fishing as long as the average expected yield, which is *TR*/*x,* is larger than the cost, *c*. Assuming that all individuals maximize their private gain, the new amount caught is where $TR/x = c$, that is, where $TR = x \times c = TC$, that is, at x_p. The collective interest of x_s boats diverges from the private interest of x_p boats. *Overfishing* thus takes place.

According to the model, some stock will remain and the flow will continue as long as fishing is costly. The point x_p may, however, be close to the point of depletion, x_d. The closer x_p is to x_d, the greater the risk that a small negative variation in the stock of fish will cause depletion. The risk of depletion depends, therefore, on how far to the right the *TR* and *TC* curves intersect.

In the past, before the appearance of new technical developments, the costs were higher, say c_{1800}. Thus the total cost curve $TC_{1800} = c_{1800}$ in Figure 3.4 is steeper. The collective and private profit maximum did not coincide, just as in Figure 3.3, but there was no risk of depletion since the private fishing fleet, x_{1800}, was distant enough from the depletion amount, x_d. A problem of our time is that technical improvements have reduced costs and the fleet has grown.

A shift upwards in the *TR* curve, as indicated in Figure 3.2, also shifts the intersection of *TR* = *TC* to the right, and thus the species comes closer to depletion. Increased prices as well as better techniques increasing the catch both cause such shifts upwards. It may be critical if demand, and thus prices, increase as the species becomes rare, and the catching techniques improve at the same time. That has been the case for many mammals hunted for sport or for their fur, or for example lobster and herring, which are 'musts' on the dining table in some cultures.

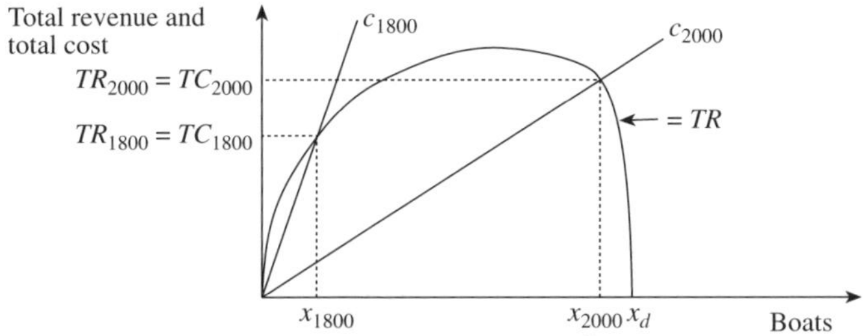

Figure 3.4 Cost and catch

The model above is static in that it illustrates catches that many continue for ever. In reality, there are variations in the stock of fish caused by factors such as the weather, pollution and political subsidy of fishing. Finally, it should be stressed that any depletion is irreversible, which, of course, is the core of the problem.

5. POLITICS AND POLLUTION

Above we demonstrated the importance of fencing off scarce resources. Biological and economic conditions for the survival of endangered species explain why species may be endangered. That may be the case if they: (i) migrate globally, such as birds and whales; (ii) require large numbers for mating and reproduction; and (iii) are caught at low cost. The most serious environmental problems are related to the global commons such as the air, the ozone layer, and the high seas, that cannot be fenced and controlled.

In Box 3.3 we present an example of how expansion of fishing boundaries may save fish from depletion. In reality, however, the picture is more complicated and problematic. Despite the introduction of fishing boundaries (property rights) for countries, the fishing industry has continued to expand at twice the rate of the global catch. The fact is that many countries subsidize fishing instead of limiting it. We must raise the question, therefore, why the fishing industry is subsidized, although to do so may result in an irreversible catastrophe.

One answer is political. That is, politicians depend on voters and pressure groups, and the fishing industry is politically important in many countries. The sector may be a large part of the industry of a nation. It is important here to note that the industry is declining. Fishermen, communities and voters require fishing rights and financial support to survive. Politicians who are concerned about re-election must consider political interests and thus tend to act in a short-sighted way. In other words, the moral obligation to consider the sustainable future losses have little priority in daily politics.

It should also be noted that many species like birds and insects and wild animals are threatened, not because they are overexploited *per se*, but because of the exploitation of their living grounds, such as rainforests and wetlands. In addition, pollution and toxic substances emitted by third parties threaten many species and entire ecosystems. Here the extinction of rare species may be due to the absence of an economic value to the species. That is, cultivation of land or pollution harms nature and thus future generations without causing concern at the time because of lack of economic interest. Above we studied free-riding and overexploitation by individuals or industries that harvest an economically valuable good in rivalry.

BOX 3.3 EXPANSION OF FISHING BOUNDARIES TO SAVE FISH FROM DEPLETION

A modern example of how the right to a scarce resource may be introduced can be seen in the expansion of fishing boundaries around Iceland during the 1970s. At that time the cod stock in the North Atlantic had fallen because of rampant fishing and effective catching methods. There was a risk that the cod would die out in the same way that the Icelandic herring had become sparse earlier. Instead of waiting for international conventions to regulate the catch, Iceland expanded its fishing territory, in spite of protests from other fishing nations. In this case overfishing of cod could be averted because the realm of the cod was relatively stationary within the area under Iceland's control. Rögnvaldur Hannesson (1974) sees this example of a one-sided declaration of rights as a condition for saving the fishery around Iceland. He maintains that in the long run this action was of benefit, not only for Icelanders but also for other nations that buy fish, or the right to fish, within Icelandic territory. In 1976 there was an agreement extending the economic aspects of national jurisdiction from 12 to 200 nautical miles offshore, thus creating the so-called 'exclusive economic zones'. With this agreement most commercially attractive fish were brought under the control of some country. Ninety per cent of all fish are today caught within an exclusive economic zone, and only 10 per cent in international waters. Before this international agreement, most fish stocks were open to everyone.

Nevertheless, many countries support *de facto* depletion by subsidizing their fishing fleet. The maximum sustainable yield of fish could possibly be achieved with as little as a fifth of the current fleet. Overfishing on a worldwide scale costs $15–30 billion yearly, according to the UN's Food and Agriculture Organization.

Source: Based on *The Economist*, 19 March 1994.

6. CONCLUSIONS

Open access to a common resource may cause extinction of species and depletion of natural resources, a phenomenon often called the 'tragedy of the commons'. Without exclusion individuals or a group may gain advantages to the harm of others if there is no control and compensation. Examples of hunting, traffic congestion and overfishing were given above. The most serious open-access problems are related to the high seas and the atmosphere, both of which cannot be efficiently fenced in, and, thus remain huge commons.

In the environmental economics literature it is often said that exclusive property rights to, for example, land, hunting or fishing, can avert the tragedy. This does not mean that exclusivity must necessarily be protected by property law. Indeed, a resource may initially be controlled through occupation, which may be against prevailing laws. Legally protected property rights will be discussed in the next chapter.

The depletion of an endangered species depends on several factors, for example: (i) low catching costs (new techniques and large-scale production methods); (ii) increased price with increased scarcity; (iii) biological characteristics of the species such as mating behaviour and food supply; and (iv) political factors such as subsidies to existing production methods. When several of these coincide, extinction may become a fact. On the other hand, some species are not threatened because they cannot easily be caught, and/or they can find food and a mate. Similarly, forests and vegetables may be harvested without depletion because reproduction is guaranteed as long as seeds are preserved.

Free-riding will normally not be the ultimate cause of depletion because of catching costs. However, any additional shock to the system caused by either a natural variation in the weather or by environmental pollution can deplete the remaining stock. Many species are threatened by exploitation or pollution of their ecosystems. A problem here is that the species is of little economic value.

It may be argued that owners should be blamed for not considering long-term effects in nature. Note, however, that politicians may be short-sighted as well as capitalistic owners. Destruction of nature may be due to subsidies to polluting and overexploiting producers. Politicians can also contribute to environmental harm by not protecting owners. If, for instance, the owner of a forest believes that there may be a confiscation by the government, or a revolution prohibiting cultivation, the best thing the long-term profit-maximizing investor can do is to cut down the forest at once and invest in some safer asset. These matters will be further discussed in Chapter 7, Sections 6 and 7.

Finally, it should be noted that there are situations where exclusive control results in depletion of nature. Exploitation of a resource like a rainforest or wetland requires initial investment. In the absence of defined property rights the resource will remain idle because of the problem of free-riders eliminating the benefit of investments. After exclusive right to the property is settled and protected, it may be profitable to invest, and later to harvest. However, it may be most profitable to invest in a monoculture or industry that harms certain species and thus reduces biodiversity.

NOTES

1. Olson (1971).
2. In this example, we analyse the problem in increments of 100 and not in increments of 1. Hence we assume a discrete change at each 100 instead of a continuous change.
3. Technically speaking, this is not completely true. MPC_1 really should be defined as the derivative of the *TPC* curve.
4. To find out the exact number of cars that would be optimal, we must have more detailed information on the cost structure.

FURTHER READING

Buchanan, J.M., and Tullock, G. (1962), *The Calculus of Consent*, Ann Arbor, MI: University of Michigan Press.

Demsetz, H. (1967), 'Toward a Theory of Property Rights', *American Economic Review*, **57** (2), 347–59.

Gordon, H.S. (1954), 'The Economic Theory of a Common-property Resource: the Fishery', *Journal of Political Economy*, **62**, 124–42.

Hardin, G. (1968), 'The Tragedy of the Commons', *Science*, 1243–8.

4. Property rights

> Human beings are ... entitled to a
> productive life in harmony with nature.
> Rio Declaration 1972, §1

1. INTRODUCTION

In the previous chapter we studied the free-rider problem and the potential overexploitation if resources cannot be exclusively controlled. This exclusivity is in the economic literature called 'property rights', on the assumption that it is enforced not only by private means but also by the public justice system. In this chapter Section 2 deals with private and public (legal) enforcement of rights. Common and collective ownership versus private ownership is studied in Sections 3–7. In Section 8 we note that property rights include different types of rights. Further applications to environmental problems are found in Sections 9 and 10. There we discuss the importance of property rights for the environment, as well as important limitations on property rights as an instrument for the protection of the environment. Section 11 concludes.

2. LEGAL RIGHTS

Examples in Chapter 3 showed how groups of people may appropriate desirable resources. That is, man creates his own exclusive 'rights' to beaver, reindeer and fishing grounds. Later on, the exclusiveness may be incorporated into the legal system and, thus, assigned as a legal right. For instance, the formation of the Sami villages and reindeer grazing rights are today included in Scandinavian law, and the Icelandic extension of the fishing limit has come to be accepted in international conventions and, indeed, has become common practice all over the world.

Legal rights and duties can be said to exist if they are found in existing laws, and if they are sanctioned by the public judicial system. The fact that rights have a basis in law has at least two important consequences: first, to end the conflict and struggle among the parties; and second, to prevent the depletion scenarios described in Chapter 3. The public sanction is central for two reasons. The first is that the right is identified by the sanction, that is, we observe the right through the sanction (for example injunctions, damages, or punishments) that comes into effect when the right is violated. It may, for instance, be impossible to describe all the rights and duties of the owner of a piece of land. However, if someone trespasses or damages the land, or if the owner harms neighbours or does not pay property taxes, there are legal sanctions that can be found in legal rules. Another aspect of the importance of sanctions is, of course, that the rights may lack force if they are not connected to consequences. In other words, if violations of rights are undetected or neglected, the rights may be of no practical significance.

The fact that a legal right is included in existing law and comes under the auspices of the public judicial system does not mean that owners do not protect their rights themselves. Most protection is undertaken by the holders of the rights. It is, for instance, up to an owner to guard buildings, fence in pasture-land, and so on. It is mainly the use of force and the levying of sanctions, and thus the definition and ultimate protection of rights, that is monopolized by the public judicial system.

There are reasons for the protection of rights to be apportioned in this fashion. The holder of a right normally has an incentive to protect it. Obviously, it would be inefficient if the public had the responsibility of fencing in and controlling private property. Yet there may be an under-investment when it comes to punishment. If a private good is stolen, the owner has an interest in getting it back, but not in deterring theft in general. This may explain why criminal punishment is usually a public matter. Privately undertaken 'justice' may also be arbitrary and cruel, furnishing yet another rationale for the public enforcement of laws. The reasons for criminal liability are further developed in Chapter 16.

Because the protection of property rights is costly, protection will normally be partial and incomplete. Hence there is no complete protection of rights by the state, or by the individual. The owner of a right has an economic incentive to protect the right as long as the benefit exceeds the cost of protection. Rights of low value will, thus, be less protected than valuable rights, and easily protected rights will be more protected than others that are more difficult to protect. Terry Anderson and Peter Hill (1975) give good examples from the American West. Barbed wire came into frequent use in the mid-nineteenth century. Yet the fencing varied according to the accessibility of grazing land. Therefore fencing started in the East and came into later use in the West as land became scarce.

The word 'right' in the economic literature is often used in a broad sense, not only in the legal sense of a subjective publicly enforced right. Thus from an economic point of view we refer to a right, even if the right is not included in the existing law. If, for example, a mother promises to take her children to the cinema but does not keep her promise, they will maintain that they have a right and the mother a duty. The promise from her side constitutes the right. The significance of the right, in turn, is determined if the breaking of the promise is attached to consequences or not. If the children can, by nagging or with the support of the father, compel the mother to take them to the cinema, the promise, and therewith the right, is of practical significance and value. Promises and rights thus exist among individuals without attaining legal status. Social controls and punitive consequences can be just as compelling as those of legal rights. For example, employees expect certain rights such as wages or promotion, corresponding to their efforts and achieved results. At the same time, the employer places certain expectations upon his employees. The type of rights and duties is partly a question of law, and partly a question of agreements made at the workplace and with respect to customs reigning in industry. Legal rights suppose that they can be enforced through the legal system. However, rights and duties are often informal, unspecified and understood. The punitive actions, likewise, can be of shifting character.

Nevertheless, from a legal point of view it is important to distinguish between those rights that are legally binding and enforceable and those that are not. In economic analysis, on the other hand, a difference is seldom made between rights in a legal sense and 'rights' and 'duties' maintained through social control, peripheral to the formal legal system. The reason for this reluctance on the part of economists to take legal qualifications into account is that they are interested in the economic consequences of rights, and this interest is independent of how the rule or right is upheld. The terms 'right' and 'contract' are used, even when a written or verbal agreement does not exist in the legal sense. *Implicit contracts* and *implicit rights* are a composite designation for informal, more or less clear expectations and conventions that influence behaviour in the economy in much the same way as legal rights.

3. COMMON OWNERSHIP

Open access to commons such as the high seas, the atmosphere, outer space and grasslands in ancient times may prevail without problems as long as the common resource is unlimited. However, scarcity causes rivalry, free-riders, and, perhaps, a tragedy of the commons as illustrated in Chapter 3. How may such a disaster be avoided?

It should be noted, first of all, that there is no simple solution to the tragedy. There are many historical examples of deserts and the extinction of valuable resources. Nonetheless, there are examples of the opposite outcome as well. One option is that strong parties appropriate a certain portion of the resource and control its use as described in Chapter 3. Later the right

BOX 4.1 THE ANCIENT VILLAGE

Initially, the surrounding forest is a large tract of common land. The access to lumber for construction and fuel is in sufficient quantity for all. The forest, in other words, is a free good with open access. It is collectively 'owned', but the question of ownership is uninteresting because there is no scarcity. However, because of changing conditions, for example, deterioration in the weather or an increase in population, the demand for wood increases. Especially near the village, the felling of trees takes place at such a pace that regrowth is hindered. The villagers need to travel an ever greater distance in order to find a wood supply. Scarcity brings with it conflicts between the villagers. How can disputes among the villagers, the plundering of the forest, and last of all the depletion of the population be avoided? We assume that there is a central power in the village strong enough to organize the utilization of the land. The deciding organ chooses to solve the problem centrally by deciding how much forest may be felled, how clearance and thinning out should be undertaken, who shall do the work, and how the results of the efforts are to be distributed. All of this may be possible to achieve, but the problem becomes more involved in that efficient utilization of the forest requires knowledge about the best available forestry and about the productivity and appropriateness of the manpower. Decisions must be made on how the work shall be undertaken and who shall work with forestry, maintenance, child care, and so on.

may be protected by the legal system. Another possibility is central regulation based on some form of *common ownership* of the scarce resource. To illustrate the pro and cons for common versus private ownership, see Box 4.1.

Common ownership raises considerable problems of control, especially in the case where individual achievements and results are not positively related to one another. Free-rider problems arise if apportionment to members of the collective does not directly correspond to disadvantages. If the results are divided, for example, among everyone regardless of performance, there is an individual interest to flout, or circumvent, directives. Hence behaviour must be controlled and force must be used through administrative systems that have come to be called '*command-and-control*' systems.

Because the information about production processes, resources and individuals is limited, central planning requires an administrative apparatus to collect information and coordinate activities. The political process that precedes decision-making about the use of resources and the apportionment of results is also costly. The same applies to the control apparatus. It is characteristic of administrative steering systems that they tend to swell and become bureaucratic.

A general problem is that the costs of information and communication increase significantly as the number of interdependent parties increases. In an organization with N members, there are

$$\frac{N(N-1)}{2}$$

links of communication between each pair. Thus an increase in the number of members brings with it a more than proportional (quadratic) increase in the number of two-way channels for communication, information and decision-making. For instance, if $N = 6$, there are $6 \times 5/2=15$ links, as in Figure 4.1(a).

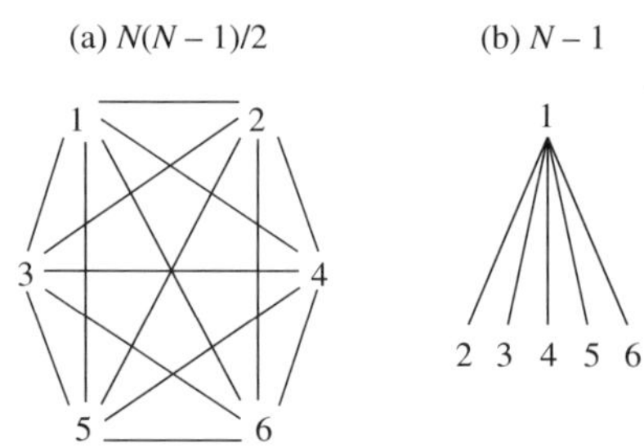

Figure 4.1 Links in a group of six

If there are 100 members, the number of links is $100 \times 99/2 = 4950$. Hence the internal coordination becomes very complicated.

The coordinator may choose between a hierarchical organization with central planning, management and steering of activities. In such a case, the communication and information channels are limited to N–1, that is, from the management to each and every one of the members; see Figure 4.1(b). With a leader who is specialized in overseeing and evaluating the efforts of the members, the conditions for creating free-riders are reduced. However, the control problem remains if many are to be coordinated, that is, if N is a large number. Moreover, information and control may be diluted as there is no direct link between the members 2–6.

4. PRIVATE OWNERSHIP

When scarcity arises, the coordination may not be solved through central planning. A reason may be that the central powers are not well informed and not strong enough to undertake command-and-control measures. Indeed, there may exist no central powers. Instead, private control may evolve more or less spontaneously through the appropriation and control of the resources by certain parties, after which the subdivision eventually comes to be accepted by neighbours and public authorities.

Another possible development is that the members of the society agree by a *social contract* to introduce and protect private property rights. Assume that the central steering organ in the ancient village above introduces private ownership. We can visualize a system such as the Swedish 'sun enclosure' from the Middle Ages, in which farms in the village were given rights to pieces of land of different types and quality. In order for the farm to be able to provide for its members, it was important that apportioned land could be utilized for the various needs of the household in question.

Assume, therefore, that the property is divided into *N* lots, as in Figure 4.2, where each farmer has the exclusive right to use the property. The costs and benefits are borne by the same party, which solves the free-rider problem. In other words, efforts and results are correlated to one another, which is why the owner is motivated towards long-term protection of the property. Indeed, the owner's right to enjoy the benefits of investments creates incentives for the effective utilization of resources.

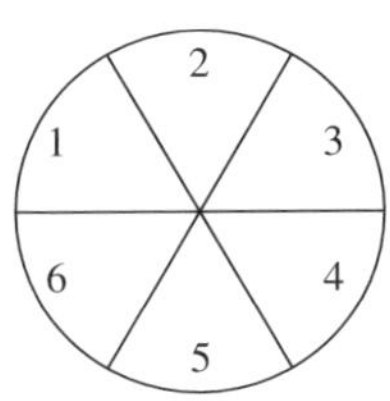

Figure 4.2 Sharing

Ownership decentralizes decision-making down to the individual farm level. The landowner determines how earth plots and forest tracts shall be used and how the work and results shall be divided and controlled. The functions that were the responsibility of the central planner are now transferred to the farmer. The same type of administrative problems which were relevant to society as a whole are now transferred to the individual household – however, on a much reduced scale because of the smaller number of members.

Note that the right to ownership limits the role of the central powers considerably compared to the case of command and control. The introduction of the right to ownership means, in effect, decentralization. Because decision-making and economic responsibility lie with the same party, an incentive is created for the effective use of resources. The main function of the state powers, accordingly, is to uphold the right of ownership. Disputes and conflicts among the citizens are controlled through legal measures with respect to property crimes and by damages when infringements occur. The law should, hence, protect private property.

5. TRANSFERABILITY

A remaining problem in the village example may be that the slices of land could be too small and inappropriate for farming. Another problem may be that the work is still heavily inter-related, for example, when sowing and harvesting. In other words, there is an economies of scale advantage in at least coordinating certain activities. If the right exists for property owners to exchange (alternatively rent or lease) lots among themselves, the involved parties may set up more purposeful units. Moreover, freedom of contract means that a comprehensive division of work is made possible. For example, the one who would like to increase his forest tract can buy or rent land, buy felling rights, and so on, and the one who would like to specialize in handicrafts can exchange his products or services for other goods and services. Thus a division of labour and specialization may lead to an increased welfare for the society as a whole.

All systems require rules for the transfer of rights, for instance, by gift, contract, or inheritance. The transfers can be more or less centrally regulated and organized. A highly decentralized form prevails when the individual members of society have the sovereign freedom to contract with each other. If it is permissible to contract and associate freely, then the basis for a market economy is given.

The most important function of markets is that prices coordinate the activities of all the agents in the economy in a highly standardized way. The activities of many actors are coordinated via demand, supply and prices (see Chapter 5).

6. COLLECTIVE OR PRIVATE OWNERSHIP?

As we have noted, private ownership has certain advantages over collective ownership. One may ask, then, why all activities are not organized privately.

We are not going to explore into the controversial political question of collectivism versus free-market liberalism. We can, however, note that collective ownership has advantages as well, which explains why collective ownership has, indeed, been most common in ancient times as well as in capitalistic societies for specific goals and activities.

Above, we described the medieval 'sun-enclosure' as a creation of private property rights. This illustration may lead to the erroneous conclusion that Swedish villages were mainly founded on tradable private ownership. On the contrary, collective ownership systems with very limited specialization and trade survived in Western Europe until the enclosures of the nineteenth century. Many villages in the Third World, as well as, for example, in the Sami villages in Scandinavia, are collective property. One reason is presumably the small number of members in society, and thus the limited coordination problem. Small societies are a prerequisite for effective social control. Moreover, the societies and production methods have been stable for centuries. Hence information on production methods and the expected outcome is publicly

BOX 4.2 MOOSE-HUNTING IN SWEDEN

Moose-hunting is a very popular activity among Swedish hunters. The hunting rights normally belong to private landowners. A problem is that many properties are small and that the moose moves over large areas. Fencing is not appropriate. Since exclusion is not possible everyone with a hunting right could free-ride on the others by shooting a moose on his property as soon as there is a chance – if he does not, the moose will disappear and the chance will presumably not recur. All hunters would reason the same and over-hunting would thus result.

To solve this free-rider problem the hunting is organized collectively. The countryside is divided in moose-hunting areas, including a number of properties. The size of sustainable hunting is decided collectively. Each hunting-right owner receives a number of moose to be hunted on his property. The hunt also includes several properties with a team of hunters. It is up to the team to bargain with each other how to share the yield.

This shows how private owners may give up parts of their private property rights for the benefit of a collective organization. In fact, the collective organization is, as well as private property rights, motivated by the problem of free-riders. A collective solution may be preferable, if it is a prerequisite for exclusion.

known. The modernization of production methods, including the restructuring of society in favour of private property rights, began with the Industrial Revolution. It was then that a market opened up for the products of farmers, which required specialization and trade.[1]

In the typical early capitalistic, privately owned enterprise, it is the entrepreneur who owns the company. He contributes with his work and capital and is the residual claimant who may gain profits or make losses. Moreover, he is the decision-maker supervising and apportioning work. This may be an efficient organization, but only on a small scale.[2] Large enterprises have apparent advantages due to economies of scale and scope, but obviously require more capital and management capacity than that of the individual entrepreneur. Additional capital may be supplied by the stock market, but stock owners require power to control management. Note that the element of sharing turns the corporate company into a collective form of ownership. Indeed, the modern large corporation has many coordination problems in common with other large administrative systems. A difference, however, between public administrations and '*widely held corporations*' is that the shares, and thus the ownership, are traded on financial markets. Mismanaged companies can be bought up, a manoeuvre that brings with it the control and corporate governance lacking in many public bodies and collective organizations. The efficiency of financial markets will be studied further in Chapter 7, Section 4.

In fact, private and collective ownership forms coexist in capitalistic economies. Collective organizations develop and survive in such economies because of their advantages. Examples are mutual insurance firms, consumer and producer cooperatives, joint ventures and partnerships. Much effort is spent on utilizing the advantages of large organizations, and at the same time maintaining efficiency through decentralized decision-making units, and more or less self-controlling groups. An important question in most organizations is how to share responsibility and results to mitigate the internal free-rider problem.

There are also political reasons for limitations on private ownership in favour of centralized collective command-and-control systems. We will return to some of these when discussing environmental regulations. Here, we shall only note that an important reason for limited private ownership is redistributive. Once the private property rights structure is fixed, room is given to the growth of wealth according to one's own ability. In the long term, this may cause a wide spread of welfare, which may be viewed as politically unacceptable. The politicians may, then, make adjustments through measures such as income and property taxes.

7. PUBLIC AND PRIVATE GOODS

Goods and services, broadly defined, can be distinguished from one another based on their degree of excludability. Non-excludability, that is, a very high cost of exclusion, is in some cases the natural characteristic of a good. An example is clean air in the atmosphere. Another is information. Once a vaccine, for example for smallpox, is known, it can be produced by all around the world. There is no possibility (if so desired) to exclude anyone – the information is accessible to everyone. Similarly, a city wall is public in the sense that all inside the wall are protected from outside enemies.

A second distinction is made between goods that are rival and non-rival in production or consumption. A product is rival in consumption if the consumption by one consumer leaves less for other consumers. Some examples of rival goods are bread, butter, cinema seats and library books. Other products are non-rival in production or consumption, for example fresh air for breathing outdoors, national defence, lighthouses, television and radio broadcasting and the like. The typical public good is non-rival; for example, one more citizen inside the wall does not reduce the protection of the others.

In some systems exclusion of non-rival goods is a result of imposed restrictions. For instance, it is possible to charge a fee to individuals crossing a bridge or visiting nature reserves although the activity does not harm others. In many cases exclusion is possible but too costly to be practised. Examples are roads and highways that may be tolled, but are usually not. By defining goods as excludable/non-excludable or rival/non-rival, we can divide goods into four categories. Pure *private goods* that are excludable and rival are found in row 1 of Table 4.1. These goods are freely produced and traded in private markets. Excludable, non-rival goods can be enjoyed by everyone without any cost (row 2 of Table 4.1). Examples are water in a wetland or sand in a desert. The good is available at zero cost. The non-excludable, non-rival goods are called *public goods* (row 4 of Table 4.1). Existing public goods are usually not offered on private markets because no one will pay since they cannot be excluded. On the other hand, once such a good, for example a city wall, is produced, it is beneficial to all in that society. Because

Table 4.1 Taxonomy of goods using excludability and rivalry

Excludable	Rival	Pure private goods (1)
	Non-rival	Free goods (2)
Non-excludable	Rival	Tragedy of the commons (3)
	Non-rival	Pure public goods (4)

nobody has to pay for the use of the public good there is an investment and financing problem that may be solved by a political intervention, including taxes.

In the case of non-excludability and rivalry (row 3 of Table 4.1), the tragedy of the commons may arise. By defining property rights, exclusion may be established, given that the right can be enforced at a relatively low cost. The good is hereby (if possible) transferred to the excludable private good category.

8. BUNDLES OF RIGHTS

In the political debate and in the environmental discussion, private property is often presented as a more or less unlimited, publicly enforced freedom. We have, however, already concluded that property rights are not absolute and enforcement is imperfect. An owner's rights of property are, in fact, bundles of complex sets of rights, duties and freedoms. One simplistic way of classifying rights and duties with respect to private property is as follows:

- right to disposal and use
- residual right
- right to compensation
- freedom of contract.

The *right to disposal and use* of the property includes all kinds of activities that are not outlawed. Restrictions and limitations of the rights are, however, common. Zoning laws limit the use of land to certain activities such as farming or industry, and a business may be restricted by, for example, emission rights (see Chapters 11 and 12). Part of the right to use may also be collective. For instance, a landowner may have to permit trespassing by the public. As in Sweden, private property may be freely accessible for walking and picking flowers and mushrooms. Similarly, military activities on private land may also be allowed. Moreover, some resources on a property may be, *de facto*, of common accessibility. An example is groundwater, which cannot be contained by fences round the property.

The *residual right* is the right of profit and the duty to cover losses. The owner is, thereby, a risk-taker. The risk, and the chance of profit, gives the owner an incentive to maximize the utility or profit of the property. The freedom to use property may be transferred by rent or lease contracts. The residual right in such contracts is kept by the owner. A transfer of ownership requires that the right to the residual value of the property be transferred. Hence the residual right is the essence of ownership.

An owner may influence certain risks, but not others, and individuals are more or less disinclined to take risks. These facts are of great significance in the economic analysis of rights and duties. Here is an example: a person can choose between owning or renting an apartment. As a tenant, the person pays in advance and does not need to incur any debts. The tenant does not assume any risk as far as the value of the apartment is concerned the day the contract is cancelled. On the other hand, the owner has a right to profits (or losses) the day the apartment is sold. Consequently, the choice between ownership and rent influences the quality and extent of maintenance of the apartment.

The *right to compensation* is closely related to use and residual rights. In order for the right of ownership to remain in force, the owner must be able to assert his rights upon infringement, for example, when the property is damaged. Hence the right of the owner is linked to the duty of others not to infringe upon his right. With ownership comes not only the possibility of excluding others and enjoying the profit but also the obligation of bearing the costs that are attached to the property, including compensation to other owners who have been harmed. In sum, the owner has the right to enjoy profits but also bears the economic responsibility for the property and for the decisions to be made.

Freedom of contract includes the right to transfer rights by contract and gift. Note, however, that ownership does not necessarily include freedom to contract. The word 'ownership' often refers to situations where the ability to contract is strictly limited. For example, ancient farmers in Sweden with very limited rights to sell the property were seen as owners. Similarly, we may talk about ownership in a feudal, mercantile, or guild society, where the master and worker have well-defined personal rights, but lack the freedom to contract or establish competing firms. Moreover, children may be owners although they do not have freedom of contract.

For these reasons there is cause to define a *narrow concept of ownership* that encompasses use, compensation and residual rights, but not the freedom to contract. Private ownership is often said to be necessary in the market economic system, which is certainly true. However, ownership in the narrow sense is not sufficient for a market economy. What differentiates a market economy from other economic systems is the far-reaching and decentralized freedom of contract, that is, the individual owner's right through voluntary agreement to determine the transfer of rights.

Under freedom of contract we also include the legal competence to establish companies, as well as the qualifications to transfer rights to another party through the power of attorney. Central to a market economy is also free competition, which is guaranteed through the freedom of association and through anti-trust laws.

So far, we have said that decision-making power can either be centralized with a central planner, or decentralized with consumers and producers via freedom of contract. Central planning and a completely decentralized market economy are extremes, however. In reality, this is also a question of degree – a dictator cannot control everything, but must decentralize some rights, and the sovereignty of consumers and producers is limited in many ways, even in the most liberal economy. For instance, the under-aged and mentally retarded are usually under guardianship. Consumers may not be free to trade drugs, weapons and sex. Many businesses, for example the legal and medical professions, transport, and hazardous industries, need a licence to trade, and so on. Hence the criteria for decision-makers and, thus, indirectly the number of economic agents are settled by laws furnishing the legal right to contract.

Because 'property rights' represent a bundle of rights with a broad spectrum, it is usually not easy to identify rights clearly. Indeed, in order to identify an owner's rights and duties, it may be necessary to investigate a succession of different laws and statutes. Moreover, the rights may change repeatedly. An owner of a car has many rights and duties. By changing the tax rules and traffic laws, the content of ownership changes. Similarly, the owner of a cooperative flat possesses a share in an association, which in turn gives the right to live in the apartment and eventually the right to rent it out. The ownership may also include duties, for example, to pay property taxes and electricity bills, to maintain the common entrance and stairways, and the implicit obligation to behave respectfully toward neighbours. When rented out, only certain rights and obligations such as the right to disposition and the freedom to use are transferred, together with the obligation to maintain the stairways and behave respectfully toward neighbours. These examples show that rights are complex bundles determined by laws, as well as by custom. In other words, there is no absolute, given right to property.

9. PROPERTY RIGHTS AND THE ENVIRONMENT

We have demonstrated by means of several examples how exclusive use and legally protected property rights may improve the environment. Indeed, the lack of private property rights may result in an ecological disaster. Even the occupation of land may save the environment (see Chapter 3). It is, of course, better if rights are assigned and enforced within a legal system – the avoidance of conflict and war is urgent both for man and the environment.

Within a jurisdiction there is a continuous assignment of rights that is of great importance both to the economy and to the environment. Here follows a hypothetical example. An owner, A, of industrial property bordering a water source possesses in his capacity as owner many rights, including the believed usage right to discharge waste into the bordering stream. The ensuing impurities, however, create an environmental problem for owner *B*, downstream. *B* sues *A*, claiming that she has the 'right to fresh water'. However, the law is unclear on this point.

Hence the court, or the legislator, must assign the right to either *A* or *B*. A classic law and economics problem, to which we shall return in Chapter 9, is what the economic effects are if 'the right of ownership to the water' is assigned to *A* or *B*. According to the Coase theorem, we may conclude that the assignment of the right to either *A* or *B* is important (see Box 2.4). The conflict inherent in unspecified rights is hereby dissolved. Assignments of rights are, as noted above, also a prerequisite for further bargaining by the parties.

Box 4.3 provides one of many examples of how private property rights may improve both the economy and the environment. Similarly, Box 4.4 demonstrates the problem of the collective ownership and control of African elephants that are heavily hunted and threatened by extinction.

BOX 4.3 OYSTER BEDS

The advantage of property rights relative to common ownership and command-and-control systems has been studied in the US oyster-fishing industry. The legal systems of the different states provide mixtures of ownership, both common and private property, of oyster beds. According to the theory of property rights, one would expect the common ownership, or open-access regime, of oyster beds to be less productive. First, oyster beds benefit from proper preparations that obviously are not going to take place if the individual investing effort in such preparations does not have an exclusive right to harvest the oysters. The harvesting process involves the removal of parts of the shell and rock deposits from the bottom of the sea. Not replacing this residue is destructive, but since it involves a cost to the individual to carry out the replacement, this will not take place with common ownership – unless the law forces the individual to do so. Second, harvesting immature oysters is profitable to the individual in an open-access regime since the individual cannot expect to catch the oyster again if it is thrown back into the ocean. The contrary is true in a system of private ownership. If the oyster is thrown back into the ocean, it will be found later by the same fisherman when it has a higher value. Third, in particularly rich oyster areas there will, with common ownership, be a congestion of fishing boats. The private owner of an equally rich area will employ the effort that maximizes the yield.

To counter the tendency of harvesting until a resource is depleted, the states have instituted a number of command-and-control measures. It is usually stipulated that some proportion of shells should be saved on commonly owned oyster grounds. States also subsidize rehabilitation programmes. To avoid the catching of very small oysters, minimum size restrictions have been set. The use of new and efficient technologies may also be restricted.

All in all, one can expect economic efficiency to be higher in areas of private property. Empirical findings support this theory. Labour productivity and, consequently, the wages of oyster fishermen have been compared between the years 1950 and 1969. Wages in Virginia with respect to predominantly private property were on average $2453, and in Maryland with a common property system $1606. Similarly, Louisiana fishermen earned $3207, while their counterparts in Mississippi, fishing on common grounds, earned $870. Moreover, data for the years 1945–70 show that Maryland fishermen harvested earlier in the season than did the fishermen in Virginia.

Source: Based on Agnello and Donnelley (1975a, b).

BOX 4.4 PROTECTION OF ELEPHANTS

Poaching and destruction of the elephant habitats in Africa have reduced the elephant population from 1.3 million to 600 000 between 1979 and 1989. Basically, two strategies have been developed for the protection of elephants. The first command-and-control, or protective, strategy (applied in Kenya) has been to forbid hunting and all sales of elephant parts or products. Through the second property-rights-oriented active management strategy (applied in Zimbabwe), the government and private investors actively seek revenue from the hunting and sale of elephant products for profit.

The protective strategy holds that the only permitted source of revenue from elephants should come from viewing, thus all hunting is banned. Since the tusks and other parts still have a considerable value on the world market, the elephants must be protected and poachers controlled and punished. A problem here is corruption of rangers and officials protecting the elephants. Another problem is that without hunting, there are no adequate funds for the detection of poaching and for compensation to farmers for damages caused by elephants. Farmers are thus harmed, and may wish to see the elephants eliminated, at least within the immediate vicinity. Hence, the command strategy without efficient control will presumably fail.

In contrast, the active management strategy establishes an incentive to reinvest in the protection of the elephants for future hunting and selling. Support and protection by the local population are attained by sharing the profit with farmers and tribesmen. The shared residual right provides an incentive to participate in the protection of the elephants. In Zimbabwe the local council in the Nyaminyami district was given a number of elephants that could earn them a long-term income of $125 000 per year if fully utilized, approximately the same sum the area had received in foreign aid for nutrition and primary education programmes. Some ranchers have fenced in their land and set up anti-poaching patrols and wildlife management programmes because they have found it to be more profitable to use their land for hunting than for raising livestock. This has given rise to a number of private nature reserves.

The property rights approach is supported by some empirical facts. In Kenya, the population of elephants dropped during the 1980s from 65 000 to 19 000 (with a similar drop in other countries using the same strategy). The elephant population in Zimbabwe grew during the same period from 30 000 to 43 000 (and in Botswana, also using an active management strategy, the elephants have increased to 56 000).

Source: Based on Heimert (1995).

Nevertheless, at the same time there are many regulations and limitations of property rights that are used for the protection of the environment. Later, we will examine such regulations. Here, we shall briefly describe a few. First, the right to the use of, for example, land is restricted by national, regional, and local planning and zoning laws. Hunting, farming, emissions and waste treatment are also regulated areas that limit the rights of property-owners. Second, the right to the residual is limited by taxes. Taxes are necessary for financing the public good, for example the legal system, and are thus at least to some extent necessary for the protection of property rights, as well as the environment. Third, the right to trade is commonly restricted to the protection of rare species and ancient cultures. For instance, the Sami people in Scandinavia have the right to use the grazing land for their reindeer, and the right to fish and hunt for their own needs, although they do not own the land. They are not allowed to let or sell this right to others for the use or non-use of the grazing land. If the right were tradable, it would presumably have been sold to landowners disturbed by reindeer, or to farmers using other methods and possessing cattle. In both cases the unique Sami traditions and culture would disappear.[3]

10. PROPERTY RIGHTS VERSUS SOCIAL AND HUMAN RIGHTS

In Chapter 2 we discussed the importance of environmental principles and rights. In this chapter we focus on the importance of property rights to protect the environment. Now we shall ask the question how these different rights relate to each other.

The Rio declaration of 1992 starts with the following two principles:

1. Human beings are ... entitled to a healthy and productive life in harmony with nature.
2. States have the sovereign right to exploit their own resources ... and the responsibility to ... not cause damage to the environment of other States ...

We shall not deal with the legal status of declarations of this type. We are, however, interested in their similarities and differences with respect to property rights. The second principle appears to be a declaration of property rights at the state level. The first declaration is different. It belongs to a class of rights that may be named *social rights* or *politically active rights*. The statement points out what the state and future politicians ought to do for its citizens; in this case: provide a healthy and productive life in harmony with nature. For instance, the Swedish constitution includes similar rights regarding education, healthcare and a healthy environment (see Chapter 2, Section 6).

The state's political responsibilities and the citizens' rights to social services are usually weaker and less binding than property rights. Social rights in constitutions or international declarations are regarded, first of all, as ambitions and general recommendations for the future. Consequently, if education, healthcare, or the environment is poor, the citizen cannot usually sue the government successfully. Indeed, social rights may be withdrawn or neglected through political decisions without the right to compensation. Moreover, social rights, of course, are not transferable. For instance, a right to public schooling or pension can usually not be sold or used as collateral.

In spite of these limitations social rights may, of course, be of great moral and political significance. The Rio declaration, by which a large number of states have agreed on substantial efforts to protect the environment, will certainly have an impact on politics around the world. It is, however, beyond the scope of this book to explain or estimate its impact and value.

While social rights are active in that they place demands on the state, *human rights* such as freedom of speech, freedom of religion, and freedom to meet and associate are *politically passive rights* in the sense that the state, or other citizens, shall not interfere with these rights. Indeed, human rights differ from social rights in that they limit the sphere of politics. The purpose is to protect the political immunity and privacy of individuals. Such rights have been included in the UN Declaration on Human Rights of 1948 and sometimes in national constitutions.

Human rights are of great importance for the protection of humanity against cruelty and political mischief. However, the enforcement of human rights has been proven to be weak, even when the rights are included in national and international constitutions. One reason is that minorities are poorly represented in politics. Human rights must, therefore, be continuously defended and upheld through moral and ethical arguments. One such moral defence is to claim that human rights are *natural rights*, that is, rights given to humanity by God or by nature, over and beyond political decision, perhaps even embedded in the human gene. The idea of being bound to a hypothetical *social contract* not to harm each other may also be seen as '*natural law*'.

Some political philosophers and legal thinkers claim that property rights are also natural rights. We will not argue against this stand. It should be noted, however, that property rights differ considerably from human rights. First, property rights to land, for example, contain a complex bundle that changes continuously through various forms of legislation and political reforms. Property rights are, thus, more flexible than, for example, the right to freedom of religion or speech. Second, changes in property rights cause windfall gains and losses to property-owners that cannot always be, or are, compensated. In addition, incomes to the state must be generated somehow. Hence, if the political system has the purpose of financing, for example, public goods and the redistribution of wealth, limitations of property rights by taxation and regulation must be accepted.

Note that human rights have the purpose of protecting the private sphere from politics, while the sphere of freedom of contract regulates what should be allocated via the market and not via the collective (political) system.

Similarly, limitations in the freedom of contract indicate what should be handled in the political or private sphere. For instance, a market for the adoption of children may be outlawed, and adoptions, instead, handled by a public agency, together with parents.

We may also talk about *environmental rights*. Here we do not include property rights, although property rights may preserve the environment. Environmental rights include both politically active rights, that is, responsibilities of the politicians to protect the environment, and politically passive duties to leave certain species, ecosystems, or cultures protected from politics as well as from markets (see Chapter 2).

11. CONCLUSIONS

Over the years there have been situations where people occupy areas of desirable resources and thereby create their own exclusive 'rights'. Those occupied areas can later on turn out to be incorporated into the legal system and, thus, assigned as legal rights. Although occupation may save the environment, it is, of course, better if rights are assigned by law. The avoidance of conflicts and wars is an urgent issue to both man and the environment.

The establishment of property rights may follow a certain pattern. First, there is open access to an unlimited resource. Second, problems arise when the resource becomes scarce. The free-rider problem and rivalry cause a conflict. Third, the conflict may, at best, be resolved through the establishment of rights. Fourth, given assigned rights, it may be possible to trade rights, that is, the preconditions for contracts and markets are established.

We have demonstrated the important function of private property rights. Private ownership decentralizes decision-making. Because both decision-making and economic responsibilities lie with the same party, an incentive is created for the efficient use of resources. The main function of the state is then to uphold the legal rights.

This is not to say that unregulated markets protect the environment. In fact, the 'free' market is based on a set of institutions and regulations. Moreover, the analysis does not conclude that a liberal market economy based on private property rights is the best political solution to most problems. In fact, the free-market economy includes many forms of collective ownership that apparently have certain advantages.

Property rights are a bundle of rights including a complex set of freedoms to use and trade and duties to compensate others for infringements in their rights. With ownership comes also the residual right to the surplus (or deficit). These freedoms, rights and duties are specified in various laws that may be changed by, for example, legislation. Hence the content and meaning of property rights may vary considerably over time. In other words, property rights in this book is a relative concept.

Human rights are sometimes said to be absolute, natural rights, and as such independent of the current political or economic system. Similarly, rights of the environment are sometimes said to be independent of current politics or human wants – nature, including animals and forests, have their own natural claims to life. Libertarian philosophers may also claim that property rights are a part of natural law.

One feature that property rights, human rights and environmental rights have in common is that they are negative rights in the sense that the political system shall protect the rights, but not intervene in the private domain or ecosystem respectively. Human rights have been proven to be weak. One reason is that the minorities protected are poorly represented in politics. Human rights must, therefore, be defended by moral and ethical arguments. One such defence is to claim that human rights are rights given by God or nature. The same may be true for environmental rights. A strength of property rights is that they must not be defended as natural law – they have a straightforward economic motivation.

NOTES

1. Dahlman (1980).
2. Alchian and Demsetz (1972).
3. Rose-Ackerman (1985).

FURTHER READING

Agnello, R.J. and Donnelley L.P. (1975a), 'Property Rights and Efficiency in the Oyster Industry', *Journal of Law and Economics*, 521–33.

Alchian, A. and Demsetz, H. (1972), 'Production, Information Costs and Economic Organization', *American Economic Review*, **62**, 777–95.

Anderson, T.L. and Hill, P.J. (1975), 'The Evolution of Property Rights: A study of the American West', *Journal of Law and Economics*, no. 18, 163–79.

Coase, R.H. (1937), 'The Nature of the Firm', *Economica*, **4**, 386–405.

Dahlman, C. (1980), *The Open Field System and Beyond: A Property Rights Analysis of an Economic Institution*, Cambridge: Cambridge University Press.

Heimert, A.J. (1995), 'How the Elephant Lost His Tusks', *The Yale Law Journal*, 1473–06.

Hohfeld, W.N. (1923), *Fundamental Legal Conceptions as Applied in Judicial Reasoning and Other Legal Essays*, New Haven, CT: Yale University Press.

Olson, M. (1971), *The Logic of Collective Action*, Cambridge, MA: Harvard University Press.

Ostrom, E. (1990), *Governing the Commons: The Evolution of Institutions for Collective Action*, Cambridge, Cambridge University Press.

Rose-Ackerman, S. (1985), 'Efficiency, Equity and Inalienability', in G. Skogh and M. Schulenburg (eds), *Law and Economics and the Economics of Legal Regulation* The Hague: Martinus Nijhoff.

PART II

Resources, Prices and Sustainable Growth

5. Prices and markets

The Stone Age was not ended because of the shortage of stone, but because of the inferiority of stone when new techniques were discovered.

1. INTRODUCTION

In the discussion of the proximity principle in Chapter 2 we noted a resistance to trade in environmental policy – waste should in principle be treated at the source, that is, not traded as ordinary goods or services. Yet the modern economy is based on far-reaching division of labour and economies of scale, which requires trade, often worldwide. It may, therefore, be economically efficient to trade waste to some specialist rather than to treat it at the source. Is such trade harmful to the environment? Obviously, it is important to examine conditions under which trade is mutually beneficial to the parties and to society. Yet the benefits of trade, the function of prices, and the meaning of 'economic value' are not obvious.

In this chapter we address some basic questions about prices, economic value, and their relation to environmental law and policy. In Section 2, we start with an exchange in a simple barter economy. Thereafter, in Sections 3 to 6 we clarify the function of markets and prices. In Chapters 3 and 4 we studied the extinction of *non-renewable resources* such as fish, mammals and other living species. In Section 7 we apply the theory of prices to *exhaustible resources* such as minerals and fossil fuels. Existing virgin ores are diminishing, which has resulted in environmental policy and legislation supporting renewable energy such as wind power and recycling.

In Sections 8 and 9, we present the concepts of consumer and producer surplus, and the 'paradox of value', that is, the confusion of total and marginal values. The misunderstanding is common in the environmental debate. We apply the economic concepts to water, that is in many areas a scarce environmental resource, given in quantity (on the global level) but not in quality. Conclusions are presented in Section 10.

2. MUTUALLY BENEFICIAL EXCHANGE

The study of complex phenomena requires simplifying assumptions. Our study of trade starts by assuming that: (i) the economy includes a limited number of agents; (ii) each owns a set of resources or assets (rights) that may be used for consumption or trade for the maximization of the utility of the agent or the group the agent represents; (iii) the economy is first a pure barter economy where the production is given; and (iv) there are no *transaction costs*, that is, costs of searching for counter-parties, bargaining, or controlling the agreement. Transaction costs are dealt with in Chapter 9.

A man in this model economy specializes in hunting rabbits. He has, therefore, a surplus of rabbits that he would like to exchange for bread. He is willing to exchange one rabbit if he receives at least *A* loaves of bread. He meets a baker who is willing to exchange *B* loaves for at least one rabbit. It is easy to show that both can gain by the exchange if *B* is larger than *A*, that is, the baker is willing to give up more bread for a rabbit than the hunter requires at a minimum. As the specialized hunter has many rabbits but few loaves, while the baker for the same reason has many loaves but no rabbits, it is reasonable to presume that *B* is larger than *A*. Thus a mutually beneficial exchange can take place.

If they meet other agents that are willing to exchange at a rate beneficial to both, the exchanges may continue. However, as the agents receive more and more of the goods they demand, they will be less willing to exchange. The exchange will cease when all require the same amount to accept an exchange. When no one is willing to exchange further, the 'market' is in *equilibrium*.

In equilibrium there is a common rate of exchange, for example, *C* loaves for *D* rabbits for *E* eggs, and so on; that is, *relative prices* are established. The price is the *opportunity cost* of eggs in terms of rabbits, and so on. In general, the price tells how much of a good must be given up in order to receive a unit of another good. The price is equal to *economic value*. Hence economic value is a relative concept – the economic value of a good exists only in relation to resources, goods, or services that must be given up in order to receive the good.

3. PRICE THEORY

Let us now move to a market with many buyers and sellers. The functioning of markets has been thoroughly analysed in economics. The theory of demand and supply in the market is primarily a theory of prices. Its purpose is to answer questions such as: what happens to the price of a good with changes in income, costs, or technology? These types of questions are of general interest, and also relevant with respect to environmental law. For

BOX 5.1 THE ROLE OF THE MIDDLEMAN

Assume that the hunter is willing to exchange one rabbit for a loaf of bread, and the baker is willing to give up four loaves for one rabbit. Since the hunter requires only one loaf for a rabbit, while the baker is willing to pay four, we should have the basis for a barter. Yet the barter may not take place if they cannot find each other. In the main text we assumed that there are no costs associated with searching and finding a counter-party with whom goods may be exchanged. Now, we assume transaction costs and introduce a middleman.

The role of the middleman is to reduce transaction costs. He is specialized in trade just as the hunter is specialized in hunting, and the baker in baking. He has learned where the buyers and sellers are located, and he has built up a reputation and credibility to make his offers trustworthy.

Suppose, now, that the middleman offers the hunter two loaves of bread at a specified time in the future for one of his rabbits. The middleman is trusted by the hunter, who accepts and gives away his rabbit without an immediate delivery of loaves. The reason for the acceptance of the barter is the expected gain of one more loaf than that required as a minimum. The middleman brings the rabbit to the baker and offers the rabbit for three loaves. The baker accepts since he would be willing to pay four loaves but now needs only to pay three (and is thus 'one loaf better off'). The middleman thereafter brings two loaves back to the hunter, who is also one loaf 'better off'. The middleman now has one loaf left, which he keeps as payment for his work.

Note that the middleman, as well as the hunter and the baker, are creating value. Goods have an economic value only if they – in the end – satisfy human needs. The fruits of hunting and baking, therefore, have no value if they cannot be distributed to the buyers. It is another matter, of course, how the goods and services will be priced and valued in the market.

instance, if the authorities forbid the sale of a pesticide, what happens to the prices and traded quantities of other pesticides? How is the demand for public transportation influenced by an act regulating private city transport? How will taxes on energy influence the use of energy, and what effect can we expect on the public budget?

In order to make such predictions, a theory and a model of the economy need to be constructed. The model is based on a series of simplified assumptions about the actors in the market, technology and available resources. Given these assumptions, the theory points to certain implications, for example, that an increased tax on oil raises the price of oil, and, with this, the demand for oil and complementary goods such as cars decreases. The state's tax revenue increases, given that the reduction in the demand for oil is not so great that it is counterbalanced by a decrease in the quantity sold. These and other predictions can be tested empirically.

The price theory model includes the following basic assumptions:

1. There is a given number of utility-maximizing consumers who are informed about all goods and prices.
2. There is a given number of profit-maximizing firms, also fully informed about goods and prices.
3. Buyers and sellers are price-takers; that is, there are so many in each group that no single actor can influence the price.
4. There is a given set of resources and technologies by which the resources are transformed into goods.

The model may seem unrealistic, but it has proved to be very useful in the area for which it was developed. As in all models, just like a road map, many details have been eliminated to highlight the essentials.

Note that the model is positive (descriptive). It explains prices, but has nothing to say about economic policy. For policy judgements we need a normative theory on what is 'good' or 'bad'. Explicit norms for policy will be presented later, in Chapters 9 and 10.

Although price theory is positive and 'value-free', there are normative underpinnings. The model is 'atomistic', that is, built on the assumption of many independent actors. The model has an ideological analogy in the classic, liberal view of the relationship between the state and its citizens. The state's role is to stipulate and enforce legal order. By apportioning property rights, the initial distribution of wealth is determined. The right to contract involves endorsing the decision-making capacity and sovereignty of legally aged citizens and legal entities. The unimpeded right of contract, together with the freedom of association and entry, opens up possibilities to engage in mutually beneficial agreements through trade on the competitive market.

This 'neoclassical' model is sometimes said to be a model of the free, unregulated market economy. Nonetheless, the model implicitly assumes a friction-less market without any transaction costs, that is, a complete and costless system of institutions and legal regulations. Trade of goods and services concerns complex bundles of rights (see Chapter 4, Section 8).

Likewise, households and firms, which in the model are described as consumption and production units, are in fact legal entities. We will return to an analysis of these institutions, with a focus on environmental law, in Part III.

The most controversial simplification in the price theory model is the assumption about economic man; that is, that market agents maximize their own utility, given the scarcity that is at hand. The economic agent is an atomic, independent unit. The agents (buyers and sellers) are assumed to have preferences that are given. More goods provide greater utility, but the marginal utility declines the more the individual already possesses. It is also assumed that the individual can, in a rational manner, rank and prioritize available alternatives. In Chapter 16 we discuss whether punishments deter environmental crimes. The answer depends on whether the criminal considers benefits and costs, including the risk of punishment, in a rational manner.

Note that the model does not say anything about the underlying biological, psychological and sociological forces that determine human desires. Social and moral aspects are thus disregarded in the analysis. This does not mean, however, that the analysis is 'amoral'. The model has to assume away a number of aspects to explain what is taking place in the markets.

Do, then, the many econometric studies showing that price increases lead to reduced demand mean that the individuals are rational utility-maximizers?

BOX 5.2 SKIRT FASHION AND WOOL PRODUCTION

Here is a classic example of what the theory of demand and supply may, and may not, explain: ladies in eighteenth century England wished to have longer skirts. This increased the demand for cloth. The price of cloth increased, which generated an increased demand for wool. The farmers increased their count of sheep, after which the supply of wool increased, which dampened the price of wool. Under certain assumptions about the production technology and competition, the supply of wool could increase so much that the price level of wool could be forced down to its original level.

Initially, the change of preference occurred in favour of long skirts. The economic analysis has nothing to say about taste or fashion. However, given these preferences and the fundamental assumptions about the choice of the consumers, clothing manufacturers and farmers, the economic analysis can elucidate market and production-related consequences.

Perhaps the most frequent answer among economists is that the assumption does not need to apply to all individuals, but only to an average or typical individual. Another point of view is that it does not make any difference how the individual makes her decision. The important issue is that the results of the decision are the same *as if* the individual had behaved in a rational, utility-maximizing manner. As long as *as if* applies, the 'correct' predictions can be made and tested. The wide applicability of price theory, and the relatively good predictions that can be made, shows that the assumption about economic man is useful, although the underlying structure of human feelings and decisions is not fully understood.

4. DEMAND

When buyers and sellers exchange goods on a market with many buyers and sellers of similar goods, they do not have to bargain and inform themselves about the willingness of counter-parties to exchange. They only need to consider the prices that indicate the opportunity cost in terms of money.

Money functions here as a numerator. Requirements of any such numerator are that its value is sustainable, dividable, and easy to transport. This explains why shells, gold, silver, and publicly guaranteed bank notes and credit cards are used for exchange.

The most common manner of explaining the meaning of prices and economic value is to derive demand-and-supply curves in markets. The curve in Figure 5.1(a) shows the demand of a good, for example rabbits, in terms of money. At a high price, p_1, few will be demanded, and at a lower price, p_2, more will be demanded, other things such as income and prices of substitutes (for example pork) and complements (for example bread) being given. If the price falls from p_1 to p_2, the quantity demanded will go up from q_1 to q_2. The well-established fact that buyers are normally willing to

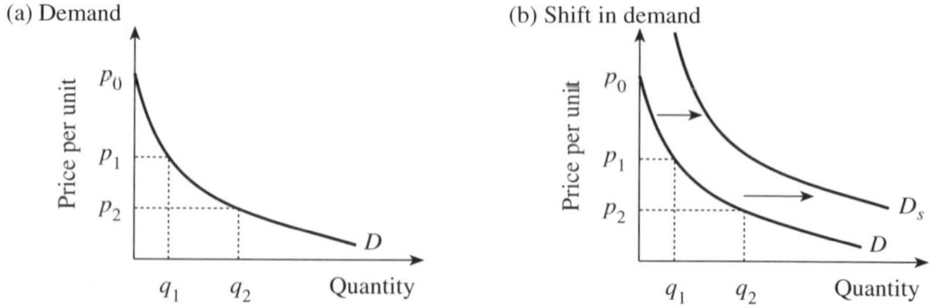

Figure 5.1 (a) Demand and (b) shift in demand

buy more (less) at a lower (higher) price is sometimes referred to as the *law of demand*.

The demand curve is of interest to the sellers because it tells them how large a quantity they can sell at various prices. The curve also tells us about the buyers' valuation of the good. Imagine a line of people ordered according to their *willingness to pay*, WTP, for the good. The one willing to pay the most is placed at the origin. She is willing to pay p_0, which is also the highest price at which the good can be sold at all.

The demand curve is two-dimensional; that is, it shows the relation between two variables: price and quantity. Other factors like income, prices of substitutes or complements, the climate and so on, also influence demand. All such factors are assumed as given in Figure 5.1(a). When there is a change in the outside factors, for example an increase in income, there is a shift in demand, indicated by the *Ds* curve in Figure 5.1(b). This shows the case where the demanded quantity, due to the increase in income, is larger at all price levels. Accordingly, the WTP is greater at all quantities.

5. SUPPLY

The amount of a good that suppliers would like to sell also depends on the price. The higher the price, the more the suppliers are willing to offer. We can think of it as an ordering of the suppliers along the horizontal axis, the vertical axis showing the minimum price they would be willing to accept to sell various quantities of the good. This price equals the cost of providing the marginal unit.

The supply curve can have different shapes, but is normally positively sloped. The shape depends, among other things, on how much time the industry has to respond. Generally, we work with the assumption that the supply curve is positively shaped, as shown in Figure 5.2(a). However, we are also interested in two extremes. The horizontal supply curve in Figure 5.2(b) mirrors the case when the good is offered on the market in unlimited numbers at price p_1. This may be the case for, say, a national market where the good is imported and the price is given on the world market. Figure 5.2(b) also illustrates a long-run supply of a good that can be produced and sold at a constant average cost in large amounts, for example certain vegetables.

Figure 5.2(c) illustrates the supply curve when the quantity is given, independent of the price. One such case prevails when a certain amount of a perishable good, for example fish or vegetables, must be sold the same day. Note that the supply curve for fish over a longer period of time depends on the fishing fleet and the profitability of the industry. Hence the long-run supply curve slopes as in Figure 5.2(a).[1] An approximate quantity of land is

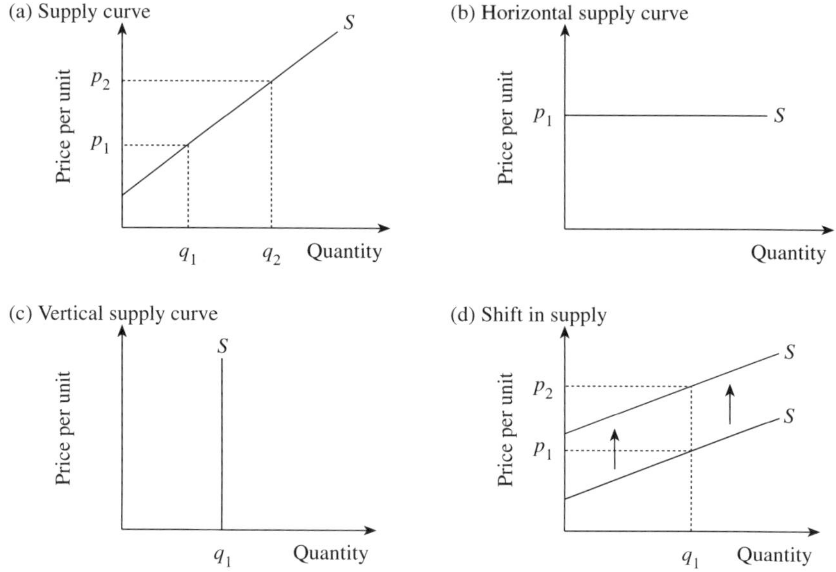

Figure 5.2 *(a) Supply curve, (b), horizontal supply curve, (c) vertical supply curve, and (d) shift in supply*

also given and independent of price. The vertical supply curve of Figure 5.2(c) may, thus, illustrate the supply of real estate within a given region.

What was said about shifts in demand is also applicable to supply. The two-dimensional picture covers only two variables, price and quantity. When, for example, the price of inputs increases, the suppliers will presumably require a larger price for each quantity, which in Figure 5.2(d) is indicated by the upward shift.

6. THE MARKET

In Figure 5.3 the demand curve and the supply curve are combined to show how prices and quantities bought and sold are determined on a competitive market. A *competitive market* prevails when there are a large number of buyers and sellers supplying the same good. The buyers in such a market are 'price-takers'; that is, no one is large enough to influence the price.

The point where supply equals demand is called the market *equilibrium*, and the price, p_e, and quantity, q_e, are called equilibrium price and quantity (or market price and quantity). Equilibrium means a point that is in balance. The balance may be stable or unstable. If a movement or shock away from

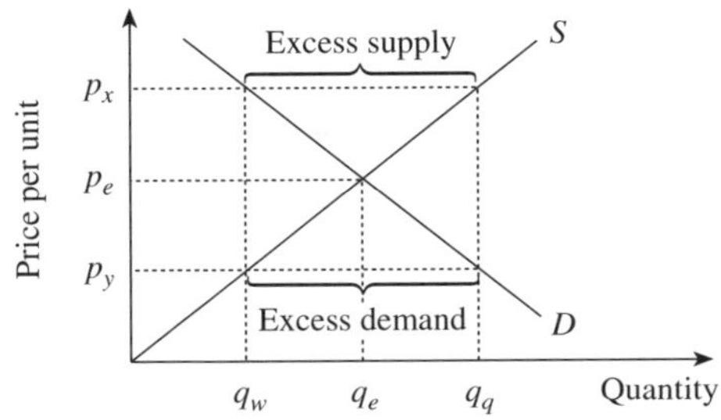

Figure 5.3 The market, excess demand, and excess supply

the market equilibrium automatically starts a process back to equilibrium, the system is stable.

If, for example, the price is set arbitrarily at p_x in the market illustrated in Figure 5.3, the suppliers offer q_q and the consumers demand q_w. Since the quantity, q_q, is greater then the q_w and no one can force the consumer to buy, the supplier will be stuck with the difference. The supplier can only get rid of the surplus by lowering the price. When the price goes down, more people demand the product and fewer wish to supply it. The price-lowering process continues until supply and demand are equal. Similarly, if the price is arbitrarily set at p_y, there will be a shortage since the demanded quantity, q_q, is larger than the supplied quantity, q_w. This will cause the price to go up until the quantities demanded and supplied are equal.

Let us now use a diagram, Figure 5.4, to illustrate the wool market sketched in Box 5.2. We start at the equilibrium point represented by the price p_0 and the quantity q_0. Now there is an increase in wool demand due to a change in taste for long skirts. This increase in demand causes a shift outward to D_1. The price of wool will, therefore, in the short-term equilibrium increase to p_1 and the wool production will increase to q_1. However, the higher price of

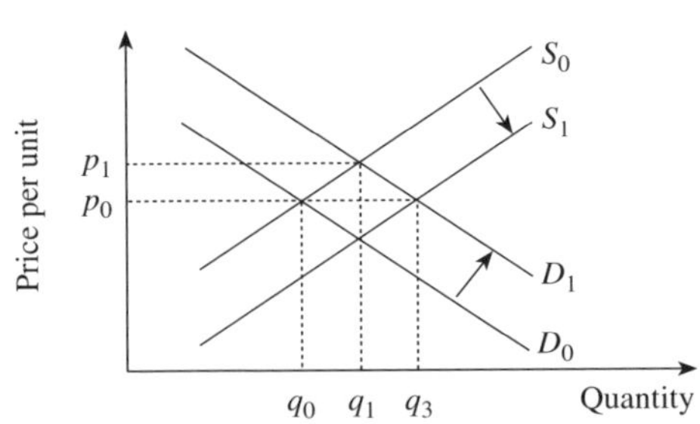

Figure 5.4 Shifts in supply and demand

wool creates profits in wool production, which presumably increases investments and the long-run supply, which pushes down the long-run price of wool. In the figure this is illustrated as an outward shift in supply, S_1. How large the increase in supply will be depends on production technology. If *constant returns to scale* prevail, a percentage increase, k, in inputs (land, labour and sheep) causes the same percentage increase, k, in wool and meat. In this case the average cost of wool production will remain unchanged (assuming constant prices on inputs). Competition will thus increase supply and push down the price to the initial level p_0, now with the quantity q_3. If, on the other hand, for example, land suitable for sheep farming is scarce, the long-run price of land may increase and, thus, the long-run shift in supply will become smaller and the long-run price of wool become higher than p_0. Similarly, if there are *economies of scale*, meaning that increased production volumes reduce the average cost of the output, the long-run supply may increase beyond S_1 and the price will decline below p_0.

7. THE MARKET FOR EXHAUSTIBLE RESOURCES

The classical economist William Stanley Jevons wrote in the mid-nineteenth century that England, due to its finite coal resource, had to choose between a rapid, prosperous exploitation and a low, long-term utilization of the resource. The optimal exploitation of a finite resource was later modelled mathematically by Hotelling (1931). Inspired by this thinking, Meadows et al. (1972) argued that economic growth leads to an overexploitation of natural resources. An important environmental issue here is whether natural resources will become extinct in the future.

In examining this issue it is useful to separate resources into renewable and non-renewable, or exhaustible, resources. Examples of *renewable resources* are forests, water, solar energy, fish and other animals. Carefully used, these resources will be available for ever. Nevertheless, many animal and plant species as well as clean water reserves are depleted or threatened. The 'tragedy of the commons' and the 'overfishing problem' have already been discussed in Chapter 3.

Exhaustible resources such as minerals and fossil oil are limited by the fact that they are not reproduced. Extracted ores and other valuable natural resources are transformed into metals in products and later spread around after use as waste, or reused. Fossil fuels such as coal and oil are burnt and will never be seen again. Existing available resources are, thus, diminishing, which frightens many in the environmental debate. The situation has also led to environmental policy and legislation, for example on recycling, with the purpose to maintain the resource base for future generations.

Yet economists are not usually worried about this. The reason is that increased scarcity will be reflected in prices that will modify behaviour. If the demand curve shifts upwards, the price will go up. Higher prices increase the search for new resources and substitutes. In fact, the price of most metals and other raw materials has not gone up since the beginning of the nineteenth century, and many, including energy, have become cheaper. There is no evidence that oil prices will increase in coming decades. The situation can be illustrated in Figure 5.4 above. There has been a continuous increase in demand, illustrated by D_1. At the same time supply has shifted outwards due to technical improvements and economies of scale.

Table 5.1 gives a picture of the development of copper and oil. The world production of both copper and oil have increased by many times during the second part of the twentieth century. So have the world reserves. Further production at the current level (the R/P ratio) can continue for 50 and 36 years respectively. Meanwhile new resources will be detected. Note that the present reserves depend on the current price. If prices go up, the search for new, including less available, resources will take place. The indexed copper price has declined while the oil price has doubled since 1950, which can be explained by the OPEC cartel, discussed further in the next chapter.

Table 5.1 Copper and oil figures, 1950–2000

	1950	1970	1990	2000
Copper				
World production, million tons	2.53	6.34	9.02	12.90
World reserve base, million tons	210	390	560	650
R/P ratio	83	62	62	50
Price, $/ton	493	1 415	2 661	1 810
Price-indexed	3 024	5 637	2 661	1 676
Oil				
World production, million tons	540	2 355	3 164	3 850
World reserves, million tons	13 400	85 000	137 000	140 000
R/P ratio	25	36	43	36
Price, $/bbl	2.0	2.1	22	28
Price-indexed	12.27	8.37	22	25.93
Index of international inflation				
Dollar-based, 1990 = 100 (World Bank)	16.3	25.1	100	108

Source: M. Radetzki, Centre for Business and Policy Studies, Stockholm.

What will happen in the future? There is, of course, a limit, although not absolute, at some time in the future. Certainly there will be less oil in the ground, but there will always be reserves left that are relatively costly to detect or exploit. When scarcity increases, the price will go up[2] and extraction will increase, but so will the search for alternatives, for example, recycling, solar energy, wind and nuclear power. Indeed, the current search for, and investments in, 'green' alternatives can be seen as an indication of strong belief in future rising prices of oil and other energy. Indeed, oil for heating houses and running cars may be obsolete long before it is very costly to exploit. Coal is an example of a resource that has become obsolete long before depletion (see the quotation at the head of the chapter).

The fact that the scarcity of non-renewable resources such as minerals and fossil fuels is not the problem should not be confused with the pollution problems related to the production and use of toxic metals and oil. A problem with virgin ore is the pollution in the surroundings, and, needless to say, the burning of fossil fuels is highly polluting.

In fact, the environmental problem related to, for example, crude oil is *affluence* rather than shortage. This is easy to see from the following experiment: assume that all reserves of natural resources and energy are halved overnight. The prices would then increase, transport would be reduced, growth would come to an end, and people would become poorer and consume less. Hence the greenhouse effect and traffic congestion would diminish. In other words, less accessible natural resources would improve the environment. Similarly, the problem of nuclear power is not the lack of uranium but the potential pollution and accidents.

Environmental policy in many countries is, nevertheless, aiming at a general decrease in the use of raw materials and energy. But the greenhouse effect, traffic congestion and enormous landfills are not due to scarce resources. On the contrary, the reason for these problems lies in the cheap and easily accessible, but polluting, energy and raw materials. Hence the problem is to control the pollution, not the exploitation of the resource *per se*. The use of very general methods aiming at reduced use of virgin resources, such as subsidized recycling or taxed energy, are costly and blunt instruments for protecting the environment, as will be shown on several occasions below.

8. CONSUMER AND PRODUCER SURPLUS

Once a market equilibrium has been reached, and thus the market price and quantity are established, the consumer's and the producer's surpluses of the marketed good can be demonstrated. The '*consumer surplus*' is the accumulated difference between the market price and the price the individual consumers would, at a maximum, have accepted to pay for the products purchased. If, for example, one consumer is willing to pay 10, at most, but only needs to pay the market price of 5, her consumer surplus will be 5. The consumer willing to pay 7 (6), at most, will likewise have a surplus of 2 (1). The consumer willing to pay 5, at most, will have no surplus. The consumer's total surplus is the sum of all the individual surpluses, that is, 5 + 2 + 1 + 0 = 8.

As noted above, the demand curve can be interpreted as the buyers' willingness to pay, WTP. In Figure 5.5, the buyers are ordered from left to right, with the one willing to pay most at the origin. Similarly, in Figure 5.5(a) we have ordered the buyers in the numerical example above according to their WTP. The total WTP equals the sum, that is, the *area*, of the bars. The total consumer surplus, 8, equals the area of the bars above the price, 5.

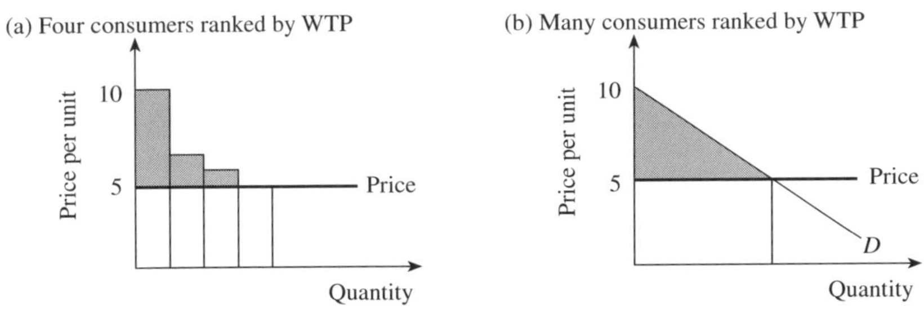

Figure 5.5 Ranking consumers by WTP

The quantity sold equals 3 or 4 in Figure 5.5(a). We may, however, think of a large number, say 400, order all goods according to the buyers' WTP and draw a continuous demand curve such as *D* in Figure 5.5(b). The whole area below the demand curve thus illustrates the total WTP when 400 are sold, while the shaded area above the price 5 illustrates the consumer's total surplus. The '*producer surplus*' is, likewise, the accumulated difference between the equilibrium price and the minimum price the producer would accept for the good. If, for example, a producer would be willing to sell a product for 2 but received the market price 5, he would have a surplus of 3. The producer willing to sell for 3 would have a surplus of 2, and so on. As in the case of consumer surplus, the producer surplus is the sum of all individual sellers' surpluses.

In Figure 5.6 the consumer surplus is illustrated by the dark grey triangle and the producer surplus by the lighter grey triangle.

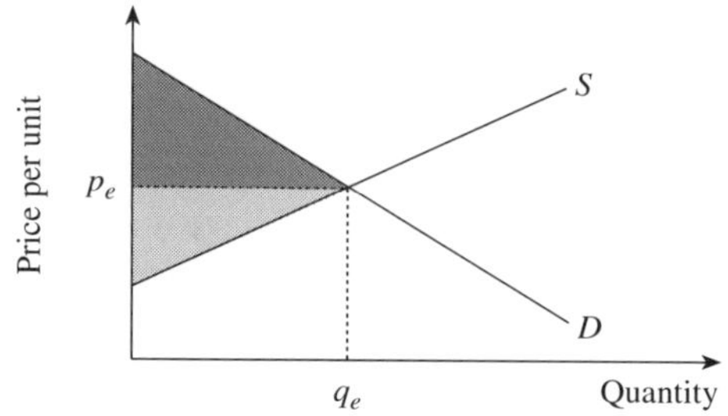

Figure 5.6 Consumer and producer surplus

9. THE PARADOX OF VALUE

In the eighteenth century Adam Smith formulated the classic '*paradox of value*': how can, for example, water, which is essential to human life, be worth less than an almost useless diamond? Since we would die without water, the demand for water must be very high; that is, we should be willing to pay an almost infinite amount of money for water. Still, in most situations no one pays more than very little for a glass of water.

There was a simple answer to the paradox once the difference between the *total* and the *marginal* nature of economic value was understood. The answer was formulated independently by three economists, William Stanley Jevons, Carl Menger and Leon Walras, about one hundred years after Adam Smith posed the question. They showed that prices are determined by the marginal willingness to buy and sell, not by the total willingness.

The total willingness to pay is very high for water. In Figure 5.7 the total willingness to pay for water is represented by the area below D_W to the left of the market quantity, q_W. The total consumer surplus equals the area below D_W

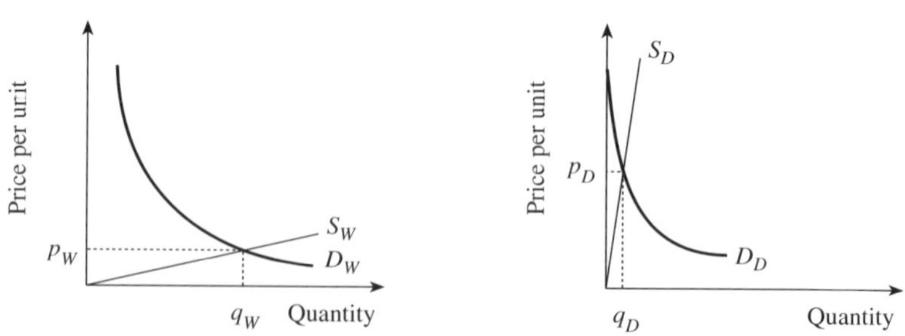

Figure 5.7 The paradox of value

and above the price, p_W. The demand curve is open upwards to the left, which indicates that the value of small amounts of highly needed water is very large and, indeed, not measurable. In the case of diamonds, the total consumer surplus is represented by the area beneath the D_D and above the price line, p_D. The total value of diamonds is certainly lower than the total value of water, although we cannot measure it.

At quantities to the left of the equilibrium quantities q_W and q_D, the buyers are willing to pay more than the amount the suppliers require in compensation. The price will, therefore, tend to increase until the equilibrium point is reached. The equilibrium price is determined by the willingness to buy and sell one additional unit. The price, thus, is the opportunity cost. Water can be supplied cheaply although demand is large. The opportunity cost, or price p_W, for an additional unit at equilibrium will, therefore, be low. Diamonds, on the other hand, are rare and costly to produce. The price, p_D, will therefore be high in equilibrium, although the total utility is small. In other words, the opportunity cost is higher in the case of diamonds than it is in the case of water.

The meaning of marginal costs and benefits is crucial in economics. What matters for a decision is the *opportunity cost*, that is, what has to be given up due to the specific choice. If a firm has to decide on an investment with the cost, X, and expected benefit, Y, the expected profit is $Y - X$. Given the investment, the firm may consider selling one more unit of the produced good. The marginal cost, that is, the opportunity cost, is the cost of producing this additional unit. Hence the investment cost, X, is a 'sunk' cost that does not count in a decision on marginal changes in production. What matters is whether the price of the final good exceeds the marginal cost of producing it.

Total and marginal values are often mixed up or misunderstood in politics. It is, for instance, often argued that necessities, that is goods like water with a very large or infinite total value, should not be allocated via the market. Instead of charging a price equal to the opportunity cost it should be distributed in a just manner by the political system, which usually means that it should be sold at a subsidized price. If so, it must be publicly financed, presumably by taxes. A problem here is that there are so many necessities: food, housing, healthcare, schools, transport, water and so on. The public budget is limited, and so is the ability publicly to offer the necessities.

Water may for political reasons be offered at a price below the opportunity cost, which causes a social loss. The loss of regulated prices can be illustrated as in Figure 5.8.

The figure illustrates a market of, for example, water where the price is fixed at a maximum level p_m. At this price the supplied quantity is q_m, while the demanded quantity is q_d. The difference $q_d - q_m$ illustrates the shortage at the regulated price. Deregulation would increase the price to the equilib-

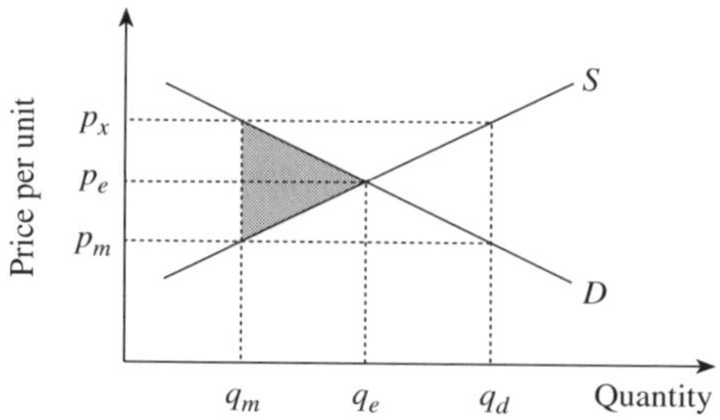

Figure 5.8 Maximum price

rium price, p_e, and thus increase the supply and reduce the demand so that the shortage is eliminated. At q_e demand equals supply. Note that the marginal consumer is willing to pay p_x at the maximum price p_m. Hence there is a marginal consumer surplus of $p_x - p_m$ for one more unit of water. At equilibrium price and quantity the surplus of consumers and of producers has increased to a sum equal to the shaded triangle in Figure 5.8. Producers as well as consumers are thus better with deregulation of the price.

Because of the excess demand at the maximum price, not all can be satisfied. Quotas may therefore be applied. If more than q_m is licensed at the price p_m, production has to be subsidized. A reason why price regulations remain could be strong lobbying among those who receive water quotas. Because water is not priced on the market it may be used, although the user is not willing to pay the opportunity cost, that is, the value to other marginal consumers, p_x. In this case we talk about inefficient use of water. The losers may be taxpayers, newcomers and other politically poorly organized groups without access to the water.

10. CONCLUSIONS

A first important point made in this chapter is that mutual exchange is valuable to both parties. The benefit of barter, as well as trade in markets, is strongly related to specialization, which creates a surplus of specific goods and a shortage of others.

A demand curve shows the quantity that will be sold at various prices. It also shows the willingness to pay for the good. If the price decreases, the quantity demanded will increase. The higher the price, the more goods will be supplied by the sellers. In other words, the supply curve is normally positively sloped. A horizontal supply curve means that price is independent

BOX 5.3 WILLINGNESS TO PAY FOR WATER

Inefficient regulation of prices is common for many goods of great importance to the environment, such as water and energy. On the other hand, there are many cases where efficiency is sought. Studies of India show, for instance, that the citizens are prepared to pay for a safe and adequate water supply. Consumers respond positively to tariffs set at a level based on real costs, if the tariff increases secure the required levels of service. A 1996 study carried out in Dehradun showed that 80 per cent of households are willing to pay more than the current tariff for improved water supply. However, governments seem unwilling to match this. The policy-makers fear that 'the people' will not want to pay, which may result in low revenues, high costs and unsatisfactory services.

Source: http://www.wsp.org/pdfs/sa_willing.pdf

Note also that water regulated by quotas, for example by (fair) distribution of water rights, may be efficiently traded on a market. If a water licence is valued less by a specific owner than by the market, the user may sell the right. The water is thereby consumed by the party that values it most. Investments are undertaken when it is profitable. In Chile this principle has been practised for over 15 years. The Limari Basin is the area where water markets are considered to function well. It is important for the functioning of water markets that transaction costs are low, and that water law is interpreted consistently. In Limari there are short-term sales of specific volumes of water, annual leases and permanent sales of rights. The prices reflect both temporary (seasonal) scarcity as well as longer-term scarcity.

Source: http://www.worldbank.org/html/fpd/water/topics/economics.html

of the quantity supplied on the market. A vertical supply curve, on the other hand, indicates that a quantity is sold, independent of price.

A competitive market is characterized by a large number of buyers and sellers. The buyers are 'price-takers', that is, no one can influence the price. The point where supply and demand are equal is called the market equilibrium. If the price is set lower than the equilibrium price, the demand will increase and supply decrease, which causes a shortage. A price equalizing demand and supply is the opportunity cost, that is, how much of a good must be given up in order to receive a unit of another good (money).

This price theory is applied to the market for non-renewable resources. An issue in environmental policy is whether natural resources such as metals and oil will be depleted in the future. Yet economists are not normally worried about this. The reason is that when the scarcity increases, the price will increase as well. Profit-seeking entrepreneurs will search for new ores and wells, as well as for substitutes including recycling, as they have done so far. The resources will never be totally eliminated. There will always be reserves that will be too costly to exploit. Indeed, the shortage is not an environmental problem – a decrease in all reserves of natural resources and energy would lead to price increases and transport reductions that may benefit the environment. The problem is the pollution when utilizing these affluent resources. An environmental policy promoting a general reduction of the exploitation of virgin ores and fossil fuels may, therefore, be blunt instruments in protecting the environment. Later in the book we will suggest a number of more specific instruments that we think will improve the environment as well as the economy.

Finally, we deal briefly with the issue of water. Fresh-water scarcity is a serious problem in large parts of the world. We cannot live without water. In other words, the total willingness to pay for a necessity like water is infinite. This may explain why the supply is often a political issue, managed by public authorities rather than by the market. Quotas and administered prices may, however, result in an inferior use of the scarce resource.

NOTES

1. We disregard the fact that the fish may in the long run be depleted, as explained in Chapter 4.
2. Note that it is the policy of the Organization of Petroleum-Exporting Countries (OPEC) to control the supply and thus artificially create scarcity to keep oil prices high. This policy may, however, have adverse effects in the long run since these high oil prices will stimulate research into alternative energy sources. We will come back to the role of OPEC in Box 6.1.

FURTHER READING

Price theory can be studied further in any standard textbook on principles of microeconomics, for instance:

Lipsey, R.G. and Courant, P.N. (1996), *Economics*, 11th edn, New York: HarperCollins.

The economics of various natural resources can be studied in textbooks on environmental economics, for instance:

Perman, R. et al. (1999), *Natural Resource and Environmental Economics*, 2nd edn, Essex, UK: Longman.
Tietenberg, T. (2000), *Environmental and Natural Resource Economics*, 5th edn, New York: HarperCollins.

6. Market failures

> It is not from the benevolence of the butcher, the brewer, or the baker that we expect our dinner, but from their regard of their own interest.
>
> Adam Smith, *The Wealth of Nations*.

1. INTRODUCTION

Prices of water, diamonds, and all other goods and service, coordinate the very complex market economy. This is possible because prices mirror opportunity costs. Restricted by prices and income, the choice of sales and purchases are made. The firms supply goods and services to the extent that it is profitable, that is, until it is possible to obtain a better outcome of alternative production. Consumers, in the same way, buy to the extent that they can obtain more satisfaction.

The price of a good covers compensation to vertically involved suppliers, producers and dealers. For instance, the price of a ceramic cup – one of the many products that are produced and distributed via markets – includes compensation to the person who dug up the clay, formed it, invested in the oven, burned it, supplied the energy, transported the final object, and sold it. Goods and services are, in fact, produced, distributed, used and paid for practically without public control or central planning. The ability of the market and the price system to solve the complex coordination problem with many producers, consumers and goods without coordination of all self-oriented individuals is a phenomenon called 'the invisible hand'.

However, the market is imperfect and the prices may be misleading, which may cause 'market failures'. Transaction costs hinder the actors from contracting and thus from regulating all activities in a mutually beneficial way. This is discussed in Section 2, dealing with external effects. Section 3 then presents market failure of monopolies, while Section 4 discusses the excess burden of taxes. In Section 5 we apply the price theory and market failure analysis to environmental policy, which aims at sustainable development through recycling. Section 6 concludes.

2. EXTERNAL EFFECTS

Trade takes place when parties believe that they will obtain a benefit from it – sellers and buyers do not usually give up something freely without compensation in terms of other goods or money. Trade can, therefore, be assumed to be mutually beneficial, at least at the moment when the parties agree. This is also true when many are involved in market exchanges. The prices give information about the opportunity costs, which include the compensation to all involved.

However, this vision of the invisible hand is based on a crucial assumption – namely, that *all* affected by the trade are included in it and accept the terms. In other words, to reflect the opportunity cost and, thus, to coordinate the behaviour of all buyers and sellers, prices must include compensation to all affected parties. If not, there is an imperfection – an 'external effect' – in the economy.

External effects may be positive or negative. *Positive external effects* (or 'externalities') prevail when benefits are not considered in the pricing of goods or services. Examples of positive externalities are investments, research and knowledge that may benefit many in society. As those who benefit from new information do not have to pay for it, there is underinvestment in information-seeking activities. It may, therefore, be of common interest to support such activities, for example through the public funding of research or by patent laws that protect innovations.

Good music or flowers in the garden may give pleasure to neighbours without payment. Hence there may also be underinvestment in music or gardening. Note, however, that although there is no explicit compensation for gardening efforts, there may be an *implicit contract* including some form of compensation, or a mutual understanding that all homeowners are expected to maintain their gardens in order to please the community.

'*Negative external effects*' prevail when someone causes harm without considering the consequences to others. Music may disturb as well as provide enjoyment to neighbours. However, if the noise is accepted due to some implicit understanding (music until 11 p.m. is accepted), it is an integrated part of the social and economic life, and, thus, no negative externality exists.

Externalities mislead the decision-makers in the economy as prices do not reflect the full opportunity cost. Assume, for instance, that the price of a plastic cup is lower than the full production cost because someone in the production chain has inflicted damage without having to pay compensation. Thus the price does not reflect the opportunity cost in using the cup. The low price will presumably cause a larger consumption of plastic cups and less of ceramic cups, compared to what the consumers would purchase at opportunity cost prices.

At a price above the opportunity cost, a good may correspondingly come to be consumed too little, that is, possible consumer's or producer's surplus will be lost. The reason for the high price may be that, when setting the price, certain positive external effects were not considered. High-tech production, for example, can raise the level of knowledge in general, which may be advantageous beyond the business that produces the knowledge. If the business is not subsidized, the production decisions are not adjusted to the positive external effects and the produced good becomes comparatively expensive. The high price will limit the positive effects that the knowledge brings with it, because the price does not reflect the good's value in relation to other (correctly priced) goods.

BOX 6.1 NUCLEAR POWER

Legislation protecting a certain industry can lead to relatively low prices of a harmful product. This low price will lead to a too high demand and thus a high supply of this harmful product. An example can be found in the area of accident law where the nuclear power plant operator is protected through financial caps that limit his exposure to liability. In some statutes the limitations are set at a much lower amount than the losses of an average nuclear accident. In that case, not only would the right of victims to compensation be seriously limited, but there would also not be a full internalization of costs due to the nuclear risk. Indeed, if the legislator limits the compensation due to victims, the energy prices for nuclear power will not reflect the true social costs of nuclear power, which will lead to an overconsumption of nuclear power. This point was also raised in the Netherlands during the parliamentary debate preceding a change of the nuclear liability statute. The amount of guarantee provided by the Dutch state was increased to the exceptional amount of 5 billion Dutch guilders. It was mentioned in the legislation that the ministry of finance would have to charge the licensee of a nuclear power plant for this guarantee. If this were not the case the nuclear energy would remain too cheap, since the energy price would not reflect the true costs of the nuclear risk.

Source: Based on Parliamentary Documents of the Second Chamber of Representatives, 23 April 1991, 72-4054. See also Faure (1995b).

Individuals and firms cause negative externalities in various ways. One is illustrated by the traffic congestion case of Table 3.1, where individual drivers increase the travel time of everyone on the road. In other words, free-riders cause externality problems. The tragedy of the commons can similarly be treated as an externality problem. Here, the actors within an industry, for example fishery, harm each other in a way that may cause depletion.

Pollution is another type of externality. Activities which may as such be beneficial to society can nevertheless cause negative side effects for third parties. These effects are external to the industry since the companies that commit the pollution are not affected.

The starting-point of traditional economic analysis of environmental pollution is that a decision-maker will not take into account an externality when it makes decisions. A great portion of environmental economics is coupled to the question of how negative external effects can be internalized in economic decisions. Examples of such measures are legal regulation of property rights, as discussed in Chapter 4, and charges on pollution, discussed in Chapter 13.

3. MONOPOLIES

In price theory external effects are treated as 'imperfections', compared to the perfect competitive economy where prices mirror opportunity costs. An additional imperfection, or reason why prices differ from opportunity costs, is monopolies. The disturbing effect on the economy is due to a high monopoly price above the opportunity cost. Moreover, the high price redistributes wealth in favour of the monopolist.

In a monopolistic market there is only one seller, or in the case of a cartel several sellers that coordinate their activities and thus act as one. There are three ways a monopoly or cartel can come into existence: the first is that there is only room for one firm in the market; the second is that the monopolist has some skill that cannot be copied by others, for example an artist may be able to produce something unique; the third is that sellers in a market join a cartel to reduce supply and, thereby, increase the price and the profit. The cartel can be created by the firms themselves, or by public authorities limiting entry into the market.

The case of the cartel is illustrated in Figure 6.1. The demand curve of the good, *D*, is downward sloping. In competition we assume that supply can be illustrated by a horizontal line, *S*, indicating that an infinite number of the good is offered at a given price, p_c. For instance, the figure illustrates a domestic market for imported oil. The oil is bought by independent importers to an international market at the price given, p_c, which is also the marginal

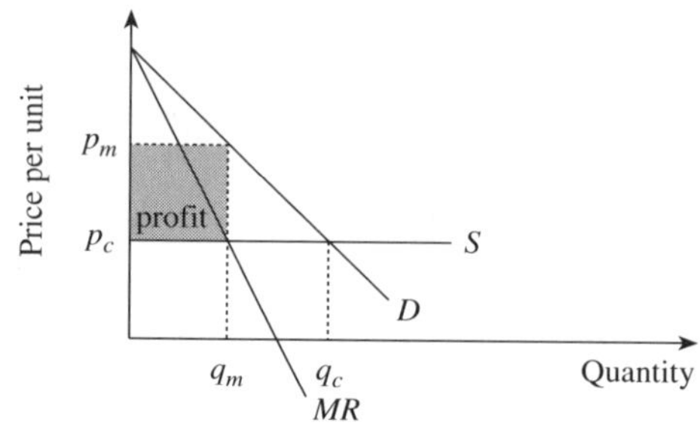

Figure 6.1 *Profit of a monopolist or cartel*

(opportunity) cost for the importers. The independent importing firms will in competition sell the equilibrium quantity q_c at the price p_c.

In the case of collusion, firms decide jointly how much to sell. The demand curve is sloping downwards, which means that a smaller quantity sold results in a higher price. The cartel will maximize the joint profit of the member firms if it sets the quantity to q_m. Here, the marginal cost of, for example, importing one more unit of oil on the world market, p_c, equals the marginal revenue, *MR*. The price will be p_m. The monopoly profit will be $(p_m - p_c)q_m$.

The reason why the marginal revenue of the cartel is smaller than the charged price, p_m, is that, when sales are increased, the price will go down. Hence the profit on goods sold previously will be lower. The quantity sold by a cartel is, therefore, less than the sum of that which would have been sold had the market been competitive, q_c.

Figure 6.1 shows that there is a profit to be made through a cartel. However, there is always a problem of holding the cartel together. The reason for this is that the cartel faces a free-rider problem. Any of the member firms may gain by breaking the agreement and selling more, although more on the market pushes down prices for the others. If the cartel is upheld by the industry itself, part of the profit may be used to uphold the cartel. Indeed, the cartel may be willing to spend up to the entire profit to establish and protect itself. Resources may be spent to police members or to lobby the government in order to protect the monopoly. This type of lobbying is usually called *rent-seeking*. This phenomenon will be further discussed in Chapter 10, Sections 4–6.

4. TAXES

While a fee comprises a payment for a good, a tax does not have any direct equivalent. A tax is a compulsory transfer of a means. It can be differentiated

BOX 6.2 OPEC

The Organization of Petroleum-Exporting Countries (OPEC) is one example of a worldwide cartel. In 1973 the OPEC members restricted their output by negotiating quotas among themselves. Although OPEC only had about 70 per cent of the oil reserves in the world it could act almost as a monopoly. When OPEC reduced its output, the prices increased and the members, and even non-members, earned huge profits. After some years of success the typical problems of cartels appeared. The high prices resulted in development of new supplies and reduced demand. Fuel-efficient cars became popular and innovations reduced the use of oil in many industries. In 1981 the peak was reached with a price of $35 per barrel. The production level was then half of OPEC's capacity. OPEC could not maintain this low level, and the member states increased output. In 1986, the price fell to $11. $12 per barrel is close to the competitive price.[1] The oil prices have increased again because of further limitations in the supply.

Note: Lipsey and Courant (1996), pp. 224–5 and 250–51.

from confiscation in that it follows predictable principles prescribed by law, for example in the form of property taxes, income taxes, or sales taxes.

Property tax means that part of the value of the individual property is given over to the state. It also implies a systematic pruning of the value of the right of ownership. Likewise, income and value-added tax draw away part of the value that otherwise would have fallen to one of the partners in a voluntary transaction.

Taxes thus influence not only the ownership and property distribution in society, but also the incentive structure. If part of the profit of a purchased good or salary is drawn in through taxes, the incentive to buy/work is not the same as if the tax did not exist. Taxes distort the economy in that prices inclusive of taxes do not reflect opportunity costs; thus prices give incorrect information. This phenomenon is named the '*excess burden*' of taxes.

Nevertheless, taxes are needed for the financing of public goods such as defence, infrastructure, schooling, national parks and the public justice system (including the protection of property rights). They are also used for the redistribution of income. Politics is much concerned with the distribution of wealth. This is especially true for welfare-oriented states. In Sweden, for

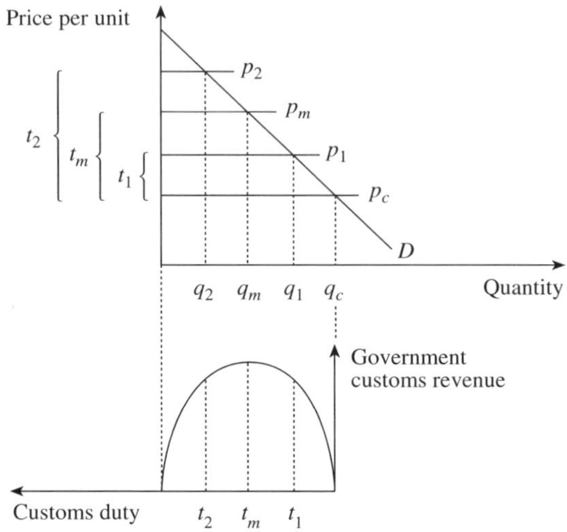

Figure 6.2 The revenue effect of raising the customs duty

instance, public spending is more than 60 per cent of the gross domestic product. Taxes are mainly on income, property, and on sales (value-added). Half of the proceeds are spent on public services such as healthcare, utilities, schools, police and defence. The other half is spent on various forms of distributive transfers back to households.

The revenue of taxes can be demonstrated in Figure 6.2, using the example of a tax on imported oil. Again, supply is a horizontal line, as in the case of oil imports in the monopoly example in Figure 6.1. The initial equilibrium is at p_c, q_c. Now a customs duty, t_1, is imposed on the oil in order to reduce oil use, and to obtain revenues for the state. The price will be increased to p_1, oil import will be reduced to q_1, and the revenue for the state will become $q_1 \times t_1$. If the toll is increased to t_2, the oil consumption will be reduced to q_2 and the tax revenue will be $q_2 \times t_2$. Note that the tax revenue is about the same as before, although the customs duty has been increased. The reason is that the tax base, that is, the amount of imported oil, is reduced because of the high price paid by the consumers. Indeed, the tax revenue varies as shown in the lower part of the diagram. If the state is aiming at a maximum tax revenue, the toll should be set at t_m. The figure shows how government revenue varies with different customs duties on a specific good.

The problem of a shrinking tax base (customs duty being a form of tax) with increased tax rates is a general phenomenon. If taxes on, for example, income are increased, the tax base (taxable income) will be reduced. At a high tax rate an increase in the tax rate will actually reduce the revenue

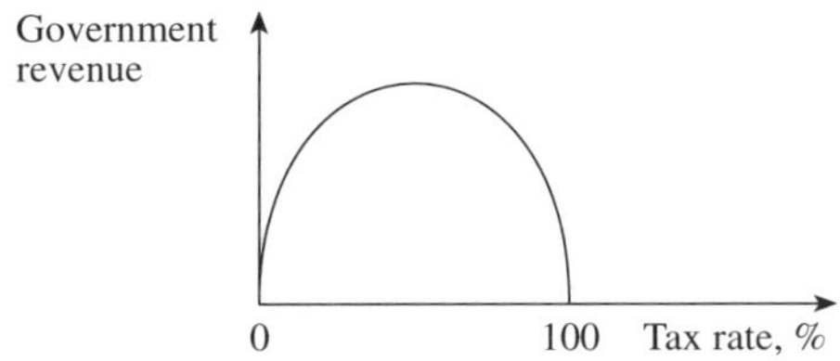

Figure 6.3 The revenue effect of raising taxes

because of the reduced base. This has been illustrated in a similar curve, named the 'Laffer curve' (Figure 6.3).

It has been argued that many welfare-oriented nations have reached the point where increases in tax rates will reduce the tax revenues. The burden of taxes, and their disturbance to the economy, has increased the interest in reduced public spending. A dilemma, of course, is that a smaller public budget reduces the possibilities for subsidies and public investments, including those meant for the environment. It also increases the interest in privatization, including legislation that makes the industry responsible for environmental impacts. This interest may, in fact, be a reason why, for example, the polluter pays principle and private handling of waste are widely accepted by governments. In other words, the environmental goals may, to

BOX 6.3 GREEN TAXES

The excess burden of taxes has increased the interest in '*green taxes*'. The idea is to expand the tax base by taxing, for example, traffic and energy instead of income. This may result in a double dividend. That is (i) a reduction in the excess burden of the income tax, and (ii) a reduction in environmental harm. The tax revenue of the state is supposed to be maintained by a reduction of the income tax that is balanced by the environmental tax. A problem, however, is that the income as a base for taxation is much larger and more stable than, for example, traffic or energy. In fact, a tax increase on traffic may not result in increased tax revenues at all. If an additional tax on traffic (gasoline) is successful from an environmental point of view, reducing traffic effectively, it may reduce the revenue from the tax on gasoline.

Source: Paulus (1995).

some extent, be a cover for a need for reduced public spending and privatization rather than due to environmental concern.

5. RECYCLING

An ecological critique of industrial society became influential in the 1970s. Waste came to be seen as a bad thing in its own right and should, thus, be minimized. Or, more radically, there would be no waste – all should be treated as valuable and thus reused in some form. Industry was criticized for its 'linear' way of thinking, that is, neglecting the 'circular' flow of resources necessary for a sustainable ecological environment.

The 'linear' economic system was characterized by a process of extraction of raw materials, production, distribution, consumption and finally by an accumulation of waste. Environmental problems were said to originate from linear use of resources, and the subsequent large amounts of waste. A sustainable (ecological) society requires, on the contrary, less extraction and more reuse of materials. Goods should be returned to the (eco)system by the closure of the loop; see Figure 6.4.

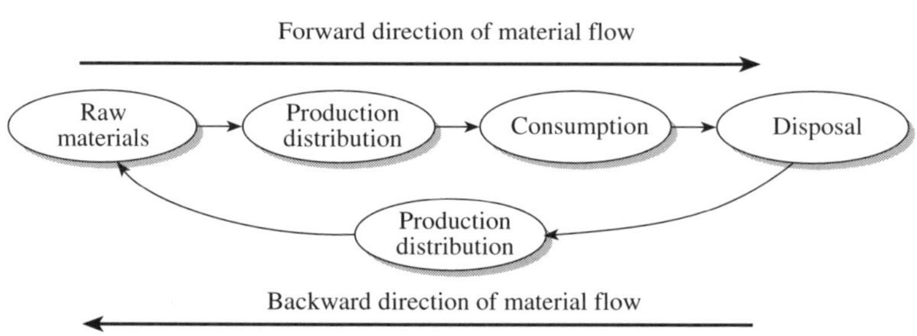

Figure 6.4 A product's lifecycle

The ecological view of production and waste has also resulted in a priority of waste treatment, as shown in Figure 6.5. An extended life of goods is supposed to be the best alternative. Next comes reuse of parts and recycling, while measures like incineration and landfill are the worst alternatives.

The circulation concept assumes that the biological, circular systems can also be applied as a norm for the production of goods and services. It is certainly true that all living organisms depend on each other in a complicated way. This has been carefully examined by biologists and ecologists. The research has inevitably been of huge importance for our understanding of the interdependence and fragility of ecosystems.

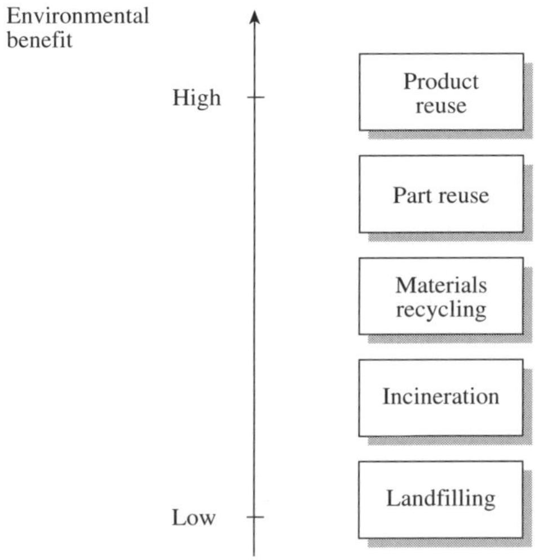

Figure 6.5 Priority of waste treatment options

The 'circular flow' concept became important in environmental policy and law. The economic arguments for regulated and subsidized recycling are weak, however. One 'environmental' argument for recycling is the need to limit the use of non-renewable resources such as metals and fossil fuels. It is argued that metals will be transformed and spread around after use as waste with low entropy, while fossil fuels are burnt and will never recur. Existing available sources are thus diminishing, which is supposed to run counter to a sustainable future. We have already discussed these ideas in Chapter 5, Section 7. The conclusion was that the reduction in non-renewable resources, and in the long run increasing prices of virgin materials and ores, is not the problem.

The environmental problems are, rather, related to negative externalities in connection with mining, burning of fuel, traffic, landfills and so on. These negative externalities should be treated in various ways depending on the circumstances. There is no reason why a specific form of waste treatment should, in general, be preferred to another. Yet a first simple rule of thumb could be that the cheapest treatment is also the least harmful. Low costs indicate a relatively small use of inputs. A careful choice of environmental policy measures requires an examination of potential market failures in various waste treatment systems.

Pollution is not a new phenomenon. In history pigs and horses polluted the roads, similar to car pollution in our time. Profit-maximizing producers and consumers recycle, burn or store in a cost-minimizing way depending

BOX 6.4 WASTE SORTING

People and local communities in Sweden devote much effort to sorting garbage so that paper and plastics can be recycled in a 'sustainable' manner. That is, paper should remain paper and plastics remain plastics. However, sorting, return and cleaning are costly, that is, they require resources like energy and manpower. An alternative is to burn paper and plastics directly and use the energy for heating. Sweden imports much oil for heating, so why not substitute oil by burning garbage? As long as the use of oil is reduced, there is no additional burden on the atmosphere. Hence, if there is no additional externality against a specific treatment, there is no economic reason for an environmental policy favouring a specific form of treatment.

Similarly, large amounts of waste are dumped today in landfills. Unsorted toxic waste in leaking landfill of course causes serious pollution. However, it is the leakage that is the problem, not the landfill *per se*. Landfills cannot generally be seen as inferior to recycling. Dry storage of non-leaking waste in, for example, deserts is sometimes relatively cheap, and may, indeed, save resources for the future. Concentrations of waste may, in a future with new technologies and new scarcity, become valuable resources.

on the relative cost of raw materials, capital and labour. Non-renewable resources like oil will diminish and may become hard to find. However, long before that occurs, increased scarcity will be reflected in prices that will modify the behaviour. Looking back a century or two, we find much more reuse of materials than today. The main economic reason was poverty, that is, scarcity of (available) resources and thus high prices relative to labour wages. Similarly, the main explanation as to why so many resources used today are based on virgin ores instead of reused or recycled materials is their cheapness. Once the increased scarcity of raw materials is realized in higher prices, billions of humans will be activated to save, substitute and find new resources. One of many ways of doing so is to recycle to a larger degree than today.

Once again, the environmental problem is related to negative externalities. Trash like paper and bottles may cause nuisance and damage that is not internalized in economic decisions. Smoke and waste in the form of polluted soil, water and air are dangerous for humans, as well as for the ecological system. Assignment and enforcement of property rights, regulations on waste treatment, charges and deposits may, therefore, be urgent measures.

Note further that the industry structure of the waste-handling industry could also be a market failure problem important to consider in environmental policy. Waste handling has in many areas developed from a small-scale to a large and concentrated industry. In some sectors of the industry there may be a concentration with monopoly power. The reason could be economies of scale, but also a strong lobby in the politically important waste-handling industry (see further Chapter 10, Section 4).

Finally, besides the economic arguments there are moral or ethical arguments in favour of recycling; the individual should be more caring, the 'throwaway' attitude should be abandoned, and nature should be more respected in industry. Economics has nothing to say about these statements *per se*. Personally we feel sympathetic to these general ideas. What we can do as economists is to make clear the economic consequences if the norms are implemented without reflection. Morals and ethics in relation to economics are further discussed in Chapter 8, Section 6.

6. CONCLUSIONS

Prices coordinate our extremely complex economy, with millions of buyers, sellers, goods and services. This is possible because prices reflect opportunity costs, that is, what the buyers and sellers have to give up, or can receive, in terms of resources and final goods. However, if the price does not include compensation to all affected parties there is a market failure – an external effect. Externalities mislead decision-makers in the economy as the prices do not reflect the full opportunity cost. Legal regulation, charges and subsidies may be used to limit the negative externalities and encourage positive externalities.

Monopoly causes another type of market failure. In a market with only one seller the profit of the firm will be maximized by setting the quantity lower than would have been the outcome in a competitive market. The price will then be higher, and it will differ from the opportunity costs. The high price also redistributes wealth in favour of the monopolist. Monopolies in the waste-handling industry may become important as the industry becomes a large-scale and concentrated industry.

The theory of market failures is applied to recycling. Profit-maximizing producers and consumers will recycle, burn or store in a cost-minimizing way depending on the relative cost of raw materials, capital and labour. The explanation as to why so many resources used today are based on virgin ores instead of reused or recycled materials is their cheapness. Once the increased scarcity of raw materials is realized in higher prices, humans will be motivated to save, substitute and find new resources. One of many ways of doing so is to recycle to a larger degree than today. The environmental problems arise when damage to humans or to the environment is not internalized in economic decisions.

Biological research on ecosystems is important. However, from our knowledge of ecosystems it cannot be concluded that waste should be treated in a specific 'natural' way. The proposed 'linear thinking' in industry is also misleading. All produced goods do not become waste. Resources like gold, silver, iron in scrapped rails and cars, paper and so on are recycled spontaneously. A large fraction of metals and chemicals used are treated at the lowest possible cost. Virgin sources are used instead of old recycled sources if they are relatively cheap, that is, they require few resources. If prices reflect opportunity costs and no considerable externalities exist, recycling would be a waste of resources.

Finally, it should be noted that resources are transformed not only into waste but also into new capital, physical as well as human, which is important for the future. This will be discussed further in Chapter 8.

FURTHER READING

Ayres, R.U. and Ayres, L.W. (1996), *Industrial Ecology: Towards Closing the Materials Cycle*, Cheltenham, UK and Brookfield, USA: Edward Elgar.

Baumol, W.J. (1977), 'On recycling as a moot environmental issue', *Journal of Environmental Economic Management*, **4**, 83–7.

Lipsey, R.G. and Courant, P.N. (1996), *Economics*, 11th edn, New York: HarperCollins.

Posner, R. (1975), 'The Social Costs of Monopoly and Regulation', *Journal of Political Economy*, **83** (4), 807–27.

Skogh, G. (1976), 'The Social Costs of Monopoly and Regulation: Some Comments', *Journal of Political Economy*, **84** (6), 1319–23.

Stiglitz, J.E. (2000), *Economics of the Public Sector*, 3rd edn, New York: Norton & Co.

7. Capital, investments, interests and risk

In the long run we are all dead.
J.M. Keynes

1. INTRODUCTION

Risk is important in our daily life, for example when we take decisions on food, transportation, education and investment. The formation of physical as well as human capital depends on risk-taking. The accumulation of capital is crucial for economic growth as well as for sustainable development. Environmental risks are of major importance. Indeed, prevention and precaution are two basic principles of environmental policy (see Chapter 2, Section 3). New knowledge brings new substances, techniques and processes that may be toxic, dangerous or stressing to the environment, especially in combination with other substances and so on. Lack of experience causes uncertainty about potential consequences. These issues will be discussed further in Part IV. An understanding of credit and risk is of importance, however, throughout the book.

That is why we introduce credit, investment and risk in this chapter. We start in Section 2 with a description of demand and supply of credit, disregarding risk. In Section 3 we introduce decision-making under risk. The treatment of risks in financial markets is thereafter briefly presented in Section 4. In Section 5 there is a short introduction to rational choice and risk perception. Section 6 introduces the valuation of risky assets and the economic value of property rights. In connection with that we discuss in Section 7 the value of legal certainty and the impact of expropriation for the protection of the environment. Conclusions are presented in Section 8.

2. DEMAND AND SUPPLY OF CREDIT

Needs, as well as benefits and costs, do not appear at the same time. The investment costs of a project usually come before the benefits, which may be spread over a long period of time. We must therefore consider how costs and benefits spread over time are valued in economics.

Let us start with a simple illustrative question: how will a benefit of 100 that will come up in a year from now be valued compared to an immediate benefit of, say, 90? In the marketplace the valuation will depend on interest and risk. Risk will be disregarded here, but studied shortly. Thus we neglect uncertainty about when costs and benefits occur. The market interest rate is assumed to be 10 per cent. There is no inflation. Saving 90 in a bank for a year will give $90 + 0.1 \times 90 = 99$ after one year. Consequently, it is better to accept 100 in one year than 90 today. The gain will be 1. We may also discount the 100 in one year from today's value by asking: which amount (x) is equivalent to 100 in one year? By solving $x + 0.1x = 100$, we obtain $x = 100/(1 + 0.1) = 90.91$. Hence the gain of taking 100 in the future will, in this calculation, be 0.91.[1]

Most individuals have a long-term reason for saving in that their earning capacity is concentrated within their productive years, while they have a need to consume during their entire life; see Figure 7.1. Children rely on their parents, and perhaps on public support, while the elderly cannot always rely on their grown-up children or public pensions. Hence there is a reason for saving during the productive years. In most modern societies, some of the redistribution of income over a lifetime has been appropriated by social welfare systems. The government taxes the productive segment of the population and transfers part of the taxed income in the form of pensions back to the segment of the population that is retired, and to the young in the form of schooling, day care, and child allowances.

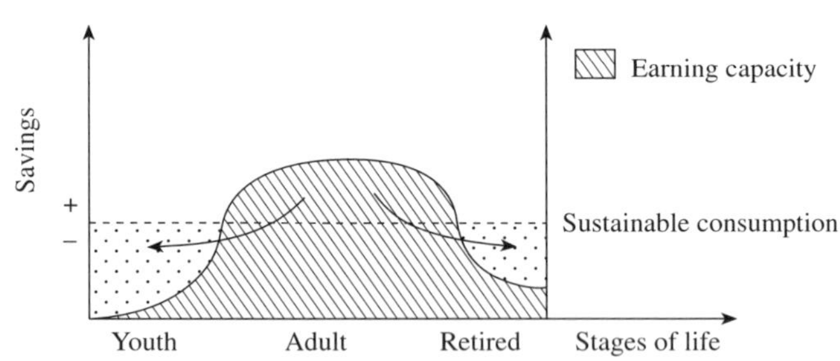

Figure 7.1 Lifecycle earning capacity

There are, of course, many other reasons for saving, for example to obtain money for durable goods. Savings in bank accounts, bonds, investments in shares and so on constitute the supply of credit on the capital market.

A reason for demanding credit is the expected benefits of investments. The problem is that costly investments must be made in advance, while the expected benefits come later. Graphically, this can be illustrated as in Figure

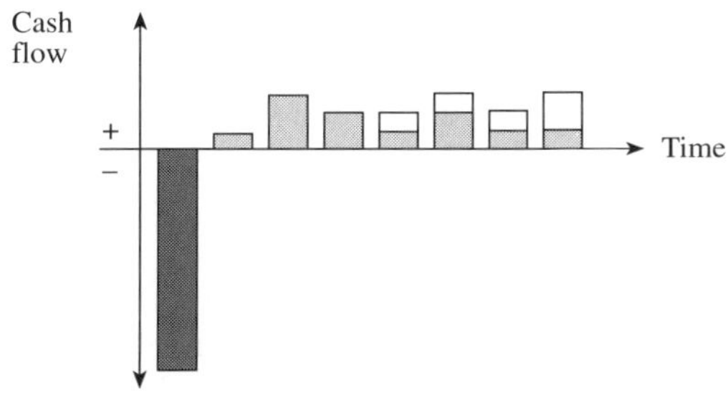

Figure 7.2 Cash flow of a project

7.2 by showing the sharp negative cash flow at the beginning of a project, for which borrowing may be needed (dark grey area). Thereafter, there will be an expected positive cash flow, which (it is hoped) will enable the entrepreneur to repay her debt (light grey) and retain a profit (white).

The interest rate is determined by the demand and supply of credit. The supply of credit can be expected to have an upward slope, as *S* in Figure 7.3; that is, at higher interests there will be more savings and thus more money to borrow. Accordingly, the demand curve is downward sloping, as *D* in Figure 7.3. The reason is that lower interest makes more investments profitable, and thus the demand for credit increases. Bargaining forces the price to equilibrium, which gives the market interest i_f and the total credit q_e in Figure 7.3.

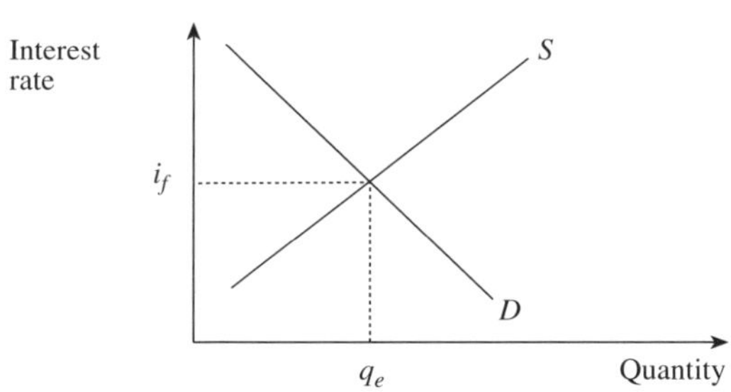

Figure 7.3 Market determination of risk-free interest rate

In a competitive equilibrium, all borrowers and lenders are faced with the same interest rate (disregarding administrative costs and risk). The marginal borrower must pay the opportunity cost of money today versus tomorrow. In other words, the interest rate is the compensation to consumers if they postpone consumption.

3. RISK

In the illustrations above we have assumed that the future stream of benefits and costs is known. In reality, of course, it is not possible to be certain about the future. All judgements are based on belief. Business as well as ownership is, thus, risky.

Risk and uncertainty are also an environmental matter. Indeed, a reason for the huge unsolved environmental problems of our time is the introduction of new substances, techniques and processes without full knowledge of the consequences. On the other hand, some trial and error is unavoidable, even if thorough investigations are undertaken according to the precautionary principle.

We will come back to these fundamental matters later. Here, we shall limit ourselves to the question of how risk is priced in the market.

The starting-point in economic risk analysis is gambling. How should a set of probabilistic outcomes be valued? For example, throw a die. You take for granted that each face has a probability of 1/6. Assume that you are paid a dollar for each eye on the face that appears. How much are you willing to pay for the right to participate in the gamble and throw the die? First, let us assume that you are *risk-neutral*. This means that you set the value of the gamble equal to its mathematically *expected value*, *EV*.

$$EV = 1/6 \times 1 + 1/6 \times 2 + 1/6 \times 3 + 1/6 \times 4 + 1/6 \times 5 + 1/6 \times 6 = 3.5$$

Hence, if you have to pay less than 3.5 for the right to the gamble, you will accept the terms and expect a profit. You are indifferent if it is an actuarially fair game, that is, if the cost is equal to 3.5, and thus the expected gain is zero.

A decision based on *EV* is rational, profit-maximizing behaviour that can be expected, especially when (i) gambling takes place repeatedly and (ii) potential losses are small in relation to the assets of the gambler (firm). The reason is the statistical *law of large numbers* that states that if an event happens independently with a certain probability, p, in each of a large number of instances, the proportion of cases in which the event is realized approaches p. This means that if you throw the die in the example above a large number of times, you will on average gain 3.5 each time. Similarly, if you in your business repeatedly take independent, risky actions, they will in the end give a return according to the *EV*.

If the potential loss of a gamble is large in relation to the assets of the firm or an individual, we would expect *risk-aversion*, that is, an unwillingness to accept a fair gamble. Assume, for instance, that an individual will gain or lose 100 with the probability of 2/3 and 1/3, respectively. Then, $EV = 2/3 \times 100 - 1/3 \times 100 = 33.33$.

Suppose the individual is invited to participate in the gamble at a cost of 20 but does not accept due to risk-aversion. The underlying reason may be that a loss of 100 would cause a larger loss in utility than the gain of 100. In other words, a reduction in wealth is more serious than a corresponding gain. Indeed, a loss may be catastrophic, while the utility of affluence may be marginal.

Consequently, risk-averse individuals are willing to pay more than the *EV* for the avoidance of large potential losses. Most people seem to be risk-averse, which opens the door to insurance business. By insuring a large number of uncorrelated, independent risks, an insurer can, due to the law of large numbers, eliminate the risk. Suppose, for example, that the probability of a fire that would destroy homes valued at $100 000 each is 0.0005 over a year time-span. For the individual homeowner, the loss is zero or 100 000 each year. However, among one million homes covered by an insurer, we can be (almost) sure that the number of destroyed homes will be close to 500, and thus the compensations paid by the insurer will be close to $50 million. In other words, the variance is small due to the law of large numbers. The *actuarial fair premium* for coverage of fire in one home, disregarding administrative costs and profit, is equal to the average, or expected, accident cost of $50. The risk-averse homeowner who fears a catastrophe is, by definition, willing to pay more. Hence trade with a risk-neutral insurer could be mutually beneficial.

4. FINANCIAL MARKETS

Risk-aversion of firms can be explained as an extension of the individual risk-aversion of the owners, and by their access, or not, to financial markets. A *closely held firm*, that is, a firm with no access to financial markets, has less ability than a *widely held firm*, that is, a firm with access to financial markets, to benefit from diversification via the market.

Diversification can be undertaken internally in a firm, or externally via financial markets. An example of internal *diversification* is a ship-owner who employs several small ships instead of one large one, or a peasant who plants various crops to limit the risk of famine. Internal diversification is normally costly, primarily due to the loss of economies of scale. A better option for the owners of a widely held firm is, according to portfolio theory: (i) to utilize economies; (ii) to maximize expected value; and (iii) to diversify through the holding of a mixed portfolio of financial assets and liabilities.

The willingness to pay for risk-reduction (reduced variance in the outcomes) is used in portfolio theory as a proxy for risk-aversion. A well-known result is that specific, independent, or uncorrelated risks can be diversified away, while the contribution to the total risk caused by the co-variances cannot be diversified.

A general result of the portfolio theory is that the best a widely held corporation can do is to maximize expected value. This is also true if the shareholders are risk-averse, because they can diversify the risk by holding shares in many different firms. *Systemic risks*, on the other hand, that hit the entire financial market cannot be diversified away within the firm, or by the shareholders.

A most diversified portfolio, usually called the *market portfolio*, contains all stocks traded.[2] The market portfolio eliminates diversifiable risks. Yet it contains the systemic macro-risks that hurt the entire market, for example inflation, cyclical spins and taxes. Movements on the stock exchange mirror the variance of systemic risks in the market portfolio.

Because systemic risks cannot be diversified, and because actors in the financial markets are for the most part risk-averse, there is a price attached to risk. To identify the price of risk, we can compare an investment on the stock exchange with a fixed-interest government bond that gives a stable, guaranteed rate of interest (i_f). This is usually seen as the rate of interest needed as compensation for delaying consumption, as discussed above.

The risk-free interest of a secure bond is in many countries around 2–4 per cent in an economy without inflation. The risks and returns on the stock markets are normally larger. In many countries the expected return or interest on the market portfolio is around 10–15 per cent. The return or interest on capital may, thus, be divided into two parts. First, there is the safe return, i_f, of on average 3 per cent, and, second, the additional compensation for the business risk, i_r, of roughly another 10 per cent.

Figure 7.4 shows the relation between interest and risk. The vertical axis shows interest or rate of return, while the horizontal axis shows the level of risk, that is, the variance in return. On the vertical axis we have indicated the no-risk secure bond interest, i_f. We have also marked the risk of the market

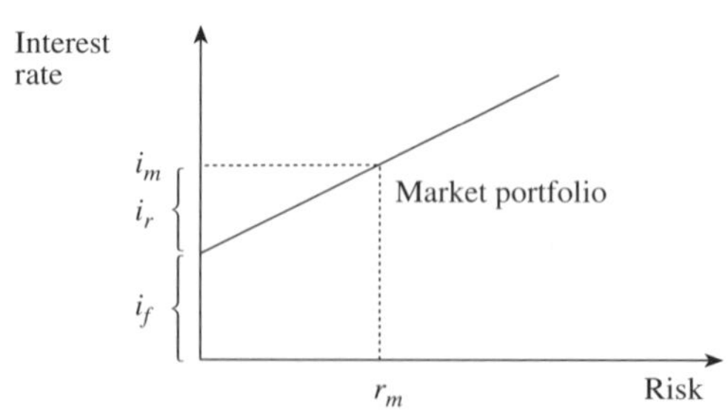

Figure 7.4 The effect of risk on the interest rate

portfolio, r_m, and the corresponding return, i_m. The return, i_m, includes the return, i_f, equivalent to the return of a safe state bond, and the compensation for the risk of the market portfolio, i_r.

Through a combination of safe bonds and the market portfolio, the individual can choose an interest and risk level according to individual preference. Risk-averse individuals will choose a large portion of safe bonds. The risk-lover, on the other hand, prefers more, but riskier, return. Risky positions to the right of the market portfolio can be obtained by loans used for investments in the market portfolio. Hence all combinations of interest and risk-taking illustrated by the straight line are available to individuals.

5. PERCEPTION OF RISK

The economic man of the standard economic model is informed about all goods and prices. In risk calculations and decisions this actor or agent is assumed to have access to probabilities and potential outcomes. Nevertheless, it is evident that humans do not have access to all information, and the capacity to elaborate and evaluate information is limited. This limited capacity motivates the assumption of '*bounded rationality*', that is, the intention remains to be rational and utility-maximizing; but as the human mind has limits, it is necessary to economize on information. The individual, therefore, suppresses, filters and focuses information, and acts according to simplified rules of thumb.

Human behaviour in a world with limited information, transaction costs and bounded rationality gives a picture of the economic decision-maker as a '*contractual man*' who relies on rules, customs, reputation and relationships instead of the perfectly rational, informed and self-contained decision-maker. The contractual man is certainly closer to reality. Note, however, that this is not to say that the model of the economic man is wrong or misleading. This assumption remains a useful simplification in traditional price theory that studies well-functioning markets.

Limited human capability and cognition are of particular importance when it comes to judging risks, especially very low-probability risks with disastrous consequences. Nuclear accidents and other major environmental catastrophes of low probability are examples. Humans tend either to neglect the risk altogether, that is, to regard the situation as 'safe', or to consider the risk to be a 'reality'. And if the risk is considered, the probability is usually overestimated. It appears as if humans are able to distinguish between relatively small probabilities, but when it comes to probabilities of less than one in 10 000 or 100 000 (which is, indeed, a remarkable capability), the risk is simply 'very small' or 'negligible'. Risks of a very small probability, say, one in a million or hundred million, can simply not be distinguished. Hence, if it is considered real, it is just 'very small', which means something like 'one in 100 000 or less', which results in a systematic overestimation of these small, but very important, probabilities.

This bounded rationality may explain phenomena such as the difference of opinion about nuclear power. A part of the population regards nuclear power as 'safe', that is, neglects or suppresses the risk, and is, thus, in favour of nuclear power, while many others consider the potential disaster, but overestimate the very small probability of a meltdown, with the consequence that they are against nuclear power.

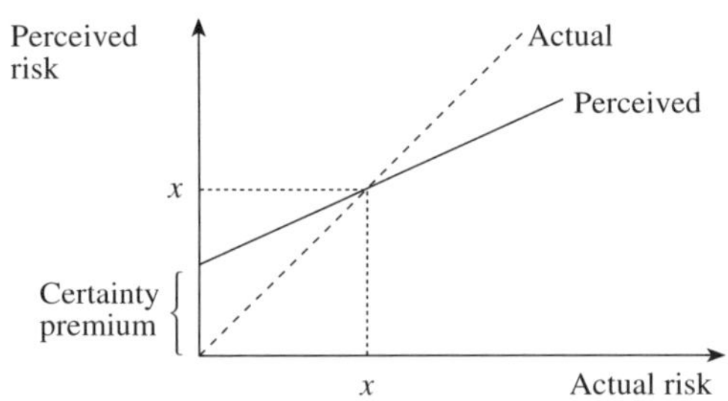

Figure 7.5 Actual and perceived risk

Figure 7.5 presents interesting results of psychological research. On the horizontal axis we measure the actual risks (probabilities) of different events (diseases, earthquakes and so on) and on the vertical axis we measure the perceived risk. Experimental surveys indicate that the risk we perceive differs systematically from the actual risk. We tend to overestimate the very small risks and to underestimate larger (familiar) risks.

Figure 7.5 illustrates overestimation of probabilities smaller than x, and underestimation of probabilities larger than x. If the perceived risk were on average equal to the actual risk, the lines would coincide. The more divergent the lines, the more the perceived risk differs from the actual risk.

The systematic inaccuracy becomes especially pronounced when the risk approaches zero. Note that at zero risk, there is a discontinuity down to zero perceived risk. Hence there is a distinct difference in the risk felt at very small probabilities, and at no probability at all. Indeed, research has indicated that humans tend to feel relief if they can neglect the very small risk by regarding it to be zero. In other words, the individual is willing to pay a '*certainty premium*' for being able to neglect a very small risk. This phenomenon seems to be most important in politics; that is, the public is pleased if the politicians can make it believable that various activities are 'safe'. In reality, risks will always be present.

Another interesting phenomenon is that individuals tend to underestimate risks that they are familiar with or have accepted. They are also inclined to underestimate risks that they can influence. This may explain why risks of smoking, food, drugs, car driving, sports, and poor indoor atmosphere are widely accepted although they are more dangerous than many risks about which people are much more concerned.

Furthermore, the media seem to have an important impact on the risks that are in focus and, thus, considered important. An explanation may, again, be the limited capacity of the human brain. A low-probability risk, like the 'mad cow disease' headlined in the media, is noted as a possible reality. The disastrous possible consequences are imaginable, but not the low probability. Hence there is a systematic misjudgement of the risk until the media focuses on something else that represses the first worry.

BOX 7.1 RADON

Radioactive radon exists naturally in the ground and in building materials. Many individuals in, for example the USA and Sweden are exposed to doses that may cause lung cancer. The risk is large, especially for exposed individuals who also are smokers. Radon is easy to detect. Ventilation and other radon-reducing activities in houses with more than 400 Bq/m^3 (becquerels per cubic metre) are estimated to save 150 lives per year in Sweden. The highest permitted exposure in Sweden is 200 Bq/m^3, but it is not enforced. The house-owner is responsible for damage but he has no duty to measure the radioactivity and is not forced to make precautions. Dangerous exposure of 400 Bq/m^3 is still frequent.

When the high risk of radon became obvious in the 1980s, the US authorities expected strong reactions and a huge demand for investments in sanitation and new buildings. However, the problem was rather the opposite. Individuals tended to repress and forget about the danger.

Similar reactions are common for unhealthy food, smoking, drugs, traffic, and earthquakes, which seem to be accepted in spite of the danger. Other risks, such as BSE (bovine spongiform encephalopathy – mad cow disease), contaminated drugs, and small amounts of toxic substances in water and food, which are of very little danger, create large headlines in the media and often irrational reactions by politicians, responsible authorities and the public.

6. NET PRESENT VALUE AND PROPERTY RIGHTS

6.1 Present Value

Given the discount rate – including the market return on a safe asset, i_f, plus the risk premium required for the asset or project in question (i_r) – it is possible to calculate the *net present value, NPV*, of a project. The *NPV* is the current discounted value of a future income. In the example above, we had an income of 100 a year from now and a discount rate of 10 per cent. The *NPV* of this future income is 100/(1 + 0.1) = 90.91. An income of 100 in two years is, in the same way, today worth 90.91(1 + 0.1) = $100/(1 + 0.1)^2$ = 82.64. If there is a project giving a return of 100 each year during the lifetime (t) of the project, the *NPV* is calculated as:

$$NPV = \frac{100}{(1+i)} + \frac{100}{(1+i)^2} + \frac{100}{(1+i)^3} + \ \dots \ + \frac{100}{(1+i)^t}$$

More generally, the *NPV* of a project is calculated as:

$$NPV = \sum_{t=1}^{T} \frac{(B_t - C_t)}{(1+i)^t},$$

where B_t is the benefit at time t, and C_t is the cost at time t. i is the discount rate.

For the project, the expected lifetime is denoted as t = 0,1 .... T. Here, 0 represents the present starting-point of the project, and T the ending point. For an infinite project, $T = \infty$. During its lifetime the project will generate an expected stream of benefits and costs. The sum of the *NPV* of these benefits and costs equals the *NPV* of the entire project.

If the expected return is constant (for example 100) and the expected lifetime is eternity, the formula is simplified to:

$$NPV = \frac{100}{i}$$

The *NPV* of the project equals the value of the assets or project on the market. An investor is, at the margin, willing to pay *NPV* for the asset, because it is what he can expect as an alternative use of his money, for example in a bank account or by purchasing a government bond.

If the project is a firm with an expected stream of future profit, the value of the firm (or its shares) equals the present value of the profits. The project may, of course, also be private property, for example land, machinery, or equipment, with expected returns.

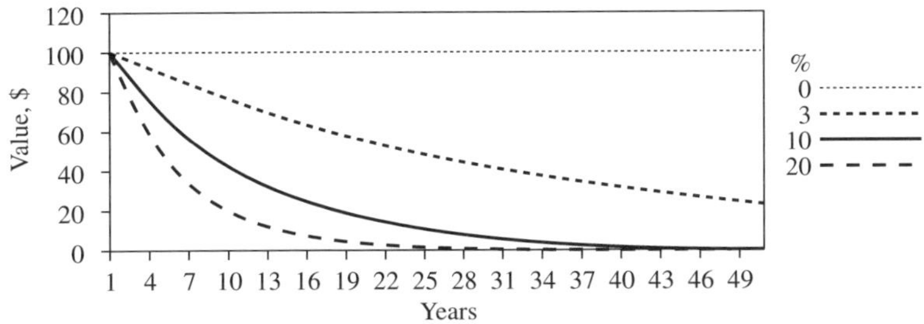

Figure 7.6 The NPV of $100 calculated for different interest rates and years

The graphs in Figure 7.6 represent the *NPV* of 100 that is gained once in coming years (until 50 years in the future) at different discount rates. The straight line at the top illustrates the extreme, with a discount rate equal to zero, which means that the value of a future income will be the same as an income of the same size today. More realistic discount rates for, for example, safe assets such as government bonds is, as noted, somewhere between 2 and 4 per cent (neglecting compensation for inflation), while risky assets such as shares require a return of 10–15 per cent on the market.

From Figure 7.6 we can make two interesting observations. First, the impact on the *NPV* of benefits and costs in the long term is strongly reduced at low discount rates as well. An income of 100 in 50 years has a present value of around 20 if the discount rate is 3 per cent, while the value is negligible at discount rates of 10 per cent and more. Indeed, benefits and costs 25 years from now at high discount rates are of very little importance for the *NPV*. This means that the economic valuation of effects beyond the first two or three decades is practically nil.

Second, the expected riskiness of a project is of great importance for the valuation of long-term effects. The risk premium is relatively large and, thus, the future value is rapidly discounted if the project is risky.

6.2 The Value of Property Rights and Legal Certainty

In Chapter 3 we examined how exclusive property rights may solve the tragedy of the commons. Private property rights, including the right to the residual, create incentives to care for the property and to undertake long-term investments. Here, we see that this conclusion must be modified. If the profit of the property is uncertain, the owner will become 'short-sighted' and disregard long-term effects. Figures 3.2–3.4 assume that the catch equals the growth of the stock. This makes sustainable catches in all future periods possible. However, if discounting is included in the model, it will be profitable to catch more of the flow and, thus, reduce the long-term stock and the sustainable catch. Particularly if the discount rate is high, the stock may come closer to depletion.

The uncertainty of the return on a project or property may be due to business risks of various types and natural risks such as earthquakes and storms. The risk may also be due to the uncertain public protection of private property. The property may be stolen, heavily taxed, or confiscated by the government. Consequently, if the risk of losing the property is large, there may be a tendency to exploit the resource more quickly, and/or to invest in some safer asset like gold, or a foreign bank account.

The fact that property owners under unstable business and political situations have overexploited scarce environmental resources and invested in safer assets has sometimes been interpreted as a failure of capitalism and of private property rights. However, from what was said above, we can conclude the opposite – the overexploitation may be caused by the absence of specification and protection of property rights.

We can also identify the important difference between taxation and confiscation. Taxes are foreseeable reductions of, for example, profits, wealth, or income. If there is a flat tax rate on income, s, the *NPV* will be

$$NPV_{tax} = (1-s)\sum \frac{(B_t - C_t)}{(1+i_f+i_r)^t}$$

Assume that the tax rate s = 10 per cent. This will give a reduction in *NPV* to 90 per cent, and the state will receive a tax revenue of 0.1 *NPV*. Confiscation of property, on the other hand, is an arbitrary or random taking of property. Now, assume that in order to cover its spending, the state randomly confiscates 10 per cent of all *NPV*. This would give the same revenue to the state as the tax. If the individuals were risk-neutral, they would be indifferent to taxation and confiscation. However, we expect them to be risk-averse. Thus they are willing to pay to avoid risk, especially if the potential confiscation is large relative to the wealth of the individual. The unwillingness to take risks can be represented by an additional political risk premium, i_p. Thus, at political risks the *NPV* is reduced to

$$NPV_{tax/risk} = (1-s)\sum \frac{(B_t - C_t)}{(1+i_f+i_r+i_p)^t}$$

Confiscation reduces the *NPV* as the tax does, that is, by $(1–s)$. In addition, however, the uncertainty of the risk-averse property owner will reduce the *NPV* in the same way as the premium for other risks. Note that $(1 + i_f + i_r + i_p)$

grows with the power of t. Hence, if the property owners are risk-averse and unable to escape the risk, this will strongly reduce the value of property, as well as the willingness to make long-term investments.

Therefore, a wise governor who wishes to collect money for the treasury without seriously disturbing the economy establishes and maintains *legal certainty*, that is, applies laws based on long-term principles, and taxes according to clear rules, instead of using arbitrary legislation or confiscation. Indeed, a prime function of the state is to maintain legal order. Note that this is not to say that politics in general should be conservative. A long-term stable tax structure and a legal system that guarantees property rights do not hinder legislation following constitutional rules. It must be possible to change obsolete laws, which is further discussed in the next section on takings.

Figure 7.6 shows further that effects for future generations (including long-term environmental damage) are *not* considered in the market economy. The discount rate depends on factors such as the expected return on investments, the need to redistribute income over the lifecycle, and uncertainty pertaining to various risks in society. No one acts on behalf of persons living more than 100 years in the future. 'In the long run we are all dead', as stated in the citation at the head of the chapter.

This pessimistic conclusion may be somewhat modified, however. In the calculations above we assumed that the net income is constant and equal to 100 each year. If we expect an increase in the price of the asset due to its increasing scarcity, the depreciation may be counteracted by the price increase. For instance, if a wetland of low value today is expected to be most valuable in the future due to the rare animals living there, it may have a high potential *NPV* motivating investments in preserving the wetland. However, the uncertainty of future prices makes investments most risky. The general conclusion must thus be that the market does not consider far-ahead effects. This is obviously an important contrast with the legal–political notion of 'sustainable development', which forces policy to take the interests of future generations into account. The implications of this conflict between the present and the future will be discussed further in the next chapter.

7. TAKINGS

7.1 Expropriation

It is fundamental to an economic system based on individual ownership and freedom of contract that the owner is compensated for infringements or encroachments on her rights. Such compensations occur at voluntary exchange. The right to compensation for damage or infringement and confiscation of rights by the public authorities is usually regulated in expropriation law. Full compensation in accordance with the *indifference principle* has the merit that changes are only undertaken as long as they do not harm the owner of the property.

If no or incomplete compensations are granted, problems arise. One is that the right to ownership becomes diffuse if compensation does not occur, or if compensation occurs arbitrarily. The right to compensation identifies the contents of the right to ownership. The owner's responsibility for costs defines in the same manner her duty toward other holders of rights; see Chapter 4. Another problem is the lack of legal certainty. Risk-averse individuals prefer foreseeable taxes or clear rules.

When the collectivization of land occurs, for example for roads or national parks, the landowner may accept the compensation freely. However, the particulars of the location may cause difficulties. First, the specific location means that the owner normally values the property more highly than the market price – otherwise, the land would be sold or offered for sale. The owner's valuation of the property may depend on relatives in the vicinity, deeply rooted customs, and so on. The price at which the owner is indifferent, that is, the lowest price the owner would voluntarily accept for giving up the property is usually called the '*reservation price*'. The reservation price is normally higher than the market price. It may, however, be impossible to estimate in more detail.

A second difficulty is that location can give the property owner a particularly advantageous position in negotiations, which in turn gives the owner a motive not to reveal her reservation price. Assume, for example, that a road is going to be built by the community. All necessary land has been bought and the owners have accepted the compensation offered, with the exception of one lot that is privately owned. The owner refuses to sell, with the motivation that it has a high personal reservation value. Regardless of whether the statement is true or false, the owner can act strategically to get a high compensation. If the owner can stop the road investment, the bargaining span is determined by the difference between the reservation price and the total worth to the community for the road to come into existence. Great negotiation leeway has a tendency to bring with it drawn-out negotiations. Besides exaggerating the reservation price, property owners along a planned stretch of road may try to out-wait others in order to be last and, therefore, in a position to negotiate a better price.

These conditions may motivate forced taking, that is, expropriation. Through expropriation, however, one is forced to an arbitrary estimate of the property's value. How high should the compensation be? Because the reservation price is normally higher than the market price for comparable properties, the compensation should be higher than the market price. Lower compensation has a distributive effect to the disadvantage of the expropriated owner. Since the owner has a reason for exaggerating her reservation price, she may be motivated to proceed from an equivalent market price with some addition beyond that.

There are examples of jurisdictions that compensate property owners to a higher level than the market price. However, it appears to be an exception rather than the common rule. The market value, sometimes with a reduction, seems to be the standard. One reason may be the problem of estimating the reservation price and the excess burden of taxes; see Chapter 6, Section 4. Note, however, that compensation below the reservation price imposes a risk on property owners who may become expropriated, which could be avoided by more generous compensation rules.

BOX 7.2 THE FREDIN CASE CONTINUED

In the Fredin case (Box 2.9), the European Court of Human Rights tested whether interference with a private property right to achieve environmental objectives was proportionate or disproportionate in the context of Article 1 of the first Protocol of the European Convention on Human Rights. The Court held that environmental protection measures could, in fact, override private property rights, which may seem contrary to Article 1 of the first Protocol.

However, details of the case make the outcome understandable. In 1973 the Swedish Environmental Protection Agency won the legal right to protect environmentally important areas from exploitation. Of special interest were natural sandy hills formed when Scandinavia was covered by ice (rullstensåsar). The law withdrawing the right of exploitation came into force ten years later, in 1983. The reason for the postponement was presumably to avoid losses of investments already made and to stop new exploitations. In spite of this, in the late 1970s Fredin bought a sandy hill and made considerable investments to make exploitation profitable. In 1983 the Environmental Protection Agency forced Fredin to stop the exploitation without compensation. Fredin then turned to the European Court and claimed compensation for investments made as well as for loss of expected profits. Fredin lost his case not only in the European Court but also in Swedish courts and received no compensation.

The reasoning so far assumes that the damage to the property owner is independent of actions taken by the owner himself. Full coverage of the damage means no risk to the owner, which may result in risky investments or carelessness. For instance, an owner knowing that there will be full compensation may invest in a swimming pool regardless of a city plan indicating a considerable risk of expropriation. Many jurisdictions, therefore, require the victim to take actions to diminish the damage. Otherwise the compensation may be reduced or withdrawn. The economics of such rules will be examined in some detail in relation to liability law in Chapter 14.

7.2 Regulatory Takings

It is possible to expropriate a portion of the property, or only certain rights, such as the right of use or to dispose. For instance, some outsider may be given the right to lay down electric cables, the public may be given the right to trespass, the right to cut trees may be withdrawn for the protection of endangered birds, and so on. Similarly, there may be limitations on the freedom to contract, for example the right to sell land to foreigners, or developers may be outlawed or restricted.

Such regulations of rights to use or contract are, in many jurisdictions, not compensated at all. Is that reasonable from an efficiency point of view? Above we concluded that the wise ruler acts as an insurer of the citizens by charging foreseeable taxes instead of relying on arbitrary confiscation. Not to compensate property owners functions as random taking, which causes uncertainty that reduces the utility of the citizens, and the value of property in general.

Yet many states do not pay compensation for losses due to regulations. One explanation is the excess burden of taxes. That is, compensation must be paid through taxes and taxes are costly to collect and disturb the price mechanism, particularly in countries with an already high taxation rate, see Chapter 6, Section 4. The interest in limiting taxation and the benefits of compensation must thus be considered. Another problem with regulatory takings is that it may be difficult to evaluate the loss due to a regulation of a right. How shall one, for example, evaluate the loss to owners if they are forced to make their property accessible to hikers? Similar problems exist, for example, in the prohibition from felling trees or cultivating land because of the historical significance of the site, and so on. This may motivate some threshold on the losses before any compensation is paid.

Some measures may also reduce the damage to property-owners, and thus lead to fewer claims for compensation. One is to postpone the implementation, as in the Fredin case in Box 7.2. Another is, in the case of trespass, to give fenced land relatively strong protection. Fencing may be costly to the owner but it shows where the owner allows no intrusion. The fence indicates, on the other hand, a freedom to others to trespass beyond the fencing. The property owner must, therefore, weigh the costs of fencing against the advantages of avoiding intrusion.

The evaluation of regulations is even more complicated by the fact that limitations on owners' rights can increase the value of the property. Urban planning means restrictions on the owner's rights. For instance, a certain type of industry may not, according to the plan, be allowed in the area. Yet the limitation does not have to mean a loss to the property owners, even if compensation does not occur. If the alternative is extensive rights – that is, freedom to develop the property, in combination with other property-owners' right to compensation for harm inflicted – there may be never-ending negotiations and thus no development at all. Here zones, as in the examples above, can mean an opening that increases the value of everyone's property.

A third explanation as to why compensation is not paid is the influence of political pressure groups. For instance, an environmental group may argue that a certain forest should be protected and, thus, not cut down. Property owners claim full compensation. However, the state does not want to spend the necessary means. The environmental group therefore counters that the ecosystem of the forest has its own environmental right. In other words, the owners of the forest never had the right to cut it down. If the environmentalists are successful in convincing the authorities, the forest may be saved without compensation to the landowners. That may be seen as a victory. Note, however, that the state's unwillingness to pay for the protection of the forest by paying owners via taxes indicates that the public is not willing to pay for the environment. If the public, via the political system, were willing to pay for the protection of the ecosystem (including the excess burden of taxes), the compensation could be financed through taxes, and the forest would be saved without conflict with the property owners. In the case of 'environmental' rights without compensation to the owners the forest is also saved, but at the cost of confiscation. The uncertainty of property owners regarding future 'environmental' takings would cause a social loss in terms of legal uncertainty. All in all, the ethical question of the 'right of the ecosystem' boils down to a question of who shall pay, the owners or the taxpayers.

8. CONCLUSIONS

The economic literature on risk is for various reasons of interest to environmental policy. First, in the theory of decision-making with risk it is assumed that individuals assess probabilities of various outcomes and make rational choices according to their attitude towards risk (normally assumed to be risk-aversion). This approach is most important in cost–benefit analysis (CBA) and in the theory of insurance that will be examined in more detail later.

Second, bounded rationality and perception of risks by individuals is important. Individuals tend in general to behave as the model of rational choice predicts, but there are important exceptions. Individuals tend to overestimate low-probability risks and underestimate risks that they are familiar with and can influence. Low-probability risks with catastrophic consequences such as major environmental hazards tend to either be overestimated or completed neglected. Systematic misjudgements of risks have important economic and political consequences for environmental policy issues, which we will discuss in more detail below.

Third, the financial analysis of credit markets and trade with risky assets is important because it illuminates valuation over time. In this literature it is common to separate the return on safe assets (interest on government bonds) and the additional 'risk premium' for risky assets like stocks. It is thereby possible to identify the social cost of riskiness due to industrial risks and political risks. Political risks include the risk of taxation, regulation and confiscation that may be important in relation to environmental policy.

The indifference principle, that is, the rule that owners harmed by, for example, expropriation should be fully compensated, reduces political risks and upholds legal certainty. Property values are hereby maintained, which is fundamental in a market-economic-property-rights-based system. Compensation is, however, not always complete. One reason is that it is costly to the government, at least in the short run. Another reason for less than complete compensation is that the owner harmed by expropriation can reduce the harm by own measures. A third reason, especially in relation to regulations, is that the loss to the owner is small or hard to calculate.

Finally, discounting of future costs and benefits means that economic consequences for generations living 100 years or more ahead are not considered in economic valuations. The reason is that economics takes individual preferences of people living today as the basis of analysis, and the interest rate reflects their preferences over time as revealed by the market. None the less, economics can estimate the willingness to pay today for monuments, art and rare species with a presumed value for future generations.

NOTES

1. The reason for the difference in gains (1 or 0.91) is the point of comparison.
2. One may think of the risk of a mutual fund that includes all shares in the market in relation to their value on the market.

FURTHER READING

Blume, L.E. and Rubinfeld, D.L. (1984), 'Compensation for takings: an economic analysis', *California Law Review*, **72**, 569–628. Reprinted in *Research in Law and Economics*, **10** (1987), 53–103.

Brealy, R.A. and Myers, S.C. (2000), *Principles of Corporate Finance*, 6th edn, New York: Irwin/McGraw-Hill.

Epstein, R.A. (1985), *Takings: private property and the power of eminent domain*, Cambridge, MA: Harvard University Press.

Kahneman, D., Slovic, P. and Tversky, A. (1982), *Judgment under Uncertainty: Heuristics and Biases*, Cambridge, Cambridge University Press.

Michelman, F.I. (1967), 'Property, utility and fairness: comments on the ethical foundation of "just compensation" law', *Harvard Law Review*, **80**, 1165–58.

Olson, M. (1982), *The Rise and Decline of Nations*, New Haven, CT: Yale University Press.

Slovic, P. (2000), *The Perception of Risk*, London: Earthscan.

Viscusi, W.L. (1998), *Rational Risk Policy*, Oxford: Clarendon Press.

8. Sustainable growth

The greatest improvement in the productive powers ... seems to have been the effects of division of labour.
Adam Smith, *The Wealth of Nations*, ch 1.

1. INTRODUCTION

The economic development during the twentieth century could hardly have been foreseen a hundred years ago. The world population has increased from one billion to six billions. Many people are still starving, but food supply has increased as measured by production per consumer, grain prices and so on. Income is certainly unevenly distributed, but has increased in most countries around the world. Life expectancy at birth has increased from around 40 years to an average of 64 years in 1994 in the poor countries and 70 years in the rich countries, partly due to improved agriculture, sanitation and medicine. In most wealthy countries like the USA, Japan and Germany the real per capita income increased twenty-fold during the century.

Most governments aim at furthering economic growth. One reason is, of course, that people ask for more money, better healthcare, increased safety and so on. Many political leaders certainly believe that industrialization, and growth in production and income, result in improvements for humanity, both in the short and in the long run. In fact, most people today have higher incomes, live longer, and are better educated than before. Yet, even if politicians do not believe in wealth as happiness, they may still aim at economic growth. That is because the growth rate indicates the level of economic activity in a nation. Growth ceases in a time of recession, which causes unemployment, bankruptcies, less ability to repay interest and mortgages, and, hence, less willingness to invest. Recession also reduces tax revenues and, thus, the ability to fulfil political programmes.

An environmental obstacle is that economic growth has been combined with an enormous exploitation of natural resources, pollution and reduction in biodiversity. The dominating industrial optimism, spurred on by the unbelievable development since the beginning of the Industrial Revolution, has turned into precautionary or pessimistic attitudes; see Chapter 2, Section 3.

Nonetheless, most environmentalists seem to believe in betterment by industrialization and economic growth. The issue is rather to maintain wealth in the future – to grow in a sustainable way for the protection of nature and future generations.

In this perspective it is understandable that sustainable development has become a major principle of environmental law. The principle may be interpreted in various ways. Here we limit the study to economic growth under the constraint of sustainability, compare Chapter 2, Section 2. The basic motivation for the principle is the fear for overexploitation of natural resources. Pollution of the environment may result in degradation, with devastating consequences for future generations. The sustainability principle is also a reaction to the overly optimistic view that economic growth solves all problems. The optimistic approach is common among industrialists and economists. Nonetheless, pessimism has a long tradition among academic economists.

This chapter starts in Section 2 with a review of the pessimistic view that has, so far, contrasted strongly with actual economic growth. The issue is, however, whether there will be a decline in the future. To make forecasts, it is important to understand the driving forces behind economic growth. A problem is that there are several more or less related explanations of economic growth. These will be presented in Section 3. In Section 4 we focus on economies of scale. Thereafter, we study different problems related to measurement of wealth, utility, satisfaction or happiness in Sections 5 and 6. Section 7 discusses possible ways of integrating future generations in the economic calculus. Section 8 concludes.

2. PESSIMISTS

Many environmentalists and economists who are pessimistic about the future take, as a starting-point in their analysis, the fact that resources on earth are limited. By continuous exploitation of exhaustible resources, and over-exploitation of renewable resources, human civilization on earth will come to an end, sooner or later.

This approach is closely related to the economic law of *diminishing returns*. This 'law' refers to a situation where the resources are given, for example land, but they are utilized more and more intensively. The intense use increases the output, but to a decreasing rate.

The classical economists Thomas Malthus (1766–1834) and David Ricardo (1772–1823) argued that more people working the existing capital (land) would, in accordance with the law of diminishing returns, result in less production per capita. The fixed resources meant that as population grew the per capita supply of food would decline. The standard of living would,

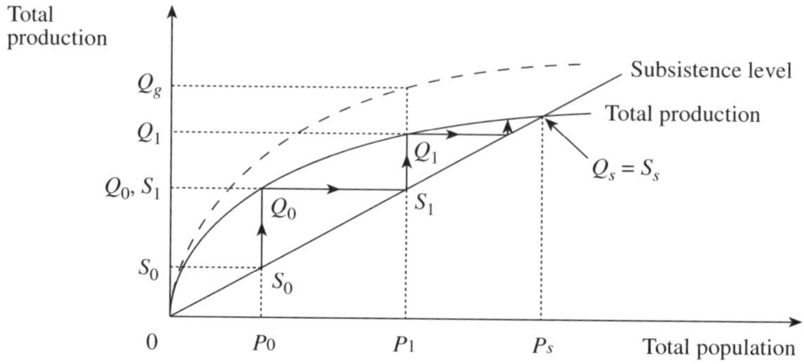

Figure 8.1 The law of diminishing returns and population growth

therefore, decline and be forced down to subsistence level. The end result would thus be a steady state with a starving population.

The law of diminishing returns can be illustrated as in Figure 8.1. The model assumes that there is one given resource (land) and one flexible resource (labour). The labour force (total population) is on the horizontal axis and the total production (food) on the vertical axis. The diminishing returns are illustrated by the sharp curve – more labour increases production but at a decreasing rate. The straight line illustrates the subsistence level at various sizes of the population. Starting at population P_0 we see that the total production is Q_0, which is larger than the subsistence level S_0. Therefore, the population can increase to P_1 with the production Q_1 and subsistence level S_1. Since Q_1 is larger than S_1 the population will continue to grow, until the stationary state where $Q_s = S_s$ is reached.

This Ricardian model assumes that the land and other natural resources are given. However, if there are savings, investments and/or technological change, this may counteract the trend. In Figure 8.1 this is illustrated by the dotted curve. When the population is P_1 the total product equals Q_g instead of Q_1 because of growth in other factors than labour.

Ricardo was pessimistic from an environmental point of view – given the limited natural resources and rapid growth of the population, he expected long-run starvation. There are several other influential economists with pessimistic approaches. One famous contribution is by Hotelling (1931). He models the optimal use of an exhaustible resource over time. He raises the somewhat discouraging question: shall we exploit the resource now and die soon, or save it and die slowly? His analysis results in a formula that says that the best we can do is to deplete the resource over time so that the price increases as much as the discount rate. The increased price is here due to the continuous increase in scarcity.

One very influential pessimistic calculation in the environmental debate is presented in D.H. Meadows et al. (1972), *The Limits to Growth*. The authors make a prognosis from a model based on historical data 1900–70. Food, industrial output and population grow exponentially, until the rapidly diminishing resource base forces a slowdown in production. Population growth turns around the year 2000 into a decline because of a lack of resources. Pollution and the population decrease in the mid-twenty-first century due to a reduced resource base and lower economic activity. That is, soon our expanding civilization is at an end. This simplistic model effectively illustrates the issue, but the simplicity is also a major drawback. The model illustrates the case where no external forces intervene in the process towards starvation. Thus it does not account for behavioural changes, technical changes, reaction in markets and so on.

The model could equally well illustrate the process in a test-tube with microbes living on a limited resource, as described in Figure 8.2, which illustrates the growth of a micro-organism, for example yeast, in a given amount of nutrient. The microbes grow exponential until they die by their own waste, that is, alcohol.[1]

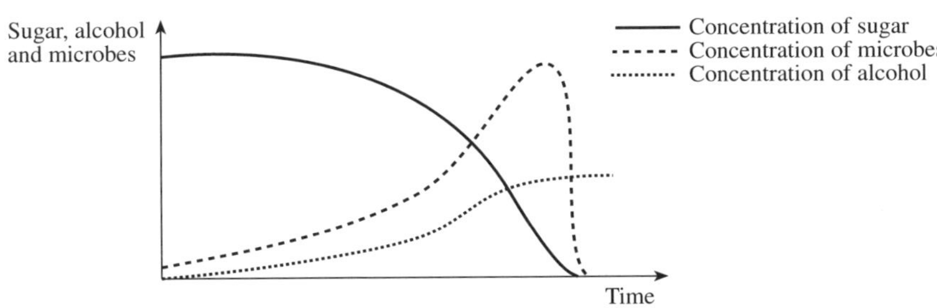

Figure 8.2 Sugar, alcohol and microbes

3. EXPLANATIONS OF GROWTH

Modern history has, so far, not supported the pessimistic forecasts. Per capital income has, since Malthus, increased in most of the world, and the world population has not started to decline due to increased poverty as the Meadows et al. model suggests. A large part of the Third World has recently succeeded in avoiding the 'poverty trap' characterized by a population growth larger than economic growth. Indeed, prices of most resources and basic products like grain have decreased, indicating less scarcity.

How, then, should this historically exceptional growth during the latest three hundred years be explained? Many economists have, of course, paid attention to this question. Yet there is no simple answer. Instead a series of factors may together explain the development.

One such explanatory factor is access to natural resources. A country rich in, for example, metals, waterpower and farming land has, of course, obvious advantages. This is, however, not enough to explain economic progress. Abundance of resources is not enough to explain development. For instance, the former Soviet Union, Africa and South America are rich in natural resources but still they have not prospered as, for example, Western Europe, Taiwan and Japan have done all with relatively few resources.

Another factor is physical capital. Investments in infrastructure and machinery have been regarded by many economists as crucial for economic development. Indeed, much development aid during the postwar period has been based on loans and grants for investments in infrastructure and industrial capital. Still, capital alone cannot explain success. Many industrially less developed countries have a large burden of debt without the expected returns. In fact, the Soviet leaders were extreme believers in capital accumulation for economic growth. They held back private consumption and favoured heavy capital investments – without success.

A third explanatory factor is technical knowledge. No one denies that technical development has been of importance for the economic progress in most countries. Nevertheless, here too more than one explanation is needed. Technical knowledge is not in itself a guarantee of economic growth. The knowledge is, except for new, non-exploited or protected findings, publicly accessible to everybody in documents and libraries. Still, it is most unevenly used, which indicates that there are differences in skill, ability or incentive to utilize new scientific and technical findings.

This brings us to a fourth factor – human capital – based on investment in education and individual competence in various respects. Human knowledge and skills are nowadays often held to be the most important factor in explaining economic development.

Yet there are also important basic institutional factors that are still missing. Institutional explanations are stressed in much recent research. One such institutional component is the property rights system discussed in Chapters 3 and 4. The point is that the driving forces towards an efficient use of natural resources, as well as efficient investments in physical capital, in human capital, and in innovations, are economic incentives, that is, the ability to gain profit from efforts and investments. In other words, an individual may have access to physical resources and knowledge to make socially beneficial efforts, but still not act because it does not pay. Similarly, free-riding may cause inefficiencies and hinder economic development, as well as result in a misuse of natural resources.

Basic institutions such as the public justice system of a nation are part of its social capital. Legal certainty, and upheld property rights including rights to trade, contract and associate are here of vital importance. Unspecified rights, economic criminality and corruption may be devastating for national as well as global development. Democratic political institutions and the market are also most important for the avoidance of the development in Meadows et al.'s model described by the microbes outlined in Figure 8.2. That is, with well-functioning political and market institutions there will be reactions to scarcities before the catastrophe occurs. As soon as there is a shortage in some resources there will be a change in prices, and investment in alternatives. Similarly, attitudes will change and cause political and legal changes. In fact, the contemporary environmental movement is in itself a reaction that may contribute, via the political system and prices, to prevent future disaster.

4. DIVISION OF LABOUR AND ECONOMIES OF SCALE

Studies on innovations for economic development have traditionally focused on natural sciences and on technological improvements. Equally important, as noted above, is the organization of production and rewards. Property rights and the freedom of contract and association are here fundamental. A related organizational issue is the division of labour. It is common knowledge in economics that division of labour, specialization and the utilization of economies of scale are fundamental for economic development. This finding goes back to Adam Smith's famous work *Wealth of Nations*, whose first sentence is quoted at the head of this chapter. Later, in his first chapter, Smith presents several examples of the importance of division of labour, including the famous pin-factory example quoted in Box 8.1.

Specialization of production and the utilization of economies of scale require investments in physical capital, as well as in knowledge and production systems. Similarly, individual specialization requires investments in knowledge and skills, that is, in human capital. Similarly typical of modern industry is large investments and decreasing average costs of production. That is, large production units reduce costs. Competition and the search for profit makes industries larger and larger. Productivity has also increased repeatedly, as in the pin-factory example. Parallel to the increase of production units we can observe an increase in the markets. In fact, a prerequisite for modern production methods is the international market and international trade. Today many markets are international and quite a few are global. Consequently, there is an enormous increase in transport. The concentration in products in industries and people in big cities requires transport all around the world.

BOX 8.1 THE PIN-FACTORY EXAMPLE IN *THE WEALTH OF NATIONS*

… the pin-maker; a workman not educated to this business … could scarce, perhaps, with his utmost industry, make one pin in a day, and certainly could not make twenty. But in the way in which this business is now carried on, not only the whole work is a peculiar trade, but it is divided into a number of branches, of which the greater part are likewise peculiar trades. One man draws out the wire, another straights it, a third cuts it, a fourth points it, a fifth grinds it at the top for receiving the head; to make the head requires three distinct operations; to put it on is a peculiar business, to whiten the pins is another; it is even a trade by itself to put them into the paper; and the important business of making a pin is, in this manner, divided into about eighteen distinct operations, which, in some manufactories, are all performed by distinct hands, though in others the same man will sometimes perform two or three of them. I have seen a small manufactory of this kind where ten men only were employed, and where some of them consequently performed two or three distinct operations. But though they were very poor, and therefore, but indifferently accommodated with the necessary machinery, they could, when they exerted themselves, make among them about twelve pounds of pins in a day. There are in a pound upwards of four thousand pins of a middling size. Those ten person, therefore, could make among them upwards of forty-eight thousand pins in a day.

Source: Adam Smith, *The Wealth of Nations*, 1979, pp. 109–110, first published 1776.

5. DEVELOPMENT MEASURES

Gross domestic product, GDP, measures the economic value of the sum of all goods and services produced during a year. Since the payment of all production and services generates income, the measure also reflects the total national income. Economic growth prevails when there is an increase in GDP from one year to another.

An advantage of the GDP measure is that it is one-dimensional – all is counted in money. All incomes or production values are simply added together. As a measure of welfare, GDP has the shortcoming that only the total or average income counts. Hence the distribution of wealth in the population is not considered. Another shortcoming is that many factors, such as quality of life and depletion of rare species, are not taken into account. Indices have, therefore, been constructed for income distribution, expected lifetime, literacy, and so on in order to obtain a better picture of human welfare. Nevertheless, the problem of comparing many dimensions, for example literacy with average income and income distribution, remains. The necessary valuation is political or ethical rather than economic.

The *net domestic product*, NDP, is a measure that adjusts for the depreciation of capital. The standard NDP estimates do not, however, adjust for the reduction in the total stock of natural resources and for the depletion of environmental values. To correct for this, economists have calculated the loss due to pollution and natural resource depletion. These calculations have, however, considerable weaknesses and are, therefore, debatable. Environmentalists may, for instance, argue that the loss of biodiversity cannot be valued economically at all. Hence the NDP is still an overestimation. An industrial optimist, on the other hand, may claim that the GDP and NDP measures do not include the positive value of all capital and knowledge available in modern society. Capital is accumulated through savings and investments. There is huge capital in infrastructure, buildings and machinery. That is, a substantial portion of the natural resources is transformed to other resources of value to humanity. This capital will contribute to future wealth, which in turn will generate further investments in capital for succeeding generations, and so on. Similarly, the accumulation of human capital, which includes increased knowledge and skills of various kinds, is equally important. New findings in information technology, medicine, psychology, and so on contribute to our wealth, and this knowledge will survive in the future, if it does not become obsolete due to future extensions in knowledge.

6. WEALTH AND HAPPINESS

When GDP is used as a measure of welfare several important simplifying assumptions are made, explicitly or implicitly. Only money counts and is added for different individuals. That is, distribution is disregarded – or everyone is supposed to have the same marginal utility of money. Moreover, the calculations are based on a neoclassical model of independent, utility-maximizing individuals where preferences are individual and assumed given. Hence economics does not include a theory on the formation and changes in human, ethical, or moral values. This does, of course, limit the use of economics. Nonetheless, economics has important insights related to ethics and environmental policy. It is, therefore, important to clarify the contributions as well as the limits to economics.

A shortcoming of economics that assumes independent (atomic) individuals is that it is not compatible with relative utility (jealousy or altruism). If an individual is in a worse (or better) position just because another is in a better position, the situations cannot simply be compared. If, for instance, a neighbour buys a Mercedes and the utility of all Volkswagen owners thereby decreases, the total utility of cars is not reflected by the sum of the value of the cars. On the other hand, if altruism prevails, everyone is happy because of the neighbour's new Mercedes, and the total utility increase is, therefore, larger than the buyer's own utility. This kind of interdependence of utility is usually neglected in economic analysis, but is important in, for example, sociology and psychology. Social interdependence in economics is limited to the interactions via contacts and markets.

A general assumption in economics is that the marginal satisfaction of goods is positive but decreasing, that is, individuals would like to have more of scarce goods, but the satisfaction or utility decreases. According to these assumptions, we should reach the 'bliss-point' in the affluent society, that is, a level of consumption where individuals are satisfied. It seems, however, as if preferences change over time, and the demand for more goods remains, even in wealthy societies.

If it is true that individual preferences change systematically over time so that one demands more as one consumes more without becoming more satisfied, it is a sad state of affairs for humanity. The possibility of individuals striving for relative positions in a vicious circle of *consumerism* is much discussed in the environmental debate, but is, with some exceptions, disregarded in economic analysis. A reason, again, is the limitation of economic theory, which assumes preferences as given. It is left to psychology, sociology, biology and so on to explain underlying human wants and needs.

The environmental movement is much occupied with changing attitudes in favour of consumption that is friendly to the environment. Established waste treatment methods have also been attacked, and recycling and cleaner production methods suggested for a better environment. The changing attitudes show up in the economy through changes in demand and supply. Consumers demand 'green' products, and 'green' firms supply them. The environment has rapidly become big business in highly industrialized countries. These new attitudes may have an important impact on consumption and production and may be of long-term benefit to humanity. If so, this will have important effects on the world economy as well. Nevertheless, economics has little to add to the question of how the changes in ideas and attitudes take place.

Moreover, economics cannot value utility changes due to changing attitudes. Individuals may be either more or less satisfied or happy through environmental awareness. The willingness to pay for environmental investments may increase, and that can be valued economically, but not the total well-being or satisfaction of the population. This brings us back to the old question: is it better to be a satisfied fool or an enlightened Socrates?

Another ethical issue is the fact that the earth today feeds six billion people. That may be seen as a major problem, but is it only a burden? The many humans constitute an important resource, promoting further growth. Moreover, the existence of more humans may be seen as an improvement *per se*, even if it is at the expense of other species, and the environment.

These issues of wealth, happiness, religion and the value of humans relative to other species belong, however, to morals and ethics, and are beyond the scope of this book.

7. FUTURE GENERATIONS AND SOCIAL PREFERENCES

In Chapter 7, Section 6 we concluded that future incomes and costs are discounted. Long-term effects are, therefore, of less importance. Indeed, benefits and costs coming up in 30–50 years and further ahead will be given practically no significance in cost–benefit analysis. An underlying reason for the discounting is uncertainty about the future. The willingness of the individual to save for the future is dependent, among other things, on life expectancy. The willingness to borrow is dependent on expected future gains and risks of available projects. All in all, uncertainty about future survival, technology, markets, taxation, confiscation and so on makes considerations in respect of over 50 years uncertain and unproductive. Hence the capital market indicates that people do not take into account things more than one or two generations ahead.

Nevertheless, more long-term considerations are evidently necessary for the survival of an advanced human civilization. There is a conflict between individual rationality, as expressed in the markets, and collective rationality of mankind or society in a broad sense. Refer to our first example of free-riding in congested traffic, discussed in Chapter 3, Section 3. Here, it was individually rational to drive as long as there was a private benefit, although it was collectively harmful. Similarly, to commit an environmental crime may be individually rational given a small risk of detection, but harmful to society. Hence individual rationality differs from what is socially rational. Similarly, what is rational in the socioeconomic perspective for those living today may not necessarily be the best alternative from the perspective of the human race. There appears to be an understanding of this, internalized, somehow, in human nature or preferences. Otherwise, it would be hard to explain why olive trees are planted, and why houses are built to withstand the wear of centuries. Statues in stone, paintings in oil, and crafts in gold, silver and wood that endure for hundreds of years are created and admired. Such very long-term investments are especially difficult to explain economically in the context of past history, where life was both shorter and riskier and where a higher discount rate would have been expected.

Economists and philosophers have tried in various ways to incorporate very long-term considerations in human decisions. One approach is to calculate long-term investments or environmental investments with a smaller discount rate than other investments, which means, in other words, that the environment (or culture) should be subsidized as compared to other (private) investments. This may be ethically or politically motivated, but there is still no economic explanation as to why we should consider generations living hundreds of years in the future.

Moreover, how shall the subsidy to 'environmental' investments be decided? And who should pay? The fact that the economy is short-sighted does not mean that politics is more able to make long-term decisions. Indeed, it may be argued that there are major failures in the political decision process. Politicians who wish to be re-elected may have the perspective of only a few years, just beyond the next election, and they are, perhaps, dependent on the support of special interests. The influence of special interests on political decision-making is further discussed in Chapter 10, Section 4. Thus the politicians may be even more short-sighted than the market.

Another approach to the issue is to say that the environment or a certain species has an 'option' value. Option value refers to irreversibility – once a species is depleted, it will never return, yet its genes, for example, may prove useful in the future. Options certainly have a market value, but option values are also discounted, and, thus, options generations ahead are negligible.

The ethics of sustainability, as discussed from a legal perspective in Chapter 2, Section 2, or as the duty we feel to leave the same chances to our successors as we ourselves have received and not to 'borrow' from future generations, may be socially preferable from the perspective of the future of humanity. There is, however, no straightforward explanation for it. One approach is to refer to a hypothetical *social contract*, including all generations, ours as well as past and future generations. By means of this contract each generation has a commitment to leave the earth in a condition that guarantees future generations at least the same opportunity or utility.

This idea certainly has some appeal, but many philosophical problems are involved. The metaphor of a social contract may be applicable in situations where the involved parties can, at least hypothetically, come together and agree on, for example, property rights and government. The 'contracting' parties may, as John Rawls (1972) suggests, also agree on the distribution of income under a veil of ignorance, not knowing who they will become. A Rawlsian contract on equity may be seen as an agreement on mutual support, and such contracts exist in reality, although on a more limited scale. A problem with an agreement over many generations is that the coming generations have nothing to give earlier generations in return.

Another problem is how utility should be measured and summarized. How should the utility of a humanity of six billion today be compared with a future humanity of, say, ten billion? Should the average utility at least remain the same, or is the fact of more individuals living a value *per se*? In other words, are we, who live today, responsible for the birth of our grandchildren?

If the goal is to provide the same opportunities to further generations, there are similar problems with the concept of 'opportunities'. Opportunities, today, are quite different from what they were a hundred years ago, and they are difficult to compare. Should future generations have the same opportunities that we have? Another interpretation is that we should leave nature as it was, in harmony. Again, what is the norm? Should nature be as it was a hundred years ago or before industrialization? And where is harmony in nature more than in our imagination? Life is, in fact, a struggle for most species, the human one included.

BOX 8.2 RIGHTS OF FUTURE GENERATIONS

The problem of valuation of rights of future generations arises in CBA undertaken to simplify environmental policy decisions. The question is how benefits to future generations should be balanced against costly measures today. There is no straightforward economic choice but there are various ethical opinions on the matter. For instance, Revesz (1999) argues that a distinction should be made between, on the one hand, harm caused as a result of environmental contamination with a low latency period, and, on the other hand, actions which may affect future generations. He claims that discounting is appropriate in the case of latent harms that occur later in a person's lifetime. However, in case of harms to future generations, discounting is ethically unjustified. It would simply be a means of privileging the interests of the current generation. He also argues that upward adjustments of the value of life need to be undertaken to account for the dread and involuntary nature of environmental carcinogens, as well as for the income level of victims. By not performing these adjustments the regulatory process risks undervaluing human life, Revesz claims.

The idea of rights of the environment, or of generations far into the future, belongs to the many ideas under the heading 'natural rights' – that is, principles ordained by God or by nature that must not, or cannot, be explained as an outcome of human actions or agreements; see Chapter 4, Section 9. Beliefs in intrinsic values, a natural order, or harmony that humans should try to reach, and sustainability and so on cannot be derived from traditional, individual-oriented, welfare-economic theory.

In sum, it is difficult to find an economic basis for the notion of 'sustainable development' as the principle has been interpreted in legal and political documents like the Rio declaration. In these documents 'sustainable development' always refers to the need to protect future generations. Such a protection may have an ethical or religious appeal, but is hard to fit into economic logic.

8. CONCLUSIONS

The historically unique economic development that followed the Industrial Revolution has, in our view, greatly favoured humanity. However, mankind is now faced with a number of environmental problems that need to be considered and solved in a rational manner. To reach a sustainable future, whatever that means, it is important to understand the forces behind economic growth. There are several explanatory factors that we have pointed to: utilization of economies of scale, formation of physical and human capital, and social capital in the form of trade customs, legal certainty and well-functioning public and private institutions.

A simple focus on the fact that virgin ores diminish with exploitation is not very helpful. Indeed, subsidization of, for example, non-fossil fuel, and taxation of non-renewable resources may result in a waste of various scarce resources. Natural resources are transformed to other types of capital and human skills. The problems are rather related to negative externalities in mining, production, transportation and consumption. For example, the greenhouse effect is not due to the scarcity of fuel in the ground, but rather the opposite. It is the accessibility and free-riding problem in the pollution of the atmosphere that are the problems. Thus the problem is free-riding and a lack of mechanisms that promote consideration of interdependences.

Social capital in a broad sense plays a central role here. The establishment of efficient legal regulations is of great importance as a first measure of environmental protection. This is especially true for ownership issues related to new knowledge and new techniques. There are fatal examples of the consequences of new knowledge and the lack of property rights. One is the splitting of the atom, the construction of the bomb, and the production of nuclear power. This new knowledge unleashed an incredible resource. However, the legal right to use this power, and the duty to control the externalities, has not yet been properly solved. Similarly, new medicines, including gene techniques, open up fantastic possibilities, but also create unsolved property rights and ethical problems.

All in all, the accumulation of capital, human resources and knowledge compensates, at least partly, the depletion of natural resources. There are, on the other hand, other very demanding environmental problems. Economic growth is based on new knowledge, new techniques, and a more extensive use of resources which creates new scarcity and, thus, conflicting interests and property rights problems, as well as 'tragedies of the commons', and pollution problems. New knowledge is, to a large extent, a public good available to the benefit of humanity, but free use of knowledge causes serious externalities. To find solutions to the current problems, we search for new knowledge, which causes economic growth and new property rights problems, and so on.

It is a matter of philosophy whether goods and services accounted in monetary terms indicate utility or happiness. The relationship between happiness and wealth is an old question that has no simple answer. It has been raised again in the environmental debate, often regarding the question of consumerism and the need for changed attitudes. A typical question is: 'Is mankind going under, striving for more and more wealth without improved satisfaction?' Many religions deny the possibility of happiness through wealth – starvation with true belief is better than richness without true belief. On the other hand, there are many materialists like us who believe that increased wealth makes people happier. This is especially true for people suffering from poverty, illiteracy, illness and lack of security.

Normative economics studies the well-being of members of a certain economy. Methodological problems arise when the utility of strangers or not yet born members of the economy should be considered. An available method is to investigate what the current population is willing to pay for the well-being of strangers and future generations, or how much people give up today for future benefits. The discounting factor (the market interest rate) indicates that considerations of the future are limited to, at most, two generations. Economists have tried in various ways to incorporate more long-term considerations in economic models, but without success. Ethical norms based on other values than utilitarian economics are needed, for instance in CBA where the very long-term considerations are essential.

NOTE

1. M.C. Kielland-Brandt, J. Nielsen, T.L. Nillsen and J. Villadsen, 'Optimization of Ethanol Production in Saccharomyces cerevisiae by Metabolic Engineering of the Ammonium Assimilation', *Metabolic Engineering*, **2** (1), 2000.

FURTHER READING

Hart, S.L. (1997), 'Strategies for a Sustainable World', *Harvard Business Review*, **75**, 67–76.

Hirschman, A. (1982), 'Rival Interpretation of Market Society: Civilizing, Destructive or Feeble?', *The Journal of Economic Literature*, no. 4.

Howarth, R.B. and Norgaard, R.B. (1992), 'Environmental valuation under sustainable development', *American Economic Review*, **82** (2), 473–7.

Krutilla, J.V. and Fisher, A. (1985), *The economics of natural environments: studies in the valuation of commodity and amenity recourses*, rev. edn, Washington, DC: Resources for the Future.

Rawls, J. (1972), *A Theory of Justice*, Oxford: Clarendon Press.

Revesz, R.L. (1999), 'Environmental regulation, cost–benefit analysis and the discounting of human lives', *Columbia Law Review*, **99**, 941–1017.

Rose-Ackerman, S. (1999), *Corruption and Government: Causes, Consequences and Reform*, Cambridge: Cambridge University Press.

Scitovsky, T. (1993), *The Joyless Economy*, Oxford: Oxford University Press.

PART III

Transaction Costs and the Law

9. The role of law

> If there are no transaction costs in changing rights, the outcome will be efficient by private agreements. Hence, the initial allocation of rights does not influence the efficiency of the final allocation.
>
> Coase's theorem

1. INTRODUCTION

Price theory is usefully applied to legal and environmental matters. Several examples are given in Part II. Nevertheless, the traditional price theory model is not fully fitted to analyse law, institutions and the environment. To understand legal institutions, price theory needs to be complemented with a theory that explains the formation of institutions such as firms, customs and the law. Fortunately, since the 1960s, a theory of economic institutions – of which Law and Economics is a part – has developed. A fundamental thought in this *new institutional economics* is that transaction costs can explain social institutions of various types. The formation and protection of property rights in Chapters 3 and 4 are examples of rule-making that may be explained by transaction costs. Similarly, the middleman in the example of the mutually beneficial exchange (Box 5.1) has the function of reducing transaction costs. Money itself can also be seen as an institution that has a transaction-cost-reducing function. Similarly, the cost of finding counter-parties and the problem of comparing prices explains the existence of common marketplaces. A marketplace with competitors also simplifies negotiations. In a marketplace where there are many buyers and sellers of homogeneous goods with given prices, there is no room for bargains.

A general point made in the new institutional approach is that institutions are prior to the market. The model of free competition is based on assumptions about firms, consumers, market place, tradable rights and so on, that is, on a given set of institutions. Environmental problems arise because of negative external effects, that is, effects that are not considered by the parties in the economy. According to institutional economics the reason why the effects are not internalized in the economy is transaction costs, broadly defined, including limited information, problems of negotiation and bargaining, and of enforcement.

In Part III we treat the institutional economic theory applied to environmental law. In this chapter we present the role of law in environmental economics. In Section 2 we give a description of transaction costs. Thereafter, we turn in Section 3 to normative economics, that is, 'good' law in terms of economic efficiency. In Section 4 we treat the Coase theorem in some detail, including its legal application when transaction costs are present. A practical example of Coasean analysis of regulations is presented in Section 5, which examines producers' responsibility for recycling. The regulation of pollution by agreements on an international level is discussed in Section 6. Section 7 concludes.

2. TRANSACTION COSTS

2.1 Impediments to Trade

Transaction costs are usually divided into search costs, contract costs and control costs. Search costs include costs to find counter-parties, as well as costs for information about prices, conditions and qualities. Contract costs include costs to negotiate and draw up contracts. Control costs are a consequence of the possibility that the counter-parties do not fulfil their agreements. This division is according to the purpose of the costs; there are no watertight barriers between the different categories. Search costs, for example, may include the problem of finding a party that is credible and controllable. Similarly, the more careful one is when drawing up the contract, the easier it is to supervise the agreement. There is, thus, a mutual dependence between the different transaction cost categories.

The division of transaction costs can also be made into costs which are present *ex ante* and those which are incurred *ex post*. Search and contract costs are present before the transaction is undertaken, which is why they are of the *ex ante* type, while the problems with control, enforcement and execution arise *ex post*. In conformity with what has been said about search, contract and control costs, there is a mutual connection between transaction costs *ex ante* and *ex post*. By making a contract specific from the beginning and by requiring ample security, later costs can be limited.

There is also a close connection between production costs and transaction costs. If, for example, a good is packaged in a certain manner, it may be easier to offer it for sale. Conversely, the conveyor-belt principle means that production takes place according to clearly defined and controllable segments, which facilitates the price-setting (agreement) and control of the results. If all actors knew one another and possessed perfect knowledge about prices and characteristics of goods, there would be no transaction costs *ex ante*. Furthermore, if control and trust were no problem, there would be no transaction costs *ex post*. Uncertainty and lack of information and trust contribute, therefore, to transaction problems.

2.2 Bounded Rationality

Yet, if all information about actors, prices and qualities was present and correct, problems would still remain. Humans do not have the capacity to elaborate and evaluate all information. The human brain has limited capacity, that is, *bounded rationality* prevails.[1] This may explain why humans act according to simplified rules of thumb, and why agreements often remain incomplete and, thus, must be complemented with rules for guidance and solving conflicts. It also explains why individuals may misperceive risks as discussed in Chapter 7, Section 5.

In order to limit transaction costs, actors can choose to cooperate or trade with one another many times. Indeed, *repeated exchange* is an important phenomenon that is explained by transaction costs. The search costs lessen when one cooperates with the same partner many times. It is also easier to understand and come to agreement with a person one already knows. If the partners expect to meet and conduct business in the future, more can also be won through honesty, which contributes to lessening the control problem in the future. This predisposes to a certain far-sightedness. If the partners are short-sighted and do not care for the long term, honesty becomes of less interest.

When repetition occurs, a certain pattern will become established, either through agreement or through customary practice. Expectations and understanding between the partners may result in social norms and rules for common action, for example on weights, money and trade. The advantage of common rules is that they are applied often and in similar situations. Regular cooperation within firms and other institutions has a similar function.

2.3 The Fundamental Transformation

The longer and more strongly the partners bind themselves to each other, the less the search costs and the greater the probable partner's knowledge about the other party. This is advantageous, but it also has a drawback. The greater the investment that is made in a relationship, the more is lost if it ceases to exist. A long-term bond can also increase the risk that the partners try to exploit each other's vulnerability. The one who is not bonded has the advantage that she can, without loss, go to someone else, so-called *exit*.

Binding relationships can have many reasons. One may pertain to *location-specificity*. Neighbours are, for instance, dependent upon one another. For businesses that lie close to one another, transport-economic reasons can bind one business to another. Another reason for strong bonds may pertain to *person-specificity*. Family, friends and colleagues know one another, which eases transactions between them, but at the same time causes bonding. A third reason may be that the partners live in a special environment and possess special knowledge, which cannot be transferred. Within a firm there is firm-specific knowledge that is not applicable anywhere else. Thus, if one leaves the business, these resources are lost. The same can apply to investments in knowledge and skills, that is, *human capital*. If the individual invests in an education or in personal relationships that are specific to a company, a dependent relationship with the company arises. The company is also dependent to the degree that the individual can 'take with him' company-specific knowledge.

In a market model with unlimited exit, homogeneous goods and equilibrium prices, there is no space for negotiation and, thus, there are no contract costs. However, as soon as two partners are bonded to one another, a *bilateral relationship* occurs, with room for negotiation. There is a highest price that the buyer is willing to pay and a lowest price that the seller is willing to accept. Between these extremes is the *bargaining span*. For instance, in the case of the middleman in Box 5.1 there is a bargaining span between one loaf of bread that makes the hunter indifferent and gives the baker all the benefit, and four loaves of bread that make the baker indifferent while the hunter receives all the benefit. Similarly, in the filter case in Box 2.4 the victims suffer 600 by pollution and are willing to pay that for a filter, at most. If they do so, the filter-installing firm pays 300 for the filter and gains 300. The other extreme, or threat point, where one party is indifferent and, therefore, quits if compensated less, is a payment of 300 to the filter-installing firm. With such a contract the firm gains nothing, while the victims gain all.

Uncertainty about the outcome of the negotiations opens the way for *strategic behaviour*, that is, manoeuvres, pressuring, and false or misleading information in order to benefit from as profitable an agreement as possible. Often, *asymmetric information* is present, that is, differing access to information that the partners can attempt to utilize to their own profit. The outcome depends on factors such as negotiating strength and what the parties believe about one another. Where there is a large bargaining span, negotiations can be long-term and costly, and may never be settled.

Note that the situation is unlike *ex ante* and *ex post*. For example, with the purchase of property or in the case of employment, great scope for freedom may prevail, with a wide assortment of choices. However, as soon as the contract is written, the state of bonding arises and the costs of moving come into play. The difference between before and after is so apparent and important that it is called 'the fundamental transformation'.

The outcome of a bargain is complicated to predict at *small-number exchanges*, that is, situations where more than two, but still a few, are involved. Suppose, for instance, that five property owners are planning to build a road through the five estates. The outcome to each of the five owners depends on the payment principle they apply and the route chosen. If nothing is settled in advance, never-ending negotiations and disputes may result. This problem is a reason for legal regulations of land use, which we discussed above in relation to expropriations (Chapter 7, Section 7).

3. NORMATIVE ECONOMICS OF LAW

3.1 First Normative Principle

The price theory is positive (descriptive) and free of normative values in the sense that it does not make a statement about whether the studied phenomena (for example price and quantity adjustments) are good or bad. The theory does not make any direct statement about human nature; the buyers/consumers in the model are abstract decision units and may, for example, constitute households composed of several individuals. Yet there are implicit normative elements. The model's description of reality, with the assumption of atomic individualism where every unit attempts to maximize her own utility or profit, is such a normative element, as discussed in Chapter 5, Section 3.

Positive price theory cannot evaluate what is good or bad in an economy. A value criterion that enables one to make normative predictions was, however, introduced in the nineteenth century by the Italian sociologist and economist, Vilfredo Pareto. The *Pareto-criterion* states that one situation is better than another, if someone in the economy receives greater utility without someone else being worse off. Freely accepted trade (without negative externalities) benefiting both parties thus fulfils the Pareto-criterion. The criterion does not take a stance with respect to the utility of different individuals – it is sufficient that someone's betterment does not take place at the cost of someone else. Yet the criterion is based on normative premises that can be perceived as far-reaching, disregarding, for example, altruism or envy.

Pareto-optimality is present when it is not possible to increase the utility for someone without diminishing it for someone else. If, in a state of the world, more goods could have been produced with a given set of resources, there is *inefficient production*, or *cost inefficiency*. More products can thus be produced to the benefit of some without a loss for others. Hence Pareto-improvements are possible, and Pareto-optimality does not prevail. The same is true if goods can be traded in a mutually beneficial way. In equilibrium, however, where there are no further possible mutual gains, there may be a Pareto optimum.

In the neoclassical price theory with competition, homogeneous goods, given production technology and a given set of resources distributed among the parties in the economy, a Pareto-optimal situation obtains. The striving for utility and profit, together with a free market where all are compensated for their sacrifices, leads to the situation where more products cannot be produced or traded efficiently.

The normative economy principle has an ideological base in the classical, liberal view of the state and its citizens. The state's role is to stipulate and enforce the legal order. The right to contract means endorsing the decision-making capacity and sovereignty of legally aged citizens and juridical persons. The unimpeded right of contract, together with freedom of association and entry, opens up to Pareto-improving agreements.

This political idea of free exchange in accordance with the Pareto-criterion is adopted in many jurisdictions. Indeed, the civil law of many countries is built on the premise that agreements reached in free contracting are beneficial not only to the individuals but also to society. Contract law, for instance, is seen as an institution for the simplification of trade, with the purpose of maximizing the value of trade. A tort law principle, common in most jurisdictions, is that, provided that the conditions are fulfilled, victims should be 'fully' compensated for a loss. In economic analysis this doctrine is equivalent to the *indifference principle*; that is, compensation is 'full' when the victim is indifferent to having either no injury or the injury plus compensation. Compensation to victims according to the indifference principle certifies that dangerous activities fulfil the Pareto criterion. Accordingly, full compensation at expropriation guarantees that property rights are not violated.

The similar foundation of normative economics based on the Pareto criteria and liberal market-oriented legal systems justifies the *first normative principle* in the economic analysis of law that states:

> Law should be structured to remove the impediments to private agreements.[2]

The law should make Pareto-improving free agreements feasible by rules that define and protect property rights, including the right to trade. The law should also simplify Parteto-improving contracts by rules that reduce transaction costs.

3.2 Second Normative Principle

Private agreements are not always feasible. Transaction costs may be prohibitive. Consequently, there are external effects that are not internalized into the economy by contracts and/or prices (Chapter 6, Section 2). One example is the traffic congestion case that is presented in Chapter 3, Section 1, where individual drivers increase the travel time of everyone on the road. Multilateral agreements among the travellers before they start driving would benefit them all, but are, of course, impossible. To avoid a standstill the traffic must be regulated in some other way than by contract.

Similarly, the tragedy of the commons is an externality problem. Here, the actors within an industry, for example fishery, harm each other in a way that may cause depletion. If all involved were able to regulate the interdependence by contract, there would be a common interest in preserving the resource and controlling free-riding; see Chapter 3, Section 4.

Depletion may also be caused by toxic pollution that does not harm an industry, but outsiders. The transaction costs problem here is that the outsiders may not know the polluter, or it may be impossible to negotiate and enforce an agreement. Again, there are prohibitive transaction costs that make free contracting among the involved impossible.

A great portion of environmental economics is, therefore, coupled to the question of how negative external effects, caused by prohibitive transaction costs, can be internalized in the economic system. Can law compensate for transaction costs? This brings us to the *second normative principle of law*:

> The law shall minimize the total cost to society in the absence of, or failures in, private agreements.

Hence, if there are no agreements due to prohibitive transaction costs, the purpose of the law is to correct for this shortcoming. Note that the underlying norm for the legal regulation is still the hypothetical agreement that the parties would have agreed upon in a world of costless contracts. Optimal law thus mimics the Pareto criterion in a hypothetical world without transaction costs.

3.3 Utilitarianism

Legal regulations usually cause positive effects for some, but negative effects for others. In order to be improvements according to the Pareto criterion, the measures must induce compensation so that no one is in a worse position. However, to compensate everyone harmed brings with it practical difficulties and is often even impossible. A regulation of prices, a prohibition to fell a pristine forest, or an investment in a highway favours some and disfavours others. How, then, shall projects of this nature be evaluated?

One possibility is to retain the analogy by hypothetical compensations. A change is said to be potentially *Pareto-sanctioned* if someone gains, and compensation that fulfils the Pareto criterion are *hypothetically* possible. That is, the compensation need not take place, but the gains must exceed the necessary compensation to make all affected indifferent. This requirement is named the *Kaldor–Hicks criterion.*

The Pareto criterion, on the other hand, is built on real compensations. The Kaldor–Hicks criterion differs in that no valuation takes place according to the individual's free will expressed in mutual agreement. It is, instead, a third party who must judge the value of the change and weigh one's profit against another's loss.

While the normative requirement of revealed preferences through real compensations is named a 'contractarian approach', the Kaldor–Hicks criterion is utilitarian. In utilitarianism a change is good if the *sum* of changes in utility is positive. This principle of the greatest possible utility for the greatest number originates from David Hume (1711–76) and Jeremy Bentham (1748–1832). Bentham presupposed that utility could be quantified and summarized. In reality, however, there are no unequivocal means of evaluating utility or disutility as soon as the voluntary agreement is abandoned as a norm.

A defence of the Kaldor–Hicks criterion is that all gain at least by some politics, and politics is impossible if no measures can be taken without full compensation. Moreover, many repeated measures and political decisions even out the costs and benefits. Positive effects, in other words, are supposed to outweigh negative ones in the long run. However, severe political decisions, like forced military service, confiscation of property, industrial poisoning of the neighbourhood, and so on, are not evidently compensated in the long run by other political measures.

This is why it may be argued that compensation should be paid when (i) the victim is identifiable at relatively low costs, and (ii) the harm is great. In other words, in a utilitarian system the state should act as an insurer and compensate large losses caused by political actions. This argument is closely related to the notion of the value of *legal certainty*; see Chapter 7, Section 6. That is, the state shall collect taxes and regulate according to foreseeable rules of law. Moreover, considerable losses caused by political decisions should be compensated.

Accepting the utilitarian rule of summing benefits minus costs for various parties in the economy makes the calculation of utility easy. For instance, the calculation of the GDP is implicitly based on the simple idea that the sum of all incomes reflects total welfare. Distribution of wealth is here disregarded, which is equivalent to an implicit assumption that the utility of marginal income is equal to all citizens. This simplistic norm also underlies the statement that the consumer or producer surplus is equal to the areas in between the demand and supply curves as in Figure 5.6. The reason for the summation of money is, of course, its simplicity. It is, however, important to remember the underlying assumptions and philosophy.

4. COASEAN REGULATION

4.1 The Theorem

In Chapter 2 we briefly presented the Coase theorem when discussing the polluter pays principle, PPP, versus the victim pays principle, VPP (Chapter 2, Section 4). This goes back to the seminal work of Ronald Coase (1960), winner of the 1991 Prize of Economics in the Memory of Alfred Nobel. The prize was won for his famous Coase theorem, of which one version is presented at the heading of this chapter. The theorem says that the distribution of rights has no importance from an efficiency point of view. With respect to the PPP versus the VPP doctrine, the theorem says that either the PPP *or* the VPP results in efficient use of resources. The theorem refers to a situation where the involved parties are able to transact without any transaction costs.

The article 'The Problem of Social Costs' (Coase, 1960) was a critique of the PPP as a generally preferred solution to the externality problem. It became, however, fundamental for the new economic analysis of law. Below we will exemplify this by another presentation of the Coase theorem.

Assume that two farmers, *A* and *B*, have land bordering one another. *A* has livestock that disturbs *B* by roaming freely over *B*'s territory, and there are no economic possibilities for setting up a fence. The marginal net value to *A* of further livestock (x) is represented by the downward-sloping line MNB_A in Figure 9.1. The distance from the horizontal axis of different quantities of livestock illustrates the profit that results from further livestock additions. We have assumed diminishing marginal profit – the greater the quantity of creatures, the less the profit arising from further animals on the farm. If *A*

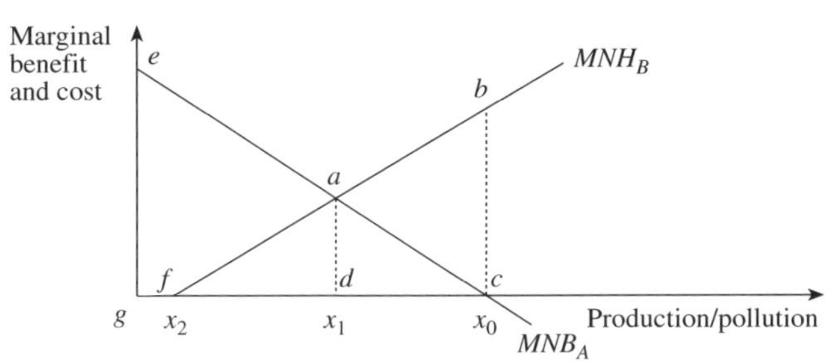

Figure 9.1 Graphic presentation of the Coase theorem

maximizes his profit without taking into account the inconvenience to *B*, *A* will choose the quantity x_0. Thereafter, further livestock generates more costs than benefits for *A*.

A's livestock causes marginal damage to *B*, corresponding to line MNH_B in the figure. We assume that the marginal negative externality is increasing, which is a reasonable assumption – a few scattered animals on the land are of little significance; but the greater the number, the greater the marginal damage to *B* of more cattle.

We now address the question: which number of cattle is optimal? We are in a utilitarian state that aims at maximal total utility in society, which in this case includes only two profit-maximizing firms. Hence the target is to maximize the joint profit of *A* and *B*.

From the two lines, MNH_B and MNB_A in the figure, we can find the socially optimal quantity of cattle. The maximum joint profit is where the profit for *A* is just as great as the disturbance to *B*, that is, at x_1 cattle. For quantities greater than x_1 a reduction in the number of cattle means an improvement because *B*'s reduced damage is greater than *A*'s gained profit. For quantities less than x_1 an increase in *A*'s livestock means in an analogous manner an improvement. *A*'s profit in increasing the quantity of livestock is here greater than the cost to *B*. Therefore, *B* can be compensated at a lower sum than *A*'s profit of having more cattle. Hence movements in the direction towards x_1 fulfil the Kaldor–Hicks criterion. Consequently, x_1 maximizes the joint profit and is socially optimal.

Coase pointed out that *A*'s choice of x_0, with a negative external effect for *B* as a consequence, presupposed that the parties do not themselves have possibilities to regulate the dependence. If there are potential improvements, these may be undertaken by the parties (given that transaction costs are not an obstacle). For instance, *B* will not quietly observe how *A* allows livestock to roam freely. *B* will be willing to (at the most) pay a sum corresponding to the area *abcd* in Figure 9.1 in order for *A* to reduce his quantity of animals to x_1. *A* can accept to do this on condition of receiving a compensation corresponding to *acd*, at least. For production to the left of x_1, *A* will demand greater compensation than *B* is willing to pay, which is why it is not appropriate to restrict the production under the level x_1. Accordingly, this level is Pareto-optimal because every deviation from this point means that at least one of the parties is in a worse position. In other words, the social optimum x_1 is reached by the parties without any central intervention.

Observe that at the optimal level, x_1, there is still a negative effect for *B*. Certain animals disturb *B*. However, no negative *external* effect is present because dependence has been taken into consideration in the agreement between the parties.

Above, we assumed that *B* had to pay *A* in order to motivate *A* to reduce the quantity of livestock. Assume, instead, that *B* has the right on his side, that is, that no animals are permitted within *B*'s area – as long as *B* is not in agreement. *B*, therefore, has a right with respect to *A*, which is why *A* is forced to pay *B* for freely roaming animals. *A* is willing to pay up to the sum *adge* in order to remain in possession of x_1 quantity of animals. *B* demands at least *adf*. The end of negotiating occurs with the optimal production x_1. How much more than *adf* that *A* pays *B* is an indefinite negotiable question. The optimal production x_1 is, thus, reached irrespective of whether *A* or *B* has the right, which is the main import of Coase's theorem. On the other hand, different rules of law have different wealth consequences – if *A* has the right to let loose livestock, *B* pays to *A*, while *A* pays to *B* if *B* has the right to grazing land.

Coase stressed the *reciprocal nature of harm*. In this particular example it refers to the fact that the damage from the cattle is not just caused by *A*; it is also due to the presence of neighbour *B*. We may see the situation as one in which farmer, *A*, harms *B*. One may, on the other hand, argue equally well that *B* limits the right of *A* to undertake cattle raising through the proximity to the ranch. One should, therefore, not ask automatically how the law should force *A* to reduce the number of cattle. The question should rather be which of the actors should be the owner of the grazing right. Coase proposed his theory mainly as a reaction to the Pigouvian tradition, which argued that imposing a duty on *A* to compensate *B* (or a charge on *B* paid to the treasury) would be *the* optimal way to internalize the externality.

The reciprocal nature of harm explains the seeming contradiction between the VPP which says that the victim shall pay, and the indifference principle that says that the victim shall be made indifferent through compensation. Here, 'victim' refers to the party that has suffered a loss. But a loss does not exist legally if it is not an infringement of a right. Once the victim has a right, the polluter has a duty to compensate the victim. The right must, therefore, be assigned first in order to render the concepts 'victim' and 'indifference' meaningful.

4.2 Prohibitive Transaction Costs

In the hypothetical Coasean world without transaction costs, traders will always find each other, negotiations will be without cost, and there will be no problems of control. Hence the parties will be able to settle Pareto-optimal contracts. In reality, however, there are always some transaction costs. Taken together, the transaction costs may be prohibitive.

A first measure by the legal system could be to assign and enforce rights. Conflict between neighbours, as in the example above, may have arisen as a consequence of increased scarcity. Over a period of time, both *A* and *B* increased their quantity of livestock. As long as the number was small, the land could be used by all without limitation. However, conflict arose due to scarcity and unspecified rights. Farmer *A* may claim the *first-use doctrine* and require the right to pursue farming without trespass. Farmer *B*, on the other hand, may claim the right to the land through his settling there. History shows that conflicts of this nature can continue for a long time and become violent. A basic function of the public justice system is thus to assign and maintain legal order. Second, once the rights are present, the involved parties can benefit from trade. Hence 'law and order' is in accordance with the first Coasean rule of law.

The cattle example above is based on the assumption that the parties can identify and control one another. Assume, instead, that *A* blows smoke over to group *B* in the neighbourhood. *B* is composed of many individuals who cannot negotiate with *A*. *A* has, then, an economic reason to choose x_0 in Figure 9.1, which is why the conflict and the negative external effect remains. How, then, can the situation be improved by law?

First, the conflict may be solved by a public assignment and enforcement of rights. One possibility is that *A* is permitted by the legal order to continue blowing smoke, with a loss of *fbc* for *B*. Another is that *A* is forbidden to blow smoke, with a loss of *ecg* for *A*. If the legislator wishes to favour one of the parties, a law may be introduced to the benefit of this group, and at the cost of the other.

If the legislator intends to maximize the social benefit, a comparison between the sizes of the areas *fbc* and *ecg* needs to be undertaken. If the law-maker is well informed about the effects on the involved parties, which corresponds to the information about *MNB* and *MNH* in Figure 9.1, the right to smoke can be regulated through a prohibition on discharging smoke greater than x_1. Such a regulation fulfils the Kaldor–Hicks criterion since improvements to all are possible in principle. The real wealth effects of such a regulation depend on whether compensations are awarded or not. If no compensations are awarded, *B* in our example makes a profit and *A* incurs a loss, compared to unlimited discharging. If the comparison is no discharge at all, *A* makes a profit corresponding to *adge* and *B* a loss corresponding to *adf*.

In order to identify the optimal law the rule-maker (often an environmental protection agency) must have access to knowledge described in the model. The net benefit curve, *MNB*, as well as the imposed damages to the victims, *MNH*, are based on a given technology. All available technologies must thus, in principle, be investigated before the *MNB* curve can be drawn.

Normally, it is only the industry, at best, that has this information. The *MNH* curve is based on knowledge of the harm to the victim, which, in fact, may not be known, even by the victims. Moreover, the drawing of the *MNH* curve is based on a simple causality relation between the production or pollution (x) and the inflicted harm, a relation that may not be known either.

A reality characterized by uncertainty leads us to the question of how pollution is *de facto* regulated when information is most limited, or is not available at all. A first choice is: *no regulation*. That may be reasonable – the benefits may, or may not, exceed the harm; so why stop an activity from which at least someone may benefit? In addition, other measures, such as zoning, charges on toxic substances and dangerous goods, or tort liability in case of accidents, may reduce the external effects. The combination of measures will be studied in Chapter 17.

Another approach is to ban toxic goods and activities, or to close down polluting industries with uncertain effects on the environment. The choice between the two alternatives depends on beliefs about potential benefits and costs. Figure 9.2(a) indicates a situation where the benefits of the polluting industry (the triangle *abc*) exceed the negative environmental impact (the triangle *cdb*). Thus, if the agency with the power to implement a law on pollution control believes in this structure, it may permit the polluting industry. Figure 9.2(b), on the other hand, shows large costs (the triangle *cdb*) and small benefits (triangle *abc*) that would make a ban preferable.

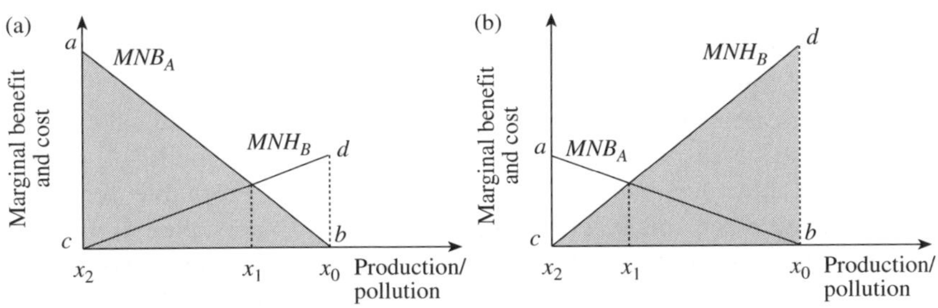

Figure 9.2 No regulation versus ban

Attitudes to precaution are briefly discussed in Chapter 2, Section 4. If the policy is that a polluting activity should be allowed if uncertainty prevails, we talk about *industrial optimism*. If, on the other hand, the general policy is that the activity should not be allowed if uncertainty prevails, this can be interpreted as the *precautionary principle*. The regulation of pollution by industry will be further discussed in Chapter 11.

5. PRODUCER'S RESPONSIBILITY FOR WASTE

5.1 Basic Questions

A current extension of environmental policy in many countries is the introduction of 'extended producer's responsibility', including collecting and recycling used goods. The general idea is that if producers in the early stages of the production process are responsible and legally liable, they will have an incentive to minimize recycling costs. This obviously fits with the policy idea that waste should preferably be recycled instead of burned or discharged in landfills; see Chapter 6, Section 5. The costs may be reduced through the choice of raw materials, design, processing, or composition of the goods. Dangerous metals and plastics may be substituted, welded parts may be applied so as to make dismantling easy, and so on. Another method of reducing recycling costs is to prolong the life of the goods through better quality and service. A long-term expectation is that different raw materials, reorganized production, new systems of returns, and dismantling and so on will make recycling privately profitable.

There are several basic matters pertaining to extended producer's responsibility that need to be analysed. A first question is: which goods should be included in the producer's responsibility – should used cars, as well as household garbage, be included? It is, in the end, consumers that pollute by littering and throwing away TV sets, furniture, and other worn-out goods. Homeowners are usually responsible for household garbage, so why should they not also be responsible for manufactured, durable goods? A second question is: how far-reaching should recycling be? Profitable recycling already takes place today. For instance, spare parts are taken from used cars, and the metal in the body and engine is reused. The social problem is the possibility of toxic substances polluting the environment. What percentage of returns is acceptable, which substances should be separated, and which should be reused? Recycling must be mandatory because of the social goal to reuse more than what is privately profitable. A third question is related to the fact that more than one producer is usually involved. Who, then, should be liable when several suppliers, producers and dealers are involved? A fourth question is related to enforcement of producer's responsibility. Fraudulent behaviour may be serious. The liable producer may also become insolvent.

Below, we focus on recycling responsibility for durable goods sold in large numbers to consumers or firms. We address the question: which party in the production and recycling process should be responsible for all, or part, of the recycling? Under 'recycling responsibility' we include responsibility for the return, collection, storage and reuse of worn-out goods. The responsible party is supposed to be legally liable if its duty is not fulfilled. We limit the study to durable goods with an expected life span of 5–20 years.

We apply a Coasean approach. Producer's responsibility is only considered from an economic point of view. That is, responsibility is the same as economic liability. The starting-point is thus efficient liability in a world without transaction costs. Thereafter, we study practical solutions in the real world with transaction costs.

5.2 Negotiations without Transaction Costs

Assume a hypothetical situation in which the party responsible for recycling can negotiate and contract without transaction costs. The firms involved maximize profits, there is no insolvency problem, and the authorities' control of recycling is costless. Moreover, there are no restrictions on the freedom of contract. The party liable for the recycling costs is, thus, free to contract work and liability to others. Given these assumptions, the Coase theorem stipulates that recycling will be undertaken in a cost-efficient way, independent of who is initially legally liable for the recycling.

To illustrate, assume that there is one supplier of raw materials, one producer, one dealer, one buyer and one recycling firm. The producer is legally liable for recycling. Due to the free transfer of rights and duties, the producer will contract with the supplier for materials that simplify the recycling process. The producer may also contract with the dealer for the collection and return of used goods. Thereafter, the dealer may contract with the buyer to return the goods (perhaps through the use of a deposit). The producer may also contract with the recycling firm for the dismantling and sale of regained materials.

Now, assume, instead, that the legislator has made the final consumer/owner liable for recycling. Because of costless and free transactions, the owner may contract with the involved parties in a way that minimizes the costs of recycling. The dealer may, thus, accept the used goods in return. Next, the dealer contracts with the recycling firm. The recycling firm may contract with the producer in order to reduce the recycling costs, and the producer may contract with the supplier of materials and so on. Similarly, if the dealer is legally liable, she may contract with the consumers to return the goods, the producer to change the design, the recycling firm to handle the recycling responsibility, and so on. Independent of the initial legal duties, it is in the common interest of the parties involved to redistribute the tasks and liabilities according to comparative advantages.

Which party in this chain will finally carry the recycling costs? It depends on the ability to transfer costs via the pricing of the separate services and the durable good. Hence there is no simple answer. However, the simplistic view that the producer carries the recycling cost of the producer's recycling liability, and that the consumer carries the cost of the consumer's liability, is not well founded. The outcome depends on market conditions. With perfect competition, with no excess profits in the industry, the consumer will usually have to pay for the recycling, independent of the initial legal recycling liability. It thus seems a reasonable first approximation to assume that consumers will end up paying for recycling, independent of the initial legal liability.

5.3 Transaction Costs

Above, we assumed zero transaction costs, which seems to be a fairly realistic assumption in an industry producing and recycling durables. Transaction costs are relatively low when a limited number of firms are involved in repeated dealings. The producers, suppliers and dealers know each other relatively well, and their performance is controlled through the value of a good reputation. The legislator may, therefore, place the recycling liability on any of the parties involved in the production and recycling processes without loss of efficiency.

If, on the other hand, recycling liability is placed on the final consumer, the outcome may cause inefficiency. The individual consumer has no comparative advantage in the recycling of durables, except for the returning of the good. He must, therefore, transact most of the recycling to other links in the chain. These transactions are not without costs because of the large number of consumers, their lack of experience, and the user's limited ability to control the quality of the recycling. For example, assume that the owner of a TV set is liable for the recycling of that item. However, it is complicated, if not impossible, for the individual owner to recycle a TV. Profit-seeking dealers and/or producers of TV sets may, therefore, offer recycling at a price. In the end, recycling may be standardized and included in the price of a TV set when it is new, but that takes time. Furthermore, it may be difficult to enforce consumer liability. TV sets may be left in the woods or stored in attics without recycling. Severe penalties may be necessary to deter a considerable portion of the TV owners.

Obviously, this is a roundabout way of making consumers legally liable for recycling. A way of reducing the transaction costs and, thus, increasing the efficiency of recycling, would be to place the legal liability directly on the party that has the comparative advantage in the recycling process. By simulating free contracting under the assumption of no transaction costs, as we did above, the legislator may identify cost-efficient recycling liability. An efficient law would make that party liable which accepts the liability freely in a world without transaction costs. Hence an efficient law makes no further transactions necessary. Unfortunately, the perfect law is not possible in practice; but by making the producer liable for the dismantling and reuse of materials, the dealers responsible for collection, and the consumers for returning the goods, further transactions are limited to low-cost transactions among the traders in the industry.

The principle of comparative advantage and the existence of transaction costs explain why, for instance, households are liable for garbage from the kitchen. There are no apparent comparative advantages in making farmers liable for the waste; and there are no direct and simple negotiations and contracts between farmers and consumers such that the liability can be transacted to the consumers. For the same reason it is efficient to make the farmers producing food liable for the waste under their control.

5.4 The Right to Transact Liability by Contract

So far, we have assumed that the public authorities can enforce recycling liability without difficulty. In reality, however, the cost of controlling the parties varies. The control of thousands of consumers may be costly, and it might also be complicated to control a large number of dealers. Foreign producers might well be impossible to control. Therefore, it matters who is liable, and the right to transfer liability by contract must be limited. For example, a legally liable producer contracts with other firms for the dismantling and storage of waste. Later, it is shown that the recycling has not been completed because of incompetence, fraud, or insolvency. If it has been legally permissible for the parties to transact the liability, then recycling cannot be enforced. Therefore, the extent to which a legislator may be motivated to limit the freedom of contract is an important question.

The question of *vicarious liability* has been addressed in the literature. A general rule is that, if a party is solvent and able to control the others involved at low cost, it is efficient to make this 'principal' vicariously liable. Hence it should not be allowed to transfer liability by contract to an insolvent, incompetent, or fraudulent party. The principal may, of course, contract for goods and services of various kinds, but at the principal's own risk. In other words, if the parties involved in the recycling do not fulfil their duties, the principal remains liable. The principal must, therefore, control the others, which may be done at low cost (relative to public supervision and control) due to repeated exchange among the parties. The legislator can, therefore, without loss of efficiency, make the principal liable for the failures of others. Public enforcement is hereby simplified – supervision is concentrated on a solvent party that, in turn, is able to control its contractors. Similarly, vicarious liability is frequently applied, for instance, in bank guarantees and in employer's liability in the workplace; see Chapter 15, Section 3.

A common problem with imports is that the producers cannot be controlled by the public authorities. This provides a reason for making another link in the chain of involved parties liable – the importer. However, importers are usually small firms that may leave the market or become insolvent, which brings us to the question of how recycling can be guaranteed in cases in which the principal goes bankrupt or disappears for other reasons. Related problems are discussed in Chapter 15, dealing with the limits to liability.

BOX 9.1 DURABLES ALREADY IN USE

The possible solutions outlined above are designed for durables not yet in use. A remaining problem, therefore, is how to handle the recycling of durables already in use. One purpose of recycling liability is to encourage the producer to design products, return systems and dismantling in a cost-minimizing way. For durables already in use, the product design is given and cannot be improved. Yet recycling liability may be used for the collection, dismantling and reuse of materials. The consumer/owner presumably has, as noted above, a comparative advantage in the return of the goods. It is thus necessary to motivate the consumers to undertake the returns. One method is to pay consumers a sum large enough to make them return most used goods. The financing of such a plan may, however, cause problems. If the dealers or producers are liable for the returns, it is they who must pay the consumers. Since the goods have already been sold, and the returns are thus not calculated in the prices, this results in windfall losses for the dealers/producers. Payment through public means is possible, of course, but presumably not politically attractive.

An alternative is to make the consumer (the owner) liable for the return. Consumer liability for returns requires that sanctions, for example fines, be used if the obligation is not fulfilled. This is not easily put into practice, even though thrown-away durables may have some form of inscription, or other markings, which make it possible to identify and, subsequently, fine the owner. Penal sanctions require that offenders are detected without too high policing costs. Yet, not all littering will be detectable. Severe penalties and comprehensive policing efforts may, therefore, be necessary. In addition, penal sanctions require that the consumer's responsibility be generally accepted.

A financial advantage to consumer return liability is, of course, that the costs of returns are carried by the consumers/owners. It may therefore be politically attractive to allocate the return duty to the consumers. However, the policing and littering costs must also be taken into consideration. The rest of the costs of recycling need to be covered by taxes, if windfall losses are to be avoided in the business.

Finally, it should be noted that a general obligation to return used durables would result in a large amount of collected waste. The recycling standard must be settled upon, and the dismantling financed for a large number of goods. Therefore, it seems reasonable to concentrate on certain goods, primarily on goods of large volume, which require considerable space on the dumping sites, and on goods containing dangerous substances.

6. INTERNATIONAL ENVIRONMENTAL CONFLICTS

So far we have mainly dealt with national jurisdictions where well-established legal institutions and conflict-solving methods are available. On an international level it is more complicated because of many involved parties, lack of institutions for negotiations, and poor enforcement. It is also at the international level where we observe the most serious environmental problems. Bilateral negotiations between single states may be possible at transboundary externalities concerning neighbouring states. In such cases there is no obvious need to use international institutions such as the EC or the UN. In most cases, however, transboundary externalities include many states. A problem in international pollution is that enforcement is weaker than on a national and bilateral level. Sovereign states may reject controls. Transboundary penalties cannot be effected, and breach of an agreement on, for example, environmental pollution is costly only to the extent that it creates mistrust in future relations.

There is a conflict between the need for effective penalties and the desire to reap the benefits of continuous well-functioning relations. Therefore, the most important, and perhaps the only, enforcement mechanism is repeated exchange, where nations are involved in a number of international transactions. The importance of repeated exchange indicates that parties involved in many relations are most prone to honour agreements. This is in accordance with the idea that trade promotes peace and economic growth.

The polluter pays principle (PPP) is an internationally recognized environmental policy principle. However, to implement the principle is not without problems. Indeed, in a large number of situations, it is not practised. One reason is that the victim pays principle (VPP) is often most efficient due to transaction costs. It may be that the international community is unable to control sovereign states and, thus, enforce payment by the polluters. Another reason for applying the VPP, which is most common in relation to nuisance or pollution in less developed countries, is simply that the polluter is unable to pay. Under such conditions the only solution may be that the victim pays the polluter in order to make her reduce the pollution. The victim may also pay for the right to control the measures upon which the agreement has been made. Hence the inability to make the polluter pay means that the polluter *de facto* receives the 'right' or power to pollute.

This reality became obvious for example, after the break-up of the Soviet Union. The wealthy Western nations would like to reduce pollution in these countries, which must be undertaken through payment and direct control. However, it was not meaningful to claim the PPP after the Chernobyl accident as the Soviet Union was practically bankrupt. Consequently, in such a situation the surrounding states, which may be victimized again, must pay for the shut-down and repair of nuclear power plants. In order to control these measures, they must also assume responsibility for the investments, for example through the establishment of joint ventures.

Many international environmental problems are of the same character; that is, industrialized states may claim that the less developed states should undertake measures to protect the environment. However, this is unlikely to take place if the victims do not organize and pay for the measures. For instance, it is often argued that the cutting down of the rainforests should be stopped by the nations in the tropics. However, local industry and population benefit from the cutting, while the victims are primarily in the most developed parts of the world. Hence the only realistic solution to the problem is that the victims pay the injurers to stop deforestation. Indeed, development aid has recently become more environment-oriented. Thus the VPP is the reality in foreign 'aid'.

7. CONCLUSIONS

Price theory assumes a given set of institutions such as markets, firms, households and property rights. To fully understand environmental policy and the role of property rights, including the freedom of contract and the duty to compensate for damages, we need the new economic theory on institutions. Transaction costs are basic in this theory. That is, costs of search, contacting and enforcement are fundamental to the development of institutions and to the choice of law. We introduced institutional economics in Part I and continue to refer to it in Parts III and IV.

In this chapter we presented the normative economics of law. That is, we value a law as 'good' or 'bad' based on economic efficiency criteria. The basic norm is the Pareto criterion: one alternative is better than another, if someone in the economy is better off without someone else being worse off. Utility is revealed by individual choice. Freely accepted trade thus fulfils the Pareto criterion. Pareto-optimality prevails when it is not possible to increase utility for someone without diminishing it for someone else. If more goods could have been produced with a given set of resources, there is inefficient production. More could have been produced to the benefit of some without a loss for others. Inefficient trade prevails if goods and services can be traded in a mutually beneficial way.

According to these norms a first normative economic rule can be established: the law should be structured to remove the impediments to private agreements. That is, the law should assign property rights and simplify mutually beneficial contracts. When transaction costs make private agreements impossible there is a second normative rule: the law should minimize the harm caused in the absence of or failures in private agreements.

The underlying economic norm for legal regulation is a hypothetical (efficient) agreement that the parties could have agreed upon in a world without transaction costs. At prohibitive transaction costs it is the aim of the legal authorities to regulate in accordance with a hypothetical efficient contract. For the central regulation to be relatively efficient the authorities must have information and/or enforcement power not available to the involved parties.

If there is uncertainty about the impact or regulation, the authorities may chose not to regulate, that is, to allow pollution as long as harm is not demonstrated, or restrict it to a certain more or less arbitrary limit. An alternative approach is to prohibit pollution when there is uncertainty. This policy could be interpreted as an application of the precautionary principle, while the first attitude could be referred to as industrial optimism.

The Coasean method of analysis is applied to legislation on producer's responsibility for recycling worn-out durable goods. Who should be economically liable when several suppliers, producers and dealers are involved? The starting-point in the analysis is the distribution of rights and duties by contracts in a world without transaction costs. The outcome is, of course, that independent of the legal distribution of the responsibility the involved parties will reallocate the duties among themselves in a cost-efficient way. Hence the choice of liable party does not matter. However, in the real world with transaction costs, legal responsibility matters. Efficient law distributes the duties according to the comparative advantage of the various parties in handling the waste. Enforcement of the rules requires that the authorities collect money from the liable party. Insolvent or foreign producers might well be impossible to control. Domestic firms may therefore be made responsible for recycling. To certify solvency some sort of guarantee may be required. The right to transfer liability by contract must also be limited to prevent the responsible party from transferring liability to others that cannot be controlled by the authorities.

On an international level it is complicated to reach enforceable agreements on environmental matters. It is also at the international level where we observe the most serious environmental problem (see Chapter 3, Section 5.) The polluter pays principle (PPP), is the general international liability rule (see Chapter 2, Section 4). Nevertheless, in reality it is often the polluted victim that has to pay the polluter, but that would not be inefficient in accordance with the Coase theorem. If the problem of establishing an enforceable international PPP agreement is great, it may be transaction-costs-reducing and more efficient to let the victim pay, that is, to apply the VPP *de facto*. Indeed, a wealth effect in favour of the polluter may effect redistribution to poor developing countries that pollute rich nations willing to pay for a cleaner environment.

NOTES

1. Simon (1959).
2. See Cooter and Ulen (2000).

FURTHER READING

Alchian, A.A., Crawford, R.A. and Klein, B. (1978), 'Vertical Integration, Appropriable Rents, and the Competitive Contracting Process', *Journal of Law and Economics*, **21**, 297–326.

Coase, R.H. (1960), 'The Problem of Social Cost', *Journal of Law and Economics*, **3**, 1–44.

Simon, H.A. (1959), 'Theories of Decision Making in Economics and Behavioral Science', *American Economic Review*, 253–83.

Turvey, R. (1963), 'On the Divergences between Social Cost and Private Cost', *Economica*, 309–13.

Williamson, O.E. (1985), *The Economic Institution of Capitalism*, New York: Free Press.

10. Balancing benefits and costs

There is no such thing as a free lunch.
Milton Friedman

1. INTRODUCTION

Damage that cannot be mitigated by private agreements should, according to 'the second rule of normative law', be minimized by the legal system (see Chapter 9, Section 3). But what can legislators or judges do to improve the situation? Do the authorities possess knowledge or competence not available to the parties themselves? A first answer is that the legal authorities have powers to enforce and to tax not available to involved private parties. Second, activities harming third parties must in some way be centrally regulated. Third, central authorities may have information on, for example, pollution and long-term degradation of the environment which the involved parties do not possess or disregard. But how should benefits and costs be estimated and valued by public authorities? The harm, as well as the virtue of activities, must in some way be evaluated before it can be efficiently regulated.

Cost–benefit analysis (CBA) provides a tool for estimating social benefits and costs. CBA is widely applied in, for example, traffic and health economics, but it is also used to evaluate legal regulations. In fact, some nations require CBA before new laws are introduced. CBA is usefully applied in the evaluation of environmental laws as well. If, for instance, the problem is traffic congestion and the regulatory issue is a speed limit, the benefits of the reduced speed in terms of less congestion and fewer accidents can be compared with the costs in terms of travel time. If the benefits exceed the cost, the CBA suggests that the speed limit should be enacted. This assumes, of course, that there are no other considerations of importance to the policy-maker, which there normally are.

We continue in Section 2 with a brief presentation of analytical methods frequently used in CBA. Thereafter, in Section 3, we question the underlying social philosophy of CBA, which presumes that the governor/law-maker is a utilitarian-welfare-, or social-profit-, maximizer. It may be argued that the outcome of the political system, as well as of legislation, is rather a result of struggling of interest groups, ideologies and bureaucracy. Another, and more fundamental, critique of CBA is that the economics is unethical and should, therefore, not be practised. In Section 4 we discuss ethical norms and the balancing problem. Special issues of importance in economics and ethics are the morality of trade, and the valuation of human life. These topics are briefly discussed in Sections 5 and 6. Conclusions are in Section 7.

2. PRACTICAL CBA

2.1 Cost-effectiveness

In a perfect CBA all benefits and costs are estimated and summarized. The result is simply a monetary positive (profit) or negative (loss) number. All costs and benefits are, in reality, of course, not measurable. The practical measurement problems remain large. The real analysis is, therefore, partial and/or indirect. Nonetheless, the analyst can do a great deal to simplify and improve the decisions of the law-makers.

A CBA is usually limited to certain aspects that can be priced, while other aspects are left to the decision-makers without valuation. A first limited option is to make an *impact analysis*, that is, a study of the consequences of considered possible alternatives. Assume, for instance, that an industry pollutes a wetland and threatens a rare species of duck. Thus, there is a depletion problem that may motivate legislation. But how should the benefits of the industry's production be valued as compared to the endangered duck? The ecologist has here an important role estimating the environmental facts. Economists can contribute with estimates of the costs, for example, of preserving wetlands, and those of reducing industry production. To judge the benefit of saving the duck in relation to the costs of the industry demands setting political priorities.

A general problem in impact analysis is that the positive and negative impacts are multi-dimensional and, thus, not easy to compare. Costs may be calculable, while benefits usually do not show up in immediate monetary gains. For instance, the time cost of a speed limit may be calculable, while the benefits in terms of non-priced effects such as reduced congestion and fewer accidents are complicated to compare with each other, and with the costs. What the impact analyst can do is to present estimates on monetary benefits and costs and impacts in terms of, for example, traffic volumes, speed and accident rates, and leave the weighing to the decision-making authorities.

A further step is to undertake a *cost-effectiveness analysis*, that is, to estimate the costs of reaching an objective given by, for example, a policy-maker. Suppose, for instance, that the goal of a law is to save human lives.

Given this objective, the analyst may compare various options such as road investments, an anti-smoking campaign, the closing down of a nuclear power plant, a vaccination programme, a clean water project, and so on. The result of the analysis will be a measure of the cost of saving a life in various ways. Given this information, it is then up to the policy-maker to make a choice. Needless to say, the policy-maker is not bound to choose the cheapest alternative – there may be other important aspects to consider – but the analysis may simplify decisions.

Cost-efficiency prevails when a certain production or objective cannot be reached at lower costs. Conversely, cost-inefficiency means that the objective can be reached at lower costs, including raw materials, capital and human resources. In other words, cost-inefficiency indicates *waste of resources*. The prime goal of cost-savings in a firm (or by a public authority) is presumably to improve profit (to limit spending), that is, to make the saved resources available to the owner (public authority). However, in the long run competition will normally push down the profit. The benefit of the reduced use of resources for a product or object is, thus, favourable to society and the environment. Therefore, whatever the objective of an investment is, there is no conflict between economic cost-efficiency and the environmental interest of saving resources.

Economists have spent much effort in estimating economic values that are not directly priced in the market. The general idea is to mimic agreements in a competitive market. Prices in an idealized market reflect the value of the marginal unit traded. Here, willingness to pay (WTP) equals the seller's willingness to accept (WTA). In other words, the marginal seller gives up a value (compensated by money) to the marginal buyer, who values it the same as the seller does. Prices thus reflect opportunity costs.

The valuation of a good becomes complicated when it is, for example, a public good that is not valued in the market. Consider, for example, the decision to invest in a national park. We assume that the park is a non-rival, open-access good. It is, however, excludable in the sense that it can be fenced off and closed (see Chapter 4, Section 7). The cost of the park is known and measurable because there is an alternative use (price) of the property. According to the Kaldor–Hicks criterion, the ideal would be to compare the cost of the park with the willingness to pay for the park by all citizens. For that, we need to estimate the demand for the park. Imagine a demand curve for the park as illustrated in Figure 10.1. The citizens are ordered in accordance with their WTP, with the highest WTP furthest to the left. The total WTP equals the consumer surplus, as shown by the shaded area in Figure 10.1. As there is no rivalry in using the park, there should be free entry, which will result in x_0 visits (assuming only visitors derive pleasure from the park). If the consumer surplus exceeds the cost of the park, the decision to invest in it is socially

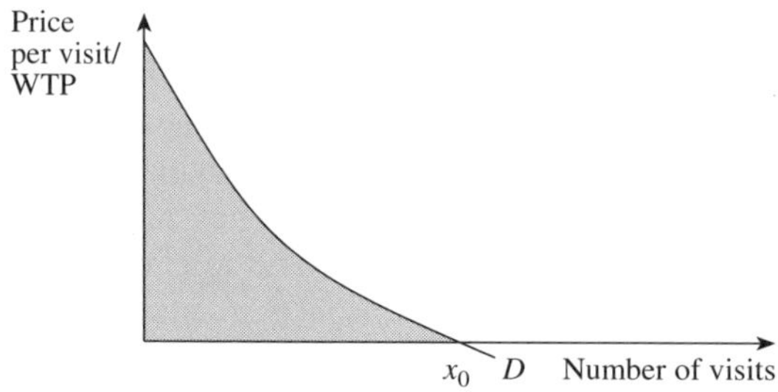

Figure 10.1 Consumer's surplus of park at price 0

optimal. Remember that this statement of social optimum rests on a series of presumptions. First, the Kaldor–Hicks utilitarian criterion is accepted as the norm. Second, costs and benefits for different groups can be added together. Prices must, thus, reflect individual marginal utility. For prices to reflect utility a series of firm assumptions must be fulfilled: the individuals must be utility-maximizers, and all markets must be in equilibrium. Then, the prices will mirror the marginal utility of different goods for every single individual. Imperfections such as external effects, monopolies and excess burden of taxes are, here, neglected.

It may be argued that a utilitarian state with the object of maximizing total utility should, first of all, redistribute wealth so that all have the same marginal utility of money. However, total equity is equivalent to a 100 per cent tax rate on earnings, which would cause a collapse of the economy. The excess burden makes it costly to tax the people (see Chapter 6, Section 4), which partly explains why redistribution does not take place to the extent that everyone's utility of money is the same.

The state may, therefore, undertake investments or political measures, for example legislation, in an attempt to favour 'weaker' groups. In such cases, the CBA must contain an element whereby benefits and costs for different groups are weighed. In our national park example, the taxpayers' money should be compared with the WTP of various groups enjoying the park. How these costs and benefits should be weighed is a political issue.

The reason why the total consumer surplus in Figure 10.1 is the marginal benefit to be compared with the cost is that the existence of the park is at stake in the decision to invest or not. Compare this with what was said about the value paradox in Chapter 5, Section 9. The reason why the total WTP for, for example, water is irrelevant is that decisions consider marginal increases or decreases, not the existence of water.

Now, let us assume that there is some scarcity and rivalry in using the national park. Too many visitors disturb the wildlife and damage sensitive

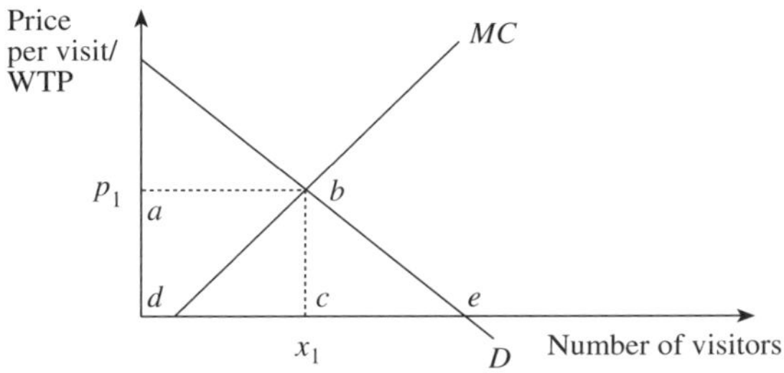

Figure 10.2 Socially optimal number of visitors

habitats. Suppose that the marginal cost of additional visitors is known and increasing, as in Figure 10.2. Given the existence of the park, the policy-maker must decide how many visitors may be allowed. The socially optimal number of visitors, according to the Kaldor–Hicks criterion, is x_1. This is so because all consumers to the left of x_1 are willing to compensate for the harm they inflict. At x_1, the marginal harm is equal to the marginal benefit of the visit; and to the right, the visitors' WTP is less than the harm. A simple means of efficient rationing is to impose an entrance fee equal to p_1. The fee will generate an income to the treasury of *abcd*. It will reduce the consumer surplus by *abcd* for those visiting the park and paying the fee, and by *bec* for those not visiting the park once the fee has been introduced.

2.2 Estimating the Willingness to Pay

The park example above requires information on the demand curve, that is, the WTP. Such information is usually not available for environmental goods such as national parks. There are, nevertheless, some techniques available to make estimates.

The *hedonic pricing* method is based on the idea that the value of property reflects all kinds of benefits and costs, including environmental impacts. The benefits can come from agricultural output, housing, or commercial income. Each piece of property has its set of attributes, some of which will be environmental, for example, the level of pollution, noise and proximity to parks and natural reserves, and so on. Altogether, these properties generate a stream of future expected earnings, which when discounted to the net present value, NPV, equal the market price of the property (see Chapter 7, Section 6).

Since the price of the property includes valuations of all attributes, it should be possible to isolate the different factors influencing the price. With the help of statistical techniques, usually multiple regressions based on time-series and/or cross-sectional data, the difference in property value due to differences in the environmental factors can be identified. Three sets of variables are usually used in the statistical analysis: neighbourhood, accessibility and environmental variables. The first set of variables approximates the WTP for factors such as quality of housing, good schools, low property taxes, and low crime rate. The second set of variables approximates the WTP for proximity to the centre of the city and/or business district, and accessibility to major roads and parking. The last set of variables approximates the WTP for environmental qualities such as lower levels of air and noise pollution and proximity to green areas.

The hedonic pricing technique is thus based on the analysis of market data from transactions in private goods and services, which are related to the characteristics of the public good under consideration. In other words, in the hedonic pricing technique the value of changes to the natural environment is analysed in relation to the perceived monetary changes this has caused in markets of influenced goods. It is then assumed, for example, that housing values will reflect the variation in the quality of environmental goods. House prices can be a function of natural surroundings such as the presence of parks and forests. On that basis an evaluation of environmental improvement can be undertaken, based on an estimation of the house price function.

The *contingent valuation method* approximates the WTP by asking a statically chosen set of persons, using questionnaire techniques, what they would be willing to pay for a benefit, or alternatively how much compensation they would require in order to accept, WTA, a loss. A similar method is to create a hypothetical market and with the help of experimental techniques, approximate the respondent's personal WTP or WTA for changes in the quantity or quality of some good. The contingent valuation method is relatively easy to apply, and it can be used in almost any context. The downside of this method is that the market is hypothetical, and, thus, actual WTP cannot be measured. Questionnaire techniques also have a number of possible biases. Establishing the validity of results measured in a hypothetical market for a good is difficult.

The *travel cost approach* approximates the WTP for environmental values like natural reserves, beautiful views and so on by direct measurement of the willingness to pay in the surrogate market of labour and travel costs. If an individual pays a certain amount, including cost of travel, forgone income and entry fee, the expected benefit must exceed the cost. By collecting information on these variables from a random set of visitors travelling from different locations, an approximation of the total WTP can be obtained.

BOX 10.1 GOTHA CANAL

Gotha Canal is a historical landmark in Sweden. The canal, which connects the east coast to the west coast through a system of lakes, became commercially obsolete with the arrival of the railways. Today the waterway is a great tourist attraction. It used to be a private enterprise but is today mainly a public good with open access to the public. Transport on the canal is priced, however. The value of this attraction has been estimated in several studies. In a hedonic pricing study the value of real estate increases on average by around 30 SEK with each metre closer to the canal.[1] Thus the canal has a significant impact on real-estate values around it. The contingent valuation method has been used to estimate the willingness to pay by cyclists, travellers visiting the canal, and shippers using the waterway.[2] Cyclists state that they are willing to pay on average 80 SEK for a trip along the canal. Visitors by car are willing to pay 12 SEK and the shippers 2000–2500 SEK per trip. The estimates are approximate and may be questioned for many reasons. Nevertheless, they present a method of calculating the willingness to pay for environmental goods. Note, however, that the value to society, including all Swedes, has not been estimated. It remains up to the politicians representing the public to consider the overall value of a historical landmark when deciding on subsidies or privatization of the canal.[3]

Notes:
1. L. Fahlgren and H. Knutsson, 'En sluss till värdering av Göta Kanal. En studie av fastighetspriser', EKI Linköping University, 20001. www.ep.liu.se/ea/gotakanal/2001/008/
2. J. Lindvall, 'Betalningsvilja för Göta Kanal', Department of Economics and Management, Linköping University, 2001. www.ep.liu.se/ea/gotakanal/2001/005
3. Bjuggren and af Donner (2002).

3. POLITICS AND POWER

3.1 Special Interest Groups

The normative welfare-economic theory presented above is based on the social norm that the government's aim is to maximize total welfare. In other words, the government is supposed to act purely in the *public interest*. The application of social CBA fits with this normative theory. The government is assumed to base decisions on the sum of all the interests of citizens.

Many objections have been raised to this welfare-economic approach, and to utilitarianism as a political philosophy. A basic critique concerns the image of the government – a benevolent despot, or political democracy – acting in the public interest. This is simply a false picture of reality, it can be argued. The political party in power has ideas and ideologies for which they fight and which they try to implement. Politicians may claim that their ideology is the interest of the people, but that may not be generally accepted by all citizens. Moreover, it may be true that the state powers execute the ideology, but the government is dependent on support from special interest groups and voters. Politics may, therefore, be understood rather as a compromise in the battle of interest groups for resources and influence.

Many economic studies show that the regulations favour special interests, although the official objective often is said to be 'the public interest', 'the environment', or 'the people'. For instance, minimum wages may be introduced to support the poor, while the regulation in reality protects those already employed. Similarly, the establishment of a national park with open access may be motivated by environmental goals, although the tourists will disturb the wildlife and damage the sensitive habitat. The special interest group gaining from the park may be, for example, upper middle-class tourists from large urban areas. The losers may be the local population and the taxpayers.

In the *public choice* literature, microeconomic models are used to explain processes of regulation. A starting-point is the assumption that the politician is also an economic or contractual man, who implements regulations that benefit the interest groups supporting him. Hence the politician is not, first of all, someone serving the public interest. Regulation is the product of supply and demand on a political market. On the demand side we find the various interest groups who want favourable regulation, and on the supply side, we find the utility-maximizing politicians who favour interest groups that give them political support and information.

Special group politics primarily functions as a wealth redistribution mechanism. That is, the gain of a special interest group causes losses to other groups. In other words, special interest groups are 'rent-seekers'. The 'rent-seeking' behaviour will, according to the literature, be especially successful: (i) if the costs are relatively low for the group to organize and bring together individuals to promote its interest; and (ii) if the costs of the public that pays the transfer (the taxpayers) are widely spread and difficult to identify. A group that is relatively small, well organized and single-issue-oriented will, therefore, have relatively low organizational costs, and may, thus, be successful.

Of special importance, here, is the idea of the *ignorant voter*. The point is that special interest groups have relatively large benefits to gain by rent-seeking, while the costs are spread over the general public via taxes. However, the individual taxpayer's share of the costs of each special interest project is small because of the large number of taxpayers; in addition, elections are rare and concern general politics rather than special projects or issues. The number of voters is, indeed, so great that no one can expect their own marginal vote to have any impact on politics. Consequently, the special interest groups may lobby and obtain benefits without eliciting reactions from the general public that pays. This phenomenon has been used to explain why the public sector has grown rapidly in most political democracies; compare Chapter 6, Section 4. There is an abundance of literature providing theoretical support, as well as empirical evidence, for rent-seeking in the case of environmental regulation.

A starting-point for environmental regulation is often a political ambition to provide some action toward environmental protection. Such demand for regulation may not be represented by a well-defined and active particular interest group. It may be initiated by a so-called *shadow interest group*. This is a group that would come into being if an accident occurred. Potential victims of environmental pollution can thus be seen as members of this latent group. If a shadow interest group ceases to be a shadow group and becomes active, it will have all the characteristics of a normal interest group. Knowing that shadow interest groups have the potential to become an effective lobby, rational politicians will, under certain circumstances, respond to these groups in the same way that they respond to normal interest groups, even though the shadow groups have not yet organized.

If legislative intervention seems unavoidable, the theory of regulation suggests that the interest groups involved will accept a general principle of regulation, but may strive to change its scope. The industrial interest groups to whom the regulation will be applied may realize that the regulation may enhance producer wealth while simultaneously correcting, or at least reducing, an externality problem.

This outcome has been stressed by Maloney and McCormick (1982) with respect to environmental quality regulation. They argue that industry, realizing that environmental regulation is unavoidable, will cooperate in the development of the regulation and try to change its contents to its own advantage. A classic example is the introduction of so-called *grandfather clauses*, which stipulate that the regulation will not be applicable to firms or products that are already in existence. Hence regulation can create a barrier to entry and, thus, protect existing industrial practices and products.

In other cases, for example as far as standard-setting is concerned, industry may lobby for lenient environmental standards to increase its profits. However, under certain circumstances, given the knowledge that environmental regulations will soon appear, more technically advanced segments of industry may also argue that the 'best available technique' should be employed, knowing that the new technique will provide them with an advantage over their competitors. In the literature this has been named *predatory regulation*.

Hence the efforts of industry may go in various directions: sometimes regulation will be favoured because it limits competition; in other cases there will be lobbying for more lenient environmental standards. With respect to the first type of lobbying, we can refer also to the function of licences, which are considered a central instrument in environmental policy. Moore (1961) has pointed to the anti-competitive effects of licensing.

3.2 The Administration

Special interest and pressure groups may lobby the legislator directly. However, since legislators usually give power to administrative agencies, the lobbying of smaller groups or individual firms will usually take place with the administrative agency.

The regulatory behaviour of administrations is also analysed in the economic literature. Administrations are not profit-maximizers in the ordinary sense, but their members may have a common interest in growth. Growth is not the ultimate goal, but it simplifies the career of the members of the organizations. A common assumption in the literature is, therefore, that organizations maximize size. The government has the problem of evaluating the demands of the agencies because much of the information is asymmetric and, thus, hidden within the administration. This may explain why complaints about inefficient administration are often met by a demand for more resources. The implementation of political reforms may thus not be efficiently implemented and controlled by the agencies.

Even if the administration only has the goal of the legislator in mind, there are important informational problems in the implementation of laws. One reason is that those regulated usually possess asymmetric information. The industry usually has information about the production and alternative techniques that the regulatory agency does not possess. An industry may also threaten, for example, a shutdown if costly regulations are imposed. Lack of information and resources may also hinder enforcement. Hence, to obtain information, the agency depends on the industry to be regulated. This explains why bargaining between the regulator and the regulated is frequently observed. These problems are further discussed in Chapter 11.

3.3 Lobbying Level

Lobbying takes place at all levels, both in central and local political and administrative bodies. Indeed, the influence of interest groups will not only play a role as far as the contents of regulation are concerned, but also when it is determined at what level of government action is to be taken. It can be argued that interest groups will prefer that level of government where their influence can be the greatest.

In the context of the European Union, Faure and Lefevere (1995) argued that this may explain why some industries will lobby in favour of environmental regulation at the European level. For new areas (where no national legislation exists), industrial lobby groups may encounter less countervailing power than at the local level where the environmental problems occur, and non-governmental organizations may oppose lenient standards. Once standards are set at the central level in Brussels, Member States will need to comply.

On the other hand, industry in Member States that already have relatively stringent environmental standards may have an incentive to lobby at the central level. The purpose of such lobbying would be to make these stringent environmental standards compulsory throughout the Union in order to force (southern European) competitors to comply as well and, thus, to create barriers to entry. In other words, predatory regulation may explain why many environmental regulations also emerge from Brussels in those cases where economic theory would, normally predict that the problem would be better dealt with at the decentralized level.

3.4 Political Failures and CBA

The special interest group theory, as well as empirical studies, has demonstrated that the traditional argument that regulation is welfare-enhancing if the market fails to internalize externalities may not necessarily be valid. There are many political failures due to asymmetric information on all levels of government. Regulations may, therefore, worsen the situation, even if there are obvious externalities.

On the other hand, it would be too one-sided to argue that, for example, environmental laws only serve private interests. Although there are strong incentives for rent-seeking, many environmental statutes are still enacted in a struggle to protect public interests. Note, also, that the interests of industry and the environmentalist may coincide, as in the case of predatory regulation; see the example provided in Box 10.2.

If the utilitarian public interest politics is a fiction, one may question whether CBA is legitimate. One defence of CBA is that public interest

BOX 10.2 LOBBYING IN FEDERAL SYSTEMS: EUROPE VERSUS THE USA

European scholars fear regulatory capture, especially in Brussels, as a result of the lack of transparency of the Brussels bureaucracy. American scholars have, on the other hand, argued that the risk of capture is larger at the state level. That may be true in the American context, with an open transparent debate at the federal level. In Europe, however, industry may be confronted with 'green NGOs' at the Member State level, at least in the 'Green' Member States such as Denmark and Germany, whereas those countervailing powers are almost absent in Brussels. Hence one can expect European industry to engage in serious lobbying efforts centrally in Brussels.

In particular cases, special interest groups representing industry might lobby in favour of a harmonization of European limit values. Interest groups in areas which are already heavily regulated may have incentives to extend their strict (national) regulations to the European level, forcing foreign competitors to follow the same strict regulation with which they already comply. The result is that industry will lobby to erect artificial barriers to entry. Green NGOs may be in favour of this lobby and may, therefore, support the demand to transfer strict national standards to a European standard. Thus industry in heavily regulated (and probably polluted) areas can (supported by green NGOs) force their stringent emission limit values upon their (southern) competitors.

arguments are frequent in politics. It is, therefore, important to confront declared goals with reality in terms of benefits and costs to various groups.

A simple example is shown in Figure 10.3. Suppose that a tax on imported oil is imposed, with the official goal of reducing the greenhouse effect. Let us first make a straightforward cost–benefit analysis of this policy. The benefit is the reduction in oil imports, q_0 to q_1. There is no direct way to measure the economic value of the reduced impact on the global atmosphere. The loss of consumer's surplus due to the tax equals *abed*; on the other hand, the state receives the revenue, *abcd*. Hence the remaining loss is *bce*. Knowing the starting-point p_0, q_0, the tax rate, and the slope of the demand curve, the area *bce* can be estimated. Thus the policy is socially preferable if the benefit to the atmosphere exceeds the area *bce*.

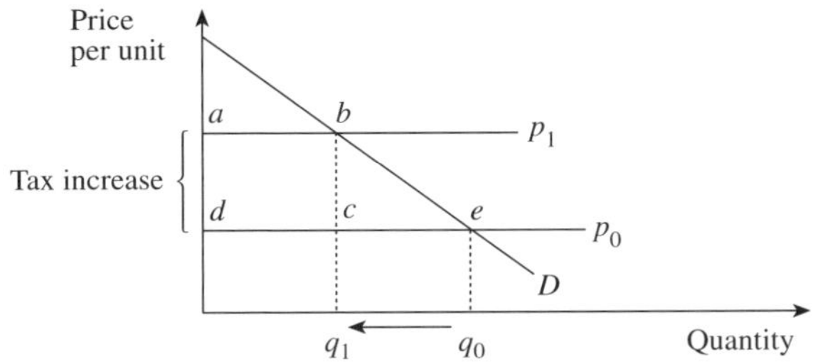

Figure 10.3 The effect of raising the tax on imported oil

Let us now compare this CBA with a listing of impacts on various interest groups. The officially announced gain is the reduction of oil used, q_0 to q_1. Other gains are the fiscal gain for the treasury, *abcd*, and the gain to domestic producers of fuels that will substitute for the imported oil (not directly illustrated in Figure 10.3). The loss to the oil consumers equals the reduced consumer's surplus, *abed*. The oil producer's loss of sales is demonstrated by q_1ceq_0.

After this listing, it may be of interest to speculate about which force is dominant behind the oil tax. A believer in the power of dominant special interests would argue that the domestic producers of fuels are the driving force. Landowners producing (subsidized) non-fossil fuels are important in national politics, while foreign fossil producers are not. Moreover, the state needs to collect tax revenues. Hence in this case the general public may be more or less misled by the greenhouse (public interest) argument.

4. ETHICAL NORMS AND THE BALANCING PROBLEM

4.1 Absolute Norms

Environmental policy is often expressed in absolute terms. For instance, water should be clean and safe to drink, or a hazardous industry should be harmless. Safety, however, is a relative phenomenon. Hazardous industries are, of course, never completely safe, and the effect of pollution on risk is gradual rather than absolute.

One may, of course, claim that the law should protect the victims and the environment and, thus, neglect the benefits of industry. In other words, as stated in many laws, pollution should be minimized, not optimized. A problem here is that, on the social level, victims will also be harmed by inefficiency. As citizens, victims have an interest in industry as employees, customers and taxpayers. Thus there is a common interest in the weighing of benefits and costs.

Nevertheless, many ethical norms are expressed in absolute terms, for example:

- Life has infinite value and cannot, or should not, be valued in monetary terms.
- You shall not kill.
- You shall not steal.

Such *categorical imperatives* are found in most religions, and are essential in some philosophies. According to Immanuel Kant (1785), an activity is morally just only if it is performed out of a sense of duty, based on a valid, ethical rule. Valid rules must be universally applicable. It may, for instance, be argued that 'you shall not steal others' property' is universal if everyone should be bound by the rule. Note that Kant's philosophy is not consequential, as is utilitarianism. For example, stealing is not bad because exclusive property rights are efficient. It is bad because it is against a universal rule.

Such rules of conduct are of great importance in religion and education. Despite the importance of ethical imperatives in human education and daily life, there are, nevertheless, always trade-offs between benefits and costs. This is known but not always articulated. We may, for instance, have good reasons for teaching our children the absolute ethical norm not to commit crimes. Yet everyone commits some crime, sooner or later. The decision may depend on expected benefits and costs of the crime when it is committed. Similarly, society accepts crime in that the criminal justice system has limited resources and must, therefore, prioritize. Indeed, there is an optimal amount of crime in the sense that the marginal benefit of reducing the crime rate is smaller than the marginal harm. This will be studied further in Chapter 16.

One may speculate why ethics and many laws are expressed in an absolute manner, although the reality is evidently gradual and relativistic. One explanation is that moral imperatives have an important normative impact. Persuasion and education may work better expressed in absolute terms.

Another explanation is that humans demand the suppression of risks or the feeling of 'safety'. Above, in Chapter 7, Section 5, we discussed the certainty premium, that is, the shift in risk estimates when moving from a very small considered risk to 'certainty'. If the politicians or law-makers can convince the public that the law guarantees safety, meaning that the risk can be neglected by already overloaded individual minds, the citizens would be released from worry by the law and, consequently, suppress the risk.

A third explanation is that laws are often a result of a political compromise, and it may be simpler to come to an agreement on absolute positive moral norms if they are not related to their costs.

Environmental laws are often expressed in absolute terms. For instance, the law may state that in order to obtain a permit, a (hazardous) industry must be 'safe', or that the groundwater must be 'clean', or the production technique should be the 'best available'. None the less, it is an illusion that (permitted) hazardous industries are completely safe. There is always some risk of accident; thus there is a trade-off between prevention and risk that must be balanced one way or another, explicitly or implicitly.

A means of maintaining the fiction of absoluteness, and getting around feelings of insecurity and the problem of complex decisions, is to introduce a threshold below which the activity or substance is said to be 'safe'. This does not, however, eliminate the balancing problem. Accumulated research in, for example, biology, physiology and economics indicates that there are variations in the acceptance level of external influences by individuals and environments. For instance, the water is never absolutely clean, and the risk of drinking polluted water gradually increases and varies with the individual, substance and concentration.

More or less absolute human guidelines and ethical norms are also of great importance in the environmental movement. Rhetorical concepts such as sustainability, green consumption, and ideas on ecological harmony and intrinsic values, and so on are examples. The purpose is often pedagogic. Needless to say, changes in attitudes in favour of increased caretaking and prevention may save the environment. Yet, if a side-effect is hostility to explicit balancing, the rhetoric results in a waste of resources, both today and in the future.

4.2 The Immoral Market

Economists have for decades suggested Pigouvian charges for the regulation of negative externalities. Examples are charges on energy, emissions and fertilizers. Such environmental measures are generally accepted today, but have been much questioned on moral grounds. The charge has been regarded as a fee to become free of the duty not to pollute. It should not be possible to buy oneself free of this duty. The moral of 'not polluting' has evidently been regarded as being in conflict with market solutions.

It may be true that some moral value is lost through sales of pollution permits. However, the moral attitude may also be due to misunderstandings about the benefit of trade and the function of the market. In addition, it may not be clear that if the market is not allowed to solve the allocation of resources, the allocation must be undertaken in some other (usually political) way, which will also have ethical as well as economic shortcomings.

Freedom of contract and, thus, the market is often restricted for moral reasons. In Chapter 4, Section 8 we listed a number of reasons why individuals are not permitted to contract or run a business. Here are some further examples: the trade of children on a market for adoption is normally outlawed; the trade of body parts is usually restricted; trade of narcotics is illegal; the international trade of waste is restricted; prostitution may be outlawed; trade with brutal regimes may also be banned; and so on. Moral indignation over the driving forces behind trade is understandable. Moral imperatives codified in a law prohibiting trade may also be highly justified. Economics has nothing to add about moral values. Economics can, however, contribute with an understanding of underlying problems and can point to important side-effects of a limited freedom of trade.

First, trade takes place because the buyers and sellers expect to gain from it. The expected gain remains although it is outlawed. Hence there is an incentive to break the law. Most traders may follow the law, but some will circumvent it, and those who are unscrupulous risk-takers will remain in an illegal business. In other words, outlawing trade causes criminality, which implies a number of problems. One is related to enforcement – if the law cannot be enforced, the trade may continue against the moral norm of the law.

Second, freedom of contract and trade are passports to the market economy. Outlawing trade thus means that coordination of demand and supply must be achieved by some other means, which may be ineffective. For instance, the demand for body parts in medicine may in a regulated or forbidden market be covered by (insufficient) donations. Similarly, adoption of children may be organized by some public authorities at high expense for adopters, if adoption is allowed at all, although there are millions of children in the world who need parents, and many adults who would love to adopt them. This is not to say that there should be an international market in, for example, adoption. One important shortcoming of such a market is that it would reveal different valuations for different children depending on, say age, sex and colour, which is against the basic ethics of equal human value.

4.3 Trade in Waste

Beneficial mutual exchange reallocates goods and services to those who value them most. This logic also applies to the world market. Given that Pareto-optimality is the norm and the sovereignty of states is generally accepted, traders will profit from free trade and so will the global community. This is also true for the trade in waste that will be stored or recycled in states where the costs will be minimized.

Nevertheless, the Basel Convention of 1992 tries to control the transboundary movement of hazardous waste. The main idea of the proximity principle (see Chapter 2, Section 5) applied in the Convention is to minimize international trade in waste. The Convention is a response to the worldwide production of hundreds of billions of tonnes annually of hazardous waste. The free trade of waste would have the effect that the industrialized world would sell a substantial part of its waste to less developed countries. According to economic theory, the buyers, as well as the sellers, would gain on this market. For instance, less developed countries with deserts for the storage of solid waste and cheap labour for dismantling and recycling would perhaps participate in and gain from the trade.

Apparently, there is a major discrepancy between the economic model of efficient trade and the principles of the Basel Convention. The assigning states obviously do not trust the international trading of waste. A problem is that sellers may not follow national laws on waste treatment. For instance, waste may be exported without specification of its true hazardous impact. Buyers may dispose of the waste in landfills, which in the long run harms their own population. Indeed, the political leaders of the receiving country may put the revenues into their own pockets, without considering the needs of the people. Not only the traders, but also the sovereignty of the buying nations are, thus, questioned. This problem is similar to the question of whether, for example, a manufacturer producing dangerous products or treating employees badly should have a licence or not; see Chapter 4, Section 8.

The Basel Convention does more than just question the freedom to trade waste on international markets. According to the Convention, hazardous waste should be minimized – not optimized and not sold. Hazardous wastes should, instead, be treated and disposed as close as possible to their source of generation. Hazardous waste generation should also be minimised at the source. This is in accordance with the idea of 'circular thinking', recycling and cleaner production methods whenever possible, which we introduced above in Chapter 6, Section 5.

4.4 Trade versus Environment

The Basel Convention can be seen as part of the environmental efforts in favour of 'green' attitudes to production and consumption. Such a change in attitude may have an important effect on the environment. Economists have, as noted, no special competence to evaluate such effects.

Yet economics has something to say about the potential costs of the ban on international trading of waste. This fits into a more general debate on the question of whether environmental protection measures may hinder international trade. Economists are traditionally sceptical of any measure that limits trade. This is for a number of reasons. First, potential gains in the international division of labour and economies of scale, and the use of national, comparative advantages in handling and storing waste will not be optimized.

BOX 10.3 KYOTO PROTOCOL: USING COMPARATIVE ADVANTAGES

The Framework Convention on Climate Change and the Kyoto Protocol (1997) provide an interesting example of how trade can facilitate an optimal use of comparative advantages. The basic idea in Article 3 (4) of the Convention on Climate Change is that policies and measures to protect the climate system against human-induced change should be appropriate for the specific conditions of each party. To that end article 7 of the Kyoto Protocol allows the parties to participate in emissions trading for the purposes of fulfilling their commitments under the Convention. The basic idea behind emissions trading is obviously that this trade could be mutually beneficial since it is much easier to realize high gains in emission reductions in some countries as compared to others. A specific application of this emissions trading in the climate change context is the concept of 'joint implementation'. Therefore article 6 of the Kyoto Protocol allows the countries to transfer to or acquire from any other party emission reduction units. The Kyoto Protocol therefore constitutes an example of a case where trade with pollutants (emission rights) may on the whole lead to better results than when such a trade is not allowed.

Second, trade is difficult to control. If there are trading parties that believe in mutual gain through trade, there are usually ways to circumvent legislation, especially on an international level. One immediate legal problem is how to define 'waste' as compared to 'raw material'.

Third, the ban on trade creates criminality, which causes other economic and moral issues. An obvious problem with the ban on the trade of waste is that illegal trade will be concentrated in areas where buyers and sellers are willing to take the risk of being caught; that is, waste will be concentrated in regions where governments are weak or corrupt.

Fourth, the underlying reason for a nation's willingness to restrict the trading of waste may be protectionism. Potential exporting countries may gain by protecting their own waste-handling industry through the limitation of exports. Hence the possibility of capture by the recycling industry in countries that would mainly export waste cannot be excluded without further examination.

Fifth, protectionism is free-riding. That is, protectionism is beneficial only if other nations do not close their borders. But once one nation closes its borders, others tend to follow. Mutual protection can rapidly freeze international trade, with a large impact on economic activities around the world. This is an important reason for GATT (the General Agreement on Tariffs and Trade) and international trade agreements.

Interruptions in international trade not only limit economic activity and growth; they also restrict international relations. Continuous interchange, reputation and relations are important for avoiding conflicts at all levels. Indeed, trade may be the most important factor for the long-term avoidance of wars. It was, in fact, the main argument for the establishment of the Treaty of Rome and the EU.

In sum, bans on trade as well as embargoes have a cost, while the benefit is usually questionable.

BOX 10.4 *SHELL* v. *GREENPEACE*

In 1995 the Shell Oil Company wanted to get rid of the oil rig, *Brent Spar*, placed in the North Sea, by transporting it to the deep Atlantic and dumping it into the waters. This was stopped, however, by Greenpeace. Instead, the rig was transported to Norway, where it was dismantled. Greenpeace regarded this as a great victory and an important move towards a complete ban of dumping in the seas. Yet the cost of dumping the rig in the Atlantic was estimated in 1997 at £4.7 million, while the cost of dismantling it, including the value of scrapped materials, was estimated to be £11–48 million depending on the method.[1] In addition, it was claimed that the dismantling was more polluting than dumping would have been. Does this economic calculus (if it is correct) show that the rig should have been dumped? Yes, if we want to minimize costs of scrapping worn-out rigs and similar equipment. However, the Greenpeace attack on Shell obviously had the wider purpose of changing attitudes in order to make an international ban politically feasible. The formation of opinions, including the value of more or less absolute principles on treatment of waste, is beyond economics. What economists can do is to demonstrate the costs of implementing such an environmental policy.

Note:

1. Det Norske Veritas, *Shell UK Exploration and Production Assessment of the Proposed Options for Disposal of Brent Spar*. Report no. 970911-0007.

5. THE VALUE OF LIFE

People often react very strongly when economists argue that a monetary value should be placed on human life. A first reaction may be that life cannot be valued. This may well be ethically correct. Nonetheless, not to put a value on human lives in the calculations of projects that obviously save or spoil human lives – whether they are investments in roads, design of cars, or risk of environmental poisoning – implies a value of zero. Hence the result of the viewpoint that life should not be considered in the economic analysis would be that too few life-saving projects would be carried out.

The inability to value life does not mean that is worthless. Indeed, it may be argued that life should, according to the moral standard, be given infinite value. However, if that is the case, any project with the slightest chance of saving a human life must be carried through, no matter what it costs. This would mean that all resources would be spent on life-saving projects, which obviously is not the best alternative as long as there are other values, for example, quality of life and the environment.

An investment in for example, a road, may lead to less congestion and fewer accidents, fatalities included. Such life-saving projects are regularly compared with other costly investments. Consequently, a valuation of life must, explicitly or implicitly, be undertaken. CBA tries to make the valuation explicit, consistent and comparable with other economic effects. Valuing life is an important aspect of cost–benefit analysis, as is valuation of the environment. CBA tries to put numbers not only on costs, but also on benefits. It is helpful if the policy-maker receives some measure of the benefits of, for example, saving one additional life as a result of additional investments in safety.

In principle there are three different ways to calculate the value of human life. The *net production method* is simple but crude. It means that the life is valued at the net present value of expected future incomes, minus one's own consumption. The method is applied when, for example, life insurance coverage is calculated. The relevant sum is compensation to survivors to ensure that they do not suffer any material loss. In the case of tort liability, the compensation awarded to surviving relatives may be calculated in the same way.

A shortcoming of the net production method is that the measure only takes into account the economic loss to other individuals, for example, the bread-winner or family. The net production method has, therefore, been called the cattle or slave method. The market value (and the economic loss) of a slave or cattle can be calculated as the net present value of the expected net profits the slave or animal will generate.

The *gross production method* values a life at the present value of lost income, that is, the value of production lost. With this method no deduction is made for the consumption of the dead person. An argument for not making the deduction for consumption is that the dead person was part of society when death occurred – thus the consumption of this individual was included in social utility. Hence both the loss of consumption and the loss of the excess production are a loss to society.

This measure has, however, important shortcomings. The gross production method includes all money income, which equals the total economic value of all goods purchased from that income (savings disregarded). This measure neglects the producer's and consumer's surplus of all goods consumed. In Figure 5.6 (in Chapter 5) the squared area $p_e \times q_e$ equals the money spent on that good, while the non-measurable shadowed triangles are the producer's and the consumer's surplus. By adding the consumer's surplus for all goods purchased, we may possibly imagine the loss of utility of the dead, but there is no way to measure it. Disregarding the consumer's surplus appears to be a gross underestimation of the loss to society of disability and/or premature death.

Note that we have, thus far, applied an *ex post* approach that is relevant when it comes to payments that compensate survivors economically. Relevant for decisions on future projects is, however, the willingness to pay for the reduction of risks, *ex ante*. The willingness to pay for risk reduction includes subjective elements such as expected sorrow, fear of death, and pain and suffering. By measuring the WTP for a reduction of the risk of injuries and death, it is possible to find out the value of reduced future fatal accidents. The method is called the *statistical life method*. The value according to this method has been estimated through the use of the contingent valuation (questionnaire) and the hedonic pricing (revealed preference) approaches. Examples of how revealed preference has been used are the studies of decisions of individuals to use underpasses when crossing roads, and statistical wage differentials due to the risks of different work. Variations in payment at very small differences in risk indicate that individuals are willing to pay a great deal to avoid injuries and fatal accidents. In the USA estimations indicate that the public is willing to pay $2–7 million. These figures can be employed in the CBA of traffic, healthcare and pollution. They can also be related to the sums spent on life-saving activities.

6. CONCLUSIONS

The specific assumptions and limitations of CBA utilitarianism do not prevent it from having a comprehensive economic application. The reason for its strong position is, presumably, the lack of consistent and systematic alternative tools. CBA is also of great importance for environmental law. In fact, in many legal systems there are regulations that stipulate in some way that costs and benefits shall be weighed against one another. This is also applicable to environmental laws. When benefits cannot be valued economically, cost-effectiveness studies may be useful to clarify and simplify political decisions.

Political as well as legal decision-making also includes aspects not considered in CBA. CBA is, thus, mainly a complement in the decision process. Indeed, as noted in section three of this chapter, there are influential special interest groups that cannot be disregarded in politics. Therefore, a modified form of CBA should be used, where the economic interests of various interest groups are presented.

The second economic principle, which says that law should substitute for contracts that cannot be reached, rests on the same contractual and utilitarian logic as CBA does. However, it is not at all certain that the law-makers' intention is economic efficiency, even if the official goal is to serve some public interest. The driving force behind laws may be special interests and rent-seeking. Indeed, many laws have the explicit purpose of redistributing rights or wealth. An example of a wealth-redistributing law in favour of families with children is a law on free school lunches and healthcare. Similarly, anti-discriminatory legislation has the purpose of distributing rights in another direction than would be the result of voluntary agreements.

As far as environmental laws are concerned, there is a common interest of cost-efficiency, and there are no obvious redistribution goals to favour a certain class of people. Yet many special interest groups are, of course, involved. We hold, therefore, that a combination of a utilitarian public interest and special interest approaches is useful in providing an understanding of how environmental regulations work. If the environmental policy does not correspond to the predictions of economic theory, it might be helpful to look at the possible influence of special interest groups.

A CBA involves several essential steps. The first is simply an enumeration of the various forms of benefits and costs inherent in the undertaking. The second step is to assign actual money values to the various forms of benefits and costs. The third step involves the selection of a rate of discount for the evaluation of benefits and costs that are expected to accrue in future years. Finally, the present discounted value of the entire expected future stream of benefits and costs will be calculated. In other words; if society is to make the most of its resources, it should compare what it receives from pollution control and environmental protection activities with what it gives up by taking resources from other users. It should measure the values of what it gains (the benefits) and what it loses (the costs). That is also applicable to human lives.

It is well known that it is impossible to attain 'certainty'. Nevertheless, many environmental laws are formulated in absolute terms. One explanation is that absolute norms may be morally appealing and possible to agree upon in the legislative process. In democratic societies laws are often an outcome of a complicated political compromise. The parties may be unable to reach an agreement other than one which all can accept in general, positive, ethical terms. Vagueness provides room for unlimited interpretations. Commitment is also weak. Moreover, it is complicated for an agency to implement a balancing of costs and benefits. An unclear law open to interpretation may in reality increase the freedom and discretionary powers of the agency. That is, a vague law requiring safety, fairness, or best technique may, somewhat paradoxically, be simpler to handle, although fulfilment of the law is impossible in practice.

FURTHER READING

Downing, P.B. (1981), 'A Political Economy Model of Implementing Pollution Laws', *Journal of Environmental Economics and Management*, **8**, 255–71.
Fuchs, V. and Zeckhauser, R. (1987), 'Valuing Health – a "Priceless" Commodity', *American Economic Review, Papers and Proceedings*, 263–8.
Hägg, P.G.T. (1997), 'Theories of the Economics of Regulation: A Survey of the Literature from a European Perspective', *European Journal of Law and Economics*, **4**, 337–70.
Harrison, D. and Rubinfeld, D. (1978), 'Hedonic House Price and the Demand for Clean Air', *Journal of Environmental Economics and Management*, **5**, 81–102.
Hoch, I. and Drake, J. (1974), 'Wages, climate and the quality of life', *Journal of Environmental Economics and Management*, **1**, 268–95.
Keenan, D. and Rubin, P. (1988), 'Shadow Interest Groups and Safety Regulation', *International Review of Law and Economics*, 21–36.
Mäler, K.-G. (1977), 'A note on the use of property values in estimating marginal willingness to pay for environmental quality', *Journal of Environmental Economics and Management*, **4**, 355–69.
Mayes, D. (ed.) (1995), *The Evolution of Rules for a Single European Market, II: Rules, Democracy and the Environment*, Luxembourg: OOPEC.
Nelson, B. (1978), *Economic Analysis of Transportation Noise Abatement*, Cambridge, MA: Ballinger.
Posner, R. (1974), 'Theories of Economic Regulation', *Bell Journal of Economics*, 345.
Vig, N.J. and Kraft, M.E. (eds) (1977), *Environmental Policy in the 1990s, Reform or Reaction?*, 3rd edn, Washington, DC: CQ Press.

11. Regulation of industry

Adopt the best available technique not
entailing excessive costs.
The BATNEEC concept.

1. INTRODUCTION

In this chapter we focus on a couple of specific problems that arise in case of regulation of industry. First we discuss, in Section 2, idealized regulation versus regulation in reality. We shall show, more particularly, that a variety of standards can be used in environmental law. We also discuss their comparative benefits. In many legal systems the standard-setting behaviour of agencies has been laid down by guidelines, which we shall also discuss. An important question discussed in Section 3 is whether the industry standards should be harmonized or should be related to location-specific circumstances. This is obviously not only important in the context of one nation state, but also within, for example, Europe. Hence the question arises how a theory of optimal specificity applies within the European context. So far we have assumed that a regulator would set standards in the public interest. However, the reality is often different. Concerning pollution abatement techniques, industry often has better information than the administrative agencies, which are supposed to regulate the industries. Hence a risk of capture emerges, which is discussed in Section 4. Conclusions are presented in Section 5.

2. REGULATION IN REALITY

2.1 Idealized Regulation

Figure 9.1 (in Chapter 9, Section 4) shows the optimal level of pollution (x_1). The optimum is possible to point out in the model because it is based on a series of simplifying assumptions: (i) there are two parties involved, one polluter and one polluted; (ii) the net profit by pollution is known by both parties (the MNB line), which implies that the profit-maximizing technology used by the polluter is given, and there is a simple linear relation between the production and pollution level (x may either indicate production or emission level); (iii) the damage to the victim is known and also measurable in economic terms (the MNH line); (iv) the goal of society is to maximize wealth, that is, the joint profit of the parties involved; and (v) there are no other addition external effects or interests involved. All of these assumptions are motivated to identify and clarify the basic economic optimization problem. The model also clearly illustrates the Coase theorem. By relaxing the assumptions one by one, we systematically obtain a fuller picture of the complex, real world.

The zero transaction costs assumption was relaxed in Chapter 9, where we formulated the normative Coasean rule saying that law should mimic the outcome that would prevail in a hypothetical world with full information and without transaction costs; see Chapter 9, Section 4. In reality, it is seldom possible to identify the optimal standard. In order to do this, the regulatory agency must have access to the information described in the model. In reality, information is most limited. The rationale for legislation is that transaction costs prevent the involved parties from coming to an agreement. To improve the situation the agency should, therefore, possess some information or power not available to the parties themselves. One answer is that the agency collects information that the ignorant free-riding polluter has no incentive to collect. Second, the agency may be able to make decisions on emissions upon which the parties are unable to agree.

2.2 Environmental Standard-setting

The balancing process of the model requires accurate information on the marginal costs of the various technical devices that could prevent harm, as well as information about the harm for the victims. In theory, information is needed on all polluters and victims. Especially in cases where there are many polluters and victims, there are obvious problems in obtaining information and in regulating all in detail. Practical simplifications are, therefore, crucial. A reduction of the problem is to abandon the search for optimal pollution and instead set politically realistic targets and try to reach them in a cost-efficient way. The target can be a total pollution of, say a maximum X tonnes of toxic emissions or Y number of cars.

In practice, the regulation is usually formulated in some general target, and in constraints or restrictions on the polluters. The general regulation is called in legal terms a *target standard* or an *environmental quality standard.* It is sometimes also referred to as an *ambient quality standard.* This standard defines the environmental quality for a certain environmental component. The target can, for example, broadly state how a particular habitat should be shaped in an ecological way or it could simply refer to specific chemical standards to which, for example, the water in a creek should comply. Economists have traditionally argued that the law should limit itself to setting these targets.

When lawyers refer to standards, they usually mean the regulatory measures, normally used and imposed by administrative agencies, that tell the factory causing the externality what measures to take to prevent harm. These measures can be imposed in general rules, but can also be found in individual licences. In the environmental area they will often take the form of emission standards, prescribing the particular quality and quantity of the emissions into the environment. Non-compliance with such standards is usually punished by administrative and/or criminal sanctions. Since in this particular case the actor is not free to choose the measures he wishes to use to reach an optimal environmental quality, economists often refer to this approach as the 'command-and-control' approach.

In order to avoid confusion concerning the notion of standards, we shall now distinguish three types of standards: target (or ambient quality) standards; emission standards; and production (or specification) standards.

Environmental policy usually starts by defining the quality that a certain environmental component should have by setting a target or ambient quality standard. However, if there were only target standards this might lead to a problem. If the environmental harm is closely connected to the regulated activity, a quality standard may suffice. In that case the administrative agency could, for example, determine the target for the water quality of a certain creek. It would be the responsibility of the only factory emitting waste water into the creek to see that the target is achieved. However, in many cases the agency costs of determining the causal connection may be very high. This is particularly the case if not one but, say, ten sources emit waste water into the particular creek. This example shows that whereas environmental policy can start from the ambient quality of an environmental component to be determined in target standards, it should also go further in laying down emission standards that take into account how the quality standards can be reached.

Quality standards may therefore become the responsibility of administrative agencies that are engaged in emission-standard-setting. They will have to take the quality standard into account when setting emission standards for individual sources. Hence quality standards and emission standards are closely related.

Quality standards typically emerged in legislation in the 1970s–80s, partly as a result of failing policy that had been based merely on emission standards. This traditional command-and-control approach, focusing only on individual emissions of separate firms, had the disadvantage that an agency could not envisage the effects of the overall pollution on the specific environmental component. Moreover, emission standards as such gave few incentives for innovation in abatement technology and further reduction of environmental harm. Policy therefore changed to an increasing use of ambient quality standards, but in many countries these target (or ambient quality) standards are still used in combination with emission standards.

The second type of standard which is often used in environmental policy, and to which we have already referred, is emission standards, also called emission limit values. These standards still leave some freedom to the potential polluter, since they usually only determine (in general rules or individual licences) the amount and quality of the substances that may be emitted into the environment. There is obviously less freedom than with mere quality standards. Quality standards leave it completely up to firms how to comply with the target set. When emission standards are used, the quality and quantities of the emissions are regulated. Still, emission standards leave much more freedom than the third category, specification or production standards, in which the process or abatement technology is also described. These will be discussed below.

BOX 11.1 EMISSION STANDARDS AND LICENCES

Emission standards can be found in almost every legal system that has environmental legislation. Most environmental legislation originated by putting emission standards in general 'permits to operate', which many factories have been obliged to have since the mid-nineteenth century. This permit was traditionally used as the instrument of the authorities to control the operation of a certain plant. As environmental awareness grew these general permits also began to incorporate emission standards. Later, in the 1960s and 1970s, various legal systems started to implement so-called sectoral legislation, protecting one specific component of the environment, for example surface water, groundwater, air or soil. Some of these general acts incorporated specific components into their standards for the emission of substances. Usually, however, the system, worked differently. The Environmental Act on protecting surface waters, for example merely stated administrative provisions, and provided powers to administrative agencies to set emission standards in individual licences. In some cases general emission standards were set industry-wide at the national level in order to guide the standard-setting behaviour of local administrative agencies. A deviation from these general standards then had to be motivated.

Specification or *production standards* go an important step further than emission standards since they will regulate *ex ante* what kind of product technology or abatement technology, for example a certain type of water treatment plant, will have to be implemented by the licensee. The advantage for the controlling administrative agency is obviously that information costs of monitoring are extremely low: it can easily be detected whether the particular factory has installed the prescribed technology. However, the disadvantages are obvious from an economic point of view. Specification standards may become obsolete very rapidly; they also give no incentive for technological innovation since all the licensee has to do is to comply with the prescribed specification. In addition, specification standards may have important anti-competitive effects, providing a monopoly to the producer of the prescribed technology. Hence the case for specification standards is generally rather weak, unless one can argue that the standard-setter has better information than firms concerning the optimal protection technology or innovation activity. This is, however, rather unlikely.

2.3 Optimal Standard-setting and Cost–Benefit Analysis

From the above it becomes clear that environmental policy needs quality standards to be set *ex ante*. A policy of mere emission standards, not taking into account the environmental quality they should achieve, has proven ineffective. If emission standards are used, ideally the optimal environmental quality is first determined and afterwards emission standards of the various plants are fixed in such a manner that the aggregate pollution coming from the various emissions will not exceed the environmental quality standards set. Therefore target standards must be set, defining the environmental quality to be achieved and, depending on the implementation instruments chosen, possibly emission standards as well. Indeed, the emission standards should not necessarily take the form of regulatory standards of the 'command-and-control' type (for example as licence conditions), but could also be implemented in emission taxes or take the form of the due care standard in a liability case.

The question arises how the cost–benefit analysis discussed above fits into this standard-setting scheme. Cost–benefit analysis will first of all play a role when environmental targets are determined, as has been indicated above. But also at this second stage, that of defining emission standards, it will play a role. In an optimal world where the regulator sets emission standards in the public interest, the administrative agency will take into account marginal costs of more stringent environmental standards and balance these against the marginal benefits of additional reduction of environmental harm. This refined balancing process requires accurate information both on the expected environmental harm and on the marginal costs of the various technical devices that could prevent this harm (and on the corresponding emission standard). Depending on whether either the parties in the marketplace or an administrative agency can be assumed to have the best information, this will lead to a choice of fixing emission standards via tort law (in which case they will correspond with a due level of care) or via regulation (in which case they will be incorporated as a condition of the administrative licence).

2.4 Integrated Pollution Control

For a long time most of the emission standards could be found in the individual licences of the specific plant. Since the basis for these licences was usually to be found in a statute dealing with the particular environmental component to be protected (say air or surface water), one plant might have to possess a variety of environmental licences, each dealing with one separate aspect of the environmental problem. These licences were, moreover, usually issued by different administrative authorities, so that there was often no coordination. A final step in this evolution has recently been seen, moving back to the early general licence. The situation now is that either the different licensing procedures are integrated or at least coordinated, or in some cases the decision-making process is totally integrated so that the potential licensee of a plant has only to address himself to one administrative agency which will, after public consultation, award one integrated licence that will set standards for the emissions relating to the various components.

This idea of an integrated pollution control system can now be found in many legal systems and has, as a result of Directive 96/61/EC, concerning integrated pollution prevention and control (IPPC), also been promoted at the European level.[1] This concept of integration can be found in Article 7 of the Directive, which states that Member States shall take the measures necessary to ensure that the conditions of and procedures for the grant of the permit are fully coordinated where more than one competent authority is involved, in order to guarantee an effective integrated approach by all authorities competent for this procedure.

BOX 11.2 CLEANER PRODUCTION, VOLUNTARY COMPLIANCE AND IPPC

To get a better understanding of the rationale behind the IPPC Directive one should appreciate that the traditional legal approach to environmental pollution used to be *ex post*. Technical corrective measures like filters and abatement technologies were imposed. However, many environmental engineers suggested a more proactive approach to environmental problems. The argument came especially from advocates of cleaner production technologies. The *cleaner production movement* stresses that a change towards cleaner production may lead to benefits to industry as well. Resources may be saved by cleaner production – customers, suppliers, creditors and personnel all value a clean production, product and environment. Information provisions are therefore required to induce industry to change to cleaner production, not primarily command-and-control regulations. One may argue that although these informational strategies may lead to benefits, there will be industries that (for a variety of reasons) will not change to cleaner production. Hence emission standards, backed up by (public) sanctions, will always remain important. On the other hand, following a cleaner production technology may in the future be a strategy for industries to reduce the costs of regulatory compliance.

More transparency and openness have also been demanded in the debate. In June 1993 the European Commission enacted the Eco-Management and Audit Scheme. Businesses from the industrial sector can hereby voluntarily participate in the *European environmental management and environmental audit scheme*, EMAS. The EMAS is a system for evaluation and improvement of environmental achievements in industry. If companies want to take part in the system, they have to submit to certain obligations: (i) the system requires a thorough audit or environmental analysis of the business. The environmental impact is looked at, as well as the weak and strong points in the organization with regard to the environment. The legal compliance with environmental law is also checked; (ii) candidates have to lay down the environmental policy that they plan to follow. This contains goals and principles aimed at a constant improvement of environmental achievements; (iii) an environmental programme is connected to the environmental policy. This programme contains the measures that have to be taken to fulfil the environmental policy; (iv) the company also has to make an environmental declaration that should give the public objective and relevant information. In return the industry obtains the benefit of an EMAS certificate.

2.5 Guidelines for Standard-setting

In legal analysis there has been an increasing occupation with the question of how a guideline for environmental standard-setting can be set. This question seemed important, first, to give the judge some indication of what the balancing of interest means in practical environmental cases he/she has to decide. Second, guidelines seem important in directing the standard-setting behaviour of administrative agencies when no clear instructions from the legislator are at hand. Third, these general principles could guide the operator of a plant when no fixed environmental standards are available to inform him about what kind of process or abatement technology should be chosen. This situation gave rise to an interest in formulating general principles of standard-setting.

Guidelines have developed in Anglo-Saxon legal systems. Traditionally, the UK has relied on the concept, *best practical means* (BPM). The concept was given legal status in the Alkali Act, 1906, and in the Health and Safety at Work Act, 1974. For each industrial branch, so-called BPM notes existed as guidelines for agencies to help them specify the BPM for a particular plant. Specifying BPM was thus in practice left to the discretionary powers of the agencies, by implication to the individual officers. The BPM notes also contained emission standards in the form of so-called 'presumptive limits', that is, non-statutory standards formulated by the chief inspector. These standards provided a basis for negotiation between industry and the agency. The same philosophy can be found behind the later adopted concept, *best available technique (or technology) not entailing excessive costs* (BATNEEC). This general guideline plays an important role in the British Environmental Protection Act of 1990.

The required 'best available technique' (BAT), does not in itself provide much guidance to an agency, or to the regulated industry. The vagueness is obvious. Guidelines such as BPM or BAT are imprecise on the balancing of costs and benefits, although one can find a reference to the economic cost–benefit test in the notion of BAT. Some guidelines approximate the economic method, and the British experience with the BPM standard shows that apparently similar questions are asked as in the economic model. For instance, in defining the term 'practicable', the question of when costs are excessive will need to be answered. The reference to economic notions becomes more explicit in the BATNEEC principle. Indeed, the notion of 'not entailing excessive costs' seems to refer to CBA. A first tentative conclusion could, therefore, be that the legal system seems to apply an economically relevant principle.

Whether this principle does relate to the economic cost–benefit test in practice cannot be determined, since these principles are still so new in the legal system that it is not yet known what the legal interpretation will be. There is no precise case law with respect to the term 'practicable' BPM, and the BATNEEC notion is still so new that it remains unclear how courts and administrative agencies will interpret the concept, 'not entailing excessive costs'.

The conclusion that the economic principles of standard-setting are followed in BATNEEC is, of course, only warranted if both the marginal benefits of reducing damage are considered as well as the marginal costs. If the practice of environmental standard-setting only takes into account whether the costs are reasonable or acceptable one way or another and disregards the benefits, this will not be compatible with the economic cost–benefit test. It will, therefore, depend upon the actual practice of standard-setting whether we can draw the conclusion that these general principles fit into the economic test or not.

All in all, it can be concluded that CBA is not in conflict with the existing guidelines. The BATNEEC notion specifically provides room for an explicit application of the marginal cost–benefit test when deciding what the 'excessive costs' are. Since BATNEEC refers to 'excessive costs', the CBA test can be used explicitly in the environmental standard-setting process. Other guidelines, such as BAT and BPM, which do not include 'costs', appear to consider them implicitly. Hence there is room to interpret the guidelines in an economic way, and to make the application of CBA explicit in environmental law. In fact, CBA is an explicit requirement in many other areas of law where it has usefully been applied.

Note, however, that CBA has many limitations, as demonstrated above, and should not, of course, be applied uncritically. Economics cannot provide an answer to all questions. The economic analysis must, in other words, be complemented. Political and ethical aspects are important in environmental policy. Hence the CBA is useful, but only as part of relevant studies on industry regulation. There is a trade-off between benefits, costs, special interests and other regulatory goals.

2.6 Environmental Standard-setting and BAT

Finally, we should stress how legal–economic principles of standard-setting such as the BAT standard discussed above can fit into this framework. The emission standard should, as discussed, in the first place take into account the environmental quality to be reached. If the goal to be reached is clear, being a specific environmental quality, BAT can provide information on the costs and benefits of various techniques that meet the target quality. As we have argued above, a BAT guideline can be interpreted as taking into account the weighing of marginal costs against marginal benefits. Given a certain target standard,

BOX 11.3 BATNEEC IN THE IPPC DIRECTIVE

We have already indicated that the notion of BATNEEC has been introduced in the UK with the new concept of integrated pollution control (IPC). This BATNEEC notion now also plays a crucial role in the Directive of 24 September 1996 concerning integrated pollution prevention and control, the so-called IPPC Directive. The concept of best available technology not entailing excessive cost (BATNEEC) has already been adopted in several other EC Directives, such as some of the so-called daughter-directives of Directive 76/464 on the discharge of dangerous substances into the aquatic environment and the more recent Directives 89/369/EEC and 89/429/EEC on the prevention of pollution from new, and the reduction of air pollution from existing, municipal waste incineration plants. The concept of BATNEEC is now removed from these directives and replaced by the new concept of BAT, as defined in a new Article 2 (11) of the IPPC Directive.

In Article 2 (11) of the Directive, BAT shall mean:

> the most effective and advanced stage in the development of activities and their methods of operation which indicate the practical suitability of particular techniques for providing in principle the basis for emission limit values designed to prevent and, where that is not practicable, generally to reduce emissions and the impact on the environment as a whole.

Reference to some sort of cost–benefit test is now made in the definition of 'available':

> 'available' techniques shall mean those developed on a scale which allows implementation in the relevant industrial sector, under economically and technically viable conditions, taking into consideration the costs and advantages, whether or not the techniques are used or produced inside the Member State in question, as long as they are reasonably accessible to the operator'.

Here one can find a clear reference to the fact that costs and benefits should be taken into account where the availability of the technique has to be considered.

the marginal cost/marginal benefit test implied in BAT can provide information on which technology is optimal to reach the target. Thus it can be determined which emission standard corresponds with the best available technology to reach the particular target standard.

These ideas are to a large extent to be found in the previously discussed IPPC Directive. Article 9 (4) prescribes that the emission limit values and the equivalent parameters shall be based on BAT, without prescribing the use of any technique or specific technology. The preparatory documents to the Directive had also made clear that the emission limit values should take into account the quality standard to be reached. Hence emission limit values should be determined, according to the IPPC Directive, both by BAT and by the quality to be achieved.

3. UNIFORMITY VERSUS FLEXIBILITY

3.1 Integrated Pollution Prevention: Challenges and Problems

As we indicated, regulatory standards can be of different types. For instance, a ban on a certain input is a restriction on industrial operations. Yet industry maintains its freedom to maximize profit within the limit set. The situation is similar with emission standards, discussed above. The agency determines through an emission standard the amount and quality of the substances that may be emitted into the environment. Such a standard is thus a restriction set without direct intervention in the production process of the regulated firm. It is left to the polluting firms to decide how to comply with the regulation.

Specific production standards go an important step further than emission standards as they regulate *ex ante* what kind of product or abatement technology (for example a certain type of water treatment plant) needs to be implemented by the licensee. To be efficient, such regulations require information on alternative techniques and a balancing between the profit to the industry and the environmental impacts of various production techniques and processes. Specific production standards may, therefore, rapidly become obsolete. Detailed and continuous information is needed for efficient regulation. Note also that specific production standards provide no immediate incentive for technological innovation since all the licensee has to do is to comply with the prescribed specification. That is why we argued in the previous section that optimal environmental standard-setting should be based on a combined use of quality and emission standards, not on specification standards. However, we also indicated that merely addressing emissions from different sources of one entity might not be optimal given *interchangeability* of emissions. That is why the idea of integrated pollution prevention and control (IPPC) was introduced.

The purpose of IPPC is to address the effects of polluting substances on the environment as a whole, instead of limiting the focus on effects on the directly polluted environmental medium. It is thus the task of the regulatory agency to find the *overall* 'best practicable environmental option' for an individual plant or factory.[2] The policy is, in addition, supposed to be proactive. It is in the rhetoric said to be superior to the old fashioned 'end-of-pipe' standards. '*End of pipe*' refers to regulation by emission standards followed

BOX 11.4 INTEGRATION VERSUS SHIFTING OF EMISSIONS

A classic problem with a non-integrated pollution control system is that it does not take into account the possible interchangeability of emissions. Because of the in practice very fragmented and sectoral pollution control, once environmental regulation is established in one sector, one can often see a shifting of the pollution to other, less controlled or less regulated sectors. Strict controls on emissions into water, for example, have frequently led to installing water purification equipment which in its turn produced sewage sludge which was again dumped on land. Instead of internalizing costs of environmental pollution, these costs only became an externality in another sector. Internalizing the externalities, however, refers to all possible forms of emissions from a certain entity, therefore integrating these different concerns in the decision-making process.

Preventing the shifting of emissions has indeed been advanced as one of the central goals of the IPPC Directive. The original proposal explicitly mentioned under the specific objectives of operation that the Directive aims to prevent pollution emissions from larger installations 'so that pollution problems are solved rather than transferred from one part of the environment to another'.[1] The considerations preceding the Directive mention that 'separate approaches to controlling emissions into the air, the water or the land alone may encourage the shifting of pollution across environmental media rather than protecting the environment as a whole'.[2]

Notes:
1. Com (93) 423 final, p. 25.
2. Ibid., p. 30.

by installing filters without direct incentives to investments in overall cleaner production methods.

The advantage of an integrated approach, therefore, is that all possible emissions, whether in the air, liquid or solid, can be integrated into one decision-making procedure as a result of which emission limit values are set in such a way that the industry has no incentives to shift its emissions from one compartment of the environment to the other. Whether the end-result of this procedure will also be efficient will obviously largely depend upon the procedure and the involved authorities, and their ability and willingness to take into account the various possible emissions and set standards in such a way that shifting is indeed prevented.

Integrated proactive planning for the environment may indeed seem appealing. The concept is certainly more ambitious than the simple 'end-of-pipe' regulation. Note, however, that the IPPC approach is very demanding. The agency shall, at least in principle, as in a centrally planned economy, not only permit and control certain emissions in specific media but also choose the best available technique or process, including considering the integrated impact on the environment as a whole. Obviously, to be successful, the agency needs information *ex ante* on the integrated environmental impact, and on the benefits of various polluting industries.

The problem is that such detailed and complex information is usually not available. The interrelations of various industries and environmental influences present a very complex coordination problem. Most industries are interrelated, and the links are many. Indeed, a large, costly and presumably bureaucratic administration would be necessary to set standards in thousands of industry plants.

The implementation of environmental policy must, therefore, in practice, be less ambitious. Praxis is, indeed, different from the idealized BAT and IPPC. The guidelines are vague, and implemented by agencies with limited powers and abilities, and the general overview on the environment is lacking. It can be argued, on the other hand, that the vagueness opens the way for flexibility, which can be used in a positive way, that is, the implementation may be stringent or lenient exactly where appropriate, according to, for instance, local conditions. The agency should also be able to react relatively smoothly to changed circumstances. This flexibility was, in fact, the declared philosophy behind the British BPM concept.[3]

3.2 Optimal Specificity

The risk that harm will be caused through, for example, hazardous waste may well vary depending upon, say population density or on specific hydrogeological conditions, where the propensity to accumulate varies. This brings us to the argument that is often advanced by economists, which is that, in general, environmental standards should not be uniform, but should be differentiated according to not only region, local needs, and branch of industry, but also preferences of the public. Indeed, it is argued that in different regions citizens may have different preferences regarding the appropriate trade-off between environmental quality and industrial production. An argument for differentiation can also be found in the economic literature with respect to optimal specificity. This theory of regulation has been advanced in Ehrlich and Posner (1974), and recently also in the work of Anthony Ogus (1994a, 1994b).

There are some obvious possibilities to differentiate as well, especially with respect to the decision to clean up polluted soils. In this case it is relatively easy to assess the future development of a certain site and to make the decision to clean up in accordance with that development. In these instances, the costs of differentiation may not be too high. Indeed, the literature has also indicated that there is a trade-off between the benefits of a detailed adaptation to location-specific circumstances on the one hand and increasing information, administrative and enforcement costs of such a differentiation on the other. The question is whether the benefits of particularization outweigh their costs. Although in some cases information and administrative costs may be too high for a detailed differentiation, in many other instances location-specific circumstances can be recognized relatively easily at low cost. The future development of a site is a good example. This leads to the conclusion that when the effectiveness of environmental law is assessed, it should also be examined whether some kind of differentiation of legal rules, standards and criteria for liability is applicable. As long as the benefits of this further differentiation outweigh their costs, the differentiation is obviously efficient.

3.3 Harmonization or Differentiation?

There is another area where the choice between harmonization and differentiation may play a role. This concerns the optimal level of government involvement in legal rule-making with respect to environmental standards. The question inevitably arises how environmental standards should be regulated in the European Community context. In answering this question, one should look at the current guiding principle for European action in the future, the subsidiarity principle. This states in Article 5 of the Treaty that the Community shall take action 'only if and in so far as the objectives of the proposed action cannot be sufficiently achieved by the Member States and can, therefore, by reason or the scale of effects of the proposed action, be better achieved by the Community'.

It is interesting to analyse how this subsidiarity principle can be interpreted in an economic way. This will be dealt with in Chapter 17. However, we can already see that the theory of optimal specificity, as discussed here, obviously has consequences for the standard-setting problem within the European Union, as well. One could make a case for harmonized quality standards, arguing that Europe should guarantee a basic environmental quality for all its citizens. The legal instruments to reach this goal would, then, be the setting of quality standards to which the environmental components (such as groundwater) should in principle correspond everywhere in the Union.

Therefore, as a result of different local circumstances, the emission limit values to reach a similar environmental quality may well vary. In principle the differentiation of emission standards should be carried through as long as the advantages of further differentiation outweigh the administrative and information costs that are incurred by a highly detailed standard-setting process.

This optimal specificity requirement not only means that the emission limit values will vary, but obviously also that BAT will vary. Indeed, the marginal cost/marginal benefit comparison will also inevitably depend upon local conditions. A technology which may be 'best' in Member State A may not be 'best' at all in Member State B, simply because local environmental conditions differ totally.

If BAT takes into account the weighing of marginal costs/marginal benefits, it means that for a particular region with, for example, little pollution and high environmental quality, a less costly technology is BAT. The IPPC Directive is, however, confusing on this point. The European Commission argues that the Directive provides for a comprehensive exchange of information and application of BAT to new installations throughout the Community.[4] The Commission apparently sees BAT as a universal concept that provides for a similar standard irrespective of local conditions. This also becomes apparent if one reads the Commission's comment with respect to the notion of 'available'. There, it is stated that available refers to techniques that are available anywhere in the world.[5]

Given location-specific circumstances, if one accepts that emission limit values should be differentiated in order to reach the same environmental quality, the same is also true for BAT, which will guide these values. Hence, taking the idea of optimal specificity from economic analysis into account, one can plead for differentiation in the use of BAT, which will allow for a local cost–benefit analysis to establish which technology is to be considered 'best' in a particular local circumstance.

4. CAPTURE

To some extent lobbying may explain why more powers are shifted to the federal level (and hence, more is harmonized) than would be efficient (see Chapter 10, Section 3). Lobbying efforts by industry may also, more generally, explain why environmental standard-setting by agencies will in practice not always take place according to the principles sketched in this chapter.

Knowledge available to the agency about techniques, benefits and damages is, of course, limited. The best informed about techniques and benefits is presumably the polluting industry, while the harm may be best known by victims. The agency has, therefore, the disadvantage of needing to search for accessible information, first of all in industry but also among victims. Hence there is an obvious problem of asymmetry and hidden information that opens possibilities for strategic behaviour by all involved. The limited information and the small-number exchange between the regulating agency and the regulated industry result in a complicated bargaining situation without any certain outcomes.

The decision of the agency is generally enforced by the power to issue and withdraw permits. That is, the industry must follow stated instructions and conditions in order to obtain a permit, which may be withdrawn on disobedience. Administrative as well as criminal sanctions may also be used (see Chapter 16). The real power of the authorities is limited, however. One reason is that the agency depends on information from the regulated industry, especially on costs and benefits, and on alternative production techniques. Without such information the regulation may fail completely. Moreover, the agency cannot, for political reasons, close down a factory without very strong reasons. Hence the threat of the agency in case of disobedience is limited. On the other hand, the industry realizes that it may benefit by supporting the agency in the short run to maintain a long-term good relationship. Therefore the relation between the regulated industry and the regulator is usually characterized as small-number negotiations. That is, the parties have to give and take, knowing that they depend on each other in a long-term repeated exchange.

Empirical results in the economics of regulation literature indicate that *capture* may result; that is, the special interest of the best-informed, organized, and most motivated group will win the game. The capture by the strongest special interest group takes place independent of the official 'public interest' (BAT) that the law intends to implement (see Chapter 10, Sections 4–6).

In the typical environmental case, where the polluting industry is best informed about technology, well organized (a few large polluters), and has much to lose (while the victims are spread and disorganized), the interests of the industry will dominate. Sometimes, however, the victims may be strong politically, which may change the outcome. Industry seems, however, on average to be successful in lobbying against pollution standards.

On the other hand, if legislative intervention seems unavoidable, the theory of regulation suggests that the involved interest groups will accept a general principle of regulation, but will strive to change its scope. The industrial interest groups to whom the environmental regulation will be applied may realize that regulation may enhance producer wealth while it simultaneously corrects, or at least reduces, an externality problem.

A way of improving the profits of the lobbying industry is for them to use the environmental regulation as a means of protecting the already-established industry. A classic example is the introduction of a *grandfather clause*, which stipulates that the regulation will not be applicable to firms or products that are already in existence. Hence regulation can create a barrier to entry and, thus, protect the existing industrial practices and products.

Similarly, more technically advanced firms in an industry may, under certain circumstances, given knowledge of environmental regulations that may come up, also argue that the 'best available technique' should be employed, knowing that the new technique provides them with an advantage over competitors. In the literature this phenomenon has been named 'predatory regulation'; that is, economically strong firms may invest in expensive, new techniques to keep out competitors with fewer resources (see Chapter 10, Section 4).

Hence the efforts of industry may go in various directions: sometimes there will be lobbying for more lenient environmental standards, or regulation will be favoured because it limits competition. Here, we can refer to studies that show that licences, which are considered a central instrument in environmental policy, also have anti-competitive effects attached to the function.

Vague regulations open the way for flexibility, which can be used in a positive way. That is, the implementation may be stringent or lenient exactly where appropriate, according to, for instance, local conditions. The agency should also be able to react relatively smoothly to changed circumstances. This flexibility was, in fact, the declared philosophy behind the British BPM concept. However, the agency should follow the intentions of the legislator, but, as noted above, the agencies may have their own goals, such as expansion or good relations with the local community or industry. Vague and diffuse guidelines may, therefore, not be implemented and controlled according to the official goal or to the 'public interest'.

Even if the agency is totally loyal to the intentions of the law-makers, the policy may not be implemented correctly because the agency must prioritize its bargaining and control efforts within a limited budget. The agency has limited bargaining power. Although it may be possible in principle for the agency to close down a factory, or impose harsh sanctions such as criminal punishment, such threats may not be effective. One reason is that a close-down might, for example, elicit protests from the local community or workforce. Another is the long-term effects of disrupting an established relationship with the industry, which may have a negative impact on the future performance of the agency. It is, in fact, a dilemma that an agency, to gain access to industry information, must consider the interests of the regulated industry. This may explain why actualized sanctions usually are few and not very harsh (see Chapter 16).

5. CONCLUSIONS

The integrated pollution prevention policy principle, as well as the BPM or BAT guidelines, are in principle central. That is, central authorities should limit and coordinate pollution. Central planning tends, however, to be bureaucratic. A general problem is that coordination of many actors requires a great deal of information; see Chapter 4, Section 3. In reality, with very limited information, the government tends to be either rigid or unclear and soft. Discretionary power to interpret and decide is very much in the hands of the agencies. However, the agencies have limited budgets considering their huge administrative task. A dilemma is that the information on best available techniques is mainly in the hands of the industry that is supposed to be controlled. The agencies are, therefore, dependent on the regulated, and may be captured by industry. The agencies may also be captured by temporary opinions and media that require 'certainty' (see Chapter 10, Section 7).

Another problem neglected in the environmental debate is that specification standards may have anti-competitive effects, providing a monopoly to the producer of the prescribed technology. Hence the case for specification standards is generally rather weak, unless one could argue that the standard-setter has better information than firms concerning the optimal protection technology or innovation activity. This is, however, rather unlikely. The outcome of the policy is, thus, arbitrary and presumably not in line with 'the public interest' or 'the environmental interest', however this is defined.

Many laws avoid the problem of balancing costs and benefits. This is also true for environmental guidelines. Yet in reality some balancing will take place, although it may be implicit. There may be political and ethical reasons for hiding the trade-offs. Nevertheless, we hold that environmental law would benefit from an explicit notion of the balancing problem. One reason for this position is that conflict of interests cannot, in the end, be avoided, and it is better in principle to handle a problem explicitly than to hide it.

Flexible management is certainly important in central planning. A dilemma is, however, that vagueness opens the door to discretionary power for the agencies, who may become captured through pressure of special interests. In sum, the consequence of vagueness may thus be that the environmental policy will remain diffuse and weak and, therefore, more or less completely in the hands of the agency or of special interests such as industry, the community, the employees and shadow interest groups, depending on their lobbying strength. This problem is one reason why economists usually recommend other methods, such as zoning, charges and liability, where applicable.

In legal analysis there has been an increasing preoccupation with the question of why a guideline for environmental standard-setting should become operative. We argue that it is, first of all, to give the judge or implementing administrator some indication of what the balancing of interest means in the practical environmental cases which must be decided. In addition, guidelines are important in guiding the standard-setting behaviour of agencies when no clear instructions from the legislator are at hand. General principles may also guide the operator of a plant when no fixed environmental standards are given. We stress that legal principles of standard-setting such as the above-discussed BAT standard can fit into the CBA framework. The emission standard should take into account the environmental quality to be reached. If the goal to be reached is clear, that is, a specific environmental quality, BAT can provide information on the costs and benefits of various techniques that meet this target. As we have argued above, a BAT guideline can be interpreted as the means of taking into account the weighing of marginal costs against marginal benefits. Given a certain target standard, the marginal cost/marginal benefit test implied in BAT can provide information on which technology (cleaner production or abatement) is optimal and, thus, it can be determined which emission standard corresponds with the best available technology to reach that particular target standard.

NOTES

1. Official Journal 1996 L257/27.
2. For an explanation of and the philosophy behind this concept (and IPPC), see, for example, the fifth report of the Royal Commission on Environmental Pollution, 'Air Pollution Control: an integrated approach' (HMSO, CMND. 6371, 1976), the tenth report, 'Tackling pollution – Experience and prospects' (HMSO, Cmnd. 9149, 1984), and the twelfth report, 'Best practicable environmental option' (HMSO, Cmnd. 310, 1998).
3. Practicability, flexibility and discretion may be considered the keywords within this philosophy. See Lomas (1990), p. 62.
4. Com (93) 423 final, p. 14.
5. Ibid.

FURTHER READING

Adler, J.H. (1996), 'Rent Seeking Behind the Green Curtain', *Regulation*, 26–34.
Baumol, W.J. and Oates, W.E. (1971), 'The Use of Standards and Prices for Protection of the Environment', *Swedish Journal of Economics*, **73**, 42–54.
Dewees, D.N. (1983), 'Instrument Choice in Environmental Policy', *Economic Inquiry*, **21**, 53–71.
Faure, M., Vervaele, J. and Weale, A. (eds) (1994), *Environmental Standards in the European Union in an Interdisciplinary Framework*, Antwerp: Maklu.
Hahn, R.W. (1990a), 'The Political Economy of Environmental Regulation: Towards a Unifying Framework', *Public Choice*, **65**, 21–47.
Maloney, M.T. and McCormick, R.E. (1982), 'A Positive Theory of Environmental Quality Regulation', *Journal of Law and Economics*, 99–123.
Moore, T.P. (1961), 'The Purpose of Licensing', *Journal of Law and Economics*, 93–117.
Ogus, A.I. (1994a), *Regulation. Legal Form and Economic Theory*, Oxford: Clarendon Press.
Richardson, G., Ogus, A. and Burrows, P. (1982), *Policing Pollution: A Study of Regulation and Enforcement*, Oxford: Clarendon Press.

12. Land-use control

Buy yourself a piece of land, they don't
make it anymore.
Mark Twain

1. INTRODUCTION

Rights assigned to owners of real estate are in most jurisdictions limited by a number of regulations. Restrictions on production and pollution on already-established sites were treated in Chapter 11. In addition, property-owners must often have permits from public authorities in order to make investments in or important changes to their property. Zoning laws regulate the location of industry, residence, farming and so on. Land use is regulated geographically through national, regional and local planning.

In this chapter we will investigate the motives for the public control of land use from an environmental point of view. In Section 2 we study the capitalization of value in land and real estate. Conflicts can easily arise among neighbours, which will be discussed in Section 3. In Section 4 we examine the reason for zoning, and the discussion on soil clean-ups. The rules on compensation to property-owners at expropriation and at restrictions in the owners' rights are investigated in Section 5. Section 6 concludes.

2. RENTS

2.1 Inelastic Supply

The price of a good is determined by supply and demand. If the demand increases, the price also tends to increase, by how much depends, among other things, on the elasticity of the supply. If the supply is elastic, small price increases will mean that relatively many new goods are brought to the market, which works against the price increase. If, on the other hand, the supply is inelastic, which is the case for land-holdings and other properties within a certain area, the prices will increase to a relatively great extent (see Chapter 5, Sections 4–6). The change in price at increased demand is demon-

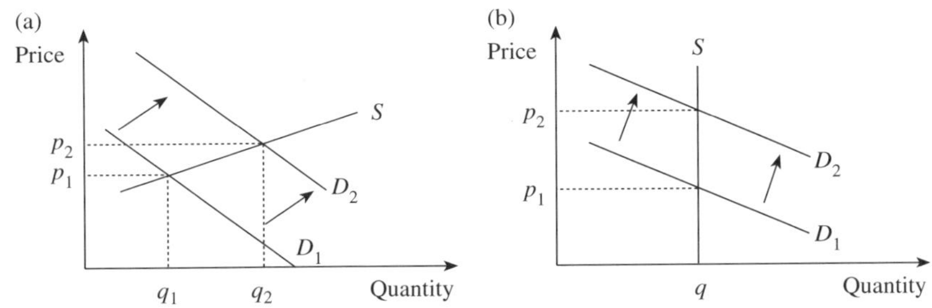

Figure 12.1 *(a) Elastic supply and (b) inelastic supply*

strated in Figure 12.1. At elastic supply, an increase in demand (shift upwards of the demand curve from D_1 to D_2) results in an increased price, from p_1 to p_2, and quantity, from q_1 to q_2 as in Figure 12.1(a). The figure could illustrate, for instance, the long-run market for housing in a nation with increasing demand due to increased population. The supply increases as well, but at increasing costs, so the long-run price will increase to p_2.

On the other hand, in a completely inelastic market with a given supply independent of the price, as in a developed city area, the supply will not increase. Only the price will go up at increased demand, as in Figure 12.1(b).

If, for example, the population in a city increases and this brings with it an increased demand for private homes, the price of these homes will increase. Perhaps the new production of homes will also increase, which will eventually limit the price increase. However, since the addition of new homes is limited, especially in developed areas, the prices may rise beyond the costs of new production. Hereby, property is given a value dependent on geographical position. In the literature, this value is called 'rent'.

Now, consider the following example of a rental property with office space that is rented out to boutiques and other shops. As the city begins to grow, the property becomes more central. Because of the increased commercial trading, the demand for boutique space increases. The rental proceeds increase, accordingly, because the sum of available boutique space (for the most part) is fixed. Hence the income streams to the landlord increase, which in a comparable manner increases the expected net present value of the property; see Chapter 7, Section 6.

Note that the rent is independent of the effort made by the tenants. Indeed, it is the property-owners who become wealthy, not the boutique owners. The reason for this is that the boutique-owners are in competition with other boutique- and shop-owners. The extent to which a boutique-owner becomes wealthy depends, instead, on her ability or on some other quality or product that the competitors lack.

Assume as a further example that a farmer intends to buy farm property. The maximum price that the farmer is willing to pay equals the net present value of the farm. If there is competition on the market for farm property, this net present value also equals the price that must be paid. If, now, the prices for the agricultural products that are produced on the farm are doubled, for example because of farming politics or due to changes in the world market, the benefit to the farmer will increase considerably. As the willingness to pay for the property depends on the expected income stream, the value of the farm will also increase. Indeed, as in the boutique example above, the increases in value will pertain to the property. The farmer, thus, will become wealthy as a landowner but not as a worker on the farm. The farmer's own labour will earn the same market wages as before, given a competitive labour market.

2.2 Politics and Value

The value of land and real estate depends on many factors. One is the care of the buildings, renovations and maintenance. The owner, therefore, has an incentive to protect the property; see Chapter 4, Section 4. However, this is not the full picture. The value also depends on the environment in the neighbourhood, on the expansion or decline of the vicinity, and so on (see Box 10.1 in Chapter 10). In the examples above, an increase in population, world market prices and agricultural politics caused the properties to increase in value. It was, in other words, external circumstances that created the wealth of the property-owners; that is, the growth of wealth was due either to luck, or to particular foresightedness (see Chapter 6, Section 4). If the development is predicted by others, expectations are included in the price that must be paid for the property. If the city had expanded in another direction, if the vicinity had fallen into neglect or become an industrial area, the development of property would instead have taken a negative turn.

Ownership is risky because of the many circumstances that influence the value of property. In order to reduce the risk, and thus increase the value, the owners may act in different ways. One is to diversify by keeping a mixed portfolio with different assets; see Chapter 7, Section 4. Another is to become politically active. Property development is strongly dependent on communal politics. If, for example, the city plan is changed, this may mean a substantial profit or loss to the individual property-owners. Property-owners may, therefore, either individually or in a group, lobby to increase the property values, say through tax-financed investments in the infrastructure. On the other hand, the relation between public investment and property values provides a motive for the government to levy taxes on property, and hereby to let developers contribute to infrastructural investments.

Homeowners, just like other property-owners, are concerned that changes in infrastructure do not reduce the value of their homes. Therefore, a steady expansion in different sections of the community with investments in the infrastructure, nice surroundings, parks and playgrounds may be advocated by politicians who seek support from large groups of voters. Correspondingly, the owners of agricultural property demand that the property values are maintained and also, if possible, increased. Similarly, tenants would like low rents, which can occur through subsidies. These subsidies also maintain the prices of property, to the advantage of the property-owners. The costs are divided over the tax collective.

These examples explain why interest groups such as property-owners, tenants, homeowners, farmers and forest-owners are engaged in questions pertaining to their land and homes. Through their activities, they can build up a defence against loss, and in the best cases a guarantee of continual increase in value.

3. CONFLICTING INTERESTS

3.1 Neighbours

When someone is considering buying property, there may be many alternatives from which to choose. The location, including the vicinity and neighbours, can influence the choice. After the purchase has been made, the situation is different: the costs of moving can be high; investments may have been made in the property, improvements that cannot be detached from the property and which a prospective buyer in some cases will not value; the family may have settled and perhaps does not wish to move.

Location-specificity applies, in other words (see Chapter 9, Section 2.3, and the discussion on optimal specificity in Chapter 11, Section 3.2). Moreover, the limited number of involved parties within the nearest vicinity brings with it a small-number exchange. Each and everyone may try to push the other toward the point where the opponent is willing to leave the area. As all are settled, the bargaining space is large. Thus there is room for strategic behaviour, including threats and misleading information. In the worst case a situation can develop, with discord continuing over generations.

A considerable portion of property rights pertains to rules for solving such conflicts (compare the first normative principle of law, Chapter 9, Section 3.2). In general, everyone is required to be appropriately considerate of the surroundings when utilizing their property. Damages for different types of intrusion, as well as the obligation to alleviate damage that arises because of such intrusion, appear in most jurisdictions. This is in accordance with the economic theory that claims that the law reduces transaction costs or substitutes and complements for bargains that do not take place due to a prohibitive small-number exchange.

3.2 Strangers

Land is of interest, not only for the owner and neighbours, but also for others, for example travellers and tourists. A difference between neighbours and travellers is that travellers do not have a long-term relationship with the owner. On the other hand, the bargaining space is not as great as long as the traveller can choose alternative pathways. It remains, however, that the choice of pathway may be limited and, therefore, the bargaining costs may be great. Moreover, the costs of searching for the owners may be important.

To see why, assume for a moment that the right of ownership is unlimited in the sense that no trespassing of any kind may be undertaken without compensation to the owner; that is, no one may trespass on another's land without contacting, negotiating with, and paying the landowner. The transaction costs will make it more or less impossible for travellers to proceed in their travels. Transport and tourism will, then, be limited to bounded territories where the landowner voluntarily grants the use of her property.

How, then, shall the interests of travellers come to the fore? A possible solution is to buy with tax money land for parks and natural reserves, and for building roads. This expropriation of land in order to build public roads is one form of collectivization. It can be motivated by the argument that the free exchange would not function because of the transaction costs, see Chapter 7, Section 7. In a world of rapid transport, the involved parties cannot negotiate with all potential landowners of property that is being crossed. Collectivization was also applicable in former times to walkers and ox-carts. Since time immemorial, there have been paths and roads that may be used by everyone.

In order to prevent chaos on the roads, traffic rules were introduced. It is of interest to note that we have, here, a transaction cost argument for common property and a planned economy: the road users do not have time to negotiate with one another, for example, whether they should yield to the left or right, which provides a rationale for centrally fixed traffic regulations. (Compare the exposé on common property in Chapter 4, Section 3.)

A collective right to trespass on the land of others may also be motivated by transaction cost arguments; that is, if everyone were obliged to negotiate with the landowner about crossing private property, much hiking and enjoyment of nature would not take place, even in cases where property-owners and wildlife are not disturbed. In Sweden, with its vast forests and mountains, there is an 'all men's right' (allemansrätt) to trespass, make fires (restricted), camp (one night), and pick berries and mushrooms. If that were not allowed without a permit from the owner, a large portion of the enjoyment would not take place and the harvest of wild vegetation would presumably rot in the forests.

The 'all men's right' is highly valued by the Swedish population, although open access is not without complications. There are conflicts with both property-owners and different environmental interests. One debated issue pertains to the free use of snow-scooters, which disturb the wildlife in the mountains. Another concerns the commercial use of the 'all men's right' in the tourism industry. Hikes, canoeing and berry-picking are sometimes organized commercially on a large scale without compensation to damaged landowners.

In such cases the private right to compensation, that is, a PPP, may be motivated. According to the Coase theorem, a VPP may also result in the efficient use of the land. However, there is an asymmetry in favour of a PPP: the owner cannot know all strangers who would like to spend time on his property, and it is costly to protect the property borders. Hence, transaction costs may be reduced, and the value of the natural resource increased, if the polluting commercial strangers have to request and pay for the utilization of the land.

4. ZONING

4.1 Voting with the Feet

Above, we used roads as an example of the collectivization of strips of land to make trespassing convenient at low transaction costs. A road is an area or zone for transport, and there are many other types of zones that may be motivated when transaction costs are high. Yet zoning is a form of encroachment on the right of the owner.

For example, assume that smoking is permitted in a train, although a number of the travellers are non-smokers. In the no-transaction-costs world of Coase the non-smokers would be willing to pay the smokers to reduce their smoking. However, due to bargaining problems, the negotiations would not be completed before the arrival at the end station. Thus these constraints may motivate a division into smoking and non-smoking compartments. The obvious benefit, of course, is that the disturbance to the non-smokers is eliminated. A potential cost, however, arises related to the choice of location, and movement to the compartments. Another problem is related to the allocation of seats to smokers and non-smokers in case a compartment is full or congested. In other words, there is a problem of optimal zoning areas where the benefits of a zone must be compared with its costs.

BOX 12.1 NEGOTIATIONS WITH NUDES

As an illustration, we can imagine that there are two types of bathers on the beach. One group would like to bathe in the nude, while the other prefers swimsuits. The swimsuit group is disturbed by the nudists and perhaps vice versa. If the bathing population is to be able to solve this through negotiation and compensation, they must first know the law, that is, if bathing in the nude is permitted or not. Otherwise, they will not know who should pay whom. Assume that nude bathing is forbidden, in which case the nudists must compensate the others in order to go unclothed. It is apparent that such negotiations may never be resolved; and if they are, they may not be completed to mutual satisfaction.

If the swimsuit group is permitted to decide, the prohibition of nudity will be upheld, to the disadvantage of the nudists. If the nudists are permitted to decide, it will mean negative consequences for the swimsuit group. Again, a solution to the dilemma may be to divide the beach into two zones, one for the nudists and the other for the swimsuit group. Thus, each may choose. The advantage to this is that no unwelcome circumstances arise.

Similarly, if a company wants to build a factory and, before beginning construction, must negotiate with and compensate all parties that might be affected, construction and production may never come about. Moreover, if there is an investment, there may be conflicts with newcomers, as will be discussed in the next section. It may, thus, be decided to designate certain areas as industrial areas, residences and parks. An important part of city planning pertains to such zoning.

All in all, zoning is an allocation mechanism that may be superior when costless contracts are not available. The benefit is that the negative interference is, at best, eliminated. To avoid harm, the parties choose their preferred location by 'voting with the feet'. The free choice of zone thus assures some freedom to the individual. An allocation problem, however, remains in identifying the optimal zones. In other words, the issue is to determine what should be parks, residential areas and areas for heavy industry, taking into account limited population increases, transport possibilities, the potential for heavy environmental degradation and so on.

The benefits of zoning are partly due to economics of specialization (see Chapter 8, Section 4). By separating areas we can undertake intensive and large-scale activities without disturbing others. Zoning is, therefore, most important for the protection of humans as well as the environment. It is the remaining externalities that may be the issue, for example, smoke from industry, noise from traffic, leaking waste sites, and so on. A problem with much zoning in the past is that the growth in population or industry, as well as toxicity, has not been foreseen. For instance, nuclear power plants should not, as has often been the case, have been located near densely populated areas. A way of promoting a better environment is, therefore, to undertake more careful zoning. Today, it can be argued that nuclear power should not be used at all. But that was not the issue in the 1960s, when industry as well as politicians wanted a rapid development of the new 'unlimited' energy resource.

So far we have pointed to the benefits of zoning, implicitly assuming that the administrative agency will determine optimal zones in the public interest. The reality may often, however, be very different. Since the definition of zones (for example for agriculture or industry) may confer significant costs or benefits upon owners, there will be serious lobbying activities. The literature has also reported evidence that zoning boards were captured by special interests. Indeed, much of what is said about regulation of industry in Chapter 11, Sections 3–4 is applicable to geographical zoning as well.

4.2 Soil Clean-up

One of the most debated issues in environmental law nowadays is probably soil clean-up. In most European countries the decision to clean up (with the subsequent question of liability to pay for clean-up costs) is made by administrative authorities. In some countries, such as the Netherlands, polluted areas have been identified since the second half of the 1970s and extensive cleaning operations have already taken place or are in course of implementation. In other countries, such as Belgium, polluted sites have only been discovered more recently, and important decisions concerning clean-up must still be taken.

This raises an interesting set of questions. First, what are the benefits and costs of cleaning up? Many investigations show that the restoration of polluted land would be very costly. The benefits, on the other hand, are not always that easily assessed. It may, of course, be claimed that the soil should be 'clean' or restored to the state that existed before pollution took place. The ethical appeal of this argument is evident. However, not to balance costs and benefits will, again, result in a loss of limited resources. Local differences in geography and so on, and the benefits of zoning need to be considered. All land cannot be held in a virgin state, and it would be extremely costly to clean up all land. Indeed, the expenditures would be larger than the benefits, including the environmental and human effects. The question of whether a site should be cleaned up will depend upon the future of that site. If, for instance, the future location is for industry and external health risks are excluded, it may not be rational to insist on a costly clean-up of that particular polluted soil.

The benefit of cleaning up, of course, also depends on the negative externalities due to toxic leakage or other disturbances to the neighbourhood. This may be due to neglect in the past or to poor foresight. If a particular site were to be used for vegetable growing in the near future, the potential health damage caused by, for example, pesticides, might well outweigh the marginal costs of clean-up action. An economist would also argue that an obvious alternative would be not to use that particular site for vegetable growing in the future.

Therefore, it makes sense to take into account the future of a particular soil when deciding upon a possible clean-up. It is thus of interest to examine the kind of criteria upon which the administrative authorities base their decision to clean up. For example, can an administrative authority decide that a particular polluted site may only be used for certain industrial goals in the future and no longer for vegetable growing? A related question is whether an administrative authority can require total clean-up of certain soil merely for ethical or ecological reasons, notwithstanding the future of that particular soil.

Interestingly enough, the necessity of balancing now seems to be accepted in recent legislation concerning soil clean-up. For instance, in the Netherlands the classic 'multi-functionality criterion' has now been relaxed, and in Flanders a new Soil Clean-up Decree provides the grounds for excuse for the owner of polluted soil who is in good faith, that is, who was not aware that the particular soil was polluted.[1] The latter point refers to the liability for unintended damage. Here, we become involved in legal matters that are treated to some extent in the discussion on the first-use doctrine in the next section. Related problems will also come up in Part IV, where we discuss the question of negligence or strict liability and other related issues.

5. NUISANCE LAW

5.1 The First-use Doctrine

Assume, for instance, that a farm is located in an isolated area. Later, it is confronted by neighbours who come late to the area and then claim compensation for nuisance. According to the first-use doctrine, there should be no compensation for the victim. If the victim would like to reduce the nuisance, he/she must, instead, pay the farmer. Hence the first-use doctrine is equivalent to VPP.

The question of whether this doctrine is efficient or not is widely discussed in the law and economics literature. The first-use doctrine, or VPP, creates an incentive not to move into areas where activities that may be disturbing are being conducted, or could be foreseen. Given that the doctrine is known, that is, that the first-comer has the right to run her business without compensation to newcomers, newcomers know that they may have to compensate the first-comer if the activity is to be reduced. Thus, when choosing a location, a newcomer has an economic motive to consider whether the cost of changing the first-comer's activity is economically feasible. If the cost of moving into the area, including expected costs of compensation to the first-comer, exceeds the benefit, it is private as well as socially profitable to locate elsewhere.

Note that the ability to foresee the future is important with respect to the choice of VPP or PPP. The comparative advantage of the VPP above is due to the assumption that the first-comer is already located and has limited ability to foresee who the followers will be and, thus, how disturbing the activity will become. However, in some cases the first-comer can foresee the development and should therefore, from a social efficiency point of view, take precautions (as well as the newcomer). A PPP would create an economic incentive for the first-comer to locate and prevent nuisance to followers. On the other hand, because the polluter pays, the followers will not have the incentive to choose their location and take precautions in an optimal way. Hence the choice of VPP or PPP depends on the parties' relative ability to prevent damage through location and precautions. A complication in real cases is that disturbing activities in a neighbourhood often develop simultaneously.

The normal starting-point in a legal case is a plaintiff's claim that compensation should be paid because of the nuisance. A first question in the economic analysis is to ask whether the harm to the newcomers can be prevented or reduced by measures to be taken by the first-comer. In addition, is the newcomer able to prevent the harm by locating somewhere else, or by undertaking preventive measures once located? If this is the case and transaction costs are zero, then Coase teaches us that the efficient location and preventive device will be implemented, irrespective of the legal rule. However, as noted above, transaction costs are important. Moreover, the conflicting parties do not know each other *ex ante*, before the location takes place. The economic question is, therefore, raised: what are the efficient prevention and location possibilities of the parties, and how can the legal system be made to support efficient outcomes? Especially in case law, these issues are normally dealt with in an *ex post* perspective, that is, when the parties have already moved to the neighbourhood and the harm has been done. A relevant question, therefore, is: could additional preventive measures have reduced the harm beneficially?

An important issue is whether the costs of nuisance have already been taken into account in the price of, for example, property, in which case there would already have been compensation and, thus, the externality would have been internalized. For instance, assume that a new railway station has been built and surrounding land is being sold at a relatively low price due to the noise. In this case the low price can be considered as a compensation for future nuisance caused by the railway. This will, then, exclude a subsequent claim by the property-owner against the railway station. This is not only true for the owner who purchased at a low price, but also for any subsequent purchaser who becomes the owner of such a piece of land. Again, he should have been informed of the proximity to the railway station (which is obviously easily visible) and realize that compensation for future nuisance caused by the railway station is included in the relatively low price being paid.

This explains why foreseeability of the nuisance is an important criterion in most of these cases. A neighbouring owner will have far more possibilities to receive compensation if, for example, the harmful activity (which was, at first, relatively innocent) expands in a totally unforeseeable way. However, if the 'surprised owner' is compensated for the harm caused by the unexpected and unforeseeable expansion by the firm, this compensation may be final in the sense that the owner, or a new buyer of the property, cannot claim further compensation. Full and final compensation implies that the loss in property value due to the nuisance is compensated. This means that the victim is compensated by the fact that the price of the property will have decreased as a consequence of the expansion of the particular polluter. A potential new purchaser will, then, purchase the land at a relatively low price because of the nuisance, but cannot claim compensation again from the factory, which already paid compensation to the previous owner.

More difficult are situations where the conflicting use of property rights cannot be dealt with by paying compensation for the unreasonable nuisance. In some cases the conflict may be so consequential that it can only be solved through the relocation of one of the two parties involved. Typically, this solution will be reached if the magnitude of the damage is much larger than the lowest relocation costs. If relocation is, therefore, the efficient solution, it will need to be established whose relocation costs are the higher in relation to the importance of the externality caused. If it can be established, for example, that the relocation costs of the existing factory would be much lower than the relocation costs of many neighbours, even if they came to the nuisance, the relocation of the factory would still be the efficient solution.

Obviously, the question of who came first will not play a role in answering the question of who will have to relocate, but possibly when answering the question of who will have to pay for the relocation costs. If the new neighbours came to the nuisance in a case of foreseeable harm, one could claim that even though the factory will need to relocate (because of the lower relocation costs), the citizens who with foresight came to the nuisance may be liable to pay (part of) the relocation costs of the factory. The latter is obviously important to give citizens in an *ex ante* perspective correct incentives to choose wisely concerning their location decisions. If they, with foresight, locate next to a factory, they can afterwards hardly claim that the factory should relocate at its own cost.

5.2 *Spur Industries* v. *Del E. Webb*

An American case sometimes cited is *Spur Industries* v. *Del E. Webb*.[2] This was a case in the 1950s in Maricopa County in Arizona, about fifteen miles west of Phoenix. The farmer, Spur, had an area suited for cattle and actually kept his cattle on that land. Del Webb, a project developer, bought 20 000 acres of agricultural land with the intention of developing a housing tract that would be called Sun City. The first houses were built 2.5 miles north of Spur's cattle grounds, but in the end 500 houses were constructed and Sun City expanded. In 1967 Del Webb's project was only 500 feet from the pastures of Spur. It was then that Del Webb found out that he was not able to sell the remaining land for residential housing because of the presence of the agricultural activities of Spur. Del Webb therefore sued Spur for nuisance caused by offensive odour and flies, Spur having at the time between 20 000 and 30 000 animals on his property, producing more than one million pounds of wet manure per day.[3] The citizens of Sun City themselves did not file a suit against Spur, only project developer Del Webb.

The case was decided by the Arizona Supreme Court, which ruled that there was a so-called 'public nuisance' because the farming activity by Spur seemed to harm a great number of citizens. In such cases, an injunction to stop the harmful activities seemed more appropriate than compensation only, according to the Court. The Court then discussed the coming-to-nuisance doctrine, that is, the first-use doctrine. Coming-to-nuisance would have constituted a valid defence if project developer Del Webb had been the only victim. However, Spur's cattle apparently caused a nuisance to a great number of people (arguing in an *ex post* perspective). Spur, on the other hand, had not acted wrongfully since he could not have foreseen that in Maricopa County, a practically new city would arise in the neighbourhood of his cattle. However, given the interests of the great number of citizens who were made victims, the Court decided that Spur would have to relocate its cattle activities. The Court held: 'Spur is required to move, not because of any wrongdoing on his part, but because of a proper and legitimate regard of the Court for the rights and interests of the public'.

However, the project developer, Webb, is obviously the cause of the duty to relocate that was placed on Spur. Del Webb, indeed, started activities in an agricultural area where it was perfectly foreseeable for him that future house-owners could be harmed by the presence of the cattle. Hence the Court decided that Del Webb must indemnify Spur for the relocation costs: 'having brought people to the nuisance to the foreseeable detriment of Spur, Webb must indemnify Spur for a reasonable amount of the cost of moving or shutting down'.

Looking at the Court decision from an economic point of view, one may claim that it was unforeseeable for the cattle-owner, Spur, that project developer, Del Webb, would come to that particular area. Nevertheless, the coming-to-nuisance defence that Spur invoked was rejected, and he was forced to relocate since his relocation costs were lower than the relocation costs of the 500 homeowners. This makes sense from an economic point of view. However,

BOX 12.2 *BOOMER* v. *ATLANTIC CEMENT COMPANIES INC.*

In the American case, *Boomer* v. *Atlantic Cement Companies Inc.*,[1] Boomer and other homeowners were the plaintiffs acting against a defendant cement company (Atlantic) that polluted the neighbourhood. More specifically, the discussions in the Court addressed the question of what remedy was most appropriate as a reaction to the nuisance caused by Atlantic to Boomer and friends. The majority in the Boomer decision argued that the plaintiffs should be awarded compensation. The arguments against a closure or relocation of Atlantic Cement Companies were that the company had just invested $45 million in the company and 300 persons were employed. This referred implicitly to the economic argument that the relocation of the company would probably cost more than the compensation to the victims. Furthermore, the Court made two rulings: first, so-called permanent (final) damages were to be awarded; and second, Atlantic Cement Company was granted a permanent future right to pollute. This right could also be claimed by the cement factory against future owners of the adjacent properties. In a dissenting opinion Justice Jasen argued against the permanent damages, claiming that this would be the same as licensing a 'continuing wrong'.[2] Moreover, Jasen argued that paying permanent damages would afterwards remove every incentive of the company to further reduce harm by investing in supplementary preventive measures. However, it appeared from facts presented that there were no obvious supplementary preventive measures that would have reduced the harm. If one applies economic analysis, one may in this case refer to Cooter and Ulen (2000), who argue that an attractive aspect of paying permanent damages is that the conflicting use of property rights is settled in a final way. As a consequence of the payments, the externality is internalized. However, Wittman (1980) has considerable criticisms. He argues that the first-use issue was not examined at all in the above case, although it appears that the homeowners were, in fact, in the area first, and the harmful activity, in this case the cement factory, came later. Wittman furthermore claims that the economic analysis the Court tried to engage in has many flaws. The Court did argue that the employment of 300 people and the $45 million investment make the relocation costs for the cement factory higher than for the homeowners. This might be true in an *ex post* situation. The judgment, however, provided a wrong signal for future companies that must make similar decisions in an *ex ante* perspective. The Boomer decision seems to signal that once a company has made considerable investments and the employees are in place, relocation is no longer necessary and a pay-off with permanent damages will suffice.

Wittman correctly argues that the Court should have examined in an *ex ante* perspective whether the cement factory had a variety of possibilities of location and whether it chose its location in the residential area wisely. It is, moreover, striking that, in the assessment of the necessity to relocate, the Court only addressed the high relocation costs for the cement factory and did not calculate the potential relocation costs for Boomer and the other homeowners.

Whether the Boomer case was correctly ruled on from an economic point of view is difficult to say since the Court did not take into account all the relevant costs in deciding the case, and did not address at all the fact that the homeowners were there first and the cement factory caused the nuisance through a potentially wrongful location decision.

Notes:

1. *Boomer* v. *Atlantic Cement Companies Inc.*, 26 NY 2d 219, 309 NYS 2d 312, 257 NE 2d 870 (Court of Appeals of New York, 1970).
2. It is the same as saying to the cement company: 'you may continue to do harm to your neighbours as long as you pay for it'.

since Webb was in the wrong in an *ex ante* perspective in locating near an agricultural area with feedlots for so many cattle, it was equally correct to decide that he must compensate Spur. Any other decision would have sent out the wrong signals to future project developers. Hence in this particular case an efficient solution was reached from an *ex post* perspective since the activity with the lowest relocation costs was required to move, and, in addition, the prospective project developers still received correct signals *ex ante* from the Court in that Del Webb was forced to pay for Spur's relocation. This solution is also referred to as a 'purchased injunction': the newcomer can 'purchase' an injunction, meaning that he can demand the closure of the activity that is causing a nuisance if he is prepared to compensate the relocation costs.

5.3 European Cases

In countries that are traditionally highly populated, such as Belgium and the Netherlands, there is relatively little discussion on first use. This has a great deal to do with the fact that it has been decided *ex ante* through zoning and planning laws which kind of activities may take place in a certain area; see Section 4. Yet there are cases where temporal priority plays a role. The Dutch Supreme Court was asked to rule on a case where Van Tol was the first user and De Jong knowingly located himself close to Van Tol's property. When De Jong sued Van Tol, claiming to be harmed by wind-blown seeds, this claim was denied, taking into account the fact that Van Tol had first use and the activities took place in an agricultural area.[4] In Belgian law one can also find cases discussing the first-use doctrine. If a Belgian chip shop[5] chooses its location next to a pig farm,[6] the shopkeeper should not afterwards complain about the smell emitted from the farm. On the other hand, Belgian law apparently also recognizes that first use is not a defence against the duty to take additional preventive measures if harm can be reduced. The duty to reduce the nuisance also exists if the victims come to the nuisance. The Court of Appeals of Ghent held in this respect that newcomers may expect that the licensee of a factory will take the necessary measures to prevent the harm as far as possible.[7] Therefore, if additional measures can reduce the problem of, for example, noise or smell, first use is no defence against a duty of taking such preventive measures.[8] If, however, the reduction of harm through further preventive measures is not possible, newcomers cannot demand the closure of the factory.[9] According to the facts, it appears that the harm caused in this particular case was relatively limited, compared to the probably much higher relocation costs of the firm. This may have been a decisive factor in the decision.

Issues of nuisance have also been addressed in, for example, Norwegian environmental law. Temporal priority has been discussed in cases on airport noise where plaintiffs have moved near an airport after it was built. In all cases the Norwegian Supreme Court denied compensation: in the first two, explicitly, on the grounds that the plaintiffs had chosen to move into the proximity of the airport and, thus, were those nearest to bearing the risk of undesirable consequences of this choice; in the other two, explicitly, by relying on the first-use doctrine, arguing that the airport was first.

In another Norwegian case, referred to as *Hunton Bruk*, a factory came to the area in 1889, but started to produce a new product in 1957 with new technology. Four homeowners, who moved to the area later than the factory was constructed but before the new technology was installed, sued the factory. The factory argued that it was in the area first and that a new method of production was an expected development of such an activity. The Supreme Court, however, found the factory liable.

The Dutch, Belgian and Norwegian cases seem to comply with the economic rules of thumb sketched above. The first-use doctrine is accepted as a defence if the newcomer knowingly comes to the nuisance: if, in other words, the harm is foreseeable. This, however, does not eliminate the duty of the existing factory to invest in efficient preventive measures, wherever possible. Foresight is apparently also a criterion in the Norwegian airport cases. The fact that plaintiffs who came to the airport after it was built were denied compensation by the Norwegian Supreme Court can be understood: they have probably already been compensated through the fact that their property could be purchased at a lower price. Thus this lower price already constitutes an *ex ante* compensation for future noise caused by the airport. This only changes if the harm caused through the activities increases unforeseeably. This was apparently the case in the *Hunton Bruk* decision. The activities began in 1889, but it was first in 1957, after the homeowners came to the area, that a harmful technology was implemented.

6. CONCLUSIONS

Earlier in this book we stressed the importance of assigned and publicly protected property rights for efficient use of resources, including the environment. Property rights give a long-term incentive to invest efficiently. That is, however, not the full picture, especially not for property that is fixed. The value of fixed property much depends on the location and the surrounding environment. For some property the value is so dependent on location that maintenance may be neglected, for example in city slums. Community politics is also of importance. Exploitation permits, investments in infrastructure, parks and so on have importance for the maintenance and the value of fixed property. Environmental issues, therefore, become political. Special interest groups mobilize to protect their interests.

A complication is that property rights in real estate may be split due to differences in use. For instance, a landowner may have the right to forestry and agriculture, while the right to trespass is public. Mining rights on the property may be owned by the state, while the air space above the land is a free good available for aviation. Environmental regulations may interfere with several interests or rights to the property.

Geographical zoning is an important environmental policy instrument. By establishing separate zones for various activities much disturbance is avoided, and by moving to appropriate zones transaction costs can be reduced. The alternative, with mutual agreements including all involved neighbours before location, may be prohibitively costly. Zoning has benefits of economies of specialization as well. It allow us to have national parks and protection of rare species, as well as industries that pollute the soil. A problem may be, of course, leakage or air and water pollution causing negative externalities. Hence the activities within zones also need to be regulated; see Chapter 11. Other problems with zoning are that the zones may be a result of specific interests rather than the public interest. Zones may, of course, in the long run prove to be inappropriately located. The environmentalists' idea that all polluted soil should be cleaned up to a 'natural' state is unrealistic. Indeed, if already-polluted land is not further used by polluting industries, there would be few resources left for the protection of remaining virgin land.

Some version of the 'first-use' doctrine is present in many jurisdictions. The doctrine says that a newcomer disturbed by those already settled in the area cannot count on compensation for the nuisance. An economic rationale of the doctrine is that the newcomer is able to choose location at a lower cost than the cost of relocation of those already settled. However, if the disturbance develops over time it may be unclear who came first, who disturbs whom, and who could most efficiently relocate. Note that environmental arguments can, depending on the situation, be used by both first- and newcomers. The first-comer may claim, for instance, that the protection of the established cultural environment requires that the first-comers' rights should be honoured. The newcomer, on the other hand, may claim that the smoke of the first-comer is a nuisance to the environment, an argument that may have a stronger impact on the law-maker.

Another important matter in conflicts of location is the presence of explicit or implicit agreements. For instance, a worker may accept a smoky environment in order to get a job or a good salary. Once the employment is settled the worker may claim that the dirty job is an environmental nuisance for which he should be compensated. If successful, the worker will be compensated twice for the inconvenience. More important from an efficiency point of view is that the costs of employing workers will become excessive, which may result in fewer than optimal employees or, in the worst case, a shut-down of the industry.

NOTES

1. According to Article 31 § 2 of the Soil Clean-up Decree of 22 February 1995, there is no duty to clean up in the case of historic pollution if the user of the soil was in good faith (see M. Deketelaere, 'Aansprakelijkheid voor historische, nieuwe en gemengde bodemverontreiniging', in K. Deketelaere (ed.), *Het decreet betreffende de bodemsanering*, Brugge, Die Keure, 1995, 135–42).
2. *Spur Industries Inc.* v. *Del. E. Webb Development Company*, 494, 2d 701 (Arizona, 1972).
3. An interesting detail is that the decision notes that a cow produces on average between 35 and 40 pounds of manure per day, so that 30 000 cows together produce more than one million pounds of manure per day, which may imaginably cause an offensive odour and attract flies.
4. Hoge Raad (Dutch Supreme Court), 3 May 1991, *Recthspraak van de week*, 1991, p. 102.
5. Chips or 'French' fries are a Belgian speciality.
6. Vredegerecht (Justice of the Peace), Beveren, 10 April 1990, *Tijdschrift voor Vrederechters*, 1990, p. 347.
7. Hof van Beroep (Court of Appeals), Ghent, 25 November 1968, *Rechtskundig Weekblad*, 1969–70, p. 429.
8. Rechtbank van eerste aanleg (Tribunal of First Instance), Antwerp, 25 June 1981, *Pasicrisie Belge*, 1982, III, p. 66; Rechtbank van Eerste Aanleg (Tribunal of First Instance), Ghent, 12 March 1981, *Rechtskundig Weekblad*, 1982–83, p. 1327.
9. Antwerp, 17 February 1988, *Rechtskundig Weekblad,* 1988–90 (Klopt niet), p. 50.

FURTHER READING

Ault, R.W. and Ekelund, R.B. (1988), 'Rent Seeking in a Static Model of Zoning', *American Real Estate and Urban Economics Association Journal*, **16**, 69–76.

Ellickson, R. (1973), 'Alternatives to Zoning', *University of Chicago Law Review*, 738–48.

Epstein, R. (1979), 'Nuisance Law: Corrective Justice and its Utilitarian Constraints', *Journal of Legal Studies*, 72–3.

Fischel, W.A. (1980), 'Externalities and Zoning', *Public Choice*, **35**, 37–43.

Fischel, W.A. (1985), *The Economics of Zoning Laws: A Property Rights Approach to American Land Use Controls*, Baltimore, MD: Johns Hopkins University Press.

Merrill, T. (1985), 'Trespass, nuisance and the costs of determining property rights', *Journal of Legal Studies*, 13–48.

Wittman, D. (1980), 'First come, first served: an economic analysis of coming to nuisance', *Journal of Legal Studies*, 557–68.

13. Tradable permits, charges and deposits

No nation was ever ruined by trade.
Benjamin Franklin

1. INTRODUCTION

An economic argument in the Pigouvian tradition is that harmful pollution can best be corrected by taxes. The idea is that the price of the produced good does not reflect the opportunity cost at negative externalities, which misleads the agents on the markets; see Chapter 6, Section 2. To correct this market failure, the state should add a tax, for example, on emissions, harmful goods, gasoline or cars, so that the prices reflect the social marginal costs. The traders will thus be guided efficiently by the prices.

In this Pigouvian language 'tax' means a fee or a charge on gasoline, on permits to pollute, and so on. A tax is, however, as normally defined, a compulsory transfer to the state or the community, for example in the form of income or property taxes, without direct benefit to the taxpayer (see Chapter 6, Section 4). The Pigouvian 'tax' comprises, on the other hand, a payment for the right to consume gasoline and to emit smoke. Below, we use Pigouvian 'tax' and 'charge' synonymously. The terminology remains unclear, however, a point to which we shall return.

Note also that the traditional presentation of economic measures to protect the environment is usually divided into central administrative 'command-and-control' measures as against decentralized market solutions. Charges as well as traded permits are typical market-oriented measures. Legal and administrative regulations are described as alternatives to market solutions, but regulations and prices can also complement each other. The Coasean approach applied in this book is more general than the Pigouvian tradition. That is, a charge is a special case of various mandatory measures to control pollution.

This will be demonstrated in the present chapter. In Section 2 we examine the economics of trade with pollution permits distributed by a regulatory agency. Thereafter, in Section 3, we investigate the economics of charges. In Section 4 we investigate deposits and charges funded for a specific environmental purpose. Section 6 concludes.

2. TRADABLE PERMITS

2.1 Regulating Many Polluters

In the normative model presented above the regulatory agency sets the emission standard in the public interest. The regulator takes into account marginal costs of more stringent environmental standards and balances these against the marginal benefits in terms of additional reduction of environmental harm; see Chapter 11, Section 2. This refined balancing process requires accurate information on the marginal costs of the various technical devices that could prevent harm, as well as information about the harm to the victims. In theory, information is needed on all polluters and victims. Where there are many factories emitting smoke, cars causing congestion in cities, tourists polluting protected areas and so on there are obvious problems in obtaining information and in regulating all polluters in detail. Administrative simplifications are, indeed, necessary.

A first simplification is, as noted in Chapter 11, Section 2, to abandon the search for optimal pollution and instead set politically realistic targets and try to reach them in a cost-efficient way. The target can be a total pollution of, say, *X* tonnes of toxic emissions in a region or *Y* number of cars in a city. A second step is to distribute permits within the target set. A cost-efficient distribution of the rights requires that the marginal benefit of a marginal permit is the same to all polluters. However, if information is poor it may be impossible to distribute permits efficiently. The distribution may, instead, be more or less arbitrary. For instance, polluters may receive rights in accordance with earlier pollution, turnover, lobbying success and so on.

The inefficiency in the case of equal quantitative distribution of permits is illustrated in Figure 13.1. In the diagram there are, for graphic simplicity only two polluters, *A* and *C*, who have different *MNB* of pollution, as demonstrated in parts (a) and (b) of the figure. We assume that the authorities have

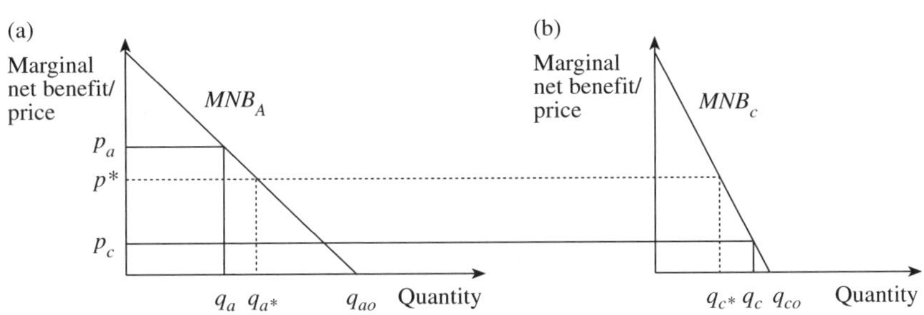

Figure 13.1 Tradable permits

decided on a total pollution target of Q, which is for some reason distributed equally between the two polluters: that is $q_a = q_c$, where $q_a + q_c = Q$.

At $q_a = q_c$ the polluters have different marginal net benefit, *MNB*, or willingness to pay. Their marginal WTP is indicated by p_a and p_c. Because of the difference in the value of a marginal pollution permit, a redistribution of pollution rights from *C* to *A*, who is willing to pay most for the right, would increase efficiency. The redistribution to *A* can be continued beneficially until $p_a = p_c$. Here, the cost of reaching the target standard, Q, is minimized. The pollution rights are distributed efficiently so that the parties receive q_{a*} and q_{c*} respectively. The sum of pollution rights should, of course, fulfil the condition $q_{a*} + q_{c*} = Q$.

2.2 Trade with Permits

The main problem of an agency that aims at a cost-efficient implementation of the target is to allocate the pollution rights in efficient quantities as illustrated by q_{a*} and q_{c*} in Figure 13.1. However, central information on the *MNB*s of the polluting firms is usually not present. To the extent information exists it is usually decentralized; that is, it is in the hands of the polluters. This fact can be efficiently utilized by a combination of regulation and trade. As soon as the polluters have received their pollution rights they may realize that they differ in their willingness to pay for additional pollution permits. If so, there is a room for trade among them. *A* is willing to pay p_a for a marginal right to pollute, while *C* is willing to accept p_c. The joint benefit of trading a marginal right is equal to the bargaining space, $p_a – p_c$. The sharing of the profit is undetermined and due to the payment of the right to pollute, upon which the parties agree. A benefit of trade remains as long as there is a difference between p_a and p_c. First, at the efficient distribution of permits, q_{a*} and q_{c*}, there is no further benefit to trade.

Such trade of permits is in accordance with the Coase theorem; given the initial set of pollution rights distributed to the parties by the legal system, the polluters have a mutual interest in cost-efficiency, and thus they will trade if the transaction costs are not an obstacle.

If the parties for some reason cannot agree on transacting permits, the inefficiency remains, of course. A different reason for inefficiency is that trade may be illegal though feasible. One reason to outlaw trade is that trade in pollution may be held to be unethical; see Chapter 10, Section 4. Another reason could be that strategic bargaining on quotas makes trade inappropriate. A lobbying firm may, for instance, claim that it will have to close down if a large amount of permits is not received. If the permits are received and thereafter sold to other firms, it will be revealed that the claim was exaggerated.

Note that permits must be distributed by some regulatory body before trade can take place. Thus the assignment of permits may be efficient if it is combined with a reallocation by trade. Quantitative regulation of rights and trade are thus complementary. The essence of the Coase theorem is that the initial distribution does not matter from an efficiency point of view, that is, the agency may distribute the quotas equally, according to production levels, seniority or whatever – trade will reallocate the rights efficiently. Hence, if the authorities want to favour small factories or early polluters, for example, this can be done by giving them relatively many pollution rights, which they can then sell to those willing to pay the most.

The important difference between distribution of quotas with and without trade is that trade reallocates without the need for central information about the WTP, that is, the shape of the *MNB* curves. Trade reveals the willingness to pay for pollution. If, on the other hand, the rights are not traded but distributed by the agency only, both *A* and *C* in Figure 13.1 may ask for more

BOX 13.1 TRADABLE PERMITS: A NOTE ON THE LITERATURE

The starting-point for most of the literature on tradable systems is the pioneering work of J.H. Dales in the 1960s.[1] Dales proposed that a market for tradable permits would be organized by the government whereby pollution rights that should be tradable would be granted for a certain period. The government would act as broker for the trade and would monitor the system. Building on Dales's proposal, other authors formulated more specific proposals with respect to the shape of this market for pollution rights. D.W. Montgomery suggested that the pollution rights should also indicate which part of the concentration of a specific compound in a particular environmental component could be emitted from a particular source.[2] Later, Hahn and Hester pointed to the importance of monitoring and enforcement in the framework of a market for pollution rights.[3]

Notes:

1. J.H. Dales, *Pollution, Property and Prices: an essay in policy*, Toronto: University of Toronto Press, 1968.
2. D.W. Montgomery, D W., 'Markets in licences and efficient pollution control', *Journal of Economic Theories*, **5**, 1972, 395–418.
3. R.W. Hahn and G.L. Hester, 'Where did all the markets go? An analysis of EPA's emissions trading programme'. *Yale Journal on Regulation*, **6**, 1989, 109–53.

permits as long as it contributes to their profits, that is, up to q_{ao} and q_{co} respectively, which exceeds the target Q and misleads the agency.

So far, we have treated the case of only two polluters sharing pollution quotas. With many polluters a market may develop with demand and supply of permits, and a price on the pollution rights. Here, the benefit of trade becomes obvious. It is, of course, in practice impossible for an agency to distribute rights cost-efficiently if there are hundreds or thousands of polluters and victims. But if the polluters have the right to trade the rights, they may reallocate the rights to the highest bidders, which is cost-effective.

The cost-effectiveness established by trading permits is usually labelled *static efficiency*. Moreover, a price on the pollution permit also creates an incentive to change to cleaner production methods to avoid costs. An even stronger incentive to reduce pollution is established if there is reason to believe that issued rights will be reduced in the future, which would increase the future price of pollution rights and, thus, increase the expected benefit of

BOX 13.2 TRADABLE SUCCESS STORIES

Most of the success stories with respect to a market for pollution rights come from the USA, although there is also a European experience with some forms of tradable pollution rights. For instance, in the Netherlands, Peeters discusses the Dutch manure legislation, which allows for a trade in the right to produce manure.[1] As far as the USA is concerned, the empirical material relating to the experience with tradable permits is overwhelming. Oates discusses the emissions trading system for air pollutants and reports that trading has made real headway in certain regions.[2] This enthusiasm is supported by other sources. Hahn and Hester (1989) claim that the trading programmes concerning the Clean Air Act have led to considerable cost savings, although they have been less than anticipated. However, they also claim that it is hard to demonstrate major environmental improvements as a consequence of these market policies.

Notes:

1. M. Peeters, '*Markt conform milieurecht? Een rechtsvergelijkende studie naar de verhandelbaarheid van vervuilingsrechten*' (Market-oriented environmental law? A comparative legal study into the tradability of pollution rights), Zwolle: Tjeenk Willink, 1992.
2. W.E. Oates, and A.M.McGartland, 'Marketable permits for the prevention of environmental deteroration', *Journal of Environmental Economics and Management*, **12** (3), 1985, 207–28.

investments reducing the demand for pollution rights. This phenomenon is called *dynamic efficiency* of tradable permits.

Trade with permits has obvious merits when the number of polluters and victims is large. It is obviously impossible for an agency to estimate benefits and costs for everybody and regulate quantity thereafter. On the other hand, if there is only one polluter within the relevant area, there is obviously no room for a market. The firm must, therefore, be regulated individually as described in Chapter 11. The outcome will be a result of either mandatory command and control, or of a bargain with the firm and the regulatory agent. The same is true in small-number exchange with a handful of polluters. A small number of polluters may possibly collude and act as one in the negotiations on pollution rights. The industry may have a strong joint interest to cooperate and to act strategically against the regulator.

3. CHARGES

3.1 The Optimal Charge

As a basis for discussion, we present the optimal charge in a simple model with one polluter and one victim. In the model presented in Figure 13.2, which has been used several times above, the polluting factory, *A*, causes harm to a victim, *B*. The optimal production, pollution, or emission level is x_1.

If there are prohibitive transaction costs and, thus, no agreement between the parties, the polluting firm *A* will choose x_0 and cause an external effect on *B*. Assume further that the state uses a charge or tax, *t*, that is constant per unit of *x*. The charge will reduce the profit and shift the marginal net benefit, *MNB*, of *A* downwards to $MNB_A – t$, and, consequently, reduce the factory's production and pollution level. The optimal charge, t^*, is such that it reduces

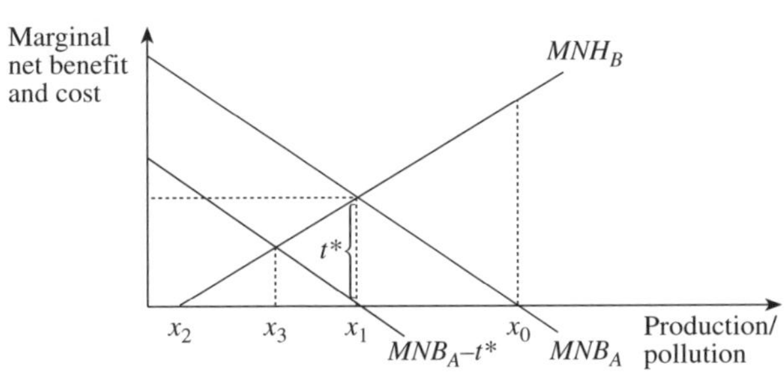

Figure 13.2 The optimal charge

A's production to the optimal level, x_1. Hence the optimal charge is equal to the marginal harm to *B* at the optimal pollution, x_1.

Now, let us compare this charge with a regulation where the factory, *A*, is commanded not to pollute more than x_1. In other words, the factory, *A*, obtains the right to pollute up to x_1 for free. On the other hand, if the tax is used, *A* must pay *t* for each unit produced, that is, $x_1 \times t$. Both measures are optimal *per se*, but regulation has a distributive impact in favour of *A* as long as the pollution rights are given without costs.

Note that if the tax is combined with regulations, the charge may have no effect on the pollution. To see why, assume that the agency has issued the permit to pollute x_1. Thereafter, the Ministry of Finance imposes the tax rate t^*. As the factory *A* already produces at x_1, there is no reason for *A* to change the production. Hence the payment to the treasury can be seen as a 'pure' tax of $x_1 x t^*$ on the industry without any impact on the pollution. Thus to use charges on the already-regulated polluter may not improve the environment, but possibly the finances of the state.

A different outcome may occur if the regulatory agency does not know the *MNB*s and regulate although there is an implicit contract. The example above assumes that there are prohibitive transaction costs and, thus, no agreement. There may, however, be a silent agreement as discussed in relation to nuisance law; see Chapter 12, Section 6. In that case a charge can worsen the situation, which is also illustrated in Figure 13.2. Suppose that there is a silent agreement by which the production is modified to the optimal x_1. Still *B* is harmed and is thus willing to pay *A* for further reductions in pollution down to x_2, but *A* requires too much in compensation for further reductions of *x*. The optimum is thus reached. Yet, due to lack of information on the agreement, the regulator may believe in a negative externality and impose a Pigouvian charge to correct for the supposed externality. If the charge, t^*, is imposed, the net marginal benefit of *A* is reduced to $MNB–t^*$. Thus the charge reduces the profitability of production, which gives room for a new silent agreement that reduces pollution to x_3, which is suboptimally low. In sum, if the interdependence of the parties disturbing each other is regulated by the parties themselves, either explicitly or implicitly, additional public regulation may cause overregulation.

If there are many factories using different techniques and causing varying degrees of harm to victims, all factories should, in principle, pay different charges, which, again, leads to overwhelming information and coordination problems. Yet recall that the problem is reduced if a subset of pollutants is damaging the same source (a water system, or a city). It may then be possible to identify a reasonable target quantity. Here, CBA may be helpful in balancing environmental quality against other interests. Once the target is set, a charge may be used for the reduction of pollution or congestion.[1] To find the

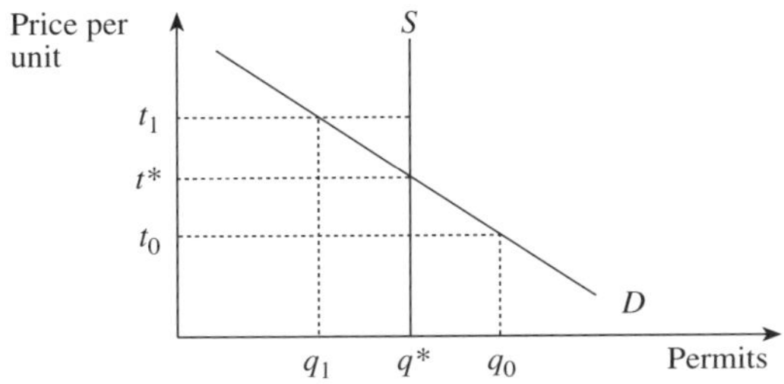

Figure 13.3 Supply of and demand for permits

cost-efficient charge reaching the target, a pricing process (auction) may be undertaken, as shown in Figure 13.3. Here, we have the demand and supply of permits. The vertical supply curve indicates the target set by the authorities. The demand is assumed to be unknown by the authority setting the charge. The chosen charge is, therefore, arbitrary, say, t_0. Excess demand for the charge will, thus, be revealed. The charge will, therefore, be increased until all demand is satisfied. On the other hand, if the initial charge is set at t_1, few pollution or traffic permits will be sold. Hence there is a reason to reduce the charge. The trail and error process continues until q^*, t^* is reached.

4. EARMARKED CHARGES, DEPOSITS AND FUNDS

An environmental tax is usually paid directly to the state without any commitments. That is, there is no obligation on the state to use the revenue for any specific purpose. It is up to the politicians to decide freely within the public budget. Yet, when taxes are introduced, there may be a promise that the means collected shall be 'earmarked' for some purpose. Such a promise may be more or less binding. The most binding and trusted commitment may be to establish an independent fund that can only be used for its specific purpose. A simpler, but less binding, way is to collect the revenue in a specific account in the books.

Note that a collection of means in a fund for a specific purpose may have double effects. One is the Pigouvian effect, that is, the charge changes prices and behaviour in the market, which may be positive. Second, the collected means are 'owned' by the fund with the specific purpose. In other words, the value of the pollution right is transferred to the fund with a certain aim, for example to improve the environment. The means may cover costs, for example, of waste-handling, clean-ups and for compensation for accidents. When future accident losses are covered by a fund it turns to insurance, which will be further discussed in Chapter 15.

BOX 13.3 CHARGES: EMPIRICAL EVIDENCE

More empirical evidence concerning experiences with charges comes from Europe than from the USA. This is typically the reverse for marketable pollution permits, which have been far more popular in the American experience than in Europe. Dewees, Duff and Trebilcock (1996, p. 326) note that charges are rarely introduced 'in the text book form'. R.W. Hahn (1989, pp. 95–114) claims that most emission charges or fees are used as a revenue-generating device for public services rather than as instruments of environmental policy, as they were prescribed by economists. However, in the Netherlands water pollution by 14 industries responsible for 90 per cent of total water pollution decreased by 50 per cent between 1969 and 1975 and by another 20 per cent by 1980; half of this reduction was due to the effluent charge. Similar success stories come from Germany, where it is reported that due to water effluent charges there were significant increases in water treatment, leading most of the firms to comply with the existing emission standards.[1] All of this European evidence seems to suggest that effluent charges provide a strong incentive to invest in water pollution abatement equipment (Frey, 1992, pp. 149–51). However, one should note that most European countries still use a combination of effluent charges and emission standards. It is therefore hard to argue that the significant investments in water treatment plants were mainly due to the charges system and not, for example, to the threat of administrative and/or criminal sanctions in case of a violation of emission standards.

Note:

1. J. Bongaerts and R.A. Kraemer, 'Water pollution charges in three countries: control through incentives', *European Environment Review*, **1** (4), 1987, 12–19.

A deposit has similarities to a charge but is in principle different. To illustrate, assume you enter a department store and take one of the baskets belonging to the store. You fill the basket, pay the bill and bring the basket with all the goods to the car. The store expects you to return the basket. You have also (silently) accepted to return it after using it. But back at the car, it is simpler for you just to leave it in the car park. Thus there is a problem in enforcing the implicit agreement. That is where a pledge or deposit may be used: you pay an amount when you take the basket to guarantee the return. The size of the pledge is of minor important as long as it is large enough to give an incentive to return the basket. Such systems where you put a coin in a locker to receive the basket, which is later refunded when the basket is properly returned, are commonly used.

Pledges, deposits and similar arrangements to guarantee the fulfilment of a duty are common in business. They are also used to protect the environment. Examples are deposits on bottles, cans, batteries, used tyres and scrapped cars.

A characteristic of a deposit is that it is paid in advance and returned when the duty is fulfilled. Note that the ownership of the deposit does not change as long as the obligation is fulfilled. The deposit may be reserved in, for example, a bank paying interest to the owner. The deposit must, of course, be administered in a trustworthy manner. This is a minor problem in the case of the mechanical locker in the supermarket. It is more problematic when the deposit is large and includes funding over a long period. A fund based on deposits may invest the money and make a profit, or it may lose the money. Indeed, it may go bankrupt.

The demand for earmarking of taxes may be based on a lack of trust; politicians may in the future use the revenues without considering earlier promises. Similarly, a requirement that means should be transferred into a fund that is independent of current politics may be due to distrust, or to a general demand for reduced risk. Thus a fund for, say, the protection of the environment is a type of guarantee. Similarly, in private business liabilities have to be guaranteed by corresponding assets and equity.

This fact is of importance in environmental matters. In Chapter 9, Section 5 we discussed producer's responsibility for recycling used cars. If producers have a duty to retake and dismantle old cars they have sold, there will be an additional liability for each new car sold. After 10–15 years the economic liability of running cars may become very large. Indeed, the producer may go bankrupt if means are not properly reserved. Hence producer's responsibility may, therefore, be combined with a requirement that sufficient means should be funded.[2]

5. CONCLUSIONS

Comparing a system of traded permits and charges, we find that the initial determination of a pollution target is equally important for both systems. Moreover, the systems are equally cost-efficient, but the path towards efficiency differs. In the case of tradable permits quotas are distributed according to some principle. Thereafter trade reallocates the permits. In equilibrium the market price for a permit will reflect the willingness to pay for a marginal

BOX 13.4 TAXES, CHARGES OR FUNDS?

Consider the following scenario: environmentalists claim that the environment should be protected, for example polluted soil should be cleaned up or nuclear power should be scrapped and the power plants dismantled. The politicians argue that such actions cannot be publicly financed because of the general burden of taxes. Instead they refer to the polluter pays principle and suggest a charge on the polluter for coverage of the restoration costs. The charge is accepted in Parliament because of the promised recovery of the environment. Nonetheless, the end may result be a tax with little connection to the promised environmental restoration.

In Sweden there is a system to promote return of used cars ready for scrapping. Buyers of new cars have to pay a fee, and final owners receive a sum when leaving the car at the scrapyard. The system reduces the number of abandoned cars in the countryside. However, the legal status of the 'car scrapping fund' is unclear. Indeed, talking about a fund is misleading. The 'scrap fee' appears to be a tax. There is no defined deposit made by the car-owners that is returned on scrapping. Consequently, no interest is paid. Reserving a deposit for 10–15 years with interest would increase its value considerably. The state is only politically committed to pay back when cars are returned. The return payment is, in fact, independent of the size of the account. If the account had been an independent fund for guaranteeing the repayments, it would have been bankrupt in the late 1980s when the stock of cars declined.

Similarly, there is a nuclear dismantling 'fund' in Sweden. After a political debate on radioactive waste in the 1980s a 'charge' of 0.01 SEK/kwh to cover future dismantling costs was introduced. A dismantling 'fund' was established by the state. Because of the vast production of electricity by nuclear power in Sweden, the 'fund' grew rapidly and is today around billion 20 SEK. In the public accounts it has been treated as an asset, ignoring the fact that there is a corresponding liability in the future to pay for dismantling the power plants. Is this a mistake, or do the authorities not expect any dismantling in the future?

pollution right. An incentive fostering dynamic efficiency will also be present due to the possibility of reducing costs in the long run by investments in technologies that require fewer pollution permits. A charge will have the same efficient result. In equilibrium the target will be reached and all will pay the same price for a marginal pollution permit. The way to equilibrium differs in that the public agency and not the market sets a charge that may cause excess demand or supply. The price can thereafter be adjusted until equilibrium is reached.

The difference between marketable pollution permits and charges is mainly distributive. Recall that, according to the Coase theorem, the initial distribution of permits has no impact on the efficiency, but on the distribution of wealth. This means that initial pollution rights can, for distribution reasons, be given to any party, who then will sell the rights to the highest bidder. Those paying the most will, thus, receive the permits in both systems, which is efficient.

A charge is collected and used by the state. It is simply a special case of tradable permits where the state is the initial owner and, thus, receives the income. Hence a main differences between charges and tradable pollution rights is that the state 'sells' the permits. An obvious reason for using charges is the need of revenues for public spending. Taxes on incomes, sales and capital causes an excess burden, which was discussed in Chapter 6, Section 4. Indeed, the argument in favour of 'green' taxes is that ordinary taxes, especially on labour, should be substituted by environmental charges. The thought is that such a change will produce a double dividend, that is, reduce the negative effects on the economy of taxes on labour and obtain positive effects on the environment.

Nevertheless, there may be political reasons for the use of tradable permits instead of charges. By distributing the rights within industry, it may be easier to reach a political compromise since industry as a whole will not lose. On the other hand, collected taxes may also be redistributed to industry. Suppose, for instance, that the government would like to introduce a charge on pesticides used in farming, but the farmers protest and threaten to vote for the opposition in the next election. An alternative may be to implement the charge, and to redistribute the revenue to the farmers as a group. Note, however, that in order to make the charge efficient in the reduction of pesticides, the returned revenues to farming must be independent of the use of pesticides by individual farmers, for example based on the size of the farm.

In sum, charges cannot be said to be more efficient, or market-oriented, as compared to administrative regulation of pollution, as long as permits to pollute are traded freely. An administrative command-and-control system prohibiting trade may, on the other hand, be inefficient. Information revealed by prices should be utilized. Industry does not have the incentive to deliver correct information as long as it receives permits by regulation.

If there is only one polluter, there is no room for trade. The regulatory agency alone has to decide on pollution level, although efficient regulation requires detailed information. This is also the case if the agency charges a tax on the polluter. If there are a few polluters it may be very complicated to find the optimal level for each polluter. Trade of permits may possibly improve the situation, but the outcome is uncertain. The outcome in small-number markets is difficult to foresee. Strategic behaviour, as well as collusion, can be expected. Still, a bargaining process including the agency and industry in a long-term relationship may lead to reasonable regulations. Knowing each other well, and knowing that misconduct is punished by the counter-party, may foster efficient solutions. A large body of literature has addressed the efficiency of various systems to reach an environmental quality standard, but without any uniform answer.

If there are ten, one hundred, or one thousand polluters, for example, farmers using pesticides, cars polluting a city, firms emitting smoke which pollutes the neighbourhood and so on it would require immense amounts of information and endless negotiations for non-tradable rights to become efficient. The distribution of tradable rights might also be costly when there are many polluters. It may be simpler and more practical to collect charges.

NOTES

1. Baumol and Oates (1971) proposed the use of such quality standards and charges for environmental protection.
2. See further on this matter Lidgren and Skogh (1996).

FURTHER READING

Baumol, W.J. and Oates, W.E. (1971), 'The Use of Standards and Prices for Protection of the Environment', *Swedish Journal of Economics*, **73**, 42–54.

Noll, R. (1982), 'The feasibility of marketable emissions permits in the United States', in R.B. Stewart and J.B. Krier (eds), *Environmental Law and Policy*, Charlottesville, VA: LEXIS Publishing.

Oates, W. (1976), 'Book review: the uncertain search for Environmental Quality', *University of Pennsylvania Law Review*, **124**, 864–91.

Oates, W., Portney, P. and McGartland, A. (1989), 'The Net Benefits of Incentive-based Regulation: A Case Study of Environmental Standard Setting', *American Economic Review*, **79**, 1233–42.

Rose-Ackerman, S. (1977), 'Market models for water pollution control: their strengths and weaknesses', *Public Policy*, **25**, 383–406.

Tietenberg, T. (1985), *Emissions trading: an exercise in reforming pollution policy*, Washington, DC: Resources for the Future.

PART IV

Risk and Liability

14. Tort law

The owner's duty ... to provide against resulting injuries is a function of three variables:
(1) The probability that she [a barge] will break away;
(2) the gravity of the resulting injury when she does;
(3) the burden of adequate precautions.
Learned Hand Rule, from the case *US* v. *Carrol Towing Co.*, 1947

1. INTRODUCTION

Information and knowledge are basic in our highly technical world. Indeed, improved products and methods have contributed to a historically exceptional economic growth. Knowledge also reduces risks. Medical research has contributed, for instance, to the elimination of many diseases. Similarly, improved insurance coverage and social welfare systems have reduced the threat of accidents. However, novelty and change create, at the same time, uncertainty and new hazards. Upcoming scarcities and the lack of property rights cause 'tragedies of the commons' (see Chapter 3, Section 3). Population growth and pollution contribute to increased environmental stress, illnesses like allergy and cancer, and so on. Moreover, advances in industry are followed by new industrial hazards. Some industrial risks may be catastrophic, for example pollution by huge oil tankers, nuclear accidents and hazardous gene manipulation. These hazards hit humanity as unexpected events, that is, as *accidents*.

Uncertainty and the risk of accidental losses are treated in various places above. Chapter 7 introduced the concepts 'expected value', 'risk premium', 'risk-neutrality', 'risk-aversion', and 'risk perception'. Cost–benefit analysis under uncertainty was discussed in Chapter 10, for example in relation to the economic valuation of a statistical life (Section 9). Regulations of emission standards, licensing, safety regulations and charges are also undertaken under uncertainty. Many of the regulations are motivated by their expected impact on safety. Such regulation is usually enforced by tort law and criminal law.

Here in Part IV we study risk and liability law. First, in this chapter, we focus on tort law. We apply a simple model that has been successfully used in the economic analysis of law. The model assumes that law has an impact on the behaviour of the involved parties and thus on the accident risk.[1] In Section 2 we present the most important liability rules: 'negligence' and 'strict liability'. We also outline various costs of accidents. Section 3 presents the model. We start with the simple case where only one party, the injurer, influences the risk of accident. The somewhat more complicated case where the victim also contributes to the accident risk is examined thereafter. Accidents may also be reduced by limited activity level. That is, reduced traffic, fewer dangerous industries or a limited utilization of a given capacity in an industry would reduce the number and/or the severity of accidents. Section 4 contains a descriptive legal case. Section 5 concludes.

2. NEGLIGENCE AND STRICT LIABILITY

In the typical *tort law* case someone (the injurer) has caused an accident that harms a victim. The victim is a stranger to the injurer – there is no explicit or implicit contract regulating the liability of the parties (if there were an agreement, contract law would apply). The victim (plaintiff) claims after the accident in a court for compensation by the injurer (the defendant). Due to the prevailing rules and the judgment of the court, the defendant will have to pay a damage or not. A damage compensating the victim is not only to the benefit of the victim. It may also have a preventive effect. This presumes that the verdict establishes a precedent that injurers may have to pay damages to their victims.

A *negligence* rule, or *fault*, is the main tort-law principle in many jurisdictions. That is, the injurer will have to compensate the victim if: (i) the injurer has caused the damage; and (ii) the injurer has been intentional or careless. If the injurer took care, he/she will not have to indemnify the damage.

There are exceptions to the negligence rule – notably in case of hazardous industrial activities and environmental damage – where *strict liability* is often applied. Strict liability means that the injurer who has caused an accident shall compensate the victim independent of the level of care taken. Strict liability is thus in accordance with the polluter pays principle.

There is an international tendency towards strict liability for environmental risks. In many areas this shift took place without the formal introduction of a strict liability rule, but instead by broadening the fault concept via case law. In some cases a very high standard of care is imposed under a negligence rule. Sometimes it is called 'objective liability' or 'risk liability'. This legal evolution has led to debates. The distinction between negligence and strict liability remains unclear. Nonetheless, one can note a tendency towards strict liability

BOX 14.1 TOWARDS STRICT ENVIRONMENTAL LIABILITY

The trend towards strict liability in environmental law is obvious. We can refer to conventions on nuclear accidents and oil pollution, as well as to the Convention of Lugano on civil liability for damage resulting from activities dangerous to the environment. At the European level we can point to the Green Paper on Remedying Environmental Damage, which was launched in 1993 and to the recent White Paper on Environmental Liability (2000), which will be discussed later. In this policy document the Commission discusses several options for regulation with respect to environmental liability. Once again one can detect a clear preference for a strict liability rule, at least for damage resulting from hazardous activities. It seems likely that whenever the European Commission takes another initiative with respect to environmental liability, it will involve the adoption of a strict liability rule. Turning to the national level, we can point to strict liability rules for environmental damage in, for example, the German Water Pollution Act of 1957 and the subsequent Umwelthafungsgesetz of 1990; other examples constitute the Danish and the Swedish Acts on Strict Liability for Environmental Damage. In case law, finally, we can point to tendencies to shift from negligence towards strict liability in the area of environmental damage. For instance, in the famous British *Rylands* v. *Fletcher* case a strict liability rule for damage caused by bursting reservoirs was instituted. This nineteenth-century doctrine is now widely applied to many cases of environmental harm.

for environmental harm, both at the international and the national level. Yet a general agreement on the rationale for liability rules is lacking. Some stress the preventive function of tort law, that is, the function to establish an economic incentive to take care. Others tend to focus on the compensation to the victim.

Here the economic analysis plays a clarifying role. The economic model of accident law has developed rapidly and has been most influential in the academic discussion. One advantage of the economic analysis is that the preventive function and the compensation goal are carefully distinguished. The influence of various legal mechanisms that one may choose among can thereby be evaluated both with respect to the prevention and with respect to the compensation issue.

The first legal scholar to analyse accident law from a law and economics perspective was probably Guido Calabresi at Yale Law School.[2] In his book *The Costs of Accidents*, Calabresi makes a distinction between primary, secondary and tertiary accident costs.[3] *Primary accident costs* are (i) the costs of accident avoidance, and (ii) the damage that occurs at accidents. *Secondary accident costs* refer to risk-aversion and incomplete or unfair loss-spreading. *Tertiary accident costs* are the costs of administering the legal system.

Tort law should, Calabresi argues, minimize the total social costs of accidents. The goal of tort law is thus to reduce accidents, but only to the limit set by the costs of reducing the total costs. A legal rule should not give incentives to avoid every possible accident, but only accidents that could be avoided by marginal costs lower than the marginal benefits in terms of accidents and other cost reductions. Liability law should, in other words, give an incentive to potential parties to adopt optimal care.

3. AN ECONOMIC MODEL ON LIABILITY RULES

3.1 The Setting

Below we present a highly simplified model that enables us to analyse the economic effects of various liability rules. To distinguish negligence from strict liability we first consider only the primary costs, that is, cost of prevention of accidents and cost of damage. Thus we neglect the secondary costs and the costs of the legal system.

The injurers and victims are supposed to be risk-neutral profit-maximizing actors. Common knowledge of the law is assumed. The injurers and victims also know their ability to reduce accident risks by taking care. Consequently, the actors will, to the extent it is beneficial, adapt to the law by taking preventive measures. Tort-law models also implicitly assume that transaction costs exclude that the parties have regulated the accident risk themselves. The *ex post* verdict by tort law is seen as a substitute for a contract *ex ante* (see Chapter 9, Section 3).

A verdict in a tort case has a direct distributive effect; that is, either the injurer must pay for the damage or the loss rests where it fell, that is, with the victim. Economic analysis of efficient liability most often assumes indifference as to who should pay in the actual case. What matters are the incentives for future prevention that the law creates. The secondary costs of accidents are thus assumed away.

There are several reasons for neglecting distribution effects in the first stage of analysis. If the law is settled in advance and thus possible to foresee – which is the case in legislation and usually also in case law – the potentially liable party can adjust by taking preventive measures and by adjusting prices. The profitability of price adjustments depends on demand and supply of the goods or services sold and on the competition in the market. In a competitive market part of the costs will be spread on customers independent of the liability rule. Benefits of prevention will similarly be spread via prices.

Risk-aversion, and thus varying utility of wealth of victims and injurers, would complicate the analysis. If the parties are risk-averse the valuation of a loss varies from person to person and may, consequently, be impossible to estimate. The analysis is much simpler, if potential injurers and victims can be, as here, assumed to be risk-neutral. The assumption is justified when injurers and victims are profit-maximizing companies, large enough to bear the cost of the accident without going bankrupt. The assumption is reasonable, especially where the firm is widely held and, thus, the owners are able to diversify via the financial markets; see Chapter 7, Section 4.

Moreover, secondary costs of risk-aversion and/or inability to pay for losses may be eliminated by insurance. We will return to the insurance issue in the next chapter.

Accidents may be reduced in various ways. One option is to limit the activity level. Reduced road traffic, reduced transport of oil, or less dangerous industries would, of course, reduce the number of accidents. Similarly, a limited utilization of a given capacity in an industry reduces risks of accidents. The most simple economic tort-law models assume that the activity level is given. Administrative costs are also neglected. The objective of the law is thereby simplified to become the minimization of the primary cost of the risky activity, that is, the costs of accident avoidance and the damage if an accident occurs.

3.2 The Unilateral Accident

In economic tort-law analysis, a distinction is made between unilateral, bilateral and multilateral accidents. In the bilateral case, two parties, the injurer and the victim, both contribute to the probability of the accident and/or the size of the resulting damage. The economic analysis must, therefore, consider the efficiency of the care taken by both parties. Unilateral influence prevails where the injurer alone causes an accident, in the sense that he is the only actor who can influence the accident risk.

Many industrial accidents are such that the potential victims have little, or no, ability to prevent accidents. For instance, the only way inhabitants in a region can escape the risk of a nuclear accident may be to leave the region. Disregarding this option, the industrial accident is unilateral. That is, it is primarily the injurer who has knowledge about the impact of precautions that may prevent the accident. In the case of industrial accidents we may also assume risk-neutrality.

Given the following assumptions: (i) a unilateral injurer; (ii) a given activity level; (iii) risk-neutrality of the injurer and the victim; (iv) in money-measurable primary costs of prevention and accidents; and (v) no administrative costs, we can find the optimal level of accident prevention and identify the efficiency of various liability rules.

Table 14.1 shows an example of a possible relationship between the cost of prevention and the cost of accident. Risk-neutrality is assumed. Thus the expected accident cost is determined as the product of probability and the damage, which is assumed given and equal to 100 at an accident. It is assumed that the risky activity takes place. Thus we do not consider the risk by allowing the activity *per se*. The optimal level of accident prevention is medium in Table 14.1. Here the total cost of the risky activity is minimized and equal to 13; see the last column.

Table 14.1 Cost of prevention and cost of accident

Level of prevention	Cost of prevention	Probability of an accident (%)	Expected accident cost	Total costs
None	0	20	20	20
Low	1	15	15	16
Medium	3	10	10	13
High	6	8	8	14
Very high	14	6	6	20

Note: The cost of the accident, if it occurs, is assumed to be 100.

From the hypothetical figures we can distinguish the effect of different liability rules; a first alternative is *no liability*. If the injurer were under no responsibility whatsoever to repair the damage, there would be no reason for the industry to take any preventive measures. If damage occurred, the victim alone would bear the cost. The probability of damage would be 20 per cent and the expected total cost 20; see the first row in Table 14.1.

In the case of *negligence* or *fault*, the court must decide on the precautionary and preventive measures that the injurer should have taken to absolve him from liability. Thereby, the court sets a standard of *due care*. If an accident occurs and the injurer has not taken due care, he will be liable for the damage. Thus potential injurers will adapt according to the level of due care to avoid accident costs. For example, assume that the due care standard set by the courts equals the medium (optimal) level in Table 14.1. The injurer will bear the total cost, including prevention cost and accident cost, if he takes precautionary measures below the medium level. If, on the other hand, the injurer takes measures equivalent to, or higher than, the medium level, the victim will need to bear the cost of the accident. The injurer will, therefore, minimize his own costs by following the court's due care standard. Consequently, injurers will avoid liability, and the victim will bear the cost of the accident if it occurs. The total outcome will be optimal because the sum of the precautionary costs carried by the injurer and the losses due to the accident carried by the victim are minimized (13).

A stringent negligence rule may be interpreted as the case where the court requires a level of due care equal to the high level in Table 14.1. Potential injurers will adapt themselves to this level. The result would be a prevention cost of 6 and an expected damage cost of 8, carried by the victim, which would result in a total cost of 14. This level is inefficient because of the high level of prevention.

In the legal vocabulary there is also the term *absolute liability*, which may have different meanings; however, all are related to very strong prevention requirements. Absolute liability is said to be more or less the same as strict liability, but the literature is unclear on this point. A possible interpretation is illustrated in the bottom line in Table 14.1. The law requires 'that all possible measures be undertaken to avoid accidents', that is, a very high level of due care (14). The expected accident cost would be reduced to 6, which is beneficial to the victim, but the total cost would be 20, due to overprevention.

Note, however, that the injurer has a more profitable choice than following the 'absolute care' requirement – he can adapt to the medium level, accept to be judged negligent, and carry the accident costs. In that case the expected costs to the firm would be 13 instead of 14. The injurer will, thus, pay for accidents and prevention, which in effect is the same as strict liability.

If, on the other hand, the due care standard is at the low level, the injurer's cost for prevention will be 1 and the victim's expected accident cost 15, which is also inefficient.

All in all, we conclude that a negligence rule can be efficient, provided that courts or legislators place the due care preventive measures at an efficient level. To succeed, the law-maker must have access to information of the type presented in Table 14.1.

With a system based on *strict liability*, potential injurers will pay for all damages. With the strict liability rule in mind, parties participating in risky activities will minimize the costs and take precautionary and preventive measures equivalent to the medium level in Table 14.1, that is, to the minimal total cost of 13.

Hence strict liability, which is equivalent to the polluter pays principle, leads to efficiency. Yet the same can be said about negligence, provided that the level of precautionary measures (due care) chosen by the court is efficient. A disadvantage of the negligence rule is that the judge must have access to information on the efficient level of care. However, to the extent that there is available information, the information will most probably be in the possession of the injurer who controls the risk. This informational asymmetry offers the most important argument in favour of strict liability.

Another informational obstacle with respect to negligence is that it must be proven, and the burden of proof is normally on the victim. If only obvious carelessness is possible to prove, the potential injurers will adapt to this and an inefficient low level of care will result.

Table 14.1 gives only a numerical example. We will now refine the argument in a graphical setting. We assume that the damage at an accident is equal to a given size, L, measurable in monetary terms. L is the same independent of the care taken by the injurer. The probability of an accident, p, is, on the other hand, a function of the level of care, x, taken by the injurer. The probability of an accident is a decreasing function, $p(x)$, of the care taken. The cost of taking one unit of care is constant and equal to w. For instance, x may be safety checks and w the price of a check. Or x may be the dimension, and w the cost of a unit of the dimension, of a tube that may explode and pollute. The cost of prevention, $w \times x$, is thus increasing with the level of care, as illustrated in Figure 14.1. The expected accident cost $p(x) \times L$ is a decreasing function of x as described in Figure 14.1. The total (primary) cost of accidents is the sum of prevention costs, $w \times x$, and the costs of potential accidents, $p(x) \times L$, which is also described by the heavy curve in Figure 14.1.

If there is no liability whatsoever, the injurer has no incentive to take care and will thus minimize his costs by taking no care ($x = 0$). If, on the other hand, the injurer is strictly liable he will minimize the total costs of accidents, TC*, at x^*, the efficient level of care. If a negligence rule prevails, the outcome depends on the legal standard of 'due care' chosen by the court. If the legal standard is $x' < x^*$, the injurer will adjust to just above this level to

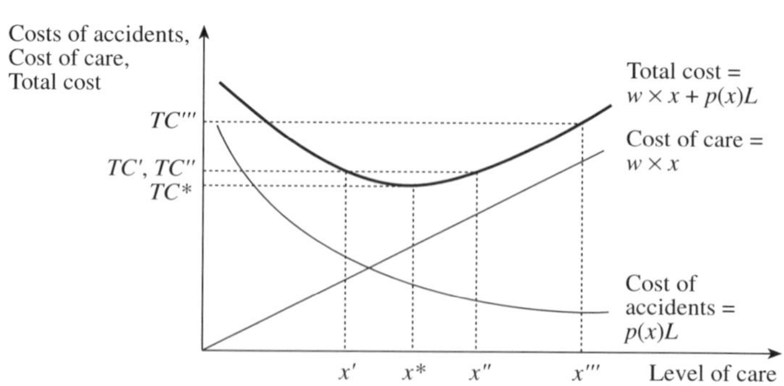

Figure 14.1 Negligence versus strict liability

escape liability. Here the total costs of accidents are TC′. This is the cheapest solution for the injurer because only the cost of care matters above the 'due care' or 'fault' standard x'. Graphically, this is illustrated with the discrete change in the firm's cost curve at the legal standard x'. With a legal standard $x'' > x^*$ the injurer will take more than optimal care to avoid liability. However, if the legal negligence standard is set so high that obedience by the injurer causes preventive costs higher than the optimal total costs, x''' (absolute liability in Table 14.1), the injurer will neglect the legal standard and thus accept the accident cost if there is an accident, which in practice means that strict liability prevails.

3.3 Bilateral Accident

Up to now we have assumed that only the injurer's behaviour has an impact on the accident risk. Normally, however, the victim also has some ability to reduce the probability of accidents, or the damage when an accident occurs. The question arises, therefore, of which liability rule is preferable, if one wishes to give both parties an incentive to take care. Are there liability rules that can provide incentives to both the injurer and the victim to take optimal care?

Strict liability will, for the above-mentioned reasons, give incentives to the injurer to take care. The victim, however, will realize that he receives full compensation and will, therefore, have no incentive to take care. A simple strict liability rule would, therefore, be suboptimal since it will not provide the victim with an incentive for efficient care.

Yet victims can be given incentives for optimal care-taking, if the strict liability rule is conditional on careful behaviour by the victim. In other words, strict liability combined with a so-called *contributory negligence defence* may make both injurer and victim behave carefully. This rule means, in its strictest form, that the victim will not receive any compensation from the injurer if the victim did not follow the due care by the victim that the law requires. A strict liability rule combined with such a contributory negligence defence will provide optimal incentives to both the injurer and the victim – provided that the due care standard set by the court is optimal. The explanation is as follows: the victim will take due (optimal) care to avoid having to bear his own loss. The injurer, knowing that the victim will take optimal care, will also have an incentive to take optimal care under the strict liability rule to minimize his expected total accident costs.

A negligence rule will also provide the victim with an incentive for optimal care-taking, if the legal due care standard is optimal. The reason is that injurers will normally, at negligence, take due care to avoid liability. Consequently, the victim expects to carry his own loss and has, therefore, an incentive to minimize his expected accident costs.

A difference between the two liability rules is that the judge has to settle the due care level of the injurer at negligence, and of the victim at strict liability with the contributory negligence defence. Hence the informative advantage of strict liability is no longer fully obvious. Nevertheless, at industrial accidents most of the prevention is related to circumstances known by the business, and not by the victim. Under such conditions strict liability would be preferred. However, the behaviour of the victim must also be controlled, which is ensured by a strict liability rule with the defence of contributory negligence. Indeed, strict liability completely unconditional on the behaviour of the victim is very rare. For instance, it is commonly required that the victim does limit the damage, otherwise compensation will be reduced or withdrawn.

Another rule which can provide incentives for care taking to both actors in an accident setting is the so-called *comparative negligence rule*. Here the victim will only receive a partial compensation for her loss. This is typically the case where the accident has been caused by joint faults of the injurer and the victim. In that case the claim of the victim for compensation will be adjusted in accordance with the degree to which the victim contributed to the accident. In other words, the victim's claim for compensation will be reduced by the amount to which the victim contributed to the accident himself. If there was, for example, negligent behaviour by both injurer and victim and the judge establishes that the victim's contribution to the accident was, for example 20 per cent, the victim's claim for compensation will be reduced by 20 per cent.

Note that at comparative negligence the court has to consider and compare the level of care taken by both the injurer and the victim. And, to be efficient, the legal standard of care must be the optimal level of care. However, the court may be poorly informed and, therefore, apportion liability randomly; alternatively the court may not take into account economic considerations at all, but apportion liability according to some principle unrelated to the efficient level of care. In this case of *shared liability* the victim and the injurer will expect to cover only part of the damage, independent of the care taken. Both parties will, therefore, normally take less than optimal care.

In sum, when both the injurer and the victim influence the accident risk, efficiency requires a liability rule that accounts for this bilateral accident situation: the victim should be given an incentive for care-taking as well as the injurer. This result may be achieved both with a strict liability rule combined with contributory negligence and through a negligence rule.

If one looks at the distributive effects, neglecting the incentives for care-taking, the comparative negligence rule becomes attractive. The victim will not completely lose his claim for compensation (which is the case under a contributory negligence rule), but still receives a partial compensation, maybe

BOX 14.2 SPARKS AND RAILROAD LIABILITY

Strict industrial liability, with the contributory negligence defence, was introduced by legislation as early as the nineteenth century in Sweden as well as in many other countries. An industry in focus was the railroads that caused fires along the tracks. The Swedish law stated:

> (1) If sparks are emitted from a locomotive, and damage is inflicted upon private property that does not stand under the administration of the railway, the railway shall reimburse the owner for the damage.
> (2) If the owner ..., in accordance with agreement, is obliged to bear consequences himself of that from the railway originating incendiary danger, he may not be entitled to compensation, where damage does not have its source through negligence during railway operations.
> (3) If the damage is caused because someone other than the railway proprietor, at a distance of less than 30 metres to the nearest railway track, deposited volatile goods without sufficient safeguard measures or erected buildings of highly flammable material or covered said buildings with such material, or has undertaken any such action which obviously increased imminent fire danger from the railway traffic to a considerable degree, the railway proprietor is exempt from the obligation to compensate in such cases. (Law of Damages, Cap., Law 12, March 1886, §5, own translation)

The first section quoted clearly states a principle of strict liability, while the second excludes regulation by contractual agreements. The third section includes contributory negligence standards that have to be fulfilled if the victim shall not have to carry the loss himself.

If a negligence rule prevailed instead, the landowners themselves would normally have to pay for the damage, because the railroad would take the care necessary to avoid liability. Therefore, to be efficient the law-maker would have to regulate the behaviour of the railroad efficiently. Since it seems less demanding for the authorities to regulate the behaviour of the property-owners along the track, strict liability with the defence of contributory negligence appears an economically well-motivated rule.

diminished proportionally by the amount to which his behaviour contributed to the loss. Obviously many legal systems have opted for this comparative negligence rule because it could alleviate some of the harsh consequences of the contributory negligence rule. The rule allows for (a partial) compensation of the victim and at least some incentives to take care.

3.4 The Activity Level

As seen in Boxes 14.1 and 14.2, the movement towards strict liability started with dangerous industries more than a century ago. Many countries introduced strict liability for ostensibly dangerous activities and later for activities harming the environment. Is there a special economic reason for the use of strict liability for dangerous activities?

In the analysis so far, we have assumed that the activity level is given. In practice, however, the activity level is of importance, especially for hazardous undertakings. In fact, the activity level is also important for ordinary, well-established industrial operations that may be environmentally harmful.

At a negligence rule, a court will usually not consider the value of the activity itself, given that it is permitted, legal and generally accepted in society. That is, the verdict will not include the social benefit and riskiness of the industry as compared to other industries. Permitted industries will, therefore, have no incentive to modify the dimensions of the system in order to avoid accidents. At strict liability, however, the firm will have to consider all benefits of the business and its costs, including costs of accidents. This strengthens the informational argument in favour of strict liability, especially if the activity is hazardous.

In the literature particular attention has been paid to the influence of the activity level. The risk of being involved in an accident is obviously not only influenced by the care which is taken when exercising the activity, but also by the number of times one engages in it. Taking the simple example of traffic accidents, one can argue that the chance that one will be involved in a traffic accident not only depends on the care which the driver (and victim) take, but also upon the number of kilometres driven in a certain period. The more one drives, the larger the probability that one will be involved in an accident.

If, once more, we assume that accidents are unilateral and only the injurer's activity can influence the accident risk, one can argue that negligence will not be optimal. Negligence indeed only provides incentives to the injurer to take optimal care, but not to adopt an optimal activity level. The reason is that when the judge will determine the due care level required in the legal system, he cannot incorporate the activity level exercised by the injurer. In other words, the judge will not be able to determine what an optimal activity level is and will not, for example, hold an injurer liable because of negligence since he engaged too often in a certain activity.

Only a strict liability rule will provide the injurer with an incentive to adopt an optimal activity level. The reason is that adopting an optimal activity level is just another way for the injurer to minimize his total expected accidents costs. Since strict liability means that the injurer will have to compensate the total accident costs, he knows *ex ante* that he will have to bear his own costs of care and the expected damage. Therefore, he will weigh not only his costs of care, but also the number of times he engages in the activity against the resulting expected loss. From this it follows that in the case of a unilateral accident only strict liability will provide incentives to the injurer to adopt an optimal activity level. At the policy level this means that strict liability seems more attractive in situations where the victim cannot influence the accident risk, neither through taking care, nor by adopting an optimal activity level.

This picture changes, however, if one moves once more to the bilateral accident situation. The problem is that in this particular case the victim will not, under strict liability with a contributory negligence defence, have an incentive to adopt an optimal activity level. The activity level of the victim will, indeed, not be taken into account when judging whether the victim was contributorily negligent or not. Only under negligence will the victim have an incentive not only to take optimal care, but also to adopt an optimal activity level since under negligence a victim will be fully exposed to his loss.

The conclusion is, therefore, that in a bilateral accident situation one should examine which activity is influencing the accident risk most, that is, is most dangerous. Strict liability is more effective in situations where one wishes to provide incentives for activity changes to injurers, whereas negligence seems more appropriate in situations where the activity of the victim is the most important factor influencing the accident risk.

4. THE TILE-VENDOR CASE

Strict liability has in many jurisdictions been introduced step by step by case law. This is the case in typically statutory law countries. There are basic economic arguments for strict liability in the unilateral case, as described above. Nevertheless, the motivation by judges is often non-economic, or economic but incorrect. Maybe due to intuition and the economic rationale of the law, many verdicts appear, generally, to be economically feasible. However, legal reasoning could be substantially improved if judges had some basic training in the economic analysis of law.

BOX 14.3 THE BURDEN OF PROOF

A reason that is often advanced in the legal literature in favour of strict environmental liability is that strict liability will help the victim to obtain compensation since he is released from the heavy burden of proving fault under the negligence rule.

However, the burden of proof argument for introducing strict liability for environmental pollution is not that convincing. Many legal systems qualify every violation of a statutory or regulatory norm as a civil fault.[1] Most industries are subjected to extensive safety regulations. Hence in these systems the victim only has to prove the violation of one of these regulations to establish liability. If, in addition, the victim can prove a causal relationship with the loss suffered, he will be able to claim compensation. In many accident cases this burden of proof will, therefore, not be as heavy as has been argued. It is, therefore, questionable whether a strict liability rule substantially improves the situation of the victim in comparison with an already-existing broadly interpreted negligence regime.

It should also not be overlooked that under the general negligence regime of tort law no limitations apply and the victim is entitled to full compensation. In many of the environmental cases where strict liability was first introduced, more particularly in the international conventions concerning nuclear accidents and oil pollution, financial caps and other limitations on the victim's rights were introduced. The alleged compensating benefit of the strict liability is therefore doubtful.

Note:
1. For Dutch case law, for example, see the so-called Jumbo II case of 1 October 1993 (*Nederlandse Jurisprudentie*, 1995, 182).

This point can be illustrated by a case in the Swedish High Court (Högsta Domstolen), hereinafter referred to as 'HC'.[4] The workshop of a bathroom tile vendor (the plaintiff) was damaged by hot water leakage in 1986. The water came from a district-heating pipeline, owned and operated by Drefvikens Energi AB (the defendant),[5] hereinafter referred to as 'Drefviken'. The leaky pipe was situated close to the plaintiff's workshop, below a street with heavy traffic. The plaintiff pleaded that Drefviken should indemnify him for the losses incurred through the hot water leakage, amounting to

672 807 SEK in total. He argued that the operation of a district-heating system was so hazardous that particularly rigorous precautionary measures should be required of the operators. He did not assert that Drefviken had acted negligently. Nevertheless, he requested that the court should try the question of liability. Drefviken argued that it should not be held liable, because it had not acted negligently.[6]

The district court and the court of appeals[7] supported the defence, arguing that they did not find that Drefviken had acted negligently. Nevertheless, the case was brought to the HC, which decided on strict liability and thus established strict liability for district-heating hot water operators.

HC acknowledged that strict liability in Sweden had been established mainly through legislation in certain limited and well-defined fields of law. The principle had also been applied by the courts in cases where no legislation existed. It was pointed out that case law in Norway and Denmark had established strict liability for district-heating operators. Nevertheless, HC held that in Sweden the main principle of civil responsibility was negligence. Thereafter, HC considered whether there were any reasons to change the liability rule. HC mentioned that although water pipes may burst and cause extensive damage, the operation of district-heating systems could not be said to constitute a hazardous activity. HC, on the other hand, noted that the type of damages caused by leaky water pipes had many similarities to those covered under the Swedish Environmental Damages Act,[8] which in turn is based on strict liability. The analogy with environmental damage was the first direct argument used by HC in favour of strict liability.

The subsequent argumentation was essentially economic. HC argued:

> The owner of the heating system basically holds a monopoly. There are good reasons why the costs of accidents should be borne by the owner, so that the costs may be spread out over all the users. If the owner of the system decides to take out insurance to cover the claims for damage, the costs of the insurance, when you take the low accident frequency into consideration, should be reasonable. A stringent liability rule for accidents such as the one in this case should also contribute to the increased safety of the system in general and thereby reduce the risk of accidents.[9]

Furthermore, HC stated that a more stringent or rigorous liability could be established in two ways: either by a stated negligence rule requiring extreme security measures within the system and its operation, or by strict liability. However, to hold the owner liable under a fault-based negligence system would have necessitated extremely rigorous safety requirements, which would mean that almost all accidents would come to be viewed as being caused through negligence. Hence HC asserted that the strict liability alternative was preferable. In addition, HC noted the simplicity of the application of strict liability – there is no need to decide what should, and what should not, be regarded as negligence when applying a strict liability rule.

There are several interesting things to say about this reasoning. First, HC did not state any explicit goal with its verdict. Nevertheless, an important objective might have been to follow the international trend towards strict liability. An analogy with the Swedish Environmental Damages Act was invoked. The term 'hazardous activity' was important in this context. HC wished to increase the safety element and reduce accidents. Although it was not pointed out, it seems evident that HC aimed at the reduction of total costs, including the cost of prevention as well as the cost of accidents.

It would therefore clarify the situation if it were made explicit that the purpose of the judgment is to contribute to the minimization of costs of accident and prevention, not only in district-heating systems, but also in other similar cases. It should also be clear that public awareness of the verdict is supposed to influence people involved in activities covered by the precedence. For the guidance of the public and courts ruling on similar cases in the future, it is important to clarify what is meant by 'similar cases'. In other words, which criteria should be fulfilled in order to make the verdict of this case applicable in other cases?

A first criterion is that two parties are involved, an injurer (Drefviken) and a victim. More complicated situations, such as the designation of responsibility of past owners or employees, may require other solutions. We will return to these problems in the next chapter.

Second, there is no contract regulating the liability of the parties. Hence it is a pure tort case.

Third, the verdict is based on the assumption that the control of the risk is unilateral. As in this case, only Drefviken controlled the risk, whereas the plaintiff could not contribute to the accident probability. The plaintiff could have mitigated the loss, of course, by storing the tiles in another way, but this want of foresight can hardly be viewed as negligence. Only two accidents had occurred during the past 20 years, and the plaintiff had no conceivable necessity to form an opinion about the probability of an accident. Drefviken, as a professional in the field, could better judge the potential accident risk than the victim, as well as control the risk by choosing the proper temperature and pressure, using adequate equipment and materials, and checking, repairing and maintaining the system. Thus it was Drefviken that controlled the risk and had information about the optimal balance between implementing preventive measures and/or assuming the potential accident risk.

Fourth, an alternative is to retain the negligence rule. Negligence may also contribute to efficiency provided that the court determines a cost-minimizing level for the duty of care. However, it is difficult for the court to balance the preventive measures against the expected cost of accidents; that is, to place the level of due care on an efficient level.

Although district heating is not regarded as a hazardous activity, its choice (as compared to other systems) may have an impact on the number and seriousness of accidents. At strict liability it is in the profit-maximizing injurer's own interest not only to minimize the total costs of accidents, but also to consider the benefits and costs of alternative heating systems.

The verdict is based on the assumption that the liable party, or the insurer, is risk-neutral and able to pay the damage. Drefviken is a relatively large company. The firm was aware of the probability of similar accidents and could calculate the costs and include them in the price it charged. The costs will, thereby, be widely spread over the company's customers, shareholders, and others.

HC apparently wanted to distribute the accident costs to the financially strong monopolist, Drefviken, in favour of the assumed weaker party, the tile vendor. Distribution effects are, as noted above, complicated to predict. Accident cost, of course, will be borne initially by the victim at negligence and by the injurer at strict liability, but normally the loss is transferred to insurers, stock-owners and customers. Judges who, with the best of intentions, try to redistribute wealth in favour of small businesses or consumers may thus fail in their ambition, and at the same time contribute to non-optimal accident prevention.

A problem with this precedent is that the absence of explicit objectives and consistent analysis leaves lower courts and the public without guidance as to what extent the verdict is applicable to other accidents. The shortcoming of

BOX 14.4 WHITE PAPER ON ENVIRONMENTAL LIABILITY

On 9 February 2000 the European Commission presented a White Paper on environmental liability (COM (2000) 66 final). In the White Paper the Commission opts for a strict liability rule for all harm which originates from hazardous activities. For all the damage originating from other activities the Commission proposes a negligence rule. This approach of the European Commission, which, incidentally, deviates from earlier signals that a general strict liability regime would be introduced, is very much in line with the predictions of the economic model as presented above.[1] Hazardous activities can often be considered unilateral, and in those situations it is important to control the injurer's activity through a strict liability rule. Even if the hazardous activities are bilateral in nature there remains a case for strict liability since the hazardous activity will have a far more important influence on the risk than the victim's activity.

However, in a bilateral case a defence should be added to the strict liability rule to take into account the victim's behaviour.[2] The same is, however, not true in the case of non-hazardous activities that may cause environmental harm. For those cases the White Paper proposes a negligence rule. The dividing line (non-hazardous/hazardous) chosen by the European Commission seems therefore to follow economic logic.

It should be noted that the White Paper does not suggest a general strict liability rule for all environmental damage, but opts for a differentiated approach with a fault rule for damage resulting from non-dangerous activities and a strict liability rule for damage resulting from dangerous activities. This follows the economic test for strict liability; it seems also more balanced than the approach taken in some Member States, which seem to have adopted some kind of strict liability regime for environmental harm, without the differentiation made in the White Paper.[3]

However, although this general approach chosen in the White Paper, of a different regime for dangerous and non-dangerous activities, seems at first sight to follow economic logic, several questions remain. One important issue which should be considered when finally judging the efficiency of the liability regime proposed in the White Paper is the fact that the economic literature has stressed, as mentioned above, that strict liability would only provide appropriate incentives for prevention if the bankruptcy risk can be cured. Otherwise strict liability would lead to underdeterrence. The potential remedies for insolvency have not been addressed in the White Paper on environmental liability, since this is the subject of various additional studies.

Notes:

1. The (non-)dangerous character of the activity as a dividing line was also suggested by Bergkamp (1998, p. 200); also Niezen, a Dutch company lawyer, recognizes that it makes sense to introduce strict liability for dangerous activities (Niezen, 2000, p. 170).
2. Such a defence is effectively proposed in the White Paper (p. 18), which confirms the conclusion that the White paper is essentially in line with what the economic model suggests.
3. Note, however, that most Member States' liability laws do not generally cover damage to natural resources.

the verdict is apparent in two later district court cases concerning damage caused by cold water.[10] In both cases there was a large, insured, unilateral injurer that controlled the accident. The main argumentation used for strict liability was an analogy with our vendor case, combined with the argument that the temperature of the water was not of crucial importance.

What, then, is of decisive importance? Is the precedent also valid for oil, traffic, and storm accidents? And, how is the distinction made between 'environmental' damage where strict liability prevails and other areas of tort where negligence is the rule?

5. CONCLUSIONS

In a no-liability situation the injurer will have no incentive for care-taking and the negative externality will thus not be internalized. If a negligence rule is adopted the injurer will take optimal care, provided the due care required in the legal system is optimal as defined in the model. Also a strict liability rule will lead to the optimum in the unilateral case; the injurer has to bear the social costs of accidents, being his own costs of care-taking and the expected cost of damage. This leads to the conclusion that both a negligence and a strict liability rule may lead to a minimization of the social costs of accidents. However, a disadvantage of the negligence rule is that the judge must have access to information on the efficient level of care. To the extent there is available information, the information will most probably be in the possession of the injurer, who controls the risk. This informational asymmetry offers the most important argument in favour of strict liability.

Differences between the rules remain as far as the secondary and tertiary costs are concerned. Under a negligence rule in principle no cases will be found since an injurer will always follow the due care standard required in the legal system and will thus never have to compensate the victim. Under a strict liability rule, on the other hand, victims will always receive compensation. A disadvantage is that a legal or administrative cost will follow with every accident since the injurer is always bound to compensate. Court costs can therefore be expected to be high at strict liability. On the other hand, the negligence cases, when they appear, require costly information since the judge has to determine in a particular case what the marginal costs and marginal benefits of care-taking were.

The burden of proof is normally on the victim at negligence, while the injurer has to show that the victim has been contributorily negligent at strict liability. This may be used as an argument for strict liability at industrial hazards.

Further, if the parties are risk-averse or unable to pay the potential accident costs, the choice of negligence and strict liability may depend upon which party is most able to pay. We return to this later issue in the next chapter.

In the bilateral case both injurer and victim influence the accident risk. A strict liability rule combined with a contributory negligence defence will in this case provide incentives to both parties to take care. Also a negligence rule will provide both the victim and the injurer with an incentive for care-taking. A difference between the liability rules is that the judge has to settle the due care level of the injurer at negligence, and of the victim at strict liability. If prevention and information are mainly in the hands of the injurer (an industry), strict liability with the defence of contributory negligence will be preferred. This argument is strengthened when the activity level of dangerous industries is also considered.

Liability alone may, for several reasons, not result in efficient prevention of accidents. First, the courts may be poorly informed and consequently the verdicts arbitrary. Second, efficient regulation of the activity levels of both parties by tort liability alone is not possible. One option is to complement liability with a charge. For instance, liability at traffic accidents may be combined with a charge on gasoline or cars to reduce the traffic volume. Similarly, city planning and land law may be used for the location or activity level of polluting or dangerous industries. Safety regulation, licensing and emission standards are other measures to regulate the activity level. Note also that regulatory standards are used as standards of 'due care' in tort cases. The presence of permits, safety checks, repairs and overloads is of importance for the verdict. Tort liability is also a penalty and thus an enforcement measure of regulations. Hence *ex ante* regulation and *ex post* liability are closely interrelated. This relationship will be studied further in Chapter 17.

NOTES

1. For an extended analysis including the activity level, see Shavell (1987).
2. See his seminal article, 'Some Thoughts on Risk Distribution and the Law of Torts', *Yale Law Journal*, 1961, 499–553.
3. Calabresi (1970).
4. The case is found in *Nytt Juridiskt Arkiv*, Stockholm, 1991, s. 720.
5. 'District heating' refers to a system with many subscribers, which provides heating to more than one building. It is not unusual for one district-heating company to provide services for a large part of a town. Normally, the systems are operated directly by the municipality or by a municipally owned corporation. 'AB' is the Swedish abbreviation for 'aktiebolag', that is, a the Swedish limited liability company.
6. The main rule in Sweden is liability based on negligence, see the Swedish Tort/Delict Act: Skadeståndslagen, Ch. 2, Section 1, SFS 1972; p. 207.
7. Tingsrätten (TR) and Hovrätten (HovR).
8. Miljöskadelagen, *SFS*, 1986, 225, Sections 1 and 3.

9. See *NJA*, Stockholm, 1991, pp. 720–25.
10. Verdict (No. DF 160, Case No. F 2619–95) of Linköpings tingsrätt, and verdict (No. DT 389, Case No. T815–94) of Södertälje tingsrätt.

FURTHER READING

Brown, J.P. (1973), 'Toward an economic theory of liability', *Journal of Legal Studies*, 323–49.

Brüggemeier, G. (1991), 'Liability for Water Pollution under German Law: Fault or Strict Liability', in J. Van Dunné (ed.), *Transboundary Pollution and Liability*, Lelystad, Netherlands: Vermande, 91–2.

Calabresi, G. (1975), 'Optimal Deterrence and Accidents', *Yale Law Journal*, **84**, 656–71.

Faure, M. and Hartlief, T. (1996), 'Towards an expanding enterprise liability in Europe? How to analyze the scope of liability of industrial operators and their insurers', *Maastricht Journal of European and Comparative Law*, 235–70.

Faure, M. and Van den Bergh, R. (1989), *Essays in Law and Economics. Corporations, Accident Prevention and Compensation for Losses*, Antwerp: Maklu.

Landes, W. and Posner, R. (1981), 'A Positive Economic Theory of Tort Law', *Georgia Law Review*, **15**, 417.

Shavell, S. (1987), *An Economic Analysis of Accident Law*, Cambridge, MA: Harvard University Press.

Skogh, G. and Rehme, D. (1998), 'An Economic Analysis of a Swedish Environmental Liability Case', *European Journal of Law and Economics*, **5**, 167–77.

15. Limits to liability

A dead man does not claim for compensation.

1. INTRODUCTION

In the last chapter we concluded that strict liability, with the defence of contributory negligence, could be preferable from an economic prevention viewpoint – especially if the activity is dangerous. This conclusion rests on a simplified model. The model assumed: (i) that only two risk-neutral parties (the injurer and the victim) are involved in the accident; (ii) that the causality between care taken and the risk of accident is known by the injurer; (iii) that the injurer and victim are identified without administrative costs; and (iv) that the damage is known and measurable in economic terms. Moreover, (v) the liable party is supposed to be able to pay the full damage to the victim, that is, there is no bankruptcy problems, and (vi) that there is no trade of liability to other parties,that is, to guarantors or insurers.

In this chapter we will investigate the applicability of liability rules when the simplifying assumptions are relaxed. We start with the assumption of risk-neutrality. This assumption may be realistic for profit-maximizing firms, but hardly for individuals. In fact, individuals are usually assumed to be risk-averse. That is, individuals are willing to pay more than the expected accident cost for the avoidance of large potential losses; see Chapter 7, Section 3. The victim or the injurer pays the insurer to accept the potential claim. Fire, storm, traffic accidents and liability are normally insured. A relevant question is thus whether such transfers of liability are in accordance with economic efficiency. In Section 2 we study the impact of insurance in the case of strict liability and negligence. In Section 3 we examine the case where the liable party is unable to pay damages. The fact that damages may not be paid creates a demand for measures certifying payments. Insurance and guarantee play here a role. The fact that the liable party may go bankrupt makes the liability rule important. Thereafter, in Section 4, we examine liability and risk-taking when the probabilities of accident are unpredictable or unknown. Many environmental hazards are new and thus unexperienced. Accidents are caused by new systems, substances and products in a complex and largely unknown way. The insurance industry is usually not willing to accept such hazards. Alternatives to insurance are, therefore, studied in Section 5, which treats risk-sharing, and in Section 6, which examines solvency requirements. In Section 7 we compare the efficiency of strict liability versus negligence at uncertainty. Compensation by liability insurance and other private insurance as well as social welfare programmes are discussed in Section 8. Incomplete claims are discussed in Section 9. Of special concern is the fact that dead victims do not claim for compensation. Conclusions are in Section 10.

2. RISK-AVERSION AND INSURANCE

2.1 Strict Liability

What are the effects of risk-aversion and the fact that liability is covered by insurance? We first examine the impact of insurance in the unilateral case with strict liability (see Chapter 14, Section 4). That is, only the liable injurer causes the accident. Here we assume that the liable injurer is risk-averse.

Assume for a moment that there is no insurance available. The fear of catastrophic damage and/or bankruptcy results in a level of care that is higher than the efficient level in the model with risk-neutral parties (as was indicated in the previous chapter). Nevertheless, the high level of care at risk-aversion is a 'second best' as long as there is no insurer willing to accept the risk. That is, a fear of disaster may cause extensive precautions and prevention, which is motivated as long as insurance is not available. Indeed, dangerous activities may not be undertaken at all because of the fear of large losses. Still, it remains efficient because there is no alternative way to reduce risks. Consequently, insurance has a fundamental role in society in that it makes risky behaviour feasible.

Now turn to a situation where insurance is available. Assume also that a risk-neutral insurer covers the whole damage. Thus the legally liable injurer has traded the liability to the insurer. The situation for the injurer is, therefore, equivalent to the liability rule *no liability*. As was indicated in the previous chapter, in this situation, the injurer has no incentive to take care. Insurance may, therefore, cause careless behaviour and an increased number of, and more serious, accidents. This *moral hazard* will normally be counteracted by the insurer. The business may otherwise break down.

A method is not to insure minor losses, that is, to offer a *deductible*. A deductible may be beneficial for the policy-holder as well. Minor losses do not cause any disaster. A deductible motivates the policy-holder to take cheap precautions that have a large impact on safety, which in a competitive economy reduces the premium.

In the market it is common for the policy-holder to cover losses within a limit set by a deductible. A small deductible gives little care and high premium, while a large deductible motivates more prevention and lower premium. The policy-holder can thus choose a combination of deductible, prevention and premium. Similarly, experience rating or a bonus system where the premium depends on earlier performance also reduces moral hazard and the premium.

Generally, the risk-averse policy-holders will insure the large loss and keep the small. In addition, insurance usually does not cover intangible losses like pain and suffering, personal losses like the loss of a family photograph album, and so on. Altogether, the remaining risk of the policy-holder maintains a considerable incentive to take care.

Administrative costs and profits of the insurance industry are added as loadings on the *risk premium*, the premium necessary to cover the expected accident damages. The size of the loadings varies, but loadings of 20–50 per cent of the premiums are common in, for example, the property and liability insurance industry. These costs in excess of the risk premium increase the tendency to 'self-insure' by a choice of deductible.

So far we have assumed that the insurer has no ability (except for the indirect influence via the deductible or bonus) to influence the behaviour of the policy-holder. Note, however, that the property and liability insurance industry is expert in the risks it insures. The industry earns profit by calculating and pricing risks, as well as by identifying the impact of various precautions and preventive measures. The industry can, therefore, offer the customers policies with various preventive requirements. For instance, an industry that installs sprinklers may get a reduced premium. Similarly, a hazardous industry may obtain a premium reduction if it promises to undertake systematic safety checks, and so on.

The control of the fulfilment of the requirements and conditions of the insurance policy is mainly dealt with in the claim settlement procedure. The compensation may be withheld or reduced if the policy-holder does not follow the contract, which can become a considerable punishment to risk-averse policy-holders. Hence the insurer has considerable control over the behaviour of the insured.

In a 'perfect' world, where the insurer can fully identify and control the injurer and modify premiums in relation to the precautions, the care level will become efficient, as in the previous chapter, where the risk-neutral liable injurer is the risk-taker. In reality the insurer has limited information, however, which explains why there are both deductibles and precaution requirements, combined with inspections and claim settlement control.

Note that liability covered by insurance turns *ex post* liability into a premium paid in advance. In other words, insurance transforms the liability into a fee or charge paid for the participation of the insured risky activity.[1] The premium depends on the risk and on the preventive measures taken. For instance, a traffic insurance premium may depend on experience of the driver, type of car and mileage. That is, the premium is more varied in relation to accident risks than, for example, a charge on gasoline.

In sum, the liable party may, as a second best, 'overprotect' itself, if no insurance is available. Insurance coverage transfers the liability to the insurer and relieves the injurer of a fear of large losses. This will reduce the level of care. If the insurer has no means of control of the care level, this results in 'underprotection'. However, if the market is competitive, it may be possible to receive insurance with mutually beneficial agreements on deductibles. The care is also directly regulated by conditions in the contracts and by enforcement at the claim settlement. The fact that the number of accidents may become relatively larger with insurance must cause inefficiencies as long as the accidental damages are fully accepted and paid for by premiums and deductibles. The problem of inefficient *moral hazard* appears first when the policy-holder has information on precautions and risks whereas this information would be hidden to the insurer.

Above, in Chapter 14, Section 6, we noted that the court is usually not able to include the activity level in the judgment. The activity level can instead be regulated by a permit to run polluting or dangerous businesses. An alternative is a charge on pollution. Here we see that insurance may include both care and activity level in the pricing, as well as regulations of policies. Indeed, the premium of, for example, a traffic insurance may include mileage (activity level), earlier record (bonus), type of car, and age of car and owner. Insurance is thus complementary to tort liability.

In the simple liability model above it was assumed that both victim and injurer know the probability of accidents, which is unrealistic, of course. The individual policy-holder is usually not able to predict the probability of accidents that occur rarely. However, the lack of information and the bounded rationality of the policy-holder do not matter as long as the risk is transferred to an insurer who possesses actuarial information. A benefit with insurance is that the liability is traded to a party that is able to calculate risks. Hence the unrealistic assumption that the liable party is informed about the risk does not diminish the power of the analysis in cases where the uninformed liable party is trading the risk to an insurer with professional actuarial information.

2.2 Negligence

How does the insurance influence the efficiency of tort law if a negligence rule prevails? To simplify the answer we first assume that the injurer alone is able to influence the risk. The injurer will in this situation avoid liability by taking the care required by the courts. Hence the victim will normally have to carry the damage. If the victim is risk-averse she will purchase insurance. No increase in accident rates will occur, because the victim's behaviour has no impact on the accident risk. The efficiency of the negligence rule thus depends on the standard of care implemented by the courts.

In the bilateral case both victim and injurer will have an impact on the accident risk. A negligence rule will give the injurer incentives to follow the law and take 'due care'. The risk-averse victim will, on the other hand, have an incentive to insure, but, as insured, the victim has no incentive to take care. The insurer may, therefore, include safety measures in the policies, and may also offer deductibles and a bonus to the policy-holder. The problem of controlling the victim is the same as controlling the insured injurer at strict liability.

BOX 15.1 THE TILE-VENDOR CASE CONTINUED

The tile-vendor case, discussed above in Chapter 14, Section 7, illustrates the unilateral case with strict liability, that is, the tile-vendor is supposed not to be able to influence the probability of leaking water tubes. This seems to be a reasonable assumption. Yet there are usually some precautions that should be taken by the victim. The tile-vendor could not influence the probability of an accident, but he could influence the size of the loss, for example by storing the tiles more carefully. A strict liability rule with the defence of contributory negligence making the hot water producer liable as long as the victim is not negligent may thus make the vendor more careful in storing the tiles. Suppose further that it is optimal to place tiles ten centimetres above the floor in case of flooding. Suppose also that the court knows this, and that this precaution is the standard of due care. The informed tile-vendor will thus store the tiles optimally as required in order to avoid liability at an accident. In addition, the tile-vendor is presumably insured by a policy covering liability as well as property and flooding. If the insurer is informed about the optimal precaution in case of flooding, in general there will presumably be a requirement in the insurance policy that the tiles should be stored ten centimetres above the cellar floor. To obtain full coverage at a flooding the vendor will thus store efficiently according to the policy. Hence insurance will contribute to efficient prevention in the same way as tort law.

If the prevailing rule is 'strict liability with the defence of contributory negligence', the outcome mirrors a negligence rule. That is, the victim will have an incentive to take due care in order to avoid liability and the injurer will carry the accident costs. The risk-averse injurer will purchase insurance and the insurer will have to control the behaviour of the injurer.

A conclusion to be drawn from this is that the model of efficient liability rules functions fairly well also at risk-aversion, when the risk is transacted to an insurer specialized in handling the risks in question.

3. BANKRUPTCY

3.1 Guarantee

In the liability model in last chapter we assumed that the liable party was able to pay the damage. However, if the damage is larger than the assets, the liability will *de facto* be limited to the assets collectable. As the maximum collectable payment at an accident is limited, the incentive to take care is also reduced. Indeed, there is no economic incentive to prevent losses above the limit set by the available assets. Available assets smaller than the damages also result in only partially compensated victims. It is important, therefore, to investigate possible prevention and coverage of losses when the liable party is unable to pay. This is especially true for costly environmental damages, where strict industrial liability may be without effect because of strongly limited means to pay.

If the liable party becomes unable to pay or manages to escape paying, this may cause distrust among those who will have to pay when the liable party does not. This is a general problem both in trade as well as in relation to environmental harm. Let us, for illustration, first consider a contractual situation. Two traders, *A* and *B*, are to contract on a risky project. They expect the project to become mutually beneficial, but are concerned about liabilities at a potential loss. Both parties are risk-neutral. *A* is willing to accept the liability, but the assets that can be collected from *A* are limited. Therefore *A* will have limited incentive to take care and to compensate *B ex post*. *A* and *B* are strangers who do not expect to trade with each other again, so there is no repeated dealing as an enforcement mechanism (see Chapter 9, Section 2). The parties may, therefore, end up with a project of low value, or with no contract at all.

A way out of the dilemma may be for *A* to offer a pledge or collateral. A pledge may serve the agreement by the increase in the collectable amount. It may also benefit the exchange by increasing the chance that a given amount can be collected. Collateral may also be a requirement for industries with environmentally dangerous activities. However, an obvious limitation in the use of collateral is the limited assets of the liable party, collateral included. An alternative, therefore, may be a guarantee. A guarantee transfers risk to an external risk-carrier, the guarantor. The guarantee functions as collateral, given that the guarantor is credible and has sufficient funds to cover the loss. To accept the risk at a relatively low price, the guarantor must be in possession of some comparative advantage as risk-carrier. One advantage may be that the guarantor is able to collect more from *A* than *B* can, perhaps because the guarantor has a long-lasting relationship with *A*. The guarantor may also be able to control the behaviour of *A* because of some specific information about *A*. The guarantor may be a bank, a relative, or a business partner who knows *A* quite well.

3.2 A Choice among Injurers

In the liability model (Chapter 14, Section 4) we included only two parties, the victim and the injurer. The reality is, of course, more complicated. Usually many are involved. We have assumed that a dangerous industry or a firm is liable, but a firm consists of many parties, and an industry may consist of many firms. A question is, therefore, how the efficiency is affected when many are involved. Obviously, when there are many parties that could be liable, more could be collected, but does this increase efficiency?

Consider a hypothetical situation where a liable firm can negotiate and contract without transaction costs with other involved firms in the production chain. There is no insolvency problem, the authorities enforce contracts without any costs, and there are no restrictions on the freedom of contract. The liable firm is thus free to contract on prevention and liability with the others. Given these assumptions, the Coase theorem stipulates that the prevention will be undertaken in a cost-efficient way, independent of who is initially legally liable for accidents.

For example, assume that there is one supplier of raw materials, one producer, one dealer, and a buyer of a pesticide used in farming. The producer is legally liable for potential damage. Due to the free transfer of rights and duties, the producer will contract with the supplier on materials to make them careful. The producer may also contract with the dealer on responsibility regarding, for example, storage and use of the pesticide. Given such an agreement, the dealer may contract with the buyer (the farmer) on education about treatment of the pesticide. The farmer may also agree to take the responsibility in case he has been negligent about following the instructions given.[2]

Now assume, instead, that the legislator has made the final user, that is, the farmer, liable. Because of costless and free transactions, the farmer may contract with the others in a way that balances prevention costs, accident costs and the impact of risk-aversion. The dealer may, thus, agree to inform the end users, and the producer may contract with the supplier of materials. Similarly, if the dealer is legally liable, he may contract with the farmer to accept liability at negligence. Independent of the initial legal duties, it is in the common interest of the involved parties to redistribute the tasks and liabilities according to comparative advantages.

The costs of prevention and accidents will in a competitive market in the end be carried by the end user, that is, the farmer or rather the consumers of the farmer's products, independent of the initial legal liability.

So far, we have assumed zero transaction costs, which seems to be a fairly realistic assumption in certain industries. Transaction costs are relatively small when a limited number of firms are involved in repeated dealings. The producers, suppliers and dealers know each other relatively well, and their performance is controlled through the value of a good reputation. The legislator may, therefore, place liability on *any* of the parties involved in the production without loss of efficiency.

However, if the transaction costs are considerable, the responsibility and prevention will not be transacted according to comparative advantage. Liability law is of special importance if the parties are strangers with no regular contact. By simulating free contracting under the hypothetical assumption of no transaction costs, the legislator may identify cost-efficient liability rules. An efficient law would make that party liable which accepts the liability freely in a world without transaction costs. Hence an efficient law makes no further transactions necessary; see Chapter 9, Section 2.

So far, we have assumed that the public authorities can enforce liability without difficulty. In reality, however, the cost of enforcement varies among parties. Some parties may go bankrupt if they are forced to pay damages. The number of involved parties may also be large. The control of, for example, thousands of farmers may be costly, and it might be complicated to control a large number of dealers. Foreign producers might well be impossible to control. Therefore, it matters who is liable.

Limited ability to collect damages also motivates limited rights to transfer liability by contract. For example, a legally liable producer contracts with the dealers to inform their customers. Later, it is shown that the information has not been given because of incompetence, fraud, or insolvency. If it has been legally permissible for the producer to transact the liability to dealers, the liability would be void.

The legal term for placing liability on a certain party, independent of the fact that somebody else may be the cause of an accident, is known in the literature as *vicarious liability*. The arguments are similar to the arguments concerning guarantors. If a party is solvent and able to control the others involved, it is efficient to make this 'principal' vicariously liable. The principal should not be allowed to escape liability through a contract with an insolvent, incompetent, or fraudulent party. The principal may, of course, contract on preventive measures, but it is the principal that pays damages in case of accidents. The principal must, thus, control the others, which may be done at low costs (relative to public supervision and control) due to repeated exchange among the parties. The legislator can, therefore, without loss of efficiency, make the principal, say a large domestic firm, liable for the failures of others, perhaps small entrepreneurs or farmers. Public enforcement is, hereby, simplified – supervision is concentrated on a solvent party that is, in turn, able to control its contractors.

3.3 Insurance

An insurance contract by which the insurer compensates losses at certain specified contingencies, for example industrial accidental pollution, is equivalent to a guarantee. The guarantor/insurer fulfils the requirements above. In a 'perfect' world in which the insurer knows the marginal impact of the control, the insurer can steer the polluting industry's behaviour toward optimal care by stipulating conditions in the policy and by varying premiums. Deductibles may be used within the limits set by the assets of the liable firm.

Insurance is often a mandatory requirement for permission to run a business, transport goods, drive a car, employ personnel,and the like. Insurance is here required as a guarantee on behalf of potential victims, including the public, that may be harmed if the liable party does not pay. Mandatory insurance contributes to efficiency to the extent that the insurer compensates the victim and monitors the behaviour of the injurer. That explains why traffic, health and liability are often mandatory requirements. Note that this demand of insurance is independent of the risk attitude of the policy-holder.

4. DEVELOPMENT RISKS

So far we have assumed that the liable party or his insurer knows the probabilities of the accident, or that they base their decisions on subjective beliefs about probabilities. However, many environmental problems involve a high degree of uncertainty. Accidents are due to new systems, new chemicals or products, or combinations thereof in a complex and largely unknown way. The economic effects of liability, insurance and guarantees at a high degree of uncertainty are therefore crucial.

We define an *actuarial risk* as a contingency that can be estimated empirically or technically. The expected accident cost can be calculated, and the risk can be priced *ex ante*. Actuarial risks are *old* risks in the sense that they have been experienced repeatedly. Examples are risks of fire and water damages that may be covered by ordinary insurance policies. The information is *public* in the sense that insurers as well as policy-holders know the probability of occurrence and how various safety measures and precautions reduce the risk.

Development risks, on the other hand, are *new* risks arising due to technological or social changes. The total lack of experience makes it impossible to foresee such risks and to make estimates regarding the probability of accidents. Any belief about the probability is, thus, arbitrary. Consequently, accident prevention cannot be based on information about marginal conditions. The only way to escape the accident risk is to avoid the dangerous activity itself.

An example is the production and use of asbestos before asbestosis was detected. Asbestos was regarded as a most useful product, although everyone knew that there was a possibility that it might be harmful (as with anything in life). As long as there was no specific information about the danger, no one considered stopping the production of asbestos. Accordingly, information was not available on how to obtain marginal reductions in the risk of incurring asbestosis. Other examples in a similar vein are risks of cancer or allergies from newly invented chemicals and new techniques. We know that a danger exists, but the uncertainty about the size of potential losses and/or their probabilities is genuine.

There is, of course, a wide gap between the two extremes of actuarial risk and development risk. In between the extremes, we define *unpredictable hazards* as observed dangers that are known to exist but are not possible to predict statistically. For instance, the probability of damage due to a new pesticide in agriculture may be unknown. Yet it is known that similar substances are harmful. Precautionary measures in terms of reduced use of the pesticide may, thus, be undertaken, although the risk is not quantifiable. After an accident or some other evidence attesting the hazard, understanding increases about the risk involved.

However, the lack of repeated experience makes it complicated or impossible to estimate with assurance the probability of an accident. While the parties may have formed certain beliefs about the risks, confidence in their beliefs is limited. Nevertheless, in the long run technical investigations and repeated experience might transfer the uncertainty into a statistically predictable actuarial risk.

Although we exemplify an actuarial risk with insurance, this does not mean that insurability requires that the risk should be predictable. Anyone may bet on a risk at a fixed premium without actuarial information. Hence statistical predictability is not a prerequisite for insurance. What matters are the subjective beliefs of the parties and their attitude towards risk.

Nevertheless, most insurers are unwilling to cover statistically unpredictable risks. It is by insuring a large number of similar risks that insurers obtain information on the actuarial relation between claims, safety devices, levels of deductibles, and costs of claim settlement. This specialization creates an informative advantage that forms the basis for profits in the industry. It also explains why statistical predictability is regarded as fundamental by the insurance industry. Risks that are unpredictable are very costly to insure, if they are traded at all on the market. Insurers are reluctant to provide cover for events where the probability of their occurrence is ambiguous, either because of limited statistical data and/or because of the different views of experts regarding the underlying causality. Losses also need to be well defined, limited, and possible to estimate.

Risk-spreading via the financial markets is here of interest. Consider a stock company traded on the financial market which is liable for a new hazard whose expected outcome cannot be estimated. The existence of the risk may be public knowledge, but is statistically unpredictable. It is well known that uncertainty does not prevent trade on financial markets. Traders bet continuously on highly uncertain projects. Indeed, the large fluctuation in stock prices is an indication of the limited confidence in the value of the assets traded.

Liability of such industrial hazards will presumably reduce the value of the firm; however, it is uncertain by how much because it is not possible to price the risk properly. Unsubstantiated news and rumours in the media may precipitate large reactions on the market. Precautions will also be uncertain and poorly priced. Some risks may not be considered at all, while others may cause inefficient overprotection.

Liability for development risks that are not at all foreseen has presumably no impact on stock prices. When information becomes available, for example an accident occurs, it will reduce the value of the firm by the accident damage, and by discounted future expected accident costs. A secondary effect of an accident of a new type is that it creates an awareness that reduces stock prices for all firms facing similar risks. The expected accident costs will, thus, be spread to the stock-owners. Hence liability for development risks causes windfall losses that can be regarded as a lump-sum tax on stocks.

Liability is limited, however, to the value of the corporate firm. In the case of losses larger than the limit set by bankruptcy, an economic incentive to take precautions or to diversify is absent.

In sum, a guarantee increases the value of the initial trade if the guarantor has: (i) assets enough to cover potential claims; and (ii) a comparative advantage in monitoring the liable party. Note that the argument for a guarantee is similar to the argument for vicarious liability in tort law. In other words, a 'judgment-proof' problem arises when a party that has become legally liable is unable to fully pay the claim. Someone else – for instance, an employer – may then be held vicariously liable. This situation may be efficiency increasing because the employer is able to observe the employee continuously and has the power to reward or dismiss him/her. Parents are often liable for damages caused by their children for the same reason. Similarly, professional associations and branch organizations with the power to control membership may be willing to guarantee the services of their members.

5. MUTUAL RISK-SHARING

Insurance, as defined in the introduction, requires that pricing has been undertaken before the occurrence of the insured event. That explains why pricing requires actuarial information. An agreement to share each other's losses does not, on the other hand, necessarily require any pre-payment. Risk-sharing thus requires less information than insurance. For instance, a group of risk-averse individuals can also benefit from sharing accident costs *ex post* if the probability of an accident is statistically unpredictable. However, here the presumption is that the expected risk is regarded as the same for all.

The simplest form of risk-sharing is a mutual guarantee whereby the pool members promise to cover each other's losses. Risk-sharing requires, however, that the parties in the pool accept and trust the presumption that they are equal, that is, that all face the same risk (although they cannot estimate it statistically), and that moral hazard and adverse selection can be controlled. Members in the same business may have some ability to control each other. They also have a common interest to obtain information, and to employ risk reduction measures. That is, the pool has a stronger incentive than the individual to undertake research and prevention.

A pool must also be large to share risks efficiently. Groups of equals tend to be small, however, and as soon as differences in the group are revealed, the mutual may be split. Groups of individuals that have long-term relationships, such as families, guilds and other societies, may be able to exert control relatively easily, and thus trust one another. They also face similar risks. Taken together, this explains risk-sharing in such groups. Throughout history, there has been mutual aid at fire, death, disease, disability, and for the loss of cargo or ships. Today, we observe mutual risk-sharing in joint ventures and in the collective ownership of risky enterprises. Contemporary insurance companies often combine insurance and mutual pooling. Many 'insurance' companies are mutuals.

Generally, sharing appears to be prior in time to insurance, which may develop at a later stage, when actuarial information is available. A first step towards insurance may be the introduction of pre-payments in a mutual pool.

Pre-payment may reduce distrust among pool members. It also evens out costs over periods of time. If the pool is large enough to spread the risks, the fund large enough to even out payments over time, and actuarial information is available, the premium can be set close to the expected accident costs plus administrative costs. A modern, large mutual pool with diversified risks may charge premiums and offer no residual rights or place obligations on the policyholders. In practice, such firms are insurers according to our definition.

A potentially liable, widely held risk-neutral firm has no incentive to insure above the limited liability. Mandatory insurance or guarantee may not be available because of the unpredictable losses. Here mutual risk-sharing may have an important role. Prerequisites for the risk-sharing of new industrial hazards are: (i) that there exists a group of firms in the industry with similar risks; (ii) that a common pool exists, or can be established without too high transactions costs; and (iii) that the pool is able to control moral hazard and adverse selection.

These conditions for risk-sharing are not always fulfilled, of course. Nevertheless, there are interesting practical risk-sharing examples. In 1967, a 120 000-ton oil spill polluted the English Channel after the *Torrey Canyon* accident. An oil spill of that size, polluting the sea and several nations, had never occurred before. Coastal nations agreed to apply strict tanker-owner liability, and only accept in their waters oil tankers that were insured or guaranteed. It was possible to establish the convention because the states had a common interest in covering clean-up costs, and because the convention was enforceable due to the power to exclude tankers from the harbours. The strict liability rule made the tanker-owners responsible for a new risk that was similar in all overseas oil shipping. The threat of potential liability and of not being accepted in the harbours gave an incentive to the oil-traders to search for guarantees. Insurance was not available. However, marine 'Protection and Indemnity Clubs' existed that shared the potential losses. Once a member of the pool, the jointly liable tanker-owners became interested in regulating safety, an interest shared with the coastal states.

Another industry where mutual guarantees may be used more extensively is nuclear power. An international convention on the strict liability of nuclear power plant owners was signed in Paris in 1960. The liability was combined with mandatory insurance, risk-sharing, or financial guarantee. Atomic pools, set up by national insurers, insure and share property and liability. Damage to the power plants may be insured. Third-party liability may also be covered, but usually to a limit set by what is supposed to be insurable. For instance, plants in Sweden are covered to around \$1.5 billion by property insurance, while the third-party liability is limited to around \$300 million. Risk-sharing agreements between the signatory states, and public coverage by the Swedish state, cover third-party losses up to \$500 million. The picture is the same in other signatory states. Hence third-party liability is severely limited, although the nuclear industry is strictly liable.

One way to increase liability at very large accidents is to require risk-sharing within the nuclear industry. According to the Ferguson–Anderson Act of 1988, mandatory risk-sharing exists in the USA, covering third-party liability up to $9 billion. Faure and Skogh (1992) have outlined a hypothetical European risk-sharing agreement covering nuclear power third-party liability one hundred times larger than today that would also make compensations possible at very large accidents and would create a joint interest in the industry for mutual control. However, the solution requires agreements by states and by plant owners that are unequal in many respects. Thus a more realistic possibility might be risk-sharing by plant owners in states with similar plants.

All in all, strict liability, with requirements on sufficient means for cover of damages as a basis for free mutual agreements in the industry on guarantees (and insurance when available), seems to have important applications. For

BOX 15.2 JOINT AND SEVERAL LIABILITY

The doctrine of 'joint and several' liability, where producers, creditors, suppliers and other stake-holders are jointly liable, has been applied to polluted soil in the USA. The background is that large claims require many contributors. Note that the mutual risk-sharing examined here is a type relating to several liabilities among firms, but the sharing is *horizontal*, not *vertical* in the same chain of production. Mutual horizontal risk-sharing differs from vertical liability in several important respects. First, by including many similar producers in the pool, the joint assets become relatively large. Second, uncorrected accident risks, and thus diversification, prevails in a mutual pool covering risks in an industry. Vertical several liabilities hit a chain of firms involved in a certain production. Third, pricing is not necessary in a horizontal mutual pool. If, on the other hand, a creditor and a vertical supplier may be held liable for the producer's accident, they must calculate a price for the risk imposed, which may be more or less impossible. Fourth, the horizontal mutual is set up by the industry specialized in the business. Hence the common pool has an interest, and possesses competence, regarding prevention. This may explain why mutuals are set up freely when extensive guarantees are required.

instance, the system could be implemented to cover losses due to breaks of water dams for electrical power. Today the liability rules vary among countries. If states decide to make water-power producers strictly liable, with the requirement of trustworthy guarantees for the licence to run the industry, the industry would search for appropriate funding systems, including international mutual sharing and insurance.

6. SOLVENCY REQUIREMENTS

So far we have implicitly assumed that the equity, as well as the solvency margin of the liable firm, is given. This may not, of course, be the case. The equity of the firm is in itself a guarantee of its undertakings. The stock-owner functions, at least indirectly, as guarantor in case of accident and liability.

Solvency margins may thus be used as an alternative to insurance and risk-sharing. Indeed, coverage of liability with equity, in combination with diversification via the financial market, appears to be a relatively cheap alternative, given the high administrative costs of insurance and risk-sharing. Independent risks will be diversified away, while systemic risks cannot be diversified. Thus, if a portfolio contains stocks of various industries and the firms are faced with accident risks specific to each firm, then the risk may be diversified. On the other hand, risks that affect all firms in the portfolio cannot be diversified. The best a widely held corporation can do is to maximize expected profits (Chapter 7, Section 7). Risk of fire, explosion, or third-party liability that occur independently in different firms can be diversified by the mixed portfolios. Old insurable risks are publicly known. Such risks not traded to an insurer will, therefore, reduce the value of the equity according to the expected accident cost. Similarly, if a firm takes preventive measures that reduce expected accident costs, the value of the firm will be increased by as much as the gain. The best choice of the firm is to minimize the expected costs of accident and accident prevention. The financial market thus solves the risk-handling problem in an efficient way – disutility due to risk-aversion is diversified away and the costs and benefits of accident prevention for an actuarial risk are reflected in the value of the firm. This outcome is equivalent to the case where the risk-averse liable party fully insures, and the insurer is fully informed about, the impact of preventive measures at zero administrative costs. Hence, in a perfect world with known probabilities and no transaction costs, diversification and insurance provide the same efficient result.

In sum, liability guaranteed by equity, especially in hazardous widely held firms traded on financial markets, appears to be relatively efficient. However, in cases of losses larger than the limit set by the assets of the firm, the economic incentive to take precautions remains inefficient. High solvency requirements and equity in firms that are involved in industrial hazards may, therefore, be considered. The equity is the owners' guarantee of the undertakings of the firm. In order to accept the risk the owners will require: (i) a competitive return on the stocks, including a risk premium; and (ii) a control of the business which is maintained via the voting right and the power to dismiss the management.

BOX 15.3 EQUITY IN HAZARDOUS INDUSTRIES

There is, as demonstrated, an argument for a high solvency requirement in dangerous industries. Nevertheless, optimistic political support to industries facing large liabilities has been to limit liability. One example is the nuclear power industry. According to the conventions on liability at nuclear accidents, the Swedish industry is only liable for losses covered by insurance or other guarantee. Hence the equity of the industry is not at risk. In other countries, for example Germany, the liability is not restricted to insurance coverage. Including equity substantially increases the liability and thus the incentives to take care. There are also ways in which industry may avoid liability. One is to organize dangerous activities in several small firms with minimal equity, and to take a bankruptcy at an accidental loss. Another way is to organize dangerous activities in countries with small potential liability. These may be less developed countries, countries with corrupt governments, but also welfare states like Sweden, which covers most personal injury by public compensation schemes.

7. STRICT LIABILITY AT UNCERTAINTY

A main argument in favour of strict industrial liability is that the injuring firm controls the activity that may cause an accident. If the injurer knows that it must cover accident costs, it has an incentive to prevent accidents efficiently. This argument is based on the assumptions that the injuring firm has access to non-public decentralized information and that the manager of the firm is able to give and enforce orders. Mandatory insurance may have the same function for large losses. That is, the insurer compensates the victim and controls the policy-holder by premiums, bonus systems, contractual constraints and in an investigating claims settlement procedure.

The assumptions about control and access to decentralized information in the firm are certainly realistic in many real-world situations – it is usually the manager of the firm who knows and controls the business. Public authorities or courts have inferior information about daily practice and the 'due care' taken in a single firm. However, this is true for the most part of old insurable risks and predictable 'business risks'.

New industrial hazards are different, however. A firm has received no private information about development risks. It may have information about unpredictable hazards, but that information is typically of public interest. As soon as evidence appears that an activity, process, or substance is dangerous, it is of common interest to spread the information. A firm may, of course, have a vested interest in keeping the information private, but there is usually a duty to disclose information about hazards. The duty may be enforced both through criminal and civil liability. Hence information about unpredictable risks is usually public in nature.

The lack of private information about development risks and unpredictable hazards weakens the argument for strict liability. It may be argued that strict liability for development risks is motivated anyway, because liability creates an incentive to collect information and undertake research. This may be true in a research-intensive industry. However, the incentive will be at an optimal degree only if the firm controls the entire market. Otherwise, additional public research is motivated because the information pertains to the common interest. Private investigations aimed toward their own gain cause underinvestments from a social point of view. Indeed, this is the standard argument for publicly financed research.

Nonetheless, there is some common knowledge about new and unforeseen accidents. We know that anything may be ultimately dangerous and that some activities appear to be more risky than others. A way to reduce risks is simply to avoid certain activities or substances. A dilemma, of course, is that the potential benefits will not actualize. An example is gene techniques, which have many very beneficial applications, yet may also be extremely hazardous, although we may be uncertain about the areas in which the hazard may lie. Yet the introduction of new techniques or products is often postponed until preliminary information on possible effects is obtained. For instance, experiments and tests are required before new drugs are released. However, experiments are costly and the delay may limit the use of products that are potentially valuable. Furthermore, experiments outside the laboratories may be necessary in order to assure newer and safer products. Other *ex ante* regulations, such as restrictions on loading, the production method, storage, pollution standard, licensing and so on, are also decided at uncertainty. The regulations have uncertain benefits in relation to the costs, but are, nevertheless, widely used. The reason is presumably the absence of alternatives at uncertainty.

For instance, what could a farmer using pesticides do in addition to what is publicly known? Not very much. However, everyone knows that pesticides should be handled, used and stored with care, and precautions are described in safety regulations for example, by instructions printed on the bags. The reasonable due care to be taken by the farmer is to use permissible pesticides and follow instructions. This furnishes an argument in favour of negligence at development risks. If a negligence rule prevails and the farmer is careless in not following issued instructions or by not disclosing information, he is negligent. To avoid damage, therefore, the farmer will normally undertake the required precautions. In other words, strict liability has no comparative advantage relative to negligence, as long as the understanding of what is reasonable 'due care' is public. Here negligence has an advantage. However, according to a negligence rule, the injurer will only pay if the behaviour is regarded as careless. Injurers will normally avoid careless behaviour in order to avoid losses. Hence the victim will carry the loss.

All in all, strict liability is a blunt preventive instrument at development risks. Any prevention that can be achieved is based mainly on public safety regulation and less on private, decentralized information. As the insurer cannot foresee and control the risks, there is no preventive impact of insurance covering development risks and new industrial hazards. The same is true of retroactive liability as in the case of asbestosis, and of 'long-tail' liability for soil polluted decades ago. The diversification of the risk can, however, be mitigated by first-party insurance or public compensation schemes.

8. COMPENSATION

8.1 First-party Insurance

A victim of an accident is primarily interested in compensation. Prevention concerns future accidents in which the present victim presumably will not be involved. Compensation is certainly also a public goal of tort law, but it is not very effective. In fact, tort law usually does not compensate victims. In the case of negligence the victim will normally not be able to prove negligence and will thus not be compensated. Strict liability will compensate the victim, in principle. There are, however, many circumstances in which the victim remains uncompensated. One is that the liable party cannot pay, or that the liability is uncovered by insurance or guarantee. Another reason is that the injurer remains unidentified. Moreover, the victim may not claim for compensation because of uncertain causation. Indeed, most serious development risks of our time will not be covered by liability.

In addition, the tort system is costly to administer. It is slow – it may take years before the liability is settled and the victim is compensated. Nevertheless, many legal systems use torts for compensation. One reason may be a distributive goal to favour poor victims at the expense the wealthy injurers. But if the legal system systematically uses the 'deep pocket' and decides in favour of poor victims, it will reduce the preventive effect, and will merely increase the costs of insurance. Retroactive liability with the obvious goal of compensation may, in fact, more or less randomly compensate victims, and at the same time cause arbitrary costs for the third-party insurer.

Hence there are reasons to search for alternative systems of compensation. Note first that potential accident victims can protect themselves, at least partly, by *first-party insurance* which covers health and disability as well as pension and life. Health treatment and income losses due to cancer, allergies, and many other diseases caused by industrial accidents, new products and techniques are covered by such insurance. A reason why it is possible to insure such risks through first-party insurance is the law of large numbers. That is, pension and life expectancy can be estimated well enough because the cause and variations of sickness, disability and better health are not fully correlated. A major benefit of first-party insurance is that liability may not be settled. Hence it is relatively cheap to administer.

First-party *property* insurance also protects victims when tort liability is not in force. The victim's property insurance covers most accidental risks and industrial hazards, but may exclude potentially very large claims, such as nuclear accidents and natural disasters. Damage that is gradual and non-accidental is also typically excluded. On the other hand, such personal damage is, at least partly, covered by health, disability and pension schemes.

A shortcoming of first-party insurance, of course, is the diluted incentive to take care. Prevention must, therefore, be undertaken by *ex ante* regulations, as discussed above. In addition, the first-party insurers may control the incentives by requiring preventive measures (from the insured victim) or exercising recourse (against the injurer).

8.2 Public Risk-sharing

It is often argued that the public should cover major catastrophes and large, unforeseen losses. Indeed, there are several reasons why states administer mandatory risk-sharing, and citizens cover losses by taxes rather than by premiums. One reason is the lack of trust in private risk-sharing agreements. The coercive power of the state, and the public organization (or supervision) of the pool, may be necessary for its credibility. Adverse selection may also be mitigated by the state's power to force the citizens into the common pool. There may also exist economies in the collection of fees. A further reason for public risk-sharing is that the national pool is large. Interdependent and/or very large accidents are *social risks* in the sense that they can (at best) be diversified nationwide or internationally.

Uncertainty about the risks may also be the reason for public risk-sharing. Hazards that are unpredictable, as well as completely unforeseen risks, may be beneficially shared collectively by all members of society. In other words, man may foresee that the unforeseeable might occur, although the uncertainty about what will happen may be genuine. Agreements on the sharing of losses 'no matter what happens' may thus be favourable. Such an agreement is, however, open to interpretations and conflicts *ex post* and, thus, may not be trusted. This may explain why agreements about mutual aid primarily exist within families, clans and societies with strong internal control and trust. Also, on a national and international level there are explicit or implicit commitments to compensate victims of unforeseen events. The interpretation of the commitment of aid and charity may be made *ex post* by a national parliament or by international organizations such as the UN.

The idea that the community should cover losses, not only at very large losses but also at illness and disability, has a long history. The welfare state is the modern symbol of this tradition.[3] Today, however, many states have introduced private, or semi-private, insurance systems with a closer connec-

BOX 15.4 FIRE INSURANCE

Many European communities organized for centuries collective sharing of losses in the event of fire. Private fire mutuals, and later insurers, took over during the nineteenth century, when actuarial information became available.

It is interesting to note that the fear of meltdowns in nuclear power plants has much in common with the fear of town fires several hundred years ago. Towns burned down, with catastrophic consequences. The risks were not insured, but to some extent the losses were covered by risk-sharing agreements, and by charity. Later, the sharing developed, and as the actuarial science grew, property and personal losses could be insured. Similarly, at a meltdown some costs will be covered by private first-party insurance and through international compensation plans. The remaining, potentially very large losses will be left to random victimization and charity. International risk-sharing may improve the situation. Later, when more information on the risks is available, insurance may be possible.

tion between premiums and benefits. A common argument in favour of these reforms is public budget deficits. In addition, we may add the uncertainty argument: earlier, when actuarial information on individual risks was absent, public risk-sharing was a rational choice. Now, the presence of actuarial information makes a more extensive use of private insurance possible.

Meanwhile, new techniques and industrial hazards place new demands on states because catastrophes due to industrial processes, chemicals, drugs and so on are not covered by insurance. However, new, potentially very large

BOX 15.5 CLIMATE CHANGE

Global warming is a hot environmental topic. A first issue is whether pollution has caused a greenhouse effect, or whether there are other reasons for the observed warming. Most experts agree that there is a climate change, with higher temperature and more rain, as well as storms and floods, but the reason for the climate change is debated. Is it man-made? What could be done to reduced the damage?

The political effort has been concentrated on the reduction of emissions by international agreements. The Kyoto Protocol is an important document. A problem is, of course, to get all nations to sign the agreements and, thereafter, to honour the commitment. Serious free-rider and enforcement problems are involved. The policy is also weakened by the fact that there is considerable uncertainty about causes and effects. We are, therefore, pessimistic about the possibility of reducing climate change by international environmental emission regulations.

Another issue is that the harm of the warming varies. Indeed, a country like Sweden may in the long run gain while, for example, the Netherlands may suffer. Some species will gain and other lose. Future generations will accommodate. All in all, the warming may in total not be a disaster to the environment or to humanity. Nonetheless, there is a serious distributive issue: some countries will be flooded and the population will have to move, while some nations will not be harmed. Indeed, already-poor developing countries will suffer most. To counteract such random victimization international risk-sharing in excess of today's charity and short-term catastrophe aid is needed.

Source: Based on Linnerooth-Bayer and Amendola (2000).

accidents require international diversification, but insurance and reinsurance are not available for these risks. It is, thus, an understandable development to seek extended international risk-sharing conventions for new risks. However, an obstacle is that voluntary risk-sharing requires that the parties face similar risks and that they trust one another.

A completely unforeseen development risk can possibly, to some extent, be reduced through diversification and by taking general precautions. However, the absence of knowledge limits the ability to act – whatever is undertaken may be inadequate. This is a general problem with the precautionary principle. Because of the absence of adequate prevention, development risks might only be mitigated by first-party insurance or by public sharing and welfare plans. Avoidance of random victimization is important in itself. Precautions and preventive actions motivated under such uncertain circumstances may be accomplished through safety regulations and negligence (see Section 7).

9. INCOMPLETE COMPENSATION BY TORT LAW

A general requirement of the tort system is that there is a loss, and that someone claims compensation. There is, however, in practice a number of reasons why there may be no claimant. One is that the victims are many, each with small claims relative to the costs of going to court. Another is that the victim does not know that he is harmed, as in the case of allergies, or may not know that he has a right to compensation. Whatever the reason, absent or incomplete claims dilute the economic incentive for prevention.

A specific problem in this respect is when the victim dies. At fatal accidents the compensation is usually directed to family members and others dependent on the victim. The loss of life in itself cannot be compensated. Similarly, life insurance pays the survivors a sum of money that the insured victim regarded reasonable when purchasing the policy. More precisely, the economic loss to the survivors can be calculated by the *net production method* discussed in Chapter 10, Section 5. That is, the economic value of a life lost is the net present value of expected future incomes, minus the victim's own consumption. The sum ensures that the survivors do not suffer any economic loss. A shortcoming of the net production method is that the measure only takes into account the economic loss to individuals in the environment. Life as such has no value. It has been named the cattle or slave method because the value of slaves, cattle and other property can be calculated in the same way.

Fortunately, there is an alternative method that is reasonable from an economic point of view. Note that relevant for decisions on future projects and preventive measures is the willingness to pay for the reduction of risk.

The individual willingness to pay for risk reduction includes elements such as expected sorrow, fear of death, and pain and suffering. By estimating the willingness to pay for a reduction of the risk of injuries and death, it is possible to find a value of reduced future fatal accidents. This *statistical life method* (Chapter 10, Section 5) has been used to value the benefit of life *ex ante*. Individuals are willing to pay a great deal to avoid injuries and fatal accidents. US estimates indicate that the public is willing to pay $2–7 million for a statistical life saved or lost. In Sweden the numbers are in the lower rank, around $2 million. Such figures are used in CBA.

The estimated value of statistical life indicates that the tort liability system (in combination with insurance) is insufficient when it comes to prevention of fatal accidents. For instance, traffic and motor insurance may cover expected costs of damaged cars, healthcare and income losses due to disability and some compensation to relatives in case of death. Consequently, the claim in the case of minor accidents and disability may be higher than the claim if the injured victim dies. Insurers and drivers will, therefore, focus relatively more on minor accidents.

Similar problems prevail in the case of environmental accidents. For example, smoke at fires in chemical industries often causes serious environmental pollution. Liability and fire insurance include property damage and liability but no compensation to 'nature'. Hence liability and insurance alone result in inefficient low prevention. The same is true of, for example, oil pollution at tanker accidents. Cleaning up is required by the claimants around the affected area, but not by the creatures on the seabed.

Different measures have been proposed to mitigate this problem, and we will discuss them further in Chapter 17. Here we observe the option to introduce a *vicarious claimant* as a stand-in for the victim. The state or some other authority or institution may be given the right to compensation on behalf of the fatally injured, or of the environment. The liable party or the liability insurer has then to consider the full cost of an accident. An alternative that partly covers the problem of underdeterrence practised in the USA is *class action*, whereby a pressure group or perhaps an environmental organization is free to claim for compensation due to damage on others unable to claim compensation themselves.

10. CONCLUSIONS

A prime concern in this chapter is whether insurance cover for liability causes inefficiency. Naturally, insurance will reduce prevention by risk-averse policy-holders simply because of the reduction of fear of large losses. That benefit is part of the agreement. Insurance is bought to make risky, but potentially utility-increasing, activities feasible. Nonetheless, the insurer must control carelessness. This is achieved by including safety requirements in the policy. Still, the insurer will not be able to observe hidden factors, that is, moral hazard. To reduce this problem of moral hazard deductibles and bonus systems are used. All in all, the insurance industry is a specialist in handling moral hazard, and control risks, and competitive firms will benefit by efficient prevention of accidents.

Basic law and economics analysis of accident law (presented in Chapter 14) assumes actuarial risks, and accidents small enough to be covered by the assets of the liable party. Risk-averse parties are supposed to be able to purchase insurance. Hence the theory neglects large and serious development risks and industrial hazards of our time.

A major problem is that the liable party may go bankrupt. Indeed, industrial hazards cause large transnational environmental accidents. The size of the potential accidents and the legal complexity will certainly give rise to incomplete cover of damages, and thus inadequate prevention and random victimization. Hence it is important to search for systems of liability and compensation that contribute to more prevention and reduced victimization of the public.

Mandatory insurance for coverage of losses in excess of the assets of the liable firm may increase the prevention and compensation. Insurance is, however, limited to risks accepted by the insurance industry, while major contemporary industrial hazards are characterized by uncertainty and high insurance premiums, if insurance is available at all. Mutual risk-sharing may, as we have demonstrated, be an alternative at unpredictable hazards. Examples from the nuclear and the oil-trading industry indicate that international legal reforms, including strict industrial liability combined with mandatory requirements of guarantees and insurance, may be important.

Another way of increasing the effective liability of an industry is to increase solvency requirements. The activities of the financial market indicate a relatively efficient consideration of benefits and costs of prevention. A problem here is that firms may escape liability by relocation of dangerous industries into small firms with very limited liability.

In addition, much damage will remain uncovered in an extended liability system such as the one outlined above. First-party and public coverage may, therefore, be increasingly motivated, especially in cases of genuine uncertainty. Similarly, global warming will cause random victimization that will motivate advanced international sharing systems.

NOTES

1. Compare this with the function of charges, discussed in Chapter 13.
2. Compare the discussion on extended producer responsibility in Chapter 9, Section 5.
3. In his famous book, *A Theory of Justice*, John Rawls (1971) presents the 'difference principle', stating that the state shall redistribute income in favour of the worst-off. The principle is based on the idea of a social contract behind a hypothetical 'veil of ignorance', that is, a situation where the individuals do not know their specific risks or which preferences they will have in the future. Under such genuine uncertainty, the solution is straightforward – the individuals accept equal sharing.

FURTHER READING

Borch, K. (1990), *Economics of Insurance*, Amsterdam: North Holland.

Faure, M. and Skogh, G. (1992), 'Compensation for Damages Caused by Nuclear Accidents: A Convention as Insurance', *Geneva Papers on Risk and Insurance*, **17** (65), 499–513.

Faure, M. and Van den Bergh, R. (1990), 'Liability for nuclear accidents in Belgium from an interest group perspective', *International Review of Law and Economics*, **10**, 241–54.

Hägg, G. (1994), 'The Economics of Trust, Trust Sensitive Contracts, and Regulation', *International Review of Law and Economics*, no. 4, 337–70.

Hirschhleifer, J. and Riley, J.G. (1979), 'The Analytics of Uncertainty and Information – An Expository Survey', *Journal of Economic Literature*, **17** (41), 371–1421.

Shavell, S. (1986), 'The judgement proof problem', *The International Review of Law and Economics*, 45–58.

Shavell, S. (1987), *An Economic analysis of accident law*, Cambridge, MA: Harvard University Press.

Skogh, G. (1999), 'Risk-Sharing Institutions of Unpredictable Losses', *Journal of Institutional and Theoretical Economics*, **155** (3).

Sykes, A.O. (1980), 'The Economics of Vicarious Liability', *The Yale Law Journal*, **93**, 1231–80.

Sykes, A.O. (1998), 'Vicarious Liability', in P. Newman (ed.), *The New Palgrave Dictionary of Economics and the Law* (3 vols), London, Macmillan, 673–7.

16. Environmental crime

> Punishment is an evil in itself and should only be employed insofar as it promises to prevent some greater evil.
> Jeremy Bentham (1780)

1. INTRODUCTION

The public often requires criminal punishments when an industry intentionally violates environmental regulations, or otherwise pollutes for profit. The seriousness of environmental pollution is a common argument in favour of criminal sanctions. One reason for retribution is moral or ethical –wrong behaviour shall be punished because morality says so. The purpose may also be educational – a way of changing attitudes. A different reason for punishments is their presumed economic deterrence effect. That is, punishments make criminal pollution more costly, which reduces the number of offences. In this chapter we shall study economic deterrence and leave the moral and ethical aspects aside. That does not mean that we think that moral aspects are unimportant. On the contrary, the reason is that we are not experts on morality, ethics and the formation of preferences or attitudes.

One argument made in favour of criminal law to protect the environment is that the severe sanctions offered by law are also used to protect traditional interests, such as property, health and honour. These are values that are protected by criminal law in many penal codes. In environmental legal doctrine it is argued that, given the deteriorating state of the environment in many industrialized countries, a clean environment is nowadays at least as important as the aforementioned values that were previously protected by criminal law. Hence, if criminal law is used to protect these traditional individual values, it should also be used to protect collective values, such as environmental interests. It is argued that individual values (such as health and property) cannot be enjoyed if the basic requirements concerning a clean environment have not been met.

Scholars in criminal law, on the other hand, claim that criminal law is an *ultimum remedium*, a last resort that should not be used too early. Other legal instruments that can deter environmental pollution, such as tort liability and administrative sanctions, should be examined first. Only if other legal instruments do not work should criminal law eventually be used.

Both the retribution argument and the ultimum remedium argument have shortcomings. A more complete calculus must consider the seriousness of the crime, the deterrence effect of criminal sanctions, and the cost of policing as well as the cost of punishments, both to society and to convicted offenders. An analysis that simultaneously considers the damage of environmental pollution (accidental as well as intentional) and relates it to enforcement costs is obviously needed. Fortunately, since the publications of Gary Becker (1968) and George Stigler (1970), a rich and abundant literature on the economics of crime and punishment has emerged.

In this chapter we will rely on this economic theory when briefly reviewing the most relevant points in relation to environmental pollution. A first issue discussed in Section 2 is the assumed rationality of the criminal. The most important difference between the economic model of tort liability and the model of criminal liability is that not all criminal polluters are detected. A low detection rate reduces the incentive to protect the environment and increases the required sanction, which, in turn, causes bankruptcy problems. A related issue is whether legal entities like firms or individuals should be criminally liable. In Section 3 we discuss the enforcement of regulations by criminal and administrative sanctions. In the policy debate, regulations for the protection of the environment are often suggested without consideration of the problem of enforcement. In reality, enforcement of environmental regulations may be weak, or even absent. Regulations are, therefore, sometimes held to be blunt environmental instruments. None the less, regulations with administrative or criminal sanctions are frequent, which may seem paradoxical. There are important economic enforcement issues to examine. Section 4 concludes.

2. ECONOMICS OF CRIME

2.1 Rational Criminals

The bottom line of the economic theory of crime is the assumption that the offender takes the decision to commit a crime or not, weighing costs and benefits. The offender is assumed to be a profit- or utility-maximizer. She does not undertake an illegal action unless the expected benefits of the crime exceed the expected costs. Taking this viewpoint, the function of the criminal law can be stated relatively simple as increasing the expected costs to deter a prospective offender.

In other words, the economic theory of crime and punishment is grounded on deterrence: threatening a potential polluter with punishments, such as imprisonment or fines, will deter him from intended or careless (environmental) crime. Criminal law is cost-efficient if a similar deterrent effect could not be reached at lower costs by using other legal instruments.

There is a long-standing debate on whether criminals are rational or not. There are, of course, many crimes such as petty theft committed by drug addicts, and violence among relatives based on hatred and passion, that cannot be explained in models of 'economic man' (Chapter 5, Section 3). Our focus, however, is on environmental crimes committed for economic reasons. Environmental pollution is in most cases a result of corporate behaviour. Such 'white-collar' criminals can be considered rational in their choice of whether or not to commit a crime.

Nonetheless, the impact of criminal sanctions on environmental pollution seems to be small. This may not be because criminals do not act rationally. Rather, it is a common criticism in environmental legal doctrine that for a potential polluter an expected sanction will often just be considered as a cost of doing business. That is, economic deterrence works, while morality is neglected.

BOX 16.1 STIGMATIZING BY MEDIA

Some jurisdictions allow the judge to order that his judgment should be published in the mass media. Although the application of such stigmatizing sanctions still varies between legal systems, there is an increasing use of such specific measures. If a polluter is prosecuted because he deposited waste illegally, he could be ordered to clean up the waste he discharged. In some legal systems it is even possible to enforce these specific duties with a severe penalty payment that will be due if the duties are not fulfilled within the time limit laid down in the judgment.

It is understandable that these specific duties can have a deterrence effect, but this deterrence depends on psychological and moral factors that are beyond economics. The stigmatizing effect connected with the publication of a judgment in a national newspaper can be disastrous for a company's reputation. Board members of a company who are prosecuted for environmental crime may consider publicity the most serious punishment. For multinational companies with a clean environmental image in particular, prosecuting a criminal case that attracts a great deal of attention from the mass media can cause a major loss in reputation and thus have a serious deterrent effect as well.

The reason for the limited deterrence effect may be that the expected cost of punishment is small relative to the benefit of pollution. If the expected cost were high enough, this would give the polluter an incentive to comply with environmental law. Yet by committing environmental pollution a lot of money may be earned. For example, investment in water-cleaning equipment that would be necessary to comply with the conditions of a licence could cost millions of dollars. In some cases the gain of crime for the company is due to a low detection rate of environmental pollution, and to the fact that the maximum punishments provided for in legislation are almost never imposed by courts in, for example, Western European countries. All in all, low probability of detection, combined with relatively low sanctions, leads to limited deterrence.

2.2 The Detection Rate

The model of efficient tort liability in Chapter 14 assumes that the liable party is identified. The assumption of a costlessly identified wrongdoer may be acceptable when, for example, an oil tanker is wrecked or a factory explodes, but presumably not when a number of firms are polluting the same water, and certainly not when the injurer escapes liability by burying barrels containing toxic liquids. At environmental hazards, or at gradual pollution, the probability of being caught and/or being forced to pay all damage is often much lower than 100 per cent. The incentive to take care will, therefore, be inefficiently low.

This may be compensated, if the sanction to which the potential polluter is exposed is higher than the amount of damage he is causing. In principle, high enough 'punitive damages' may be efficient from a preventive viewpoint, if they can be collected – a bankruptcy problem is usually apparent at large monetary sanctions. Another issue is to whom the punitive damage should be paid. Should the victim of the detected injurer receive all compensation motivated by deterrence, while other victims receive nothing? An alternative is, of course, for the state to collect monetary sanctions.

To illustrate the consequences of a small detection rate, assume that only a few intentional or careless polluters are detected. They are rational, risk-neutral, profit-maximizing owners of hazardous industries. The probability of an accident is p and the accident damage is D. The expected accident damage is thus $p \times D$. A damage of D to be paid with the probability p is, in the tort liability case, sufficient for compensation of the victim, and for the creation of an efficient incentive to prevent accidents. In the tort model the detection rate, d, is equal to 1. However, if $0 < d < 1$, the experienced expected cost of the accident is $d \times p \times D < p \times D$. Hence the care taken by the owner will be related to benefits in terms of expected costs if detected, which is the full cost reduced by the fraction $d < 1$. Liability alone thus establishes inefficient, small prevention.

To compensate for the less than 100 per cent coverage of damages, the liability may be increased by a *penal sanction*. The formula for how large the sanction (S) must be to serve the purpose of efficient deterrence is $S = D/d$, assuming a risk-neutral offender. In the tort case $d = 1$, and $D = S$. But if $D =$ £10 000 and $d = 0.1$, this means that nine times out of ten the offender escapes the clutches of the law. Hence the optimal sanction to deter a risk-neutral offender would be £100 000. Here the expected cost to the prospective offender is $d \times p \times S = p \times D$, that is, equal to the expected damage of his act, which establishes an efficient incentive to take care.

In many cases of environmental pollution the probability of being caught may not be 10 per cent, but in fact much lower. This means that the efficient sanction to deter the potential polluter should be correspondingly higher. This cannot be achieved with tort law, since strict liability in principle only forces the injurer to compensate the victim the amount of damages he caused when detected, nothing more (except for the case when punitive damages are applied). The fact that the probability of detection is less than one may, therefore, require the use of criminal law to deter environmental pollution.

Criminal sanctions have, on the other hand, limitations that are made obvious by the model. If the damage D is large and the detection rate d is very small, the efficient punishment S must be very high. If, for instance, the potential damage is one million and the probability is one in a thousand, the efficient fine is one billion, which, of course, may cause bankruptcy, even for big industries. To compensate for the limited deterrence due to small collectable amounts, non-monetary sanctions such as imprisonment, bodily harm and ultimately capital punishment may be used. Such punishments have serious consequences for the punished. Indeed they may be catastrophic, which should be considered in a social cost–benefit analysis. In model terms it means that the assumption of risk-neutrality does not apply to sanctions causing bankruptcy. Thus the inefficiency because of a limited collectable amount is the same as in tort liability, as discussed in Chapter 15, Section 3, but much more drastic.

2.3 Cost of Punishment and Policing

Above we assume that the damage of accidental, or gradual intended, pollution, D, as well as the detection rate, d, is given. The injurer/criminal is rational, risk-neutral and able to pay an efficient monetary fine, that is, a transfer to the state. Such a transfer causes no social cost in a CBA where the gain to the state is valued the same as the loss to the criminal. The optimal sanction can, therefore, be set by the simple formula $S = D/d$.

Reality is, of course, more complicated. One problem is that risk-aversion cannot be neglected, especially for large individual sanctions. The loss of wealth and freedom at imprisonment is a social cost. Moreover, the collection of fines, as well as running prisons, causes costs to society. Hence costs of punishments are in the economics of crime usually assumed to be increasing with higher sanctions.

A second problem is the cost of policing. The detection rate normally varies with the policing effort, and the reaction by the offender. Some may be

BOX 16.2 LARGE PUNISHMENTS AND LITTLE POLICING?

The product of the detection rate and the sanction constitute the expected costs of a crime to the risk-neutral criminal. A certain deterrence effect may, therefore, be maintained by reducing the probability of detection (d) and increasing the sanction (S), or vice versa. Because it is costly to increase policing, while fines, within a range, are pure transfers, there is an argument for using fines at the upper level of the range, combined with limited policing. Suppose, for example, that $S = 100\,000$ and $d = 0.01$, then the expected cost of the crime to the criminal is 1000. By doubling either the probability of getting caught or the expected punishment, the expected costs for the criminal will double. The two ways to obtain these results, however, are not equally easy to achieve. Increasing the expected punishment might demand less effort from the government than increasing the probability of catching the offender. Therefore, the point has been made in the literature that increasing punishment rather than the probability of catching offenders inflicts fewer costs on society. The argument is that a highly expected sanction leads to high deterrence, and a low detection rate has the advantage that less has to be invested in crime control. However, this works only to the extent that monetary fines are used, and the offenders are risk-neutral. Otherwise, we have to consider the suffering of the punished as well as the costs of prison. The problem is that a small detection rate often requires a harsh punishment that is a real cost to society. Therefore, many economists have shown themselves to be opponents of prison sanctions, simply because the costs of the execution of those sanctions are much higher than the fines, which can be administered relatively easily.

deterred while others may turn to other crimes. The reaction depends on available alternatives. The deterrence effect of policing effort depends on the punishment and on alternatives to the offenders. Several important factors should, therefore, be taken into account in calculating the enforcement of a certain environmental sanction: one is the costs of authorities catching and convicting the offender; another is the cost of punishment. Fines imposed on risk-neutral solvent parties are, as mentioned, pure transfers with low social costs, while imprisonment causes large individual costs and costs for the criminal justice system. On the benefit side we have the deterrence of harmful crimes.

2.4 Individual or Corporate Liability?

Criminal environmental pollution is often committed not by individual actors, but by persons acting on behalf of a company. In cases of corporate environmental crime the question arises whether the corporation, the employee, or both should be criminally liable. Criminal law can hold liable only the corporation, only the individual employee involved in the violation of the law, or both the corporation and the individual employee. What is the economic difference?

From an economic point of view, designating the liable party is unimportant so long as the sanctions are freely transferable, the parties are fully informed, and no bankruptcy problem exists. With no transaction costs the involved parties will redistribute liability among themselves according to their comparative advantages, carrying losses and taking precautions. Either the corporation can charge the employee the imposed fine it paid, or the employee may ask the corporation for reimbursement of a fine he pays, or a punishment risk he takes. Choosing to impose the fine on either the corporation or the individual is thus unimportant. The contractual relationship between the employee and the corporation governs these matters. This is obviously an application of the Coase theorem discussed many times above.

Nevertheless, the world we live in is not ideal. Arguments are advanced to hold the corporation, as well as the individuals, liable. One argument is that even monetary sanctions are not freely transferable between the employer (the corporation) and the employee. For instance, an employee can hardly trust the employer after imprisonment. Indeed, the law may prohibit contractual transfers of liability. For instance section 2679 (d) of the United States code provides that tort recovery from the employee is specifically foreclosed (28 USCA 2679 d), and paying someone else's fines constitutes a criminal offence in Germany.

An important argument in legal doctrine is that sanctions should in practice be imposed on corporations. This point is related to the principle in tort law, being that of '*respondeat superior*'. *Respondeat superior* means that an employer is vicariously liable for the torts of its employees committed in furtherance of the employment. The employer, however, is liable only for damages that result from negligence on the part of his employees. In the economic literature, this *respondeat superior* inquiry focuses on the problem of insolvency (compare Chapter 15, Section 3). For example, because the employee is unable to pay for the damage he caused, liability imposed on him alone is ineffective. Holding the employer vicariously liable for damage caused by the employee's negligent behaviour provides incentives to force the corporation to exert effective control over its employees. The employer can threaten termination, or refuse any promotion, as an inducement to careful conduct. In the context of environmental corporate crime, from an economic point of view one can, therefore, argue that given the limited funds of the employee, corporate criminal liability may be an efficient instrument to urge the corporation to issue prudent guidelines and exert effective control over its employees.

Given the potential large damage of environmental crimes, and the corresponding large fines, it appears more efficient to make the corporation, and

BOX 16.3 PERVERSE EFFECTS OF CORPORATE LIABILITY?

A criticism of the use of corporate criminal liability has been formulated by Jennifer Arlen.[1] She argues that the traditional argument in favour of vicarious liability is an indirect means of sanctioning wrongful employees, assuming that corporations subject to criminal liability will in turn sanction the wrongful agent. This regime can, however, lead to perverse incentives: it is true that a corporation monitoring its employees might reduce the number of crimes. On the other hand, enforcement expenditures may increase the probability that public authorities are informed about those crimes, whereby the corporation's expected criminal liability is increased. Thus vicarious liability could lead to the perverse incentive that the corporation will reduce the monitoring of its employees in order to avoid detection of corporate (environmental) crime.

Note:

1. Jennifer Arlen, 'The potentially perverse effects of corporate criminal liability', *Journal of Legal Studies*, **23**, 833–67, 1994.

not only the individual, responsible. However, corporate entities may also be unable to pay for the damage caused. Moreover, a polluting corporation may escape a liability suit because the damage to the environment is widely dispersed and therefore difficult to trace. Monetary sanctions may exceed the corporation's assets and thus become ineffective. Because non-monetary sanctions are hard to apply to corporations, imprisonment may be applied to individual employees as well.

3. REGULATORY CRIMES

Environmental law usually takes the form of specific administrative regulations imposed on industry. The permitted amounts and quality of, for example, polluting emissions are subject to prior approval via licences, see Chapter 11. Thus it may be a crime to operate a facility without a permit, or to violate emission standards. Most of the environmental regulations we have discussed so far are enforced through either administrative penal law or criminal law.

Monetary sanctions can be both criminal and administrative. An administrative agency, however, cannot normally impose non-monetary sanctions, such as imprisonment. According to the European Convention for the Protection of Human Rights and Fundamental Freedoms only an impartial judge following a procedure proscribed by law can impose imprisonment and other non-monetary sanctions. Imprisonment is available only as a criminal sanction, not as an administrative sanction. The economic analysis of monetary sanctions is, none the less, the same for administrative penal sanctions and damages or fines issued by courts. If environmental pollution cannot be efficiently deterred through monetary sanctions, criminal law may be used to enforce environmental regulations.

Environmental criminal law usually starts with provisions that criminal law follows prior administrative decisions and punishes *abstract endangerments* of environmental values. Criminal law applies as soon as the administrative provision (for example in the form of an emission limit value in a licence) has been violated, whether or not this causes harm to the environment.

In some legal systems these abstract endangerments are not primarily punished through the criminal law, but through fines, belonging to administrative penal law. Environmental law is thus part of administrative law, using permits and licences extensively. Hence, because most environmental crimes consist of a violation of such administrative norms, the administrative agency that sets the emission standards determine what kind of behaviour is criminal.

Authorities generally only punish the lack of a permit, or a violation of regulations.[1] Polluting only constitutes a crime when it violates an administrative norm. That is, compliance with a permit is usually sufficient justification for the polluter. An alternative would be to consider all pollution a crime, leaving the judge to decide which acts warrant punishment.

The present legal structure seems to be economically reasonable. First, the administrative authorities have an informational advantage over a judge in a regulatory case. In most cases a regulatory agency has either superior knowledge of, or far better access to, relevant ecological and technological information than a judge. Requiring a judge to acquire expert knowledge of chemical and toxic substances, and keep up to date with recent developments in the field of environmental science, might be inefficient, if not impossible. Moreover, administrative agencies acquire information that benefits a large number of people and, therefore, diminishes the costs of research for society.

Note also that as long as the environmental crime is based on endangerments, that is, violations of regulations, and not on the environmental damage *per se*, the criminal (expected) harm may be relatively small. The violation of a regulation may also be easier to identify than the environmental harm. The violations of regulations may, therefore, be deterred by feasible administrative sanctions or by criminal fines. For example, the initial assets of an offender is 1000, and the potential accidental damage is 2000. If an accident occurs and tort liability prevails, the offender will become bankrupt. The effective liability is only 1000, which yields too little care. Compare this with the violation of a safety standard. The offender violates the standard, which increases the probability of an accident by 5 per cent. The expected social cost of the violation of the safety regulations is thus $0.05 \times 2000 = 100$. The detection rate of the violation is estimated to be 40 per cent. The optimal sanction (ignoring policing costs) is thus $100/0.4 = 250$, which is within the collectable assets of the offender.

An argument in favour of criminal law enforcement is that administrative authorities often follow a compliance strategy by which they seek to achieve the voluntary compliance of the offender. In the negotiations with the polluting industries the authorities may rely on a long-term cooperative strategy. Punishment, say by closing down a factory, may be devastating. On the other hand, even when only the administrative sanction is used, the administrative authorities will have some power in their negotiations concerning the measures that have to be taken to comply with the conditions of a licence. This is especially the case if they know that they are backed by a public prosecutor, who can bring a criminal case if the company is not willing to follow the proposals made by the administrative authorities. Thus criminal law enforcement has a very useful role in backing up administrative law enforcement.

One problem with a compliance strategy of administrative authorities is that it does not give enough incentives to potential polluters to follow the requirements of the law. If all a polluter risks after detection is that he will

> ### BOX 16.4 ENFORCEMENT STRATEGIES
>
> There is a noteworthy difference in approach between public prosecutors in some Western European countries like Belgium and The Netherlands and in the USA. In Europe, prosecutors seem to focus primarily on the result of the criminal action, that is, that the investments should be made and the environmental pollution stopped, instead of focusing primarily on deterrence.
>
> On the other hand, public prosecutors in the USA, especially those from the specialized Environmental Protection Agency, seem primarily to direct actions towards deterrence through high criminal sanctions. The power of discretion of American judges is also limited through federal sentencing guidelines that set minimum sanctions that have to be followed by the judge.

have to make the investments he was forced to make anyway, deterrence will, of course, fail.

The current structure of environmental law, relying primarily on administrative agencies to determine environmental crimes, and on administrative as well as criminal monetary sanctions, appears reasonable. Nonetheless, administrative law is not the sole source of environmental criminal law. Some serious cases of environmental pollution, such as intentional emission of strongly toxic substances, could be punishable directly by criminal law, even if no violation of administrative provisions were at hand. A criminal provision could punish pollution directly. Such a law could punish emissions in general but be particularly directed to cases where the consequences were of the most serious nature, say long-lasting pollution with consequences for people's health, or a significant risk causing injuries to the population. The main difference between such a criminal law versus administrative law discussed so far is that the linkage between the criminal and prior administrative decisions can be totally ignored. Hence serious environmental pollution can be punished although the defendant followed the conditions of a licence. The dependence of the administrative law is thus set aside.

4. CONCLUSIONS

Some crimes are committed because of passion and hatred. Others are planned and committed for profit. We argue that illegal environmental pollution committed by industry mainly belongs to the latter type. A model assuming

BOX 16.5 A LEGAL TREND

It seems fair to state that there has been an evolution from the model of abstract endangerment towards punishing concrete danger. In the latter case some kind of damage, or a specific risk of damage to environmental media such as water, soil and air, is a prerequisite for criminal liability. Mere abstract danger does not suffice. In many legal systems during the 1980–90s, there was a change to a criminalization of the concrete endangerment of ecological values. To show the importance of environmental crimes, some countries have incorporated in their criminal codes provisions aimed to protect against concrete endangerment. The provisions aim at a more direct protection of ecological values, but still keep the relationship with administrative law to some extent intact. Therefore, the criminal law protection may fail if the defendant complied with the conditions of administrative regulations. Precisely with that end in view tendencies became evident in legal doctrine and (sometimes) legislation to punish some cases of serious pollution notwithstanding the fact that the conditions of a licence were followed. In some legal systems, norms other than environmental ones are used to prosecute environmental pollution. The public prosecutor may use broad notions from the general criminal code such as 'forgery' or 'participation in a criminal organization' to prosecute environmental crimes. These classic criminal provisions may sometimes be easier to prove than a violation of the environmental statutes. Indeed, sometimes a higher sanction is applicable than in case of violation of the environmental statute.

rational behaviour thus seems reasonable and useful. The model is simple as well. The basic difference as compared with the tort model presented in Chapters 14 and 15 is that not all liable parties (criminals) are identified. Undetected carelessness or intentional harm motivates efforts of policing, that is, to increase the detection rate, but that is costly. It is also costly to punish detected offenders. Thus there is a trade-off between the benefits of protecting the environment, the cost of policing and the cost of punishment. When deterrence can be achieved equally by fines and prison sanctions, fines are to be preferred since they are less costly to impose. Fines are financial transfers that move the amount from the offender to society, while imprisonment means a cost in terms of freedom, production and resources used in the criminal justice system. Recall that the probability of detection of environmental pollution is often very low. Moreover, the environmental damage may be large. In that case the optimal sanction to deter pollution becomes high. Therefore, the optimal monetary sanction required for deterrence often exceeds the offender's assets. Consequently non-monetary sanctions, such as imprisonment, may be optimal.

Our brief overview shows a variety of legal techniques that can be used to punish polluting activities. In addition it should be noted that there may be large differences as far as the scope of the particular provision is concerned. A crucial question a legislator has to address is whether the criminal law should focus on a certain activity, on an endangerment such as, for example, an emission, or on the seriousness of the pollution. The legislator also has to take into account the requirement to define criminal behaviour in a relatively precise way *ex ante* – the so-called *lex certa* principle. In addition, the legislator will have to consider the question of whether the criminal law protection of the environment is provided independent of administrative law or whether the traditional penal law upon prior administrative decisions is kept intact. Statutes other than environmental ones are in practice of great importance as far as the prosecution of environmental crimes is concerned. The way criminal provisions are formulated shows that the legislator has to struggle with these questions. The result is that each legal system uses a variety of methods to criminalize environmental pollution.

Moreover, civil liability is often combined with criminal sanctions. Thus the punished may have to pay damages as well as fines. In some environmental statutes the judge can impose direct measures on the convicted polluter, such as a duty to restore the harm committed, for example by cleaning up polluted soil. In effect, this is a tort liability that partly recovers the damage, and may be combined with criminal sanctions. Note also that the standard of care applied by courts in civil law cases is closely related to administrative regulations and punishments when the regulations are violated. Indeed, the negligence norm may follow the regulatory standards. If, for instance, a pollution permit is violated, a licence is missing, or a driver is intoxicated, this may call for tort liability as well as a penal sanction. The combination of measures will be further discussed in the next chapter.

NOTE

1. Other varieties can be found as well. Criminal provisions may not merely aim to punish emissions, but to punish when a certain state, such as degradation of a certain habitat, is reached. An obvious disadvantage of such provisions, is that it might often be difficult to prove that the particular state has been reached.

FURTHER READING

Becker, G.S. (1962), 'Irrational Behaviour and Economic Theory', *Journal of Political Economy*, 1–13.

Becker, G.S. (1968), 'Crime and Punishment: An Economic Approach', *Journal of Political Economy*, 169–217.

Bowles, R. (1982), *Law and Economy*, Oxford: Martin Robertson.

Coffee, J.C. (1980), 'Corporate crime and punishment. A non-Chicago view of the economics of criminal sanctions', *American Criminal Law Review*, 419–76.

Faure, M. and Heine, G. (1991), 'The Insurance of Fines: The Case of Oil Pollution', *Geneva Papers on Risk and Insurance*, 39–54.

Shavell, S. (1985), 'Criminal law and the optimal use of non-monetary sanctions as a deterrent', *Columbia Law Review*, 1232–62.

Skogh, G. (1982), 'Public insurance and accident prevention', *International Review of Law and Economics*, 67–80.

Stigler, G. (1970), 'The optimum enforcement of laws', *Journal of Political Economy*, 213.

Wheeler, N. (1984), 'The use of criminal statutes to regulate product safety', *Journal of Legal Studies*, 593–622.

17. Various instruments at various levels of government

Too many cooks spoil the broth.

1. INTRODUCTION

In the introduction to this book we promised to discuss a variety of legal instruments which could be used to remedy environmental harm. We said that we would also pay attention to legal instruments other than the traditional ones stressed by economists (taxes and marketable permits). Therefore, we have also paid substantial attention to property rights, safety regulation, land-use control, tort liability, insurance and criminal law.

When discussing some of the instruments in the separate chapters we indicated some of the similarities or differences between various instruments. For instance in Chapter 13, dealing with tradable permits and charges, we made it clear that when a charge is collected and used by the state this could in fact be considered as a special case of tradable permits whereby the state is the initial owner (Section 2). Hence the legal form may differ, but the effects of instruments are often not that different.

We have shown that sometimes a combined use of various instruments may be warranted. Liability rules can, for instance, be combined with charges and with safety regulation. Safety regulation (often taking the form of emission standards in environmental law) could also guide the judge in establishing fault in an environmental liability case. In Chapter 15, Section 2 we noted that a court (in establishing negligence) may not usually require an appropriate activity level from a polluter. Insurance, on the other hand, can adapt the premium to the activity level. Similarly, a charge on, for example, gasoline or pesticides may reduce the activity (traffic or farming). A charge may be a preferable instrument when it is aimed to influence large numbers of polluters.

This should not lead us to the conclusion that we should strive for a combination of all kinds of policy measures in order to achieve the highest possible reduction of environmental harm. A combination of measures and instruments without any coordination may lead to overdeterrence. One central message in this book is that environmental pollution abatement always has a price. It is an important task of environmental economics to indicate what the optimal level of pollution reduction is. An uncoordinated combination of all kinds of instruments is obviously too costly. Hence the appropriate policy answer is not to combine all measures and instruments discussed in this book at random, but to identify what types of instruments are more appropriate in a particular situation, given specific comparative benefits.

In this final chapter we briefly survey various legal instruments presented, and investigate how they may be combined to control environmental harm. We complement the analysis so far, especially by an examination of appropriate political decision levels on various environmental matters (local, national and federal). In Section 2 we recall the use of property rights as an environmental instrument. Thereafter, in Section 3, we compare safety regulation and liability. The use of regulations is of special importance in cases where tort liability does not work properly. Section 4 applies the discussion on safety regulation versus liability to environmental protection. Section 5 contains a discussion on geographical zoning and lobbying for environmental regulation, both concerning land use and safety. In Section 6 we examine arguments for various levels of government. This is most important in the European context: should environmental regulation take place nationally, or should it be on an international (EU) level? We finally discuss whether environmental standards should be uniform and harmonized, or differentiated and flexible.

2. PROPERTY RIGHTS AND ENVIRONMENTAL HARM

Open access to a scare resource may, as shown in Chapter 3, cause serious environmental harm. Similarly, many rare species are threatened by extinction because of poaching or pollution. A legal measure to solve such problems is often suggested in environmental economics literature to assess private property rights to the scarce resource.

However, there is no simply defined and efficient property rights rule. There are, in fact, many possible combinations of rules that may be named property rights. Property rights are bundles of rights and duties that include: (i) the right to use and to dispose; (ii) the residual right to the surplus and duty to cover deficit; (iii) the right to compensation at infringements; and (iv) the freedom to contract (Chapter 4, Section 8). All these parts are restricted and subject to change by law-makers. One owner's right, for example to compensation, corresponds to another's duty not to infringe in the first owner's right. Tort law as well as contract law is in this respect part of the prevailing property rights regime. So are administrative regulations restricting use. For instance, zoning gives the landowner certain rights of exploitation, but zoning is basically a restriction on use. Similarly, a licence gives the owner the right to run a business, that is, freedom to act and contract on certain matters, while it excludes others without a permit. Furthermore, licences are part of the enforcement system. Indeed, a withdrawn licence may constitute a serious punishment. Taxes are partial reductions of residual rights.

All in all, the legal instruments that are discussed in this book are parts of complex sets of rights, duties and restrictions that may be bundled together in what we name 'property rights' belonging to owners of various goods. The components of the bundle may be combined by law-makers in various ways, all with different impacts on the economy and the environment. A thorough analysis is thus needed in the search for property rights to serve an efficient economy, including the environment.

Recall that effective property rights must fulfil certain criteria (Chapter 4, Sections 8 and 9). First, the owner must be able to enjoy the benefits and influence the costs generated by the scarce resource and the owner's effort. Second, it must be possible to enforce rights and duties privately and/or publicly. Third, the owner needs to be able to contract with other parties involved. The reason is that the initially assessed property rights are usually sub-optimal. Trade is thus required to modify rights and duties efficiently.

Further, distributive consequences have to be considered for political reasons. A Pareto-improvement requires that no one become worse of. Hence all losers must be compensated. The less requiring criterion of Kaldor–Hicks (Chapter 9, Section 3) may be applied. On the other hand, legal certainty requires that no one be seriously harmed (Chapter 7, Section 7). In practice, a change in the ownership structure has to be politically acceptable. Changes in rights or duties, therefore, require compensations to those who lose, usually in terms of other rights or subsidies.

These circumstances make crucial the choice of ownership structure and compensation. In fact, there may be no effective property rights regime available to solve serious environmental problems. Indeed, the absence of effective property rights may explain why serious threats to the ecosystem remain.

Yet innovations on a case-by-case basis may, it is hoped, improve the situation. Box 4.4 on the ownership of elephants is an example. A similar solution is suggested in Box 17.1.

From the wolverine example here it is obvious that there is not only one possible property rights solution. There are many. Some may work; others will not. Indeed, institutional innovations should be sought. Another conclusion that may be drawn is that a combination of measures is usually needed. A change from the present state ownership of the wolverine to the suggested property rights regime requires changes in subsidies and the pricing of a

BOX 17.1 THE ENDANGERED WOLVERINE

The Scandinavian wolverine is a predator that kills many reindeer belonging to the Sami, the indigenous population of northern Scandinavia. The wolverine is also an endangered species. The Swedish state 'owns' the wolverines. That is, they are protected and hunting is illegal. The Sami people is collectively compensated for reindeer killed by all predators. The reason why the individual reindeer owner is not compensated is that the harm caused by individual predators cannot be identified.

The intended conservation is ineffective, however, due to poaching. To solve the problem, Sellenthin and Skogh (2002) suggest a property rights regime whereby Sami communities with reindeer herders as members are the owners of the wolverines. Reindeer breeding and wolverine protection thus become joint operations. It is suggested that remuneration for wolverine protection be received from the Swedish state, which pays for wolverines living in the grazing area. The system is supposed to be financed by a redistribution of current subsidies to the Sami.

Are conditions for efficient conservation met by the suggested property rights regime? First, the outcome of the ownership (wolverines in the area) must be measurable. There are 270 wolverines living in Sweden. The wolverine is relatively stationary and, due to new techniques, countable with high enough accuracy at relatively small costs. It is more complicated to address ownership of, for example, bears and wolves, which move over large areas. Second, property rights need to be assigned to parties that have information and control of hunting and competing activities. The Sami people is an obvious candidate. The reason why collective ownership of the Sami villages is suggested is that the reindeer farming is already organized collectively. It is essential that the owners profit from the conservation. Income from trophy hunting may be possible for animals like the African elephant, but not for wolverines, which are hunted because of their damage to farming. The public authorities, therefore, have to pay a price for their conservation. International support will be required for predators in poor countries. The motivation for international support is that the survival of the species is a global public good (Chapter 4, Section 7). Finally, the legal assignment of the property right will never be fully adequate. It must be possible, therefore, to renegotiate rights and duties. Parties involved in conservation must thus be able to contract and enforce the trade at low transaction costs. The Sami communities and the reindeer farmers seem to be the relevant partners, connected to each other in a long-term relationship. Hence they will probably succeed in regulating rights to trespassing wolverines and similar matters.

public good. Finally, it should be noted that an important merit of the suggested ownership reform may not only save the animals; it will also reduce poaching, an environmental crime. That is, an inappropriate ownership structure may cause both inefficiency and criminality.

3. INSUFFICIENT TORT LAW AND SAFETY REGULATION

In Chapter 15 we discussed the applicability of tort law and insurance. A conclusion was that these legal instruments have important applications, but also limitations. Hence there may be an argument for the use other legal measures, especially safety regulations. Here we continue the examination of circumstances where liability rules may not suffice to deter environmental harm optimally, and add a discussion on regulatory interventions that may be used as a complement. Steven Shavell (1984a and 1984b) advances several criteria that influence the choice between safety regulation and liability rules.

Information deficiencies have often been advanced as a cause for government intervention through regulation. A proper operation of a liability system according to the model presented in Chapter 14 requires information on, for example, the existing legal rules, the accident risk, efficient measures to prevent accidents and so on. In practice the choice of legal instrument depends more on who (the parties in an accident setting or central authorities) is best informed.

The parties that may be involved at an accident generally have much better information on the accident risk than that possessed by the regulatory body. The parties themselves have, in principle, the best information on the costs and benefits of the activity that they undertake and of ways to prevent accidents. This 'assumption of information' is, however, reversed if it becomes clear that some risks are not readily appreciated by the parties in an accident. Costs that hit external parties cannot always be easily assessed by the parties involved. Therefore the question arises whether either the government or the parties involved can acquire the information at least cost.

If the potential damage is so large that it may exceed the wealth of the liable party, liability rules will not provide optimal incentives. The injurer will only take care to avoid an accident equal to his wealth, which can be lower than the care required to avoid the total accident harm. This is a simple application of the principle that the deterrent effect of tort liability only works if the injurer is sufficiently solvent to pay for the damages he causes. If an injurer is protected against such liability, a problem of underdeterrence exists (Chapter 15, Section 9). If mandatory insurance is available, it could overcome the problems of underdeterrence, provided that the moral hazard problem can be cured (Chapter 15, Section 3). Safety regulations may alternatively overcome the problem of underdeterrence. Care is determined *ex ante* by regulation combined with enforcement instruments that induce the potential injurer to comply with the regulatory standard, irrespective of his wealth. However, a limitation exists if the regulation is enforced by monetary sanctions only. If the damage exceeds the injurer's wealth, the insolvency problem remains. However, if a safety regulation is introduced because of a potential insolvency problem, the regulation may in the end be enforced by non-monetary sanctions such as imprisonment, which also have serious shortcomings.

The absence of a liability claim is another argument to enforce care by means of safety regulations rather than through liability rules. There are a number of reasons why a lawsuit is not brought. Sometimes an injurer can escape liability because the harm is thinly spread among a number of victims. As a consequence, the damage incurred by every individual victim is so small that he has no incentive to bring a suit. In particular, this problem will arise if the damage is not caused to an individual but to a common property, such as, for example, surface waters, in which each member of the population has a minor interest.

In addition, a long time might have elapsed before the damage becomes apparent; in this case much of the necessary evidence may be either lost or not obtained. Another problem is that if the damage only manifests itself years after the activity, the injurer might have gone out of business.

A related problem is that it is often hard to prove that a causal link exists between an activity and a type of damage. The burden of proof becomes more significant with increasing passage of time since the damaging incident took place. Often a victim will not recognize that the harm has been caused by a tort, but might think that his particular ailment, for example cancer, had a 'natural cause', associated with bad health in general. For all these reasons a liability suit might not be brought and hence safety regulation is required to ensure that the potential injurer takes efficient care.

When examining liability versus regulation, the administrative costs of both systems should also be compared. Liability rules are clearly costly in terms of time for both parties and in court fees. A part of these costs is borne by the whole community, such as the cost of the legal system, fees for the judges and so on. Regulation incurs costs for the community, including the costs of making the regulation, setting the standards, passing the statutes and so on, and of subsequent enforcement.

Here the liability system seems to have an advantage: the administrative costs of the court system are only incurred if an accident has actually happened. The main advantage of the tort system is that accidents will be prevented by the deterrent effect of being held liable and having to pay damages to the victim. In case of safety regulation the costs of passing the regulation and of enforcing it are always there, whether there are accidents or not. Recall that enforcement of regulations by criminal law is costly both in terms of policing and punishment. It may also be ineffective because of a small detection rate and insufficient or very costly punishments (Chapter 16, Sections 2 and 3).

4. ENVIRONMENTAL POLLUTION

4.1 Reasons for Regulation

We will now discuss how these criteria of regulation relate to environmental pollution. If one takes the criteria for safety regulation discussed above and applies them to the potential risk caused by environmental pollution, there is no doubt that liability rules alone are not sufficient. On the other hand, after the occurrence in case of an accident there may always be an *ex post* issue of liability.

If one looks at the first criterion, that of information costs, it must be stressed that an assessment of the risks of a certain activity often requires expert knowledge and judgement. This is especially true for development risks that are new and unknown. Small organizations may lack the incentive or resources to invest in research to find out what the risks are. Also, there will be little incentive to carry out intensive research if the results are automatically available to competitors in the market: this is the well-known 'free-rider' problem. This problem can partially be countered by legal instruments granting an intellectual property to the results of the research. However, the problem remains that it may not be possible for small companies to undertake studies on the optimal technology for preventing environmental damage. Therefore, it is often more efficient to allow the government to support research on the optimal technology (for example in an environmental research institute). The results of this research can then be passed on to the parties in the market through the regulation. Hence the setting of environmental standards in regulation can be seen as a means of passing on information about the minimal environmental technology required.

Moreover, it is more efficient for the government to acquire information on the optimal emission standard than it would be, for example, for an individual firm to find out what additional reduction in pollution would produce an optimal reduction in the expected damages from the emission. There are undeniable 'economies of scale' advantages in regulation.

Further, the insolvency argument points in the direction of regulation. Pollution can be caused by individuals or firms with assets smaller than the damage. Also, a small firm could cause harm to a large number of individuals or to entire ecosystems. Moreover, most firms have been incorporated as a legal entity and, therefore, benefit from limited liability. That is, the individual shareholders are not liable to the extent of their personal assets. The liability is limited to the value of the shares.

In addition, the chance of a liability suit being brought for damage caused by wrongful pollution is naturally very small. The damage is often spread over a large number of people, who will have difficulty in organizing themselves to bring a lawsuit. In addition, the damage could only become apparent some years after the emission took place. This will bring proof of causation and latency problems, which will make it difficult for a lawsuit to be brought against the polluter.

For these reasons it is clear that some form of government regulation of environmental pollution is necessary.

BOX 17.2 SAFETY REGULATION IN PRACTICE

In many cases the regulation consists of licences or permits in which an administrative authority fixes an emission standard that must be followed by the potential polluter. These licences play a crucial role in environmental policy in most countries. An improvement of environmental quality will mostly be effected by imposing more stringent emission standards in administrative licences. Hence the general requirement that emissions are controlled through licences and that the quality and quantity of the emissions are regulated by the conditions in this licence is a cornerstone of environmental law. Since these licences are administrative acts, in most legal systems environmental law is considered to be a part of administrative law. Criminal law usually only comes into the picture to sanction a violation of administrative regulations or emission standards in the licences.

Although environmental pollution is in the first place controlled through these administrative licences, in individual cases there may still be damage to the environment. Then again liability under tort law comes into the picture and the question is raised of the influence of regulation on the liability system and vice versa.

Although it is difficult to examine whether the environmental regulation is generally also effective in reducing environmental harm, some studies have attempted to examine the effectiveness of safety regulation in controlling it. These studies do not address the specific quality of every environmental law, but examine whether regulation has generally been more important in reducing environmental harm than liability rules. Dewees (1992a and 1992b) demonstrated that in North America the quality of the environment has improved substantially as a result of regulatory efforts, not so much in response to legal action in tort.

This empirical evidence of the success of regulation, compared to tort law, has been stressed in Dewees et al. (1996). They hold that the large regulatory effort to improve the environment has met with considerable success when measured by the reduction of emissions, but that it is more difficult to argue that the environmental regulations of the 1970s in the USA had an equally considerable influence on the ambient environmental quality. Moreover, they also stress that while environmental regulation is a determining factor in pollutant emissions and ambient concentrations, other non-regulatory factors such as economic growth and the weather also influence environmental quality.

Thus there is a strong argument to control environmental risk through *ex ante* regulation. Nevertheless, in individual cases there will be damage to the environment. Then again liability under tort comes into the picture. The question of how regulation influences the liability system and vice versa has been addressed by Rose-Ackerman (1995), who compared US and European experiences. She noted that the fact that there are many arguments in favour of *ex ante* regulation of the environment does not mean that the tort system is obsolete. One reason to continue to rely on the tort system is that the effectiveness of (environmental) regulation depends on enforcement, which may be both costly and weak. In addition, the influence of lobby groups on regulation can to some extent be overcome by combining safety regulation and liability rules. Moreover, safety regulation, for example emission standards in licences, can be quickly outdated and often lacks flexibility, which equally merits a combination with tort rules.

Hence, from the above it follows that although there is a strong case for safety regulation to control environmental risk, tort rules will still play an important role. This obviously raises the question whether compliance with regulation will affect the liability issue.

4.2 Violation of Regulation and Liability

An interesting question to be answered in this respect is whether a violation of a regulatory standard should automatically be considered a fault under tort law and thus lead to liability of the licensee.

If the licence sets the regulatory standard at the efficient care level, a violation of the regulation ought to lead to liability. However, the costs of following the regulatory standard are not the same for all injurers. Following the standard may thus be inefficient in some cases. The question is whether this means that these injurers should not be held liable if they violate the regulatory standard. This problem can be compared with the *bonus pater familias* standard used in tort law. A detailed individualization of standards of efficient care may be the optimal solution, disregarding the costs of an individualized standard setting. Therefore, the legal system sets the required level of care at an average level, the so-called *bonus pater familias* standard. The same can be said for regulation. If various groups can reduce pollution at different costs, a separate standard for each group is efficient. In most cases, however, the regulator will not be able to identify specific types. Therefore, a single regulatory standard will be used. Although one may argue that a failure to satisfy the regulatory requirement should not necessarily result in a finding of negligence, most legal systems generally consider a breach of a regulatory duty a fault.

One of the reasons for introducing safety regulation to prevent environmental damage is, as was mentioned above, that the regulator may possess better information than the parties involved. Hence the regulation passes on information to the parties on the efficient standard of care. The regulation also gives information to the judge, who has to evaluate the behaviour of the injurer *ex post* in a liability case. The judge may lack the information necessary to find out whether in a particular case an injurer should not be held to follow the regulatory standard, for example, because he posed a smaller risk than usual. Therefore, particularly in environmental cases, a judge will accept a finding of negligence as soon as a regulatory standard has been breached. An advantage of this system is that it gives victims incentives to prove that the regulatory standard has been breached. This makes the victim an enforcer of safety regulation. He can claim compensation under the negligence rule as soon as a causal relationship between the violation of the regulatory standard and his damage is established.[1] Thus statutory standards can be applied to define negligence.

4.3 Compliance with Regulation and Liability

Whereas a breach of a regulatory standard may result automatically in a finding of negligence, the question arises whether the opposite is true; more specifically, whether following a regulatory standard excuses from liability. In environmental law this is particularly important, since the conditions under which an emission of pollutants is allowed are mostly laid down in a permit. Obviously these permits and their effects on liability can take various forms. In some cases permits and regulations are fairly general, but in other cases they specify emission limits. It is especially in the latter case, that is when specifically allowed releases in a permit have been respected, that industry often argues that as long as they follow the conditions of that licence, no negligence in tort law is possible. This is often referred to as the 'justificative effect of a licence' or the 'regulatory compliance defence'.

Many legal systems do not accept a regulatory compliance defence. There is an economic rationale for this rule. If compliance with a regulatory standard or licence automatically resulted in a release from liability, the potential injurer would have no incentive to invest more in care than the regulation asks from him, even if additional care could still reduce the expected accident costs beneficially. A first reason to hold an injurer liable (if the other conditions for liability are met), although he has followed the regulatory standard, is that this standard is often merely a minimum. The complete 'compliance defence' prevents any incentive to take precaution in excess of the regulated standard. Exposure to liability will give the potential injurer incentives to take all efficient precautions, even if this requires more than just following the licence. This, by the way, holds under both negligence and strict liability. Since the regulatory standard cannot always take into account all efficient precautionary measures an injurer can take, testing the measures taken by the injurer even though the regulatory standard was followed will provide additional incentives. Allowing a regulatory compliance defence would also largely remove the beneficial incentive effects of strict liability. As we argued above, strict liability has the advantage that it provides the injurer with incentives to take measures to reduce the risk (prevention and activity level), even if regulatory conditions were followed. Burrows (1999) argues that the complete compliance defence prevents any precaution in excess of the regulated standard. If there is serious underenforcement of standards, the role of liability as an incentive to take precautions remains important.

BOX 17.3 REGULATORY COMPLIANCE IN DUTCH CASE LAW

The regulatory compliance defence is rejected in some legal systems, such as in Belgium and in the Netherlands. It is argued that the basic idea is that the administrative authority, when granting a licence and setting permit conditions, cannot take into account the possible harm that the licensed activity might cause to all possible third parties. Their rights on compensation for damages may not be impaired simply because the operator of a plant followed the conditions of a licence. Legal doctrine and case law clearly state that keeping the permit conditions is just a minimum; in addition, the plant owner has to take all possible precautions as deemed necessary under tort law to prevent his licensed activity causing harm to third parties.

For instance, in Dutch case law it is generally accepted that following the conditions of a licence does not release a plant owner from potential liability. An exception would only exist if the interests of the potential victims were clearly taken into account when the conditions of the permit were set.[1] This point was made very clear in a famous case in the Dutch Supreme Court that dealt with pollution caused by the French salt mines in the Alsace region.[2] The Salt Mines argued that the emissions were within the limits set by their permit and, therefore, not illegal. The Court, however, judged that the licence had not taken into account the potential harmful effects of the emissions for third parties and could, therefore, not release the Salt Mines from liability.

Note:

1. M. Rus-van der Veld, 'Onrechtmatige daad en vergunning', in N.S.J.Koeman, W.J.Ouwerkerk and J.M. Van Dunné (eds), *Civielrechtelijke aansprakelijkheid voor milieuschade*, *Vereniging voor Milieurecht*, 1987–4, Zwolle: Tjeenk Willink, p. 111 and J.H.Nieuwenhuis, 'Blinddoek en balans in het milieurecht. Drie manieren om belangen af te wegen', in A.M. Hol and M.A. Loth (eds), *Dilemma's van aansprakelijkheid*, 1991, pp. 44–7.
2. Supreme Court, 23 September 1988.

A second reason is that exposure to liability might be a good remedy for the unavoidable capturing and public choice effects that play a role when permits are granted. If a permit always released a party from liability, all a plant operator would have to do would be to obtain a good permit with easy conditions from a friendly civil servant. That would then exclude any lawsuit for damages from a potential victim. Obviously the capturing and public choice effects should also be addressed via direct tools. In this respect one should mention the liability, even under criminal law, of the licensor. Liability on the licensor (and appropriate sanctions within administrative law) can provide incentives to civil servants to act efficiently when granting licences.[2] This, however, still requires tort law to take into account the fact that regulatory standards are not always set efficiently. If the optimal level of care is higher than the regulatory standard, liability will efficiently provide additional incentives.

Moreover, tort law can also be seen as a 'stop-gap' for situations not dealt with by the statute.[3] This makes it clear that the exposure to liability notwithstanding the permit is an important guarantee that the plant operator will take efficient care. Finally, Schmitz (2000) has provided an additional justification for combining liability and safety regulation, given that this combination is welfare-improving if wealth varies among injurers.

5. LAND USE AND LOBBYING

In the previous sections we focused on safety regulation and pollution in already-located industries. Geographical regulation via zoning is another dimension of environmental regulation. Industries, farming, forestry, residential areas, national parks and so on are separated to reduce disturbances. Industries receive permits to locate in specific areas. The decision on location may be local, regional, national or international. The economics of governmental level, applicable to both emission permits and zoning, is discussed in the next section.

The basic argument in favour of zoning, as compared to mutual agreements including involved parties, is the transaction costs in multilateral negotiations (Chapter 12, Section 4). The large numbers involved may make a mutually beneficial agreement impossible, although there are economies of specialization. Zoning allows us to have national parks and protection of rare species, as well as polluting industries.

Location permits are, of course, combined with emission standards, liability and safety regulations as discussed above. The discussion on optimal specificity and local preference (Chapter 11, Section 3) is also applicable to zoning.

The value of fixed property depends greatly on its location. Community planning is, therefore, important for owners of fixed property. Exploitation permits and public investments in infrastructure are thus of large value to industry. Hence special interest groups mobilize to protect their interests.

The influence of private interest in environmental law has been addressed a number of times in the various chapters (see, for example, Chapter 10, Section 3). It undoubtedly plays a role with respect to the issue of instrument choice, zoning included. We have presented a variety of instruments that can be used to control environmental pollution. The literature suggests under what kind of circumstances a particular type of instrument would be optimal. In practice, however, these economic prescriptions may not be followed. A reason why emission taxes are seldom used in the USA, for example, is that firms prefer emission standards to taxes. Standards may serve as barriers to entry to new firms, thus raising the profits of existing firms. Charges, on the other hand, do not preclude entry by new firms and represent an additional cost for existing firms on the market, as argued by Buchanan and Tullock (1975). This basic point has been elaborated by many other scholars examining the implications of rent-seeking for pollution taxation.

Hahn and Hester (1989) pointed out that the policy instruments are almost never used in the way that is suggested by economic theory. Emission charges, for example, are used as a revenue-raising device with few direct effects on polluters, and many marketable permit approaches are not really designed to create markets. Through *grandfathering*, that is, by giving a permit to the already-established firm, old firms are often protected. In addition, in cases where the economic prescriptions (incentive-based instruments) are followed, there is some evidence that emissions trading is used as a loophole by which industry can forestall compliance. Hahn (1990a) also argues that the varying interest group attitudes in, for example, the USA and Europe may account for the fact that European countries tend to rely more on the use of fees, whereas marketable permits have been introduced on a relatively important scale in the USA. Hence the selection of the appropriate mix of policy instruments will to a large extent be determined by the way political choices are actually made in different countries.

6. VARIOUS LEVELS OF GOVERNMENT

6.1 Criteria for (De)centralization

In Chapter 11, Section 3 we discussed whether environmental standards should be uniform or flexible. From a legal perspective this refers to the question whether environmental standards should be harmonized or differentiated. We will expand on this issue now by first looking at criteria for (de)centralization in general; then we will look for criteria for centralization of environmental issues and ask what the consequences are for environmental standard-setting.

BOX 17.4 INSTRUMENT CHOICE AND INTRINSIC MOTIVATION

Recently Frey (1997, 1999) pointed to the importance of intrinsic motivation of citizens in the formation of environmental morality. He argued that some instruments might encourage the intrinsic motivation, whereas others rather undermine it. Frey argues that an environmental policy which is solely based on command and control undermines environmental morality, because it reduces the self-determination of people. Moreover, complex and abstract regulations are unlikely to improve environmental morality. The same is, however, true according to Frey for tradable emission rights. To pay for being able to undertake an undesirable activity – the pollution of the environment – can be compared with the indulgences sold in the Middle Ages: the sense of punishment induced by sinning is lost as a result of the 'licence to pollute'. Emission rights of course tend to reduce pollution because they make violation costly, but on the other hand they destroy the intrinsic motivation to safeguard the environment.

The best way to promote environmental morality in the short term is, according to Frey, by appeals and participation procedures, and, in the long run, by education. Moreover, when legal regulations have an expressive function, this supports environmental morality. This is the case with easily comprehensible regulations whose punishments fit exactly the damage done to nature.

Because market-oriented policy instruments, such as tradable permits, do not always support environmental morality, Frey suggests the use of complementary environmental policies. However, a complementary policy should not be identified with a 'systems approach' in the sense that everything should be done at the same time. The aim must be to exploit the strong points of each instrument, while at the same time compensating for the approach's negative aspects.

Should (environmental) regulation be promulgated at central (European or federal) level or at a more decentralized level? This question has been addressed in the 'economics of federalism'. The starting-point for the analysis is usually the theory of Tiebout (1956) on the optimal provision of local public goods. Tiebout argued that people with the same preferences cluster together in communities. Competition between local authorities will, under certain restrictive conditions, lead to local efficiency. For instance, if there are in one community citizens with a high preference for sports and in another one a majority of citizens with a preference for opera, the first community can construct sporting facilities, whereas the second can provide an opera house. If someone living in the second community prefers sporting facilities instead of the opera house, he can move to the first community, which apparently provides services that better suit his preferences. Competition will thus prevail between communities. The idea is that well-informed citizens will move to the community that provides the local services that are best adapted to their personal preferences.

This 'voting with the feet' idea not only applies to community services, but also, for example, to fiscal decisions and environmental choices. In addition, the idea of citizens moving to the community that provides services which best correspond with their preferences can also be applied with respect to legal rules. Thus it has been argued that competition between legislators may lead to legal systems in competition with each other. The idea is that in an optimal world, citizens will cluster together in states that provide legal rules that correspond to their preferences. Well-informed citizens, who would be dissatisfied with the legislation provided, can move (vote by the feet) to the community that provides legislation that best corresponds with their preferences. Obviously, this system only works if certain conditions are met. One is that citizens have adequate information on the contents of the legal rules provided by the various legislators. Another is that it is not too costly to move.

The Tiebout model can be used as a starting-point in the analysis of current legal systems. Van den Bergh (1997) uses the theory to provide criteria for centralization/decentralization within the European Union. If competition between decentralized legislators will lead to an optimal provision of legal rules, the central question is: why centralize? Thus Van den Bergh questions a part of the current discussion in the legal literature that focuses on the opposite question: why should there be decentralization? He suggests instead an approach called 'bottom-up federalization'. That is, the analysis should start by investigating the local level. Since the local level often has the best information on local problems and on the preferences of citizens, local decisions may have an advantage. However, when there is a good reason, decision-making should be moved to a higher level. Van den Bergh also argues that there may, indeed, be a variety of reasons why the local level is not best suited to take decisions, and that central decision-making can lead to more efficient results.

We now apply the criteria for centralization to environmental problems. The Tiebout argument in favour of competition between local communities works if the problem to be regulated is, indeed, local. Once the problem to be regulated has a transboundary character, there may be an argument to shift powers to a higher legal level. This corresponds with the basic insight that if the problem of regulation crosses the borders of competence, the decision-making power should be at a higher regulatory level, preferably resting with an authority which has jurisdiction over a territory large enough to deal adequately with the problem. This argument could play a role with respect to environmental problems. Indeed, many environmental problems cross national borders.

A great many of the environmental directives in the EU fit into this economic criterion for community action. One can refer, for example, to the regulation on the transboundary shipment of waste,[4] but also to many other directives which regulate pollution of a transboundary character.[5] Many environmental directives thus deal with pollution problems that cross the borders of one single Member State. Hence they can be justified. Nonetheless, many environmental directives also deal with local problems that do not cross national borders. The question, therefore, remains whether an economic rationale can be found for European jurisdiction in those cases where the effects of pollutants are confined within the borders of the relevant Member States.

6.2 Race to the Bottom?

There is an economic argument for central regulation of local pollution problems, that is, the risk that a 'race to the bottom' would emerge to attract foreign investments. As a result of this race, countries would fail to enact or enforce efficient legislation. The argument may play a role in environmental cases as well. That is, local governments may compete with lenient environmental legislation to attract industry. The result would be an overall reduction of environmental quality below efficient levels.

This race-to-the-bottom argument, claiming that competition among jurisdictions will be destructive, corresponds with the general European legal argument that the creation of harmonized conditions of competition is necessary to avoid distortions. This argument was traditionally used to harmonize legislation of the Member States in a variety of areas. Simply stated, the argument is that complying with varying jurisdictions confers costs on industry. If the jurisdictions vary, these costs will differ. Thus conditions of competition within the common market would not be equal. The argument apparently assumes that a total equality of conditions of competition is necessary for the functioning of the common market. 'Levelling the playing field' for European industry remains the central message.

There are, however, examples showing that an economic market integration is possible with differentiated legal systems, without the distortions announced by the race-to-the-bottom argument. Public choice scholars have often advanced the Swiss federal model as an example where economic market integration goes hand in hand with differentiated legal systems. A similar argument against the race-to-the-bottom rationale for central environmental regulation can also be found in the American example. Revesz (1992, 1995) stresses that central standard setting-would not be an effective response to the race-to-the-bottom problem, since the local communities concerned would have other means to attract industry, if they wish (relaxed regulatory controls in other areas, subsidies and the like).

The mere fact that conditions of competition differ is not an endangerment of a common market. There can be differences in conditions for a variety of reasons (wages, climate, taxes, and so on). Differences in environmental legislation only pose a problem if environmental costs are considerably different between the Member States. If these differences lead to relocation of firms to the state with the lowest standards the 'race-for-the-bottom' argument is valid, as is the 'pollution haven' hypothesis (see Box 17.5).

BOX 17.5 A MOVEMENT TO POLLUTION HAVENS?

If there is a race to pollution havens, there is an argument in favour of centralization. The question therefore arises whether there is empirical evidence that states can attract industry with lenient environmental standards. The empirical evidence is rather weak. Repetto (n.d.) argues that pollution control costs are only a minor fraction of the total sales of manufacturing industries. Jaffe et al. (1995) have argued that empirical evidence shows that the effects of environmental regulations are 'either small, statistically insignificant or not robust to tests of model specification'. They argue that the stringency of environmental regulations might have some effect on new firms in their decision to locate for the first time, but that this will not induce existing firms to relocate. They equally argue that other criteria such as tax level, public services and the unionization of the labour force have a much more significant impact on the location decision than environmental regulation. This empirical evidence has been somewhat contradicted by Xing and Kolstad (1995), who argue that the laxity of environmental regulations in a host country is a significant determinant of foreign direct investment from the US chemical industry. The more lax the regulations, the more likely the country is to attract foreign investment.

This discussion shows that there is no clear race to the bottom as far as environmental standards are concerned. There is also some evidence that states try to strive for high environmental standards, even if this puts extra costs or burdens on their industry. Some countries may, in fact, be more involved in a 'race to the top' (Van den Bergh et al., 1996, pp. 141–2). The reason may be an ambition to attract customers, employees and financiers who are concerned about environmental issues.

There is an additional economic argument in favour of centralization based on transaction costs. The argument is often advanced by European legal scholars pleading for harmonization of private law in Europe: differences in legal systems are very complex – they only serve Brussels law firms. This argument neglects the fact that there may be substantial benefits from differentiation that is adapted to the preferences of individuals. The crucial question, therefore, is whether the possible transaction costs savings of harmonization outweigh the benefits of differentiated legal rules.

All in all, the economic argument to harmonize environmental rules with respect to problems that are not transboundary is relatively weak. Nevertheless, many European directives deal with, for example, drinking or bathing water, although these resources are typically national or local.

6.3 The Environment as an International Public Good

The question remains whether endangered species should be protected on an international level. From an economic point of view, one may think of the protection of habitat and entire ecosystems as an international public good (Chapter 4, Section 7). It could, for instance, be argued that the international community, rather than the Swedish state, should pay for the wolverines as described in Box 17.1. Because extinction is an international concern, some international body like the UN would be an appropriate financier. However, the UN lacks financial resources and taxation power. That may explain why national states have agreed to protect threatened species in their own area.

Suppose, for instance, there is a hypothetical turtle that only has a habitat in Greece. If the issue is merely local, the Greek population should decide on whether or not to protect the turtle. However, if the survival is a global public good, it is an international concern. The financing of the species may, nevertheless, be delegated by conventions to national states. In that case it is up to Greece to interpret the international agreement and to decide, as a second best. Another option is that the EU decides on the matter.

Wils (1994) classifies the protection of endangered species on a European level as justified by the fact that this endangerment causes 'psychic spillovers'. The argument then goes that the endangerment of a Greek turtle also harms the interests of, for example, Dutch citizens, or future generations, who will suffer a psychic spillover from the fact that the Greek turtle is extinct. In other words, Wils gives an international public good argument for protection of the turtle. A remaining question is who shall decide on the value of the turtle to humanity. Here economics has nothing to say. It is a political and ethical issue (Chapter 8, Section 7). The reason why it is suggested that the European Union should protect the turtle, instead of the UN or Greece, for example, may be that Wils distrusts the protecting capability of the global, as well as the local, body.

6.4 Guarantee of Environmental Quality

Another important policy argument states that all European citizens should be guaranteed a similar environmental quality. This is sometimes referred to as the protection of the 'European environmental and cultural heritage and human health'. If, at the policy level, one accepts this argument, it could be used to harmonize environmental quality.

Note that the reason for centralization in such a case is not the economic need for market integration, or for efficient environmental protection, but for the political desire to guarantee all citizens within the Union a similar, or at least basic, environmental quality. If one accepts that a basic environmental quality should be guaranteed, the next step is to ask how these standards can be achieved. The quality standards must be influenced by the specific emissions coming from various sources. However, according to the theory of optimal specificity of legal rules, the costs to reach a certain level of environmental protection may well vary according to location-specific circumstances. Indeed, the local conditions in, for example, Belgium or Germany may be totally different from those, say, in Portugal or Greece. Hence the emission limit values needed to reach a similar environmental quality within the Union will have to take these differences into account. The conclusion therefore is that where the environmental quality (target) to be reached is uniform, the emission limit values must vary according to the location-specific circumstances.

This approach of harmonized target standards, but differentiated emission limit values, has not been European policy so far. Indeed, the already mentioned Directive 464/76 attempts to harmonize emission limit values, and the recent IPPC Directive still explicitly refers to the setting of emission limit values at the Community level.[6] This idea of harmonizing emission limit values runs counter to the idea of reaching a uniform environmental quality. Harmonized emission limit values will obviously lead to differentiated environmental quality.

A consequence of accepting the idea that emission limit values may be differentiated is that those in less polluted Member States might be more lenient than in already more polluted states. Thus the conclusion is that if the policy goal to be reached is a uniform environmental quality, a harmonization of conditions of competition is not the aim. Harmonized competition would lead precisely to the opposite result of differentiated environmental quality.

A crucial question is why differentiated emission limit values are not followed in European legal practice. Instead, there is a tendency to harmonize emission limit values at the European level. An answer can be found in public choice theory, which pays a great deal of attention to the role of interest groups in legislation. As soon as inefficiencies in legislation are discovered, public choice scholars may investigate whether the legislation is the result of demand from interest groups. The lobbying activities at the European level are extremely strong. Also with respect to environmental standard-setting one can detect intensive rent-seeking behaviour.

It is understandable why special interest groups representing industry may lobby in favour of a harmonization of European limit values. Interest groups have incentives to force their strict (national) regulation upon the European level. Thereby, industry can force foreign competitors to follow the national regulation (with which they already comply). The result is that industry will lobby to erect barriers to entry. Indeed, industry in heavily regulated (and probably polluted) areas will force its stringent emission limit values upon its competitors. This is precisely what took place during the discussions concerning the IPPC Directive. Strong lobbying in favour of emission limit values at the Community level was undertaken by German industry. Thus it becomes clear that the 'harmonization of conditions of competition' argument is used to serve the interests of industries in heavily regulated areas to erect barriers to entry. Their (southern) competitors from Member States with more lenient environmental standards were not able to comply with these more stringent environmental standards. Hence environmental law can be used to limit market entry and environmental law may be abused to serve private-interest goals.

NOTES

1. Faure and Van den Bergh (1987).
2. Note, however, that industry argues against such a liability of the licensor, claiming that this may entail the risk that licensors would be too reluctant to allow emissions, if this could give rise to their liability.
3. Rose-Ackerman (1992), p. 123.
4. Regulation 259/93 of 1 February 1993, *OJ*, 1993, L 30.
5. This is certainly also the case for Directive 464/76 on the Discharge of Dangerous Substances into the Aquatic Environment. For other examples, see Van den Bergh et al. (1996), pp. 131–2.
6. Art. 18 of the IPPC Directive explicitly refers to the possibility of setting Community emission limit values.

FURTHER READING

Burrows, P. (1999), 'Combining regulation and liability for the control of external costs', *International Review of Law and Economics*, **19**, 227–42.

Dewees, D., Duff, D. and Trebilcock, M. (1996), *Exploring the Domain of Accident Law: Taking the Facts Seriously*, New York and Oxford: Oxford University Press.

Elliott, E.D., Ackerman, B.A. and Millian, J.C. (1985), 'Toward a Theory of Statutory Evolution: the Federalization of Environmental Law', *Journal of Law, Economics & Organization*, **1**, 313–40.

Faure, M. and Van den Bergh, R. (1987), 'Negligence, Strict Liability and Regulation on Safety under Belgian Law: An Introductory Economic Analysis', *Geneva Papers on Risk and Insurance*, 95–114.

Faure, M. and Lefevere, J. (1995a), 'Protecting Drinking Water Quality against Contamination by Pesticides: An Alternative Regulatory Framework', *Review of European Community and International Environmental Law*, 321–6.

Faure, M. and Lefevere, J.G.J. (1995b), 'Some Public Interest and Private Interest Aspects of Environmental Standard Setting in the European Community', in D. Mayers (ed.), *The Evolution of Rules for a Single European Market, II: Rules, Democracy and the Environment*, Luxembourg: OOPEC.

Gunningham, N. and Grabosky, P. (1998), *Smart Regulation. Designing Environmental Policy*, Oxford: Clarendon Press.

Hahn, R.W. (1989), 'Economic prescriptions for environmental problems: how the patient followed the doctor's orders', *Journal of Economic Perspectives*, **3**, 95–114.

Jaffe, A.B., Peterson, S., Portney, P. and Stavins, R. (1995), 'Environmental Regulation and the Competitiveness of US Manufacturing: What does the Evidence tell us?', *Journal of Economic Literature*, **33**, 132–63.

Kolstad, C.D., Ulen, T.S. and Johnson, G.V. (1990), 'Ex Post Liability for Harm vs. Ex Ante Safety Regulation: Substitutes or Complements?', *American Economic Review*, **80**, 888–901.

Lee, D.R. (1985), 'Rent-seeking and its implications for pollution taxation', *Southern Economic Journal*, **53**: 731–44.

Mackaay, E. (1982), *Economics of information and the law*, Boston: Kluwer.

Oates, W.E. and Schwab, R. (1988), 'Economic Competition among Jurisdictions: Efficiency Enhancing or Distortion Inducing?', *Journal of Public Economics*, **35**, 333–54.

Oates, W.E., Portney, P. and McGartland, A. (1989), 'The *net* benefits of incentive based regulation: a case study of an environmental standard setting', *American Economic Review*, **79**, 1233–42.

Pelzman, S. and Tideman, T.N. (1972), 'Local v. National Pollution Control: Note', *American Economic Review*.

Revesz, R. (1992), 'Rehabilitating Interstate Competition: Rethinking the Race to the Bottom Rationale for Federal Environmental Regulation', *New York University Law Review*, **67**, 1210–54. Reprinted in *Land Use & Environment Law Review*, 1995.

Revesz, R. (1996), 'Federalism and Interstate Environmental Externalities', *University of Pennsylvania Law Review*, **144**, 2341–416.

Rose-Ackerman, S. (1991), 'Regulation and the Law of Torts', *American Economic Review, Papers and Proceedings*, 54–8.

Schoenbrod, D. (1996), 'Why States, not EPA, should set Pollution Standards', *Regulation*, **4**, 18–25.
Shavell, S. (1984a), 'Liability for Harm versus Regulation of Safety', *Journal of Legal Studies*, 357–74.
Shavell, S. (1985), 'Criminal law and the optimal use of non-monetary sanctions as a deterrent', *Columbia Law Review*, 1232–62.
Skogh, G. (1982), 'Public insurance and accident prevention', *International Review of Law and Economics*, **2**, 67–80
Tiebout, C. (1956), 'A Pure Theory of Local Expenditures', *Journal of Political Economy*, **64**, 416–24.
Van den Bergh, R. (1998), 'Subsidiarity as an Economic Demarcation Principle and the Emergence of European Private Law', *Maastricht Journal of European and Comparative Law*, **5**, 129–52.
Wils, W.P.J. (1994), 'Subsidiarity and the E.C. Environmental Policy: Taking People's Concerns Seriously', *Journal of Environmental Law*, 85–90.

Bibliography

Abelson, P. (1979), *Cost Benefit Analysis and Environmental Problems*, Farnborough, Hants: Saxon House.

Ackerman, B.A. (ed.) (1975), *Economic Foundations of Property Law*, Boston: Little Brown and Company.

Ackerman, B.A. and Stewart, R.B. (1988), 'Reforming environmental law: the democratic case for market incentives', *Columbia Journal of Environmental Law*, **13**, 171–99.

Adams, M. (1989), 'New Activities and the Efficient Liability Rules', in M. Faure and R. Van den Bergh (eds), *Essays in Law and Economics. Corporations, Accident Prevention and Compensation for Losses*, Antwerp: Maklu.

Adams, M. and Shavell, S. (1990), 'Zür Strafbarkeit des Versuchs', *Goldammers, Archiv für Strafrecht*, 337.

Adler, J.H. (1996), 'Rent Seeking Behind the Green Curtain', *Regulation*, 26–34.

Agnello, R.J. and Donnelley L.P. (1975a), 'Property Rights and Efficiency in the Oyster Industry', *Journal of Law and Economics*, 521–33.

Agnello, R.J. and Donnelley L.P. (1975b), 'Property Rights in the Fisheries', *Southern Economic Journal*, **42**, 253–61.

Alchian, A.A., and Allen, W. (eds) (1974), *University Economics*, 3rd edn, London: Prentice-Hall.

Alchian, A.A. and Demsetz, H. (1972), 'Production, Information Costs and Economic Organization', *American Economic Review*, **62**, 777–95.

Alchian, A.A., Crawford, R.A. and Klein, B. (1978), 'Vertical Integration, Appropriable Rents, and the Competitive Contracting Process', *Journal of Law and Economics*, **21**, 297–326.

Anderson, T.L. and Hill, P.J. (1975), 'The Evolution of Property Rights: A Study of the American West', *Journal of Law and Economics*, no. 18, 163–79.

Ault, R.W. and Ekelund, R.B. (1988), 'Rent Seeking in a Static Model of Zoning', *American Real Estate and Urban Economics Association Journal*, **16**, 69–76.

Ayres, R.U. and Ayres, L.W. (1996), *Industrial Ecology: Towards Closing the Materials Cycle*, Cheltenham, UK and Brookfield, USA: Edward Elgar.

Ball, S. and Bell, S. (1991), *Environmental Law*, London: Blackstone Press, p. 212.

Baumol, W.J. (1977), 'On recycling as a moot environmental issue', *Journal of Environmental Economic Management*, **4**, 83–7.

Baumol, W.J. and Oates, W.E. (1971), 'The Use of Standards and Prices for Protection of the Environment', *Swedish Journal of Economics*, **73**, 42–54.

Becker, G.S. (1962), 'Irrational Behaviour and Economic Theory', *Journal of Political Economy*, 1–13.

Becker, G.S. (1968), 'Crime and Punishment: An Economic Approach', *Journal of Political Economy*, 169–217.

Becker, G. (1976), *The Economic Approach to Human Behaviour*, Chicago: University of Chicago Press.

Bentham, J. (1780), *Fragments on Government: Introduction to the Principles of Morals and Legislation.* Reprinted Basil Blackwell, Oxford, 1960.

Bergkamp, L. (1998), 'A future environmental liability regime', *European Environmental Law Review*, 200–204.

Betlem, G. (1995), 'It's no use crying over spilt chemicals', *Maastricht Journal of European and Comparative Law*, 289–305.

Bjuggren, P.-O. and af Donner, H. (2002), 'Ownership of a cultural landmark: The case of Gotha Canal', *International Review of Law and Economics*, **21** (4), 499–519.

Blume, L.E. and Rubinfeld, D.L. (1984), 'Compensation for takings: an economic analysis', *California Law Review*, **72**, 569–628. Reprinted in *Research in Law and Economics*, **10** (1987), 53–103.

Bocken, H. (1988), 'Alternatives to Liability and Liability Insurance for the Compensation of Pollution Damages', *Tijdschrift voor Milieuaansprakelijkheid*, 83–7 and *Tijdschrift voor Milieuaansprakelijkheid*, 3–10.

Bohm, P. (1971), 'An approach to the problem of estimating demand for public goods', *Swedish Journal of Economics*, **73**, 55–66.

Borch, K. (1990), *Economics of Insurance*, Amsterdam: North Holland.

Bouckaert, B. and De Geest, G. (eds) (2000), *Encyclopedia of Law and Economics* (5 vols), Cheltenham, UK and Northampton, USA: Edward Elgar.

Bowles, R. (1982), *Law and Economy*, Oxford: Martin Robertson.

Bradford, T. (1970), 'Cost–benefit analysis and demand curve for public goods', *Kyklos*, **23**, 775–91.

Brans, E.H.P. (1994), 'Liability for Ecological Damage under the 1992 Protocols to the Civil Liability Convention and the Fund Convention and the Oil Pollution Act of 1990', *Tijdschrift voor Milieuaansprakelijkheid*, 61–7 and 85–91.

Brealy, R.A. and Myers, S.C. (2000), *Principles of Corporate Finance*, 6th edn, Irwin/McGraw-Hill.

Brown, J.P. (1973), 'Toward an economic theory of liability', *Journal of Legal Studies*, 323–49.

Brown, J.P. and Holahan, W.L. (1980), 'Taxes and legal rules for the control of externalities when there are strategic responses', *Journal of Legal Studies*, **9**, 165–78.

Brüggemeier, G. (1991), 'Liability for Water Pollution under German Law: Fault or Strict Liability?', in J. Van Dunné (ed.), *Transboundary Pollution and Liability*, Lelystad: Netherlands, Vermande, pp. 83–98.

Buchanan, J.M. (1975), *The Limits of Liberty: Between Anarchy and Leviathan*, Chicago: University of Chicago Press.

Buchanan, J.M. and Tullock, G. (1962), *The Calculus of Consent*, Ann Arbor, MI: University of Michigan Press.

Buchanan, J.M. and Tullock, G. (1975), 'Polluters' profits and political response: direct control versus taxes', *American Economic Review*, **65**, 139–47.

Burrows, P. (1999), 'Combining regulation and liability for the control of external costs', *International Review of Law and Economics*, **19**, 227–42.

Calabresi, G. (1970), *The Costs of Accidents. A Legal and Economic Analysis*, New Haven, CT: Yale University Press.

Calabresi, G. (1975), 'Optimal Deterrence and Accidents', *Yale Law Journal*, **84**, 656–71.

Calabresi, G. and Melamed, D. (1972), 'Property Rules, Liability Rules, and Inalienability: One View of the Cathedral', *Harvard Law Review*, **85**, 1115–23.

Cameron, J., Demaret, J.P. and Gerardin, D. (eds) (1994), *Trade and Environment: the Search for Balance*, London: Cameron May, pp. 436–58.

Cameron, J., Werksman, J. and Roderick, P. (eds) (1996), *Improving compliance with international environmental law*, London: Earthscan, pp. 229–42.

Coase, R.H. (1937), 'The Nature of the Firm', *Economica*, **4**, 386–405.

Coase, R.H. (1960), 'The Problem of Social Cost', *Journal of Law and Economics*, 1–44.

Cocker, A. and Richards C. (1992), *Valuing the Environment, Economic Approaches to Environmental Evaluation*, London: Bellhaven Press.

Coelho, P. (1976), 'Polluters' profits and political response: direct control versus taxes. Comments', *American Economic Review*, **66**, 976–8.

Coffee, J.C. (1980), 'Corporate crime and punishment. A non-Chicago view of the economics of criminal sanctions', *American Criminal Law Review*, 419–76.

Cohen, M. (1996), 'Commentary' in E. Eide and R. Van den Bergh (eds), *Law and Economics of the Environment*, Oslo, Juridisk Forlag, pp. 167–71.

Cook, P. and Graham, D. (1977), 'The Demand for Insurance and Protection: The Case of Irreplaceable Commodities', *Quarterly Journal of Economics*, 143–56.

Cooter, R. and Ulen, T. (2000), *Law and Economics*, 3rd edn, Reading: Addison-Wesley.

Cropper, M.L. and Oates, W.E. (1992), 'Environmental Economics: A Survey', *Journal of Economic Literature*, **30**, 675–740.

Dahlman, C. (1980), *The Open Field System and Beyond: A Property Rights Analysis of an Economic Institution*, Cambridge: Cambridge University Press.

Davis, R.K. (1963), 'Recreating planning as an economic problem', *Natural Resources Journal*, **3**, 239–49.

Demsetz, H. (1967), 'Toward a Theory of Property Rights', *American Economic Review*, **57**, (2), 347–59.

Deprimoz, J. (1995), 'Regime Juridique des Assurances contre les Risques Nucléaires', *Juris. Classeur*, 1–24.

De Vries, C. (1999), 'Community action on environmental liability', in L. Wiggers-Rust and K. Deketelaere (eds), *Aansprakelijkheid voor milieuschade en financiële zekerheid*, Brugge-Lelystad: Die Keure-Vermande, pp. 141–7.

Dewees, D.N. (1983), 'Instrument Choice in Environmental Policy', *Economic Inquiry*, **21**, 53–71.

Dewees, D.N. (1992a), 'The Comparative Efficacy of Tort Law and Regulation for Environmental Protection', *Geneva Papers on Risk and Insurance*, 446–67.

Dewees, D.N. (1992b), 'Tort Law and the Deterrence of Environmental Pollution', in T.H. Tietenberg, (ed.), *Innovation in Environmental Policy, Economic and Legal Aspects of Recent Developments in Environmental Enforcement of Liability*, Aldershot, UK and Brookfield, USA: Edward Elgar, pp. 139–64.

Dewees, D., Duff, D. and Trebilcock, M. (1996), *Exploring the Domain of Accident Law: Taking the Facts Seriously*, New York and Oxford: Oxford University Press.

De Witte, B. and Forder, C. (eds) (1992), *The Common Law of Europe and the Future of Legal Education*, Deventer: Kluwer.

Diamond, P. (1974), 'Single Activity Accidents', *Journal of Legal Studies*, 107–64.

Downing, P.B. (1981), 'A Political Economy Model of Implementing Pollution Laws', *Journal of Environmental Economics and Management*, **8**, 255–71.

Easterbrook, F.H. and Fischel, D. (1991), *The Economic Structure of Corporate Law*, Cambridge, MA: Harvard University Press.

Ehrlich, I. and Posner, R. (1974), 'An Economic Analysis of Legal Rule Making', *Journal of Legal Studies*, 257–86.

Ellickson, R. (1973), 'Alternatives to Zoning', *University of Chicago Law Review*, 738–48.

Elliott, E.D., Ackerman, B.A. and Millian, J.C. (1985), 'Toward a Theory of Statutory Evolution: the Federalization of Environmental Law', *Journal of Law, Economics & Organization*, **1**, 313–40.

Elton, E.J. and Gruber, M.J. (1984), *Modern portfolio theory and investment analysis*, New York and Chichester: Wiley.

Endres, A. (1994), Umweltökonomie, Eine Einführung, Darmstadt, Wissenschaftliche Buchgesellschaft.

Epstein, R. (1979), 'Nuisance Law: Corrective Justice and its Utilitarian Constraints', *Journal of Legal Studies*, 72–3.

Epstein, R., Gregory, C. and Kalven, H. (1984), *Cases and Materials on Torts*, 4th edn, Boston: Little, Brown.

Epstein, R. (1985), *Takings: private property and the power of eminent domain*, Cambridge, MA: Harvard University Press.

Faure, M. (1991), 'De gevolgen van de "administratieve afhankelijkheid" van het milieustrafrecht: een inventarisatie van knelpunten', in M. Faure, J. Oudijk and D. Schaffmeister (eds), *Zorgen van Heden*, Arnhem: Gouda-Quint, pp. 128–9.

Faure, M. (1994), 'Eerstingebruikneming in het milieurecht: een rechtseconomische analyse', in K. Raes and H. Willekens (eds), *Economische verklaringen van het recht*, The Hague: VUGA, pp. 164–7.

Faure, M. (1995), '*Ius Commune* and transboundary environmental pollution', *Maastricht Journal of European and Comparative Law*, 215–18.

Faure, M. (1995), 'Economic Models of Compensation for Damages caused by Nuclear Accidents: Some lessons for the Revision of the Paris and Vienna Conventions', *European Journal of Law and Economics*, 21–43.

Faure, M. (1998), 'Harmonization of Environmental Law and Market Integration: Harmonizing for the Wrong Reason?', *European Environmental Law Review*, 169–75.

Faure, M. and Hartlief, T. (1996), 'Towards an expanding enterprise liability in Europe? How to analyze the scope of liability of industrial operators and their insurers', *Maastricht Journal of European and Comparative Law*, 235–70.

Faure, M. and Heine, G. (1991), 'The Insurance of Fines: The Case of Oil Pollution', *Geneva Papers on Risk and Insurance*, 39–54.

Faure, M. and Lefevere, J. (1995), 'Protecting Drinking Water Quality against Contamination by Pesticides: An Alternative Regulatory Framework', *Review of European Community and International Environmental Law*, 321–6.

Faure, M. and Lefevere, J. (1995), 'Some Public Interest and Private Interest Aspects of Environmental Standard Setting in the European Community', in D. Mayes (ed.), *The Evolution of Rules for a Single European Market,*

II, Rules, Democracy and the Environment, Luxembourg: OOPEC, 320–51.

Faure, M. and Oudijk, J.C. (1994), 'Die strafgerichtliche Überprüfung von Verwaltungsakten im Umweltrecht. Ein rechtsvergleichender Überblick der Systeme in Deutschland, den Niederlanden und Belgien', *Juristenzeitung*, 86–91.

Faure, M. and Ruegg, M. (1994), 'Environmental Standards Setting through General Principles of Environmental Law', in M. Faure, J. Vervaele and A. Weale (eds), *Environmental Standards in the European Union in an Interdisciplinary Framework*, Antwerp: Maklu, pp. 39–60.

Faure, M. and Skogh, G. (1992), 'Compensation for Damages Caused by Nuclear Accidents: A Convention as Insurance', *Geneva Papers on Risk and Insurance*, **17** (65), 499–513.

Faure, M. and Van den Bergh, R. (1987), 'Negligence, Strict Liability and Regulation of Safety under Belgian Law: An Introductory Economic Analysis', *Geneva Papers on Risk and Insurance*, 95–114.

Faure M. and Van den Bergh, R. (1989), *Objectieve aansprakelijkheid, verplichte verzekering en veiligheidsregulering*, Antwerp: Maklu.

Faure, M. and Van den Bergh, R. (1990), 'Liability for nuclear accidents in Belgium from an interest group perspective', *International Review of Law and Economics*, **10**, 241–54.

Faure, M., Koopmans, I. and Oudijk, J. (1996), 'Imposing criminal liability on Government Officials under environmental law: a legal and economic analysis', *Loyola of Los Angeles International Comparative Law Journal*, 529–69.

Field, B. (1994), *Environmental Economics, an Introduction*, New York: McGraw-Hill.

Fischel, W.A. (1980), 'Externalities and Zoning', *Public Choice*, **35**, 37–43.

Fischel, W.A. (1985), *The Economics of Zoning Laws: A Property Rights Approach to American Land Use Controls*, Baltimore, MD: Johns Hopkins University Press.

Frankel, M. (1974), *The Alkali Inspectorate. The control of air pollution. Social Audit, A special Report*, London: Headly Brothers.

Freeman, A.M. (1997), 'Economics, Incentives, and Environmental Regulation', in N.J. Vig and M.E. Kraft (eds) *Environmental Policy in the 1990s, Reform or Reaction?*, 3rd edn, Washington, DC: Congressional Quarterly, pp. 187–207.

Frey, B. (1992), *Umweltökonomie*, 3rd edn., Göttingen: Vandenhoeck & Ruprecht.

Frey, B. (1997), *Not just for the money. An economic theory of personal motivation*, Cheltenham, UK and Lyme, USA: Edward Elgar.

Frey, B. (1999), 'Morality and rationality in environmental policy', *Journal of Consumer Policy*, **22**, 395–417.

Fuchs, V. and Zeckhauser, R. (1987), 'Valuating Health – a 'Priceless' Commodity', *American Economic Association, Papers and Proceedings*, 263–8.

Gordon, H.S. (1954), 'The Economic Theory of a Common-property Resource: the Fishery', *Journal of Political Economy*, **62**, 124–42.

Gravelle, H.S.E. (1987), 'Accidents, Taxes, Liability Rules and Insurances', *Geneva Papers on Risk and Insurance*, **12**, 115–31.

Gunningham, N. and Grabosky, P. (1998), *Smart Regulation. Designing Environmental Policy*, Oxford: Clarendon Press.

Hägg, G. (1994), 'The Economics of Trust, Trust Sensitive Contracts, and Regulation', *International Review of Law and Economics*, no. 4, 337–70.

Hägg, P.G.T. (1997), 'Theories of the Economics of Regulation: A Survey of the Literature from a European Perspective', *European Journal of Law and Economics*, **4**, 337–70.

Hahn, R.W. (1989), 'Economic prescriptions for environmental problems: how the patient followed the doctor's orders', *Journal of Economic Perspectives*, **3**, 95–114.

Hahn, R. (1990a), 'The Political Economy of Environmental Regulation: Towards a Unifying Framework', *Public Choice*, **65**, 21–47.

Hahn, R.W. (1990b), 'Regulatory Constraints on Environmental Markets', *Journal of Public Economics*, **42**, 149–75.

Hahn, R.W. and Hester, G.L. (1989), 'Where did all the markets go? An analysis of EPA's emission trading programme', *Yale Journal on Regulation*, **6**, 109–53.

Hanley, N., Shogren, J.F. and White, B. (1997), *Introduction to Environmental Economics*, Oxford: Oxford University Press.

Hannesson, R. (1974), *Economics of Fisheries. Some Problems of Efficiency*, Lund Economic Studies.

Hansmann, H. (1996), *The Ownership of Enterprise*, Cambridge, MA: The Belknap Press of Harvard University Press.

Hansson, I. and Skogh, G. (1987), 'Moral hazard and safety regulation', *Geneva Papers on Risk and Insurance*, **12**, 132–44.

Hardin, G. (1968), 'The Tragedy of the Commons', *Science*, 1243–8.

Harrison, D. and Rubinfeld, D. (1978), 'Hedonic House Price and the Demand for Clean Air', *Journal of Environmental Economics and Management*, **5**, 81–102.

Hart, S.L. (1997), 'Strategies for a Sustainable World', *Harvard Business Review*, **75**, 67–76.

Heimert, A.J. (1995), 'How the Elephant Lost His Tusks', *The Yale Law Journal*, 1473–1506.

Hirschleifer, J. (1985), 'The Expanding Domain of Economics', *American Economic Review*, 53–68.

Hirschleifer, J. and Riley, J.G. (1979), 'The Analytics of Uncertainty and Information – An Expository Survey', *Journal of Economic Literature*, **17** (41), 371–1421.

Hirschman, A. (1982), 'Rival Interpretation of Market Society: Civilizing, Destructive or Feeble?', *The Journal of Economic Literature*, no. 4.

Hoch, I. and Drake, J. (1974), 'Wages, climate and the quality of life', *Journal of Environmental Economics and Management*, **1**, 268–95.

Hohfeld, W.N. (1923), *Fundamental Legal Conceptions as Applied in Judicial Reasoning and other Legal Essays*, New Haven, CT: Yale University Press.

Holmes, A.F. and Bello, J.H. (1993), 'Trade and the Environment: A snapshot from *Tuna/Dolphins* to the NAFTA and beyond', US Trade and Policy Series, No. 22, *The International Lawyer*, 169–76.

Hotelling, H. (1931), 'Economics of Exhaustible Resources', *Journal of Political Economy*, 137–75.

Howarth, R.B. and Nogaard, R.B. (1992), 'Environmental valuation under sustainable development', *American Economic Review*, **82** (2), 473–7.

Hume, D. (1739), *Treatise on human Nature*. Reprinted Oxford: Oxford University Press, 1941.

Jaffe, A.B., Peterson, S., Portney, P. and Stavins, R. (1995), 'Environmental Regulation and the Competitiveness of US Manufacturing: What does the Evidence tell us?', *Journal of Economic Literature*, **33**, 132–63.

Jans, J.H. (2000), *European Environmental Law*, 2nd edn, Groningen, European Law Publishing.

Jescheck, H.H. and Waigend, T.H. (1996), *Lehrbuch des Strafrechts, algemeiner Teil*, 5th edn, Berlin: Duncker & Humblot.

Kahneman, D., Slovic, P. and Tversky, A. (1982), *Judgment under Uncertainty: Heuristics and Biases*, Cambridge: Cambridge University Press.

Kahneman, D. and Tversky, A. (1982), 'The Psychology of Preferences', *Scientific American*, no. 1.

Kant, I. (1785) 1998, *Groundwork of the metaphysics of morals*. Reprinted Cambridge: Cambridge University Press.

Keenan, D. and Rubin, P. (1988), 'Shadow Interest Groups and Safety Regulation', *International Review of Law and Economics*, 21–36.

Kidnerr, R. and Richards, K. (1974), 'Compensation to dependants of accidents victims', *The Economic Journal*, 130–42.

Kiss, A. and Shelton, D. (1997), *Manual of European Environmental Law*, 2nd edn, Cambridge: Grotius Publications.

Kolstad, C.D. (1987), 'Uniformity versus Differentiation in Regulating Externalities', *Journal of Environmental Economics and Management*, **14**, 386–99.

Kolstad, C.D., Ulen, T.S. and Johnson, G.V. (1990), 'Ex Post Liability for Harm vs. Ex Ante Safety Regulation: Substitutes or Complements?', *American Economic Review*, **80**, 888–901.

Krämer, L. (1995), 'Community Environmental Law under the Maastricht Treaty on European Union and the Fifth Environmental Action Programme', in F. Abraham, K. Deketelaere and J. Stuyck (eds), *Recent economic and legal developments in European environmental policy*', Leuven: Leuven University Press, pp. 75–106.

Krutilla, J.V. and Fisher, A. (1985), *The economics of natural environments: studies in the valuation of commodity and amenity resources*, rev. edn, Washington, DC: Resources for the Future.

Landes, W. and Posner, R. (1981), 'A Positive Economic Theory of Tort Law', *Georgia Law Review*, 851–924.

Landes, W. and Posner, R. (1984), 'Tort law as a regulatory regime for catastrophic personal injuries', *Journal of Legal Studies*, 417–34.

Lee, D.R. (1985), 'Rent-seeking and its implications for pollution taxation', *Southern Economic Journal*, **53**, 731–44.

Lidgren, K. and Skogh, G. (1996), 'Extended Producer Responsibility: Recycling, Liability, and Guarantee Funds', *Geneva Papers on Risk and Insurance*, **21** (79), 170–81.

Linnerrooth-Bayer, J. and Amendola, A. (2000), 'Global Change, Natural Disasters and Loss-sharing: issues of Efficiency and Equity', *Geneva Papers on Risk and Insurance*, **25**, (2), 203–19.

Lipsey, R.G. and Courant, P.N. (1996), *Economics*, 11th edn, New York: HarperCollins.

Lomas, O. (1990), 'Current Survey: Environment', *Utilities Law Review*, **62**, Summer.

Lundgren, N.G. (1987), *Kampen om naturresurserna*, Stockholm: SNS förlag.

Mackaay, E. (1982), *Economics of information and the law*, Boston: Kluwer.

Maler, K.G. (1977), 'A note on the use of property values in estimating marginal willingness to pay for environmental quality', *Journal of Environmental Economics and Management*, **4**, 355–69.

Maloney, M.T. and McCormick, R.E. (1982), 'A Positive Theory of Environmental Quality Regulation', *Journal of Law and Economics*, 99–123.

Markesinis, B.S. (1994), *The German Law of Torts, A Comparative Introduction*, 3rd edn, Oxford: Clarendon Press.

Mattei, U. (1994), 'Efficiency in Legal Transplants: an Essay in Comparative Law and Economics', *International Review of Law and Economics*, 3–10.

Mayes, D. (ed.) (1995), *The Evolution of Rules for a Single European Market, II: Rules, Democracy and the Environment*, Luxembourg: OPEC.

McCormick, R. and Tollison, R. (1982), *Politicians, Legislation and the Economy: an inquiry into the interest group theory of governments*, Deventer: Kluwer.

Meadows, D., Meadows, D.L., Randers, J. and Behrens III, W.W. (1972), *The Limits to Growth – A report for the Club of Rome's Project on the Predicament of Mankind*, London: Earth Island.

Merrill, T. (1985), 'Trespass, nuisance and the costs of determining property rights', *Journal of Legal Studies*, 13–48.

Michelman, F.I. (1967), 'Property, utility and fairness: comments on the ethical foundations of "just compensation" law', *Harvard Law* Review, **80**, 1165–258.

Mishan, E.J. (1974), *Cost–Benefit Analysis: an Informal Introduction*, 2nd edn, London: Allen and Unwin.

Moore, T.P. (1961), 'The Purpose of Licensing', *Journal of Law and Economics*, 93–117.

Mueller, D.C. (1979), *Public Choice*, Cambridge: Cambridge University Press.

Nelson, B. (1978), *Economic Analysis of Transportation Noise Abatement*, Cambridge, MA: Ballinger.

Newman, P. (ed.) (1998), *The New Palgrave Dictionary of Economics and the Law* (3 vols), London: Macmillan.

Niezen, G.J. (2000), 'Aansprakelijkheid voor milieuschade in de Europese Unie', in *Ongebonden Recht Bedrijven*, Deventer: Kluwer, pp. 165–79.

Noam, E. (1982), 'The Choice of Governmental Level in Regulation', *Kyklos*, 278–91.

Noll, R. (1982), 'The feasibility of marketable emissions permits in the United States', in R.B. Stewart and J.B. Krier (eds), *Environmental Law and Policy*, Charlottesville, VA: LEXIS Publishing, pp. 116–28.

Oates, W. (1976), 'Book Review: the uncertain search for Environmental Quality', *University of Pennsylvania Law Review*, **124**, 864–91.

Oates, W.E., and Schwab, R. (1988), 'Economic Competition among Jurisdictions: Efficiency Enhancing or Distortion Inducing?', *Journal of Public Economics*, **35**, 333–54.

Oates, W., Portney, P. and McGartland, A. (1989), 'The *net* benefits of incentive based regulation: a case study of an environmental standard setting', *American Economic Review*, **79**, 1233–42.

Ogus, A.I. (1981), 'Quantitative Rules and Judicial Decision-Making', in: P. Burrows and C. Veljanovski (eds), *The Economic Approach to Law*, London: Butterworths, pp. 210–25.

Ogus, A.I. (1994a), *Regulation, Legal Form and Economic Theory*, Oxford: Clarendon Press.

Ogus, A.I. (1994b), 'Standard Setting for Environmental Protection: Principles and Processes', in M. Faure, J. Vervaele and A. Weale (eds),

Environmental Standard in the European Union in an Interdisciplinary Framework, Antwerp: Maklu, pp. 23–37.

Ogus, A.I. (1995), 'Quality control for European regulation', *Maastricht Journal of European and Comparative Law*, **2**, 325–38.

Olson, M. (1971), *The Logic of Collective Action*, Cambridge, MA: Harvard University Press.

Olson, M. (1982), *The Rise and Decline of Nations*, New Haven, CT: Yale University Press, pp. 26–7.

Ostrom, E. (1990), *Governing the Commons: The Evolution of Institutions for Collective Action*, Cambridge: Cambridge University Press.

Paulus, J.A. (1995), *The Feasibility of Ecological Taxation*, Antwerp: Maklu.

Pearce, D.W. and Turner, R.K. (1998), *Economics of Natural Resources and the Environment*, New York and London: Harvester Wheatsheaf.

Pelzman, S. (1976), 'Toward a more General Theory of Regulation', *Journal of Law and Economics*, **19**, 211–40.

Pelzman, S. and Tideman, T.N. (1972), 'Local v. National Pollution Control: Note', *American Economic Review*, pp. 959–63.

Perman, R., Ma, Y., McGilvray, J. and Common, M. (1999), *Natural Resources and Environmental Economics*, 2nd edn, Harlow, UK: Longman.

Pigou, A.C. (1920), *The Economics of Welfare*, London: Macmillan.

Pigou, A.C. (1951), *A Study in Public Finance*, London: Macmillan.

Polinsky, A.M. (1979), 'Controlling externalities and protecting entitlements: property right, liability rule and the tax-subsidy approaches', *Journal of Legal Studies*, **8**, 1–48.

Polinsky, A.M. (1983), *Introduction to Law and Economics*, Boston: Little, Brown & Co.

Polinsky, M. and Shavell, S. (1991), 'A note on optimal fines when wealth varies among individuals', *American Economic Review*, **81**, 618.

Pommerehne, W. (1988), 'Measuring environmental benefits: a comparison of hedonic-technique and contingent valuation', in D. Bös, M. Rose and Chr.Seidl (eds), *Welfare and efficiency in public economics*, Berlin: Springer, pp. 363–400.

Porges, A. (1995), 'The New Dispute Settlement: From the GATT to the WTO', *Leiden Journal of International Law*, 115–33.

Posner, R.A. (1974), 'Theories of Economic Regulation', *Bell Journal of Economics*, 345.

Posner, R.A. (1975), 'The Social costs of Monopoly and Regulation', *Journal of Political Economy*, **83** (4), 807–27.

Posner, R.A. (1980), 'Optimal sentences for white collar criminals', *American Criminal Law Review*, 400–418.

Posner, R.A. (1985), 'An economic theory of the criminal law', *Columbia Law Review*, **85**, 1193–209.

Posner, R.A. (1998), *Economic Analysis of Law*, 5th edn, New York: Aspen.
Quah, E. and Rieber, W. (1989), 'Value of Children in Compensation for Wrongful Death', *International Review of Law and Economics*, 165–79.
Rawls, J.A. (1972), *Theory of Justice*, Oxford: Clarendon Press.
Repetto, R. (n.d.), 'Trade and Sustainable Development', UNEP, *Environment and Trade Series*, vol. 1.
Revesz, R. (1992), 'Rehabilitating Interstate Competition: Rethinking the Race to the Bottom Rationale for Federal Environmental Reglation', *New York University Law Review*, **67**, 1210–54. Reprinted in *Land Use & Environmental Law Review*, **25**, 373, 1995.
Revesz, R., (1996), 'Federalism and Interstate Environmental Externalities', *University of Pennsylvania Law Review*, **144**, 2341–416.
Revesz, R. (1999), 'Environmental regulation, cost–benefit analysis and the discounting of human lives', *Columbia Law Review*, **99**, 941–1017.
Richardson, G., Ogus, A. and Burrows, P. (1982), *Policing Pollution: A Study of Regulation and Enforcement*, Oxford: Clarendon Press.
Rodi, M. (1996), 'Public environmental law in Germany', in R. Seerden and M. Heldeweg (eds), *Comparative Environmental Law in Europe. An Introduction to Public Environmental Law in the EU Member States*, Antwerp: Maklu, 151–91.
Rose-Ackerman, S. (1977), 'Market models for water pollution control: their strength and weaknesses', *Public Policy*, **25**, 383–406.
Rose-Ackerman, S. (1985), 'Efficiency, Equity and Inalienability', in G. Skogh and M. Schulenburg (eds), *Law and Economics and the Economics of Legal Regulation*, The Hague: Martinus Nijhoff.
Rose-Ackerman, S. (1991), 'Regulation and the Law of Torts', *American Economic Review, Papers and Proceedings*, 54–8.
Rose-Ackerman, S. (1992a), 'Environmental Liability Law', in T.H. Tietenberg, (ed.), *Innovation in Environmental Policy, Economic and Legal Aspects of Recent Developments in Environmental Enforcement and Liability*, Aldershot, UK and Brookfield, USA: Edward Elgar, pp. 223–43.
Rose-Ackerman, S. (1992), *Rethinking the Progressive Agenda. The Reform of the American Regulatory State*, New York: The Free Press.
Rose-Ackerman, S. (1995), *Controlling Environmental Policy: the Limits of Public Law in Germany and the United States*, New Haven, CT and London: Yale University Press.
Rose-Ackerman, S. (1996), 'Public Law versus Private Law in Environmental Regulation: European Union Proposals in the Light of United States and German Experiences', in E. Eide and R. Van den Bergh (eds), *Law and Economics of the Environment*, Oslo: Juridisk Forlag, 13–39.
Rose-Ackerman, S. (1999), *Corruption and Government: Causes, Consequences and Reform*, Cambridge: Cambridge University Press.

Rus-van der Veld, M. (1987), 'Onrechtmatige daad en vergunning', in N.S.J.Koeman, W.J.Ouwerkerk and J.M. Van Dunné (eds), *Civielrechtelijke aansprakelijkheid voor milieuschade, Vereniging voor Milieurecht*, Tjeenk Willink, Zwolle, 111.

Sands, P. (1995), *Principles of International Environmental Law I: Frameworks, standards and implementation*, Manchester: Manchester University Press.

Schmitz, P. (2000), 'On the joint use of liability and safety regulations', *International Review of Law and Economics*, **20**, 371–82.

Schoenbrod, D. (1996), 'Why States, not EPA, should set Pollution Standards', *Regulation*, **4**, 18–25.

Schultze, C. (1977), *The Public Use of Private Interest*, Washington, DC: The Brookings Institution.

Schwartz, A. (2000), 'Statutory Interpretation, Capture, and Tort Law: The regulatory compliance defense', *American Law and Economics Review*, 1–57.

Schwartz, A. and Wilde, L. (1979), 'Intervening in markets on the basis of imperfect information: a legal and economic analysis', *University of Pennsylvania Law Review*, 630–82.

Scitovsky, T. (1993), *The Joyless Economy*, Oxford: Oxford University Press.

Seerden, R. and Heldeweg, M. (eds) (1996), *Comparative Environmental Law in Europe: an Introduction to Public Environmental Law in the EU Member States*, Antwerpen–Apeldoorn, Maklu.

Seerden, R. and Deketelaere, K. (eds) (2000), *Legal Aspects of Soil Pollution and Decontamination in the EU Member States and the United States*, Antwerpen–Groningen: Intersentia Uitgevers.

Sellenthin, M.O. and Skogh, G. (2002), *Property Rights in Endangered Species, The Wolverine Case*, Working paper, Linköping University.

Shavell, S. (1980), 'Strict Liability versus Negligence', *Journal of Legal Studies*, 1–25.

Shavell, S. (1984a), 'Liability for Harm versus Regulation of Safety', *Journal of Legal Studies*, 357–74.

Shavell, S. (1984b), 'A Model of the Optimal Use of Liability and Safety Regulation', *Rand Journal of Economics*, 271–80.

Shavell, S. (1985), 'Criminal law and the optimal use of non-monetary sanctions as a deterrent', *Columbia Law Review*, 1232–62.

Shavell, S. (1986), 'The judgement proof problem', *International Review of Law and Economics*, 45–58.

Shavell, S. (1987), *An Economic Analysis of Accident Law*, Cambridge, MA: Harvard University Press.

Simon, A.A. (1959), 'Theories of Decision Making in Economics and Behavioral Science', *American Economic Review*, 253–83.

Simon, J. in G.T. Miller (1996a), *Living in the Environment*, 9th edn, Belmont: Wadsworth Publishing.
Simon, J. (1996b), 'Das Umwelthaftungsgesetz', in M. Ahrens and J. Simon (eds), *Umwelthaftung, Risikosteuerung und Versicherung*, Berlin: Erich Schmidt Verlag, pp. 13–26.
Sioutis, G. (1996), 'Public environmental law in Greece', in R. Seerden and M. Heldeweg (eds), *Comparative Environmental Law in Europe: an Introduction to Public Environmental Law in the EU Member States*, Antwerp: Maklu, pp. 193–211.
Skogh, G. (1973), 'A Note on Gary Becker's Crime and Punishment: an Economic Approach', *Swedish Journal of Economics*, **57**, 305–11.
Skogh, G. (1976), 'The Social Costs of Monopoly and Regulation: Some Comments', *Journal of Political Economy*, **84** (6), 1319–23.
Skogh, G. (1982), 'Public insurance and accident prevention: an economic approach', *International Review of Law and Economics*, **2**, 67–80.
Skogh, G. (1989), 'The combination of private and public regulation of safety', in M. Faure and R. Van den Bergh (eds), *Essays in law and economics. Corporations, accident prevention and compensation for losses*, Antwerp: Maklu, 87–101.
Skogh, G. (1998), 'Development Risks, Strict Liability, and the Insurability of Industrial Hazards', *Geneva Papers on Risk and Insurance*, **23** (87), 247–64.
Skogh, G. (1999), 'Risk-Sharing Institutions of Unpredictable Losses', *Journal of Institutional and Theoretical Economics*, **155** (3).
Skogh, G. and Rehme, D. (1998), 'An Economic Analysis of a Swedish Environmental Liability Case', *European Journal of Law and Economics*, no. 5, 167–77.
Skogh, G. and Stuart, C. (1982a), 'A Contractarian Theory of Property Rights and Crime', *The Scandinavian Journal of Economics*, no. 2.
Skogh, G. and Stuart, C. (1982b), 'An economic analysis of crime rates, punishment and the social consequences of crime', *Public Choice*, 171–9.
Slovic, P. (2000), *The Perception of Risk*, London: Earthscan.
Smith, A. (1776), *The Wealth of Nations*. Reprinted London: Pelican Classics, 1970.
Spier, J. and Sterk, C.H.W.M. (1992), 'The draft convention on civil liability for damage resulting from activities dangerous to the environment', *Tijdschrift voor Milieu en Recht*, 591.
Spier, J. (1993), 'Green book on remedying environmental damage', *Aansprakelijkheid en Verzekering*, **13**.
Stewart, R.B. (1981), 'Regulation, Innovation and Administrative Law: a Conceptual Framework', *California Law Review*, 1268–73.

Sterk, C.H.W.M. (1994), *Verhoogd gevaar in het aansprakelijkheidsrecht*, diss. KUB, Kluwer.

Stigler, G. (1961), 'The economics of information', *Journal of Political Economy*, 213.

Stigler, G. (1970), 'The optimum enforcement of laws', *Journal of Political Economy*, 526–36.

Stiglitz, J.E. (2000), *Economics of the Public Sector*, 3rd edn, New York: Norton & Co.

Stone, C. (1980), 'The Place of Enterprise Liability in the Control of Corporate Conduct', *Yale Law Journal*, 36–43.

Sykes, A.O. (1980), 'The Economics of Vicarious Liability', *The Yale Law Journal*, **93**, 1231–80.

Sykes, A.O. (1998), 'Vicarious Liability', in P. Newman (ed.), *The New Palgrave Dictionary of Economics and the Law*. (3 vols), London: Macmillan, pp. 673–7.

Taams, R. and Uithoorn, M. (1995), 'The Dutch Soil Pollution Cases: Shell, Sovay, Duphar and Fasson/Van den Brink', *Environmental Liability*, **39**.

Tiebout, C. (1956), 'A Pure Theory of Local Expenditures', *Journal of Political Economy*, **64**, 416–24.

Tietenberg, T. (1985), *Emissions trading: an exercise in reforming pollution policy*, Washington, DC: Resources for the Future.

Tietenberg, T. (1990), 'Economic instruments for environmental regulation', *Oxford Review of Economic Policy*, 17–33.

Tietenberg, T. (1994), *Economics and Environmental Policy*, Aldershot, UK and Brookfield, USA: Edward Elgar.

Tietenberg, T. (2000), *Environmental and Natural Resource Economics*, 5th edn, New York: HarperCollins.

Tolley, G.S., Graves, P.H.F. and Blomquist, G.C. (1981), *Environmental Policy: Elements of Environmental Analysis*, vol. I, Cambridge, MA: Ballinger.

Turvey, R. (1963), 'On the Divergences between Social Cost and Private Cost', *Economica*, 309–13.

United Nations (1987), The World Commission on Environment and Development, *Our Common Future*, Oxford: Oxford University Press.

Van Acht, R.J.J. (1993), 'Onrechtmatige hinder', *Milieu en Recht*, 225–6.

Van Calster, G. (1996), 'The WTO Committee on Trade and Environment: Exploring the Challenges of Free Trade', *European Environmental Law Review*, 44–51.

Van den Bergh, R. (1988), 'Le droit civil face à l'analyse économique du droit', *Revue Internationale de Droit Economique*, 234.

Van den Bergh, R. (1998), 'Subsidiarity as an Economic Demarcation Principle and the Emergence of European Private Law', *Maastricht Journal of European and Comparative Law*, **5**, 129–52.

Van den Bergh, R. and Heremans, D. (1987), 'Recht en Economie', *Tijdschrift voor Economie en Management*, 139–63.

Van den Bergh, R., Faure, M. and Lefevere, J. (1996), 'The Subsidiarity Principle in European Environmental Law: An Economic Analysis', in E. Eide and R. Van den Bergh (eds), *Law and Economics of the Environment*, Oslo: Juridisk Forlag, 121–71.

Vanden Borre, T. (1997), 'Transplantatie van "kanalisatie van aansprakelijkheid" van het kernenergierecht naar het milieu(aansprakelijkheid)-recht: een goede of gebrekkige zaak?', in M. Faure and K. Deketelaere (eds), *Ius Commune en milieurecht. Actualia in het milieurecht in België en Nederland*, Antwerpen: Intersentia, pp. 331–82.

Vanden Borre, T. (1998), 'Dekking van het nucleaire risico op nationaal-rechtelijke basis of via internationale verdragen: de Verenigde Staten versus Europa', in K.Deketelaere, M. Faure and G. Verhoosel (eds), *Grensoverschrijdende milieuproblemen: uitdagingen voor de nationale en internationale rechtsorde*, Antwerp: Intersentia, pp. 443–90.

Van Dunné, J.M. (n.d.), 'Een kamikazeactie op De Rotte. De visie van Vranken op de aansprakelijkheid uit art. 1401 BW, in het bijzonder bij bodemvervuiling uit het verleden', *Weekblad voor Privaatrecht Notariaat en Registratie*, 5976.

Van Dunné, J.M. (1988), 'De rechtspraak inzake milieuaansprakelijkheid uit onrechtmatige daad: van schuldbeginsel naar risicobeginsel', *Tijdschrift voor Milieuaansprakelijkheid*, 33.

Van Dunné, J.M. (1992), 'Environmental liability: continental style', *Review of European Community and International Environmental Law*, 396.

Veljanovski, C.G. (1982), *The New Law and Economics: a Research Review*, Oxford: Centre for Social Legal Studies.

Verschuuren, J. (1993), *Het grondrecht op bescherming van het leefmilieu*, Zwolle: Tjeenk Willink.

Verschuuren, J. (1995), 'Naar een codificatie van beginselen van het milieurecht', *Recht en kritiek*, 421–45.

Vig, N.J. and Kraft, M.E. (eds) (1997), *Environmental Policy in the 1990s, Reform or Reaction?*, 3rd edn, Washington, DC: CQ Press.

Viscusi, W.K. (1983), 'Frameworks for Analyzing the Effects of a Risk and Environmental Regulations on Productivity', *American Economic Review*, **73**, 793.

Viscusi, W.K. (1989), 'Towards a diminished role for tort liability: social insurance, government regulation and contemporary risks to health and safety', *Yale Journal on Regulation*, **6**, 65–107.

Viscusi, W.K. (1998), *Rational Risk Policy*, Oxford: Clarendon Press.

Vogel, D. (1997), 'International Trade and Environmental Regulation', in N. Vig and M. Kraft (eds), *Environmental Policy in the 1990s*, 3rd edn, Washington, DC: CQ Press, pp. 345–64.

Werksman, J. (1996), 'Designing a compliance system for the UN framework convention on climate change' in J. Cameron, J. Werksman and P. Roderick (eds), *Improving compliance with international environmental law*, London: Earthscan, pp. 85–112.

Wheeler, N. (1984), 'The use of criminal statutes to regulate product safety', *Journal of Legal Studies*, 593–622.

Williamson, O.E. (1985), *The Economic Institution of Capitalism*, New York: Free Press.

Wils, W.P.J. (1994), 'Subsidiarity and the E.C. Environmental Policy: Taking People's Concerns Seriously', *Journal of Environmental Law*, 85–90.

Wittman, D. (1980), 'First come, first served: an economic analysis of "coming to nuisance"', *Journal of Legal Studies*, 557–68.

Xing, Y. and Kolstad, C. (1995), 'Do Law Environmental Regulations attract Foreign Investment?', *Working Paper in Economics*, University of California, Santa Barbara, Department of Economics, 16–95.

Yamin, F. (1996), 'The use of joint implementation to increase compliance with the climate change convention', in J. Cameron, J. Werksman and P. Roderick (eds), *Improving compliance with international environmental law*, London: Earthscan, pp. 229–42.

Yohe, G.W. (1976), 'Polluters' profits and political response: direct control versus taxes: Comment', *American Economic Review*, **66**, 981–2.

Index

Italicized entries contain a brief definition at their first reference in the text.